THE FRAMEWORK OF CORPORATE
INSOLVENCY LAW

THE FRAMEWORK
OF CORPORATE
INSOLVENCY LAW

Hamish Anderson

OXFORD

UNIVERSITY PRESS

OXFORD

UNIVERSITY PRESS

Great Clarendon Street, Oxford, OX2 6DP,
United Kingdom

Oxford University Press is a department of the University of Oxford.
It furthers the University's objective of excellence in research, scholarship,
and education by publishing worldwide. Oxford is a registered trade mark of
Oxford University Press in the UK and in certain other countries

Published in the United States of America by Oxford University Press
198 Madison Avenue, New York, NY 10016, United States of America

British Library Cataloguing in Publication Data
Data available

Library of Congress Control Number: 2017931339

ISBN 978–0–19–880531–1

Printed and bound by
CPI Group (UK) Ltd, Croydon, CR0 4YY

For Amanda

FOREWORD

Hamish Anderson brings to the task of writing this book a working lifetime of experience in the practice of insolvency law as it affects companies. To this he harnesses a scholarly interest in the subject and the underlying principles that animate it. This is an invaluable combination, so that the reader knows that his analysis of statute and case law is informed and tempered by his knowledge of how it works in practice.

In his Preface, the author comments that when he (and indeed I) started in practice, the subject had not then attracted much academic attention. It was a patchwork of primary and secondary legislation and decided cases. In a sense, that is still true, but developments over the last forty years have been remarkable.

First, the pioneering work of Sir Roy Goode and Professor Ian Fletcher in bringing some overall coherence, as well as penetrating analysis, to the law of corporate insolvency has led to a flowering of academic interest, with significant work being done on numerous topics. This has been matched by a notable level of engagement by practitioners not only in their own cases but in the subject generally.

Secondly, legal and economic changes have transformed the whole area. This book rightly takes the Cork Report and the ensuing reforms in insolvency legislation in the 1980s as a starting point. The area of international co-operation has undergone a huge change with the EU Insolvency Proceedings Regulation and the enactment by the UK and other countries of the UNCITRAL Model Law on Cross-Border Insolvency. The need for those reforms, and more, was borne out to an extent that could not have been predicted by the succession of major insolvencies (actual and potential) that have followed, culminating in those triggered by the financial crisis in 2008.

The courts have been heavily engaged in seeking to resolve the many issues that have arisen. Some of the major insolvencies have produced enough judgments to fill several volumes of law reports. It is striking, when reading those cases, that for all the contemporary significance of the issues and the mass of new law, recourse is frequently necessary to cases decided over the last 200 years. This underscores that the present law, although new in many respects, is underpinned by some long-established principles.

It is these principles as well as the major features of current insolvency law that the author examines in a way that is never less than illuminating. Further, by avoiding a recitation of the minute detail of many of the applicable rules, he gives himself the space to discuss these principles and features in depth.

This work is an important addition to the literature on this subject. A second edition will soon be needed. I look forward to the author's views on the approach taken by the Supreme Court to section 127 of the Insolvency Act 1986 in *Akers v Samba Financial Group* [2017] UKSC 6 and, at the time of writing, judgments are awaited from both the Supreme Court and the Court of Appeal in the Lehman Waterfall cases.

The Rt Hon Lord Justice David Richards
April 2017

PREFACE

I belong to a generation of insolvency lawyers who were largely self-taught because the subject had not then attracted the academic attention which it has subsequently received. Insolvency law is now the subject of numerous text and reference books but, when I started in practice, there were few titles. The scarcity of resources and the lack of an academic introduction to the subject had the beneficial effect of necessitating thought about the purpose and function of the various rules which I encountered. I have set out to write the book that I wish I had had to hand on that journey. It is neither a textbook nor a reference book but I hope that it will be complementary to both.

Black-letter corporate insolvency law is now much more detailed than it was in the days before the Cork Report and the Insolvency Act 1986. The need for a proper understanding of the purpose and function of the rules remains as great as ever and the task of achieving that understanding is, if anything, made more complicated by the sheer volume of the law and the detail of the rules. I hope that my book will assist the academic study of insolvency law and equally be of use to all who apply it. I also hope that the examination of the conceptual framework of the current rules in the book will inform consideration of future developments of English insolvency law.

I have had it in mind to write this book for a number of years but the pressures of practice made it impossible to devote enough time to the project until I retired from the partnership at Norton Rose Fulbright LLP earlier this year. Even then the book would probably have remained unwritten were it not for the encouragement of two people. The first was my erstwhile partner Richard Calnan who, as well as being a most stimulating colleague, was also enthusiastic about the concept of the book and supportive of my belief that it would fill a gap in the literature. The second was my wife Amanda who made it clear that she abhorred the idea of idleness in retirement! She has been very generous in allowing me the time and space to complete the text. She and the rest of my family now know much more about corporate insolvency law than they think necessary.

An acknowledgement is due in respect of Chapters 19 to 21 dealing with distribution of the insolvent estate, expenses, and the ranking of creditors. Those chapters benefitted greatly from previous work on the same subjects done with Charlotte Cooke, of South Square, and Louise Gullifer, of the University of Oxford, when writing our joint contributions to *Treatment of Contracts in Insolvency* and *Ranking and Priority of Creditors* (OUP 2013 and 2016 respectively, full references will be found in the text).

Subject to two major departures, I have tried to state the law as at 1 December 2016. Both those departures concern changes which are due to take effect on 6 April 2017, which I know will be before the publication of the book. The first concerns amendments to the Insolvency Act 1986 made by the Small Business, Enterprise and Employment Act 2015 where I have anticipated the replacement of creditors' meetings with decision and consent procedures. The second concerns the Insolvency (England and Wales) Rules 2016 which were laid before Parliament when this text had almost been completed (and subsequently amended). I have substituted references to the new Rules for all the references that had been made to their predecessors. In both cases I have ignored all transitional provisions. A similar issue confronted me over the European Regulations (principally in connection with Chapter 22). The Recast Regulation will apply to proceedings opened from 26 June 2017 but, having regard to the potentially long gestation period of questions under the existing EC Regulation, both Regulations will continue to be relevant for some time to come. I have therefore referred to both.

Hamish Anderson
December 2016

TABLE OF CONTENTS

TABLE OF CASES

United Kingdom

xix

Australia

Court of Justice of the European Union

Hong Kong

New Zealand

Singapore

TABLE OF LEGISLATION

LIST OF ABBREVIATIONS

the Act	Insolvency Act 1986 (as in force on 6 April 2017)
BEIS	Department of Business, Energy & Industrial Strategy
CDDA	Company Directors Disqualification Act 1986
COMI	Centre of main interests (part of the terminology of cross-border insolvency law as explained in Chapter 22)
CVAs	Company voluntary arrangements
Cork Report	Report of the Review Committee, *Insolvency Law and Practice* (Cm 8558, June 1982)
Dear IP	A series of letters addressed by the Insolvency Service to authorized insolvency practitioners which can be accessed on the Service's website at <https://www.insolvencydirect.bis.gov.uk/insolvencyprofessionandlegislation/dearip/dearipindex.htm>
EC Regulation	Council Regulation (EC) No 1346/2000 of 29 May 2000 on Insolvency Proceedings [2000] OJ L 160/1
European Regulations	the EC Regulation and the Recast Regulation
JIC	Joint Insolvency Committee (see Chapter 9)
R3	Association of Business Recovery Professionals
Recast Regulation	Regulation (EU) 2015/848 of the European Parliament and of the Council of 20 May 2015 on Insolvency Proceedings [2015] OJ L 141/19 (RR)
RPB	Recognized professional body (within the meaning of section 391 of the Act)
the Rules	Insolvency (England and Wales) Rules 2016 (SI 2016/1024) as amended by the Insolvency (England and Wales) (Amendment) Rules 2017 (SI 2017/366)
SIPs	Statements of Insolvency Practice promulgated by the JIC which can be accessed on the R3 website <https://www.r3.org.uk/what-we-do/publications/professional/statements-of-insolvency-practice>
SME	Small and medium-sized enterprise
SPV	Special purpose vehicle
UNCITRAL	United Nations Commission on International Trade Law

1

INTRODUCTION

1. Scope of the book

The title of this short book borrows from those of the White Paper, *A Revised* **1.01** *Framework for Insolvency Law*, which preceded the 1985/86 reform of insolvency law, and, more recently, the Insolvency Service's May 2016 consultation paper, *A Review of the Corporate Insolvency Framework*.[1] The book is an examination of the purposes of English corporate insolvency law and the various rules and procedures for dealing with insolvent companies under the Insolvency Act 1986.

English corporate insolvency law is very detailed and can be obscure. It sometimes **1.02** conveys the impression of comprising a set of arbitrary rules which lack coherence. The question 'why?' has rarely been addressed since the seminal Cork Report in 1982, with the result that the law has developed in a piecemeal fashion both in the courts and in legislation. By concentrating on that question, this book aims to promote a better understanding of the present law and to show how that understanding might inform future developments.

The book avoids being a detailed (still less comprehensive) commentary on the **1.03** insolvency procedures under the Act. Instead, the focus is on providing a relatively succinct account of English corporate insolvency law which identifies a rational explanation for the form that the rules and institutions of the modern law take or,

---

[1] Department of Trade and Industry, *A Revised Framework for Insolvency Law* (White Paper, Cm 9175, February 1984); The Insolvency Service, *A Review of the Corporate Insolvency Framework – A consultation on options for reform* (May 2016).

where there is no other obvious explanation, at least the history which has resulted in the present position.

1.04   Not only is much of the detail of insolvency proceedings under the Act omitted in the interests of producing a comprehensible examination of the subject as a whole, but considerations of space have also precluded more than passing references to insolvency procedures in special situations, save for where they serve to illustrate a point of more general interest. A 'company' for the purposes of this book is therefore an ordinary public or private limited company which is amenable to the insolvency jurisdiction of the Act without engaging any of the special regimes and carve-outs which are mentioned in Chapter 5 (where the sources of the law are examined).

2. Insolvency law and insolvency procedures

1.05   It is tempting to think of English corporate insolvency law purely in terms of the three procedures available under the Act—liquidation, administration, and company voluntary arrangements—but any such approach is misleading. Quite apart from the special regimes referred to in the previous paragraph, there are two broader reasons for treating the procedures under the Act as being parts of a single body of law that is greater than the sum of those parts. First, the procedures themselves are less discrete than they initially appear. This is because of the comparative ease with which an insolvent company can be moved from one procedure to another and the versatility of the procedures themselves which can, directly or indirectly, deliver either a terminal or reorganizational outcome (a subject which is considered in Chapter 6). Secondly, focusing on the differences between the procedures disguises their very substantial underlying commonalities.

1.06   In summary, the common characteristics of proceedings under the Act are:

a)   insolvency proceedings are not necessarily opened by a court order;

b)   the court does not manage the day-to-day conduct of the proceedings;

c)   the conduct of the proceedings is entrusted to an office-holder;

d)   only a qualified insolvency practitioner can act as the office-holder (unless the official receiver is acting as liquidator);

e)   insolvency practitioners are highly regulated and an office-holder's failure to conduct the proceedings in accordance with prescribed standards exposes him/her to disciplinary action in addition to legal liability;

f)   office-holders have special powers and privileges to enable them to perform their functions;

g)   creditors' interests are paramount;

h)   creditors are treated as a class and individual rights within the proceedings must be exercised consistently with the interests of the class;

i) the role of the court during the course of proceedings is to resolve disputes and determine questions of law;

j) the court will not substitute its own commercial judgment for that of the office-holder; and

k) there is a common distribution scheme (which applies unless the creditors collectively contract out by means of a company voluntary arrangement (CVA) or Companies Act scheme of arrangement).

For all these reasons, liquidation, administration, and CVAs are better regarded **1.07** as variations on a common approach to insolvency process, where the differences reflect only the more specific purposes for which those particular procedures have been developed. That perception of the overall structure of English corporate insolvency law informs the treatment of the subject in this book where topics are, as far as practicable, considered generically.

3. Policy, principles, and practicalities

An explanation of why the law takes the form that it does involves consideration **1.08** not only of policy but also various principles of insolvency law which have either developed alongside the statutory framework or been inherited from earlier bankruptcy law. However, the law as a whole cannot adequately be explained simply in terms of policy and principles. A recurrent theme of the functional analysis offered in this book is that the very nature of insolvency process dictates many of the more detailed features of the procedures which are available under the Act. The interaction between policy, principles, and practicalities can be illustrated as follows.

English corporate insolvency law meets the social and economic need for rules **1.09** to deal with the assets and undertaking of a defaulting debtor company in a way which does not stifle economic activity. It does so by providing a small suite of terminal and reorganizational procedures which can be accessed by both debtors and creditors. A terminal procedure is essentially distributive in character whereas a reorganizational procedure promotes corporate rescue. The need to provide procedures and the balance between terminal and reorganizational procedures are all questions of policy for the legislature.

Insolvency proceedings prevent disorderly and unproductive competition between **1.10** creditors to their own collective detriment and contrary to the wider interests of society as a whole. The practical effect of such proceedings, when invoked, is to restrain individual actions by creditors who are then treated as a class. This gives rise to a number of principles: for example, that creditors should not be permitted to subvert the true purpose of insolvency proceedings for private advantage and that creditors should not be free to bargain for preferential treatment. Such principles are largely the product of judicial decisions, although some have also come to be reflected in the terms of the legislation.

1.11 The mechanisms of the procedures are inevitably very detailed. For example, where a procedure involves making distributions to creditors, it is necessary to have rules to identify the available assets and for the submission and quantification of claims. This, in turn, necessitates cut-off dates to determine the composition of the insolvent estate and by reference to which the participating claims are ascertained. Such rules almost inevitably have arbitrary consequences and thus some transaction avoidance rules apply to mitigate those consequences. These necessary concomitants of giving effect to policy and principle are, in themselves, essentially matters of practicality.

4. Arrangement of commentary

1.12 The remainder of this book is informally divided into eight parts:

a) Chapters 2 to 5 set the scene. They examine the nature and purpose of insolvency law and the concept of insolvency proceedings. They consider what is meant by 'insolvency' in English law and identify the diverse sources of English corporate insolvency law.

b) Chapters 6 to 10 consider the procedures under the Act. They identify and contrast the salient characteristics of liquidation, administration, and CVAs and the purposes which they each serve. The concept of creditors' rights being a class remedy is also examined to identify how and why the exercise of those rights is regulated by the courts.

c) Chapters 11 to 13 concern the administration, supervision, and regulation of insolvency proceedings. The intention is to show how the role of the office-holder has developed and how the resultant need for oversight and control is met by a combination of the jurisdiction of the court to control the conduct of insolvency proceedings and a complex system of extra-curial regulation.

d) Chapters 14 and 15 consider the concept and composition of the insolvent estate. This establishes the background for what follows later concerning the distribution of the estate. Chapter 15 examines the nature and purpose of insolvency transaction avoidance rules as a necessary adjunct to determining the composition of the estate and facilitating its distribution.

e) Chapters 16 and 17 concern investigation and wrongdoing by directors. They examine the special powers which office-holders enjoy and the limits placed upon the exercise of those powers. They identify the dual purposes of those powers in enabling the office-holder to discharge his functions as regards the insolvent estate and, at the same time, serving wider social and economic interests in the exposure of malpractice, the application of suitable sanctions where it has occurred, and the deterrence of future misconduct.

f) Chapter 18 examines the controversial subjects of phoenixism and pre-packing. It considers the inescapable tension between the office-holder's duty to maximize realizations and the policy responses to public disquiet which constrain the unfettered exercise of his/her powers.

g) Chapters 19 to 21 deal with distribution of the insolvent estate. They take in turn the creation of a distributable fund and the quantification of eligible claims, the concept of the expenses of the proceeding and their priority and, lastly the ranking of creditors. The process of distribution is in many ways the best exemplar of the rules resulting as much from practicalities as from policy and principles.

h) Lastly, Chapter 22 considers the subject of cross-border insolvency law, identifying the aims of the law and the various mechanisms which the law provides for the achievement of those aims.

Throughout the text the 'Act' means the Insolvency Act 1986 and the 'Rules' means the Insolvency (England and Wales) Rules 2016 (both as in force on 6 April 2017) unless the context otherwise requires.

2

FUNCTION AND OBJECTIVES OF INSOLVENCY LAW

1. Credit and default

2.01 Why have insolvency law? The simple answer to that question is that credit is indispensable in a modern free market economy but credit brings with it the possibility of default. The extension of credit in whatever form, and whether in large or small amounts, creates a need for the law to provide remedies to deal with that default when it occurs. The ordinary remedies are private remedies; the creditor obtains and enforces a judgment for its private benefit but sometimes the debtor cannot pay because its liabilities are greater than its means. Insolvency law then provides the method by which the remaining assets are administered in accordance with a predetermined scheme, replacing private competition between creditors with an orderly distribution to all in so far as there are assets to support it.

2.02 The reliance of modern society upon credit to facilitate commercial activity may explain the need for insolvency law but it does not explain how insolvency law addresses that need. To put this another way, insolvency law may be an indispensable part of English commercial law but it does much more than regulate the outcome of transactions where the counterparty is unable to discharge its obligations.

2. Objectives

As the Cork Report observed:[1]   **2.03**

> The law of insolvency takes the form of a compact to which there are three par-
> ties: the debtor, his creditors and society.

But the balance between those three parties is unequal and susceptible to change
in line with changes in policy. Given that insolvency law deals with a loss where
the interests which are at stake are not aligned (and, in the case of creditors, even
the interests of different creditors are not necessarily consistent), an overriding
objective of insolvency law must be to provide a set of rules for allocating that loss
which are recognized by all stakeholders as being a just solution. The UNCITRAL
Legislative Guide on Insolvency Law noted that:[2]

> ... insolvency law must be complementary to, and compatible with, the legal and
> social values of the society in which it is based and which it must ultimately sus-
> tain. Although insolvency law generally forms a distinctive regime, it ought not to
> produce results that are fundamentally in conflict with the premises upon which
> laws other than the insolvency law are based.

Perceptions of what is 'just' or 'fair' in the context of corporate insolvency
will differ according to the nature of the insolvent undertaking and the solution being pursued but a fundamental precept of general application is that
there should be equal treatment of creditors who have comparable rights and
interests.

Insolvency law must not only offer proportionate solutions which meet the needs of **2.04**
stakeholders in a variety of differing circumstances but also deliver those solutions
efficiently and at an acceptable cost.

The need for insolvency law to provide solutions to default which command the **2.05**
respect of stakeholders is important because of the scope for creditors to structure their business relations in a way which mitigates or even avoids the unwelcome aspects of an unsatisfactory insolvency law. It is also important because
ultimately it will influence choices about where investment is made and business
is undertaken.

a. Economic perspectives

A highly influential economic view of the role of insolvency law is that it replicates **2.06**
a hypothetical bargain between creditors which they would have reached if they

---

[1] Report of the Review Committee, *Insolvency Law and Practice* (Cm 8558, June 1982) para 192.
[2] UNCITRAL, *Legislative Guide on Insolvency Law* (United Nations 2005) 10.

had negotiated a solution in advance of their problems with the debtor and under which they would recognize the need for individual enforcement action to be stayed for the common good.[3] The law is designed to facilitate the outcome which a sole owner of the enterprise would have decided was in his best interests but to deliver that outcome for the benefit of the company and its creditors as a whole. Since a sole owner would use assets in the way that is most economically efficient, the result is to deliver the best returns for creditors. Effective insolvency regimes promote the extension of credit.[4] A refinement of this approach identifies the role of insolvency law in ensuring that capital in the economy is put where it will be best used.[5]

2.07 Just as there is a need for processes which produce fair results between competing creditors, so too there is a societal interest in having processes available which prevent a disorderly collapse. Insolvency procedures dealing with financial institutions are generally outside the scope of this book but problems in that sector conveniently illustrate two issues of much wider application. First, insolvency can present a risk of systemic failure (the domino effect). Defaults resulting from the insolvency of one market participant can bring down others and threaten the survival of the market as a whole. Another, more prosaic, example of such risk is where an insolvent company has a prominent market position, which could be national or merely local, so that its failure will lead to the insolvency of its suppliers and other aligned businesses such as sales outlets and franchises. Secondly, there is the problem of companies being 'too big to fail' thus requiring rescue at the taxpayers' expense—the privatization of profit coupled with socialization of loss. Society has a very clear interest in its laws preventing any repetition of the expensive rescues which followed the financial crash of 2008 and extensive new measures have been introduced in respect of the insolvency of financial institutions with precisely that end in view. In addressing these issues, insolvency law complements and interacts with regulatory law.

2.08 A rather different societal interest arises out of the privatization policies of the late twentieth century which resulted in previously state-owned utilities and other

---

[3] The work of Thomas Jackson stands out in this connection. For an early example, see Thomas Jackson, 'Bankruptcy, Non-Bankruptcy Entitlements and the Creditors' Bargain' (1982) 91 Yale LJ 857.

[4] A useful review of empirical evidence in this respect is provided in A Menezes, 'Debt Resolution and Business Exit' <http://documents.worldbank.org/curated/en/912041468178733220/pdf/907590VIEWPOIN003430Debt0Resolution.pdf > accessed 3 October 2016.

[5] See further: Kenneth Ayotte and David A Skeel Jr, 'Bankruptcy Law as a Liquidity Provider' (2013) 80 U Chi L Rev 1557; Thomas H Jackson and David A Skeel Jr, 'Bankruptcy and Economic Recovery' (2013) *Faculty Scholarship*, Paper 476 <http://scholarship.law.upenn.edu/faculty_scholarship/476> accessed 31 August 2016; Sarah Paterson, 'Rethinking the Role of the Law of Corporate Distress in the Twenty-First Century' LSE Legal Studies Working Paper No 27/2014 <http://ssrn.com.abstract=2526677> or <http://dx.doi.org/10.2139/ssrn.2526677> accessed 31 August 2016.

monopoly suppliers being exposed to the risk of failure. In those cases, the societal interest lies in the maintenance of essential supplies which has led to a proliferation of special procedures under which the interests of creditors are subordinated to the wider public interest. Those special procedures are considered in Chapter 3 in so far as they cast light on the concept of insolvency proceedings but, that apart, they too are outside the scope of this book.

These are all macro-economic considerations but not all the objectives of insol- **2.09** vency law reflect economic priorities—or at least not directly. Bankruptcy has lost some of its stigma but it remains a core objective of insolvency law to promote commercial prudence—so called 'moral hazard' and the imperative of discharging obligations as fully as circumstances permit.

b. Government policy

Government policy in respect of insolvency law is directed towards the promo- **2.10** tion of enterprise, but this is not a one-dimensional perspective. The White Paper which followed the publication of the Cork Report and preceded the sweeping 1985/86 reforms of English insolvency law set out a convenient summary of the purposes of insolvency law which, despite the many changes which have subsequently been made, remains a fair appraisal of the policy underpinning the Act:[6]

> The fundamental objectives of the Department of Trade and Industry are to encourage, assist and ensure the proper regulation of British trade, industry and commerce, and to promote a climate conducive to growth and the national production of wealth. In pursuing these objectives, the principal role of the Insolvency Legislation is (i) to establish effective and straightforward procedures for dealing with and settling the affairs of corporate and personal insolvents in the interests of their creditors; (ii) to provide a statutory framework to encourage companies to pay careful attention to their financial circumstances so as to recognise difficulties at an early stage and before the interests of creditors are seriously prejudiced; (iii) to deter and penalise irresponsible behaviour and malpractice on the part of those who manage a company's affairs; (iv) to ensure that those who act in cases of insolvency are competent to do so and conduct themselves in a proper manner; and (v) to facilitate the re-organisation of companies in difficulties to minimise unnecessary loss to creditors and to the economy when insolvency occurs. The main task in furthering the department's objectives is to ensure that action is taken at an early stage in insolvencies under the control of the Court to protect insolvent's assets in the interests of creditors, and to investigate the affairs of insolvents where it appears that malpractice rather than misfortune has been the cause of liquidation or bankruptcy, so that undesirable commercial or individual conduct is sufficiently deterred.

---

[6] Department of Trade and Industry, *A Revised Framework for Insolvency Law* (White Paper, Cm 9175, February 1984) para 2. (The department is now called the Department for Business, Energy & Industrial Strategy.)

The continuing relevance of these objectives was restated by the Insolvency Service in May 2016:[7]

> The UK Government believes in the promotion of entrepreneurship, investment and employment. Having an efficient and effective insolvency regime is one of the ways through which the Government is seeking to achieve this. It helps to create a business environment that supports growth and employment by ensuring that viable businesses in distress can be rescued. Where businesses cannot be rescued, the insolvency regime should provide a low cost procedure for liquidating businesses and returning funds to creditors quickly.

In so far as there is a discernible difference in the underlying approach taken in these policy statements, separated as they were by more than thirty years, it is an increased focus on the role of insolvency legislation in the rescue and rehabilitation of companies in difficulty. English insolvency law, in common with other modern legal systems, includes both terminal and reorganizational insolvency procedures.

3. Terminal and reorganizational responses to default

2.11 The Cork Report had earlier observed:[8]

> Insolvency law is not an exact science and it is not possible to design a set of rules which will be valid for all times...

Given the social and economic significance of insolvency law, it is inevitable that it will be in a constant state of evolution as it responds to new problems and changing circumstances.[9]

2.12 Historically, the treatment of debtors was harsh. Maine noted:[10]

> ... the extraordinary and uniform severity of very ancient systems of law to debtors, and the extravagant powers which they lodge with creditors.

In English common law, insolvency was analogous to crime with debtors being liable to imprisonment as an alternative to the seizure of their assets by individual

---

[7] The Insolvency Service, *A Review of the Corporate Insolvency Framework – A consultation on options for reform* (May 2016) para 2.1.

[8] Cork Report (n 1) para 196.

[9] This is likely to limit the European Union's ability to harmonize the insolvency laws of member states without full political union and without a uniform fiscal policy (see further: European Commission, *Proposal for a Directive of the European Parliament and of the Council on preventive restructuring frameworks, second chance and measures to increase the efficiency of restructuring, insolvency and discharge procedures and amending Directive 2012/30/EU*, COM(2016) 723 final <http://ec.europa.eu/information_society/newsroom/image/document/2016-48/proposal_40046.pdf> accessed 23 November 2016).

[10] Sir Henry Maine, *Ancient Law* (John Murray 1861).

creditors, but legislation intervened from the sixteenth century onwards. Acts of 1542 and 1570[11] introduced procedures for rateable distribution amongst creditors and an Act of 1705[12] made provision for discharge from bankruptcy. Thus it can be seen that the twin concepts of rateable distribution amongst the general body of creditors and relief from debt were established features of insolvency law long before the advent of companies and corporate insolvency.

There is a crucial distinction between personal and corporate insolvency in that, in personal insolvency law, there is an inescapable need to address the future status of the individual debtor because he/she will survive the process. (That does not necessarily mean discharge, although that is how the issue has been addressed in English law.) There is no equivalent inescapable need in the case of corporate insolvency because the result can simply be the dissolution of the company. Indeed, the Cork Report proceeded on the basis that:[13] **2.13**

> In the case of an insolvent company, society has no interest in the preservation or rehabilitation of the company as such, though it may have a legitimate concern in the preservation of the commercial enterprise.

A terminal procedure is the foundation of most systems of insolvency law (as was bankruptcy in English law). The model is the imposition of a stay, the seizure of the debtor's assets, and their orderly distribution amongst the creditors. In an English bankruptcy, as such, the concept of discharge retains its original form whereby the result of the administration of the insolvent estate is the protection of the debtor from further claims by his creditors. However, modern circumstances require a greatly expanded approach to discharge in the context of both personal and corporate insolvency whereby a debtor can obtain relief from his/her or its obligations without submitting to a terminal procedure. In corporate insolvency law, that is the role of reorganizational procedures. **2.14**

Insolvency law has to strike a balance between terminal and reorganizational procedures and associated rules, for example those dealing with transaction avoidance, which go with them. UNCITRAL said of this in its *Guide*:[14] **2.15**

> An insolvency law needs to balance the advantages of near-term debt collection through liquidation (often the preference of secured creditors) against preserving the value of the debtor's business through reorganization (often the preference of unsecured creditors and the debtor). Achieving that balance may have implications for other social policy considerations, such as encouraging the development of an entrepreneurial class and protecting employment. Insolvency law should include the possibility of reorganization of the debtor as an alternative to liquidation, where

---

[11] 34 and 35 Hen 8 c4 *'An act against such persons as do make bankrupts'*; 13 Eliz c7 *'An act touching orders for bankrupts'*.

[12] 4 and 5 Anne c17 *'An act to prevent frauds frequently committed by bankrupts'*.

[13] Cork Report (n 1) para 193.

[14] UNCITRAL, *Legislative Guide on Insolvency Law* (United Nations 2005) 11.

creditors would not involuntarily receive less than in liquidation and the value of the debtor to society and to creditors may be maximized by allowing it to continue. This is predicated on the basic economic theory that greater value may be obtained from keeping the essential components of a business together, rather than breaking them up and disposing of them in fragments.

Different legal systems strike the balance in different ways and are sometimes classified as 'creditor-friendly' or 'debtor-friendly' according to the severity of their rules. Those terms themselves reflect policy objectives. Creditor-friendly sets of rules adopt a restrained approach to depriving creditors of the benefits of the enforcement of their contractual rights and are thus perceived as facilitating the extension of credit. Debtor-friendly measures, on the other hand, adopt a much more liberal approach to interfering with those rights and are seen thereby to be more supportive of rescue and restructuring. It is doubtful whether such classifications any longer serve a useful purpose. First, all developed systems recognize the value of both objectives and will adjust the balance from time to time to reflect changing economic conditions and social attitudes. England, which has been traditionally regarded as a pro-creditor jurisdiction, is no exception in this respect. Secondly, it is increasingly clear that unbridled freedom to exercise individual creditor rights may itself be inimical to the rights of a company's creditors as a whole and that the existence of effective rescue and reorganization procedures is therefore a necessary part of the legal armoury to make a jurisdiction 'business friendly'.

2.16 In the United Kingdom, the social interest in the rescue and rehabilitation of companies in financial difficulty is now seen as extending to the fostering of an enterprise culture which encourages the creation of new businesses. As the Insolvency Service has said:[15]

> It is in the nature of risk-taking that, on occasions, there will be failure. But in a society which is genuinely enterprising the cost of failure must not be set so high that it acts as a deterrent to economic activity.

This was written in the context of proposals to lessen the stigma of bankruptcy but the same sentiment was applied to companies in financial difficulty in the Secretary of State's foreword to *A Review of the Corporate Insolvency Framework* where he said:[16]

> ... I have a very singular ambition: to make Britain the best place in the world to start and grow a business.
>
> If we're going to make that vision a reality, entrepreneurs have to know that they can restructure when times are tough, without removing much-needed protection for

---

[15] Department of Trade and Industry, *Insolvency – A Second Chance* (White Paper, Cm 5234, July 2001) para 1.23.

[16] The Insolvency Service, *A Review of the Corporate Insolvency Framework – A consultation on options for reform* (May 2016).

creditors and employees. Getting the balance right will help more businesses survive, save more jobs and, in the long run, increase productivity.

The common theme is the need to mitigate the rigour of a terminal response to insolvency, not only by a judicious approach to the application of sanctions but also by the provision of procedures which enable businesses or viable parts of businesses to survive unburdened (or at least partially unburdened) by historic debt.

It is questionable how far the preservation of the company itself, as opposed to its **2.17** business, should be a priority but doing so accords with the policy of stimulating entrepreneurial activity.[17] It is also questionable how far supporting failing businesses yields longer term benefits in the wider economy. Three basic points can be made to illustrate the difficulties of formulating policy in this area: first, that part of the role of insolvency law, according to economic theory, lies in ensuring that capital in the economy is relocated to where it will be best used; secondly, that the preservation of jobs in a failing business may be at the longer term expense of job creation in other businesses; and, thirdly, that sustaining under-performing businesses risks exposing other operators in the same sector, which are discharging their liabilities, to unfair competition. Questions such as these illustrate the wisdom of the Cork Report's premise that it is not possible to provide a set of rules that will remain fit for purpose in all future circumstances.

---

[17] As will be seen in Chapter 8, rescuing the insolvent company as a going concern is the primary objective of administration. This contrasts with the approach of the Cork Report noted in para 2.13 above.

3

THE CONCEPT
OF INSOLVENCY PROCEEDINGS

1. Introduction

3.01 Insolvency proceedings, whether of a terminal or a reorganizational nature, are the proceedings which can be invoked by or in respect of a company so as to subject its property and affairs to the rules of insolvency law applicable to the administration of an insolvent estate.

3.02 Insolvency proceedings are the principal means by which the objectives of insolvency law are achieved but they are not the only such means. For example, the rules whereby transactions defrauding creditors can be set aside are capable of being invoked outside insolvency proceedings and the rules for the disqualification of unfit directors operate independently of any insolvency proceedings in which the relevant misconduct may have been uncovered.

3.03 The purpose of this chapter is to examine the concept of insolvency proceedings before proceeding to any detailed consideration of the attributes of the various procedures which are currently available under the Act. This is, to some extent, a question of international jurisprudence for two reasons. First, whether or not proceedings qualify as 'insolvency proceedings' may affect the recognition of such proceedings in other jurisdictions and, secondly, in so far as there are applicable definitions, they are either derived from or to be found in international sources.

2. The special nature of insolvency proceedings

The nature of insolvency proceedings was considered by the Privy Council in **3.04**
*Cambridge Gas Transportation Corpn v Official Committee of Unsecured Creditors
of Navigator Holdings Plc*. Part of the Board's reasoning involved determining
whether an order made by a court in New York in the course of insolvency proceedings was an order *in rem* or *in personam*. Lord Hoffmann said:[1]

> … their Lordships consider that bankruptcy proceedings do not fall into either cat-
> egory. Judgments in rem and in personam are judicial determinations of the exist-
> ence of rights: in the one case, rights over property and in the other, rights against
> a person. When a judgment in rem or in personam is recognised by a foreign court,
> it is accepted as establishing the right which it purports to have determined, with-
> out further inquiry into the grounds upon which it did so. The judgment itself is
> treated as the source of the right.
>
> The purpose of bankruptcy proceedings, on the other hand, is not to determine or
> establish the existence of rights, but to provide a mechanism of collective execu-
> tion against the property of the debtor by creditors whose rights are admitted or
> established.

Having drawn that distinction, and thereby avoided the established rules of private
international law for the enforcement of judgments *in rem* and *in personam*, the
Board gave effect to the New York order. The outcome of the case proved highly
controversial and it was subsequently held to have been wrongly decided in *Rubin v
Eurofinance SA*.[2] Although the Supreme Court in *Rubin* decided that orders made
in the course of insolvency proceedings were not *sui generis*, the special character of
insolvency proceedings as such was recognized.[3]

3. Defining characteristics of insolvency proceedings

It has been necessary to delineate what is meant by 'insolvency proceedings' for the **3.05**
purposes of European Regulations which allocate jurisdiction to open insolvency
proceedings between member states.[4] Under those Regulations, the proceedings
to which they apply are expressly and definitively identified in annexes, but the
Regulations also contain provisions which determine eligibility for inclusion in

---

[1] [2006] UKPC 26, [2007] 1 AC 508 [13]–[14]. Lord Hoffmann was adopting US usage of the
term 'bankruptcy' to refer to both corporate and personal insolvency. (See also *Pattni v Ali* [2006]
UKPC 51, [2007] 2 AC 85 [23].)

[2] [2012] UKSC 46, [2013] 1 AC 236; see further Chapter 22.

[3] Ibid at [91], [106] (Lord Collins SCJ).

[4] Council Regulation (EC) 1346/2000 of 29 May 2000 on Insolvency Proceedings [2000] OJ L
160/1 to be replaced by Regulation (EU) 2015/848 of the European Parliament and of the Council
of 20 May 2015 on Insolvency Proceedings [2015] OJ L 141/19 (RR). See generally Chapter 22.

those annexes and which are of more interest for present purposes. Paragraph 1 of article 1 of the later of these Regulations now provides that:[5]

> This Regulation shall apply to public collective proceedings, including interim proceedings, which are based on laws relating to insolvency and in which, for the purpose of rescue, adjustment of debt, reorganisation or liquidation:
> (a) a debtor is totally or partially divested of its assets and an insolvency practitioner is appointed;
> (b) the assets and affairs of a debtor are subject to control or supervision by a court; or
> (c) a temporary stay of individual enforcement proceedings is granted by a court or by operation of law, in order to allow for negotiations between the debtor and its creditors, provided that the proceedings in which the stay is granted provide for suitable measures to protect the general body of creditors, and, where no agreement is reached, are preliminary to one of the proceedings referred to in point (a) or (b).

> Where the proceedings referred to in this paragraph may be commenced in situations where there is only a likelihood of insolvency, their purpose shall be to avoid the debtor's insolvency or the cessation of the debtor's business activities.

3.06 Similarly, it was necessary for the purposes of the UNCITRAL Model Law on Cross-Border Insolvency, dealing with the recognition of foreign insolvency proceedings, to identify the nature of the proceedings to which it would apply. Article 2(a) of the Model Law provides:[6]

> 'Foreign proceeding' means a collective judicial or administrative proceeding in a foreign State, including an interim proceeding, pursuant to a law relating to insolvency in which proceeding the assets and affairs of the debtor are subject to control or supervision by a foreign court, for the purpose of reorganization or liquidation;

The accompanying Guide to Enactment supplements this definition in the following way:[7]

> The attributes required for a foreign proceeding to fall within the scope of the Model Law include the following: basis in insolvency-related law of the originating State; involvement of creditors collectively; control or supervision of the assets and affairs of the debtor by a court or another official body; and reorganization or liquidation of the debtor as the purpose of the proceeding ...

3.07 It is important to bear in mind the context of both the European and UNCITRAL formulations; in both cases they serve to control the scope of the particular instruments in which they appear, which are concerned with questions of private

---

[5] See further paras (9) to (17) of the Preamble. (The criteria for inclusion in Regulation 1346/2000 were more restricted.)

[6] United Nations 2014. See generally Chapter 22. The definition was repeated without amendment in the Cross-Border Insolvency Regulations 2006 (SI 2006/1030) by which the Model Law became part of English law.

[7] At 39, para 66.

16

international law, and neither purports to be a definition of insolvency proceedings of universal application. They nonetheless provide considerable assistance in identifying an emerging international consensus as to the characteristics of insolvency proceedings which distinguish them from other proceedings. It is suggested that those distinguishing characteristics are:

a) The proceedings must be 'collective'. (This crucial requirement is more easily stated than explained. Its meaning is examined in the next section of this chapter.)
b) The proceedings must be premised upon the actual or anticipated insolvency of the subject company (as opposed to being proceedings under general laws which may be invoked without any actual or anticipated insolvency—for example schemes of arrangement under the Companies Act 2006).
c) The purpose of the proceedings must be terminal or reorganizational.
d) The proceedings must involve some element of official control over the subject company's conduct of its own affairs.

Each of those characteristics is necessary in order for proceedings to be insolvency proceedings but, subject thereto, the proceedings need not take any particular form. The fact that English law has hitherto eschewed debtor in possession procedures does not mean that such procedures are not insolvency proceedings. The requisite degree of external control may be satisfied by aggrieved persons having a right of recourse to the court.[8] Insolvency proceedings can be court proceedings or out of court proceedings and they need not be directed to any particular outcome—provided that it is either terminal or reorganizational. The requirement is for the proceedings to be part of the body of insolvency law, not that the subject company should necessarily be insolvent.

The correct identification of the true nature of insolvency proceedings may inform **3.08** the court's approach to the use of such proceedings. In *Secretary of State for Business, Innovation and Skills v PAG Management Services Ltd*, a public interest winding-up petition was presented against a company which was operating an artificial scheme to avoid business rates involving the grant of leases to special purpose vehicles (SPVs) which were then put into solvent liquidations. The SPVs thereafter took the benefit of a rates exemption available to companies in liquidation, whilst the leased properties were refurbished and marketed. In making a winding-up order, Norris J said:[9]

> [Counsel] gave evidence from the Bar that many corporate reconstruction schemes involve the interposition of a company to receive assets and then to be wound up (perhaps for tax reasons or as a mechanism of distribution) and that it had never

---

[8] See further para (10) of the Preamble to Regulation (EU) 2015/848 of the European Parliament and of the Council of 20 May 2015 on Insolvency Proceedings.
[9] [2015] EWHC 2404 (Ch), [2015] BCC 720 [67].

been suggested that this was improper; and that many schemes of very many sorts require directors to take steps which are wholly predetermined (in relation to which it was never contemplated that they would exercise independent judgment). Of such schemes I say nothing, save that if the liquidation is not genuinely a collection and distribution of assets then its propriety might need to be reconsidered. For me it is the use of the company in liquidation as an asset shelter and the inherent bias towards prolongation of the liquidation that is subversive of the true purpose and proper functioning of insolvency law. So I cannot accept [counsel's] submission that the operation of the scheme through the medium of insolvency is not commercially improper.

4. Collectivity

3.09 What is meant by insolvency proceedings being 'collective' proceedings? Whilst it is not the only defining characteristic of insolvency proceedings, it tends to be the characteristic most frequently cited. The Cork Report provides a good example:[10]

> Insolvency proceedings are inherently of a collective nature; their prime beneficiary is the general body of the insolvent's creditors, each of whom is affected, though clearly by no means necessarily to the same extent, by the common disaster. If each such creditor is denied by law the right to pursue separate remedies against the insolvent and is obliged to rely on the outcome of collective proceedings, then his interest in those proceedings ought to be, so far as is consistent with the claims of his fellow creditors, as fair and reasonable as circumstances will permit, to compensate him for the loss of his individual rights.

According to this explanation, insolvency proceedings are collective because individual remedies are no longer available and the company's creditors must instead look to the insolvent estate for distribution in accordance with a prescribed scheme. This is clearly apt to describe the nature of a terminal insolvency proceeding and accords with Lord Hoffmann's description of bankruptcy proceedings in *Cambridge Gas* as a form of 'collective execution'. It fits less comfortably with a reorganizational procedure which does not necessarily involve any form of distribution. In this context, collectivity means only that the interests of the general body of creditors take precedence over the rights of individual creditors.

3.10 This, slightly more limited, explanation of collectivity was implicitly adopted by the Insolvency Service when it proposed that administration should replace administrative receivership (a form of security enforcement[11]) saying:[12]

---

[10] Report of the Review Committee, *Insolvency Law and Practice* (Cm 8558, June 1982) para 232.

[11] See further Chapter 6 Section 3.

[12] Department of Trade and Industry, *Insolvency – A Second Chance* (White Paper, Cm 5234, July 2001) para 2.5.

The Government's view is that, on the grounds of both equity and efficiency, the time has come to make changes which will tip the balance firmly in favour of collective insolvency proceedings – proceedings in which all creditors participate, under which a duty is owed to all creditors and in which all creditors may look to an office-holder for an account of his dealings with a company's assets.

A similar approach is discernible in the *Virgos-Schmit Report on the Convention on Insolvency Proceedings*:[13]

Insolvency proceedings are collective proceedings. Collective action needs clearly determined legal positions to provide for an adequate bargaining environment. This is true not only once the insolvency proceedings have been opened, but also before they have been opened (when the debtor is already in economic difficulties), as the rights 'in bankruptcy' will influence negotiations for a possible 'pre-bankruptcy' reorganization.

In the recast European Regulation of 2015, collective proceedings are defined thus:[14]

'collective proceedings' means proceedings which include all or a significant part of a debtor's creditors, provided that, in the latter case, the proceedings do not affect the claims of creditors which are not involved in them....

This definition further reduces the concept of collectivity to its most important element which is that the proceeding should regulate the rights of most, if not all, of the company's creditors.

The concept is explored more fully in UNCITRAL materials. The UNCITRAL **3.11** *Legislative Guide on Insolvency Law* states:[15]

... one of the fundamental principles of insolvency law is that insolvency proceedings are collective proceedings, which require the interests of all creditors to be protected against individual action by one of them.

and (earlier in the context of terminal procedures):[16]

A collective proceeding is designed to provide equitable treatment to creditors, by treating similarly situated creditors in the same way, and to maximize the value of the debtor's assets for the benefit of all creditors. This is normally achieved by the imposition of a stay on the ability of creditors to enforce their individual rights against the debtor and the appointment of an independent person whose primary duty is to maximize the value of the debtor's assets for distribution to creditors.

---

[13] EU Council reference 6500/1/96, REV1, DRS 8 (CFC), 3 May 1996, para 8. The report on the Convention (which never took effect but from which the Regulations referred to in footnote 4 are derived) is regarded as an authoritative commentary—see *Re Olympic Airlines SA* [2015] UKSC 27, [2015] 1 WLR 2399 [9] (Lord Sumption SCJ).

[14] Regulation (EU) 2015/848 of the European Parliament and of the Council of 20 May 2015 on Insolvency Proceedings, art 2(1).

[15] United Nations 2005, at 83, para 26.

[16] Ibid at 31 para 35.

and in the *Guide to Enactment of the Model Law on Cross-Border Insolvency* which provides:[17]

> For a proceeding to qualify for relief under the Model Law, it must be a collective proceeding because the Model Law is intended to provide a tool for achieving a coordinated, global solution for all stakeholders of an insolvency proceeding. It is not intended that the Model Law be used merely as a collection device for a particular creditor or group of creditors who might have initiated a collection proceeding in another State. Nor is it intended that the Model Law serve as a tool for gathering up assets in a winding up or conservation proceeding that does not also include provision for addressing the claims of creditors …
>
> In evaluating whether a given proceeding is collective for the purpose of the Model Law, a key consideration is whether substantially all of the assets and liabilities of the debtor are dealt with in the proceeding, subject to local priorities and statutory exceptions, and to local exclusions relating to the rights of secured creditors. A proceeding should not be considered to fail the test of collectivity purely because a class of creditors' rights is unaffected by it.

3.12 Thus it can be seen that the concept of the collectivity of insolvency proceedings which has developed is that:

a) The proceeding must address the claims of all of the company's creditors who are affected by it and those creditors must constitute the generality of the creditor base.

b) Subject to the enforcement of proprietary rights and the like, creditors have rights in the proceeding in lieu of their rights to take individual action in competition with other creditors.

c) Creditors of equal standing have the same rights in the proceeding.

The outstanding point of conceptual difficulty is how far collectivity demands that insolvency proceedings should be proceedings in which the company's creditors are the prime beneficiaries (as perceived by the Cork Report). It is suggested that, with the increased emphasis on rescue and reorganization, the more important consideration is whether creditors are being treated as a constituency according to a scheme of universal application rather than whether their interests will necessarily trump those of the debtor.[18]

5. Modernizing the concept

3.13 One of the most marked developments since the enactment of the Act has been the emergence of numerous special procedures to deal with failing companies engaged

---

[17] United Nations 2014, at 39 and 40, paras 69 and 70 of the Guide.

[18] Although it should be noted that creditors' interests remain paramount in the existing procedures under the Act.

in specific types of business or transaction.[19] The companies which are subject to these special regimes range from banks and insurance companies through to companies in the health, transport, and energy sectors and other utilities. The bespoke procedures to which they are subject adopt a number of different approaches ranging from light-touch adaptation of the insolvency procedures under the Act to accommodate the distinguishing characteristics of the nature of the business in question, through to regulatory intervention with no pretensions to being analogous to an insolvency proceeding.

The most interesting of these special procedures, for present purposes, apply to **3.14** providers of essential public services. The common denominator is that these are undertakings where the failure of the company will, or at least may, affect a wider range of interests than those of the company's own stakeholders and the question which arises is how far these special regimes, which for other purposes are outside the scope of this book, are true insolvency procedures or whether their emergence calls for some revision of the concept of insolvency proceedings.

Despite considerable differences of detail in the governing legislation, in each case **3.15** the fundamental purpose of the special procedure is to sustain the provision of the relevant service, if necessary by transferring the appropriate parts of the property rights and liabilities of the existing operator to another provider. The interests of creditors are subordinate and the proceedings are not necessarily triggered by insolvency. The policy imperatives for doing so are uncontroversial. Rail is one such sector where a special regime applies and, as Lord Woolf CJ observed in *Re Railtrack Plc*:[20]

> The legislative preference is that the company should not be wound up and that all or part of its undertaking should be transferred to another company as a going concern, its relevant activities having been carried on in the meantime ...
>
> The reason for the preference is obvious. It is because it is in the national interest that the railways should continue to function as effectively as possible, even if it is necessary for a railway company to be subject to a railway administration order.

Broadly, these procedures all have the following in common. Ordinary insol- **3.16** vency proceedings under the Act are either not available at all or cannot be commenced without notice to the appropriate authorities. If given notice, the authorities can respond with a petition to the court for the appropriate special proceeding. An order results in the appointment of a 'special administrator' who must be an insolvency practitioner and who manages the company for the special purposes of the applicable legislation, instead of for the ordinary purposes of an administration under the Act. Under some of these regimes, the purpose of the order is simply transfer, and management pending transfer, but

---

[19] See further Chapter 5 Section 3a.
[20] [2002] EWCA Civ 955, [2002] 1 WLR 3002 [11]–[12].

in others it is expressed in terms of an objective to secure the continued provision of the services and to make continuation of the order itself unnecessary. This is to be achieved either by rescuing the company as a going concern or by transferring the whole or parts of its undertaking to a new provider. In this later model, it is further provided that transfers shall only be effected if rescue is impractical or will not secure continued provision without transfers, or if the interests of creditors would be better served by transfers. Transfers are the subject of separate provisions which involve not only a new appointee to provide the service but may also transfer the property, rights, and liabilities of the subject company to the new appointee. Such transfers require the approval of the appropriate authority.

3.17 These proceedings are not proceedings undertaken for the benefit of creditors (or the debtor) because the clear intention is to give preference to the interests of society as represented by the consumers of the services. Although the procedures can indirectly result from creditor action, only the authorities can petition. The petition may or may not be grounded on insolvency. The procedures include provisions to protect the interests of creditors but those interests are subordinated to the regulatory purpose of achieving continuity of provision.[21] Transfer does involve a form of execution against the property of the company but it is not an execution which is conducted by or on behalf of the creditors of the company even if the company is insolvent.[22] On the contrary, the effect of the order is to suspend creditor remedies whilst the special purpose or objective is pursued—the pursuit of which may actually be at the expense of creditors. The fact that an insolvency practitioner acts as the administrator does not determine the nature of the procedure; insolvency practitioners are the obvious choice of independent professional to administer such proceedings because the requisite skills and resources are those which are employed in insolvency proceedings.

3.18 The procedures are, at best, hybrids which are conventional insolvency proceedings in form rather than substance. The points of particular difficulty are that:

a) the proceedings may be triggered for reasons unrelated to the solvency of the company;

b) proceedings undertaken with the objective of securing continuity of supply for the benefit of the public cannot be regarded as proceedings undertaken for

---

[21] The court drew this distinction between railway administration and 1986 Act administration in *Railtrack* ibid at [32].

[22] *Re Metronet BCV Ltd* [2007] EWHC 2687 (Ch), [2008] Bus LR 823 [29] (Patten J): 'It seems to me that there could easily in certain circumstances be a tension between the need to secure the transfer of the existing appointees undertaking to the new appointee in order to maintain the underground network and the interests of creditors in obtaining the best return from an otherwise insolvent company.'

terminal or reorganizational purposes because termination or reorganization is no more than an incidental consequence of the true objective; and,

c) proceedings in which the interests of both the debtor and its creditors are subordinated to social interests cannot be regarded as collective insolvency proceedings (in the sense that that term is usually understood).

Such proceedings are very far removed from the creditors' bargain theory of insolvency law whereby insolvency law is viewed as replicating a hypothetical bargain which the creditors would have struck if they had negotiated a solution in advance of their problems with the debtor.[23]

Although it is a development of the emerging international norm, it is suggested **3.19** that proceedings of this nature should nonetheless be regarded as genuine insolvency proceedings when used in the context of actual or anticipated insolvency. The existence of a social interest in the operation of insolvency law was recognized in the Cork Report[24] but the new dimension is to treat that interest as being paramount instead of being part of a 'compact' in which society, creditors, and the company are all parties. In most cases this will be a distinction without a difference because the social interest in an 'ordinary' insolvency lies in there being a conventional insolvency proceeding exhibiting all the characteristics identified in paragraph 3.07 above. In those instances where special measures are necessary to preserve continuity of service in the public interest, it seems appropriate to allow such preference to be a legitimate function and characteristic of insolvency proceedings and to develop the concept accordingly.

---

[23] See further Chapter 2 para 2.06.
[24] Cork Report (n 10) para 192.

4

THE MEANING OF INSOLVENCY

1. Introduction

4.01 Insolvency proceedings relate to insolvent companies. Insolvency is therefore a central concept and the law requires a test of insolvency which can be used to determine whether a company is amenable to such proceedings and to regulate the availability of certain other rights and remedies concerning transaction avoidance which apply to protect the integrity of an estate which is the subject of insolvency proceedings. It is a curiosity of the Act that despite its title it provides no definition of 'insolvency' for these purposes but refers instead to 'inability to pay debts'.[1] The advantage of this looser terminology is that it embraces both cash-flow (or 'commercial') and balance sheet measures of a company's financial difficulty.

4.02 The application of the test of inability to pay its debts to a company's entry into insolvency proceedings under the Act is not uniform but the variances are easily explained by reference to the particular characteristics of the different proceedings. A company may be wound up by the court if it is unable to pay its debts.[2] A company goes into voluntary liquidation if its shareholders pass a winding-up resolution and the liquidation will be a creditors' voluntary liquidation if it is not preceded by a directors' declaration of solvency ie, a statutory declaration that the directors believe that it will be able to pay its debts in full with interest during a period not exceeding twelve months.[3] The difference between the two entry routes

---

[1] Different tests are applicable for the purposes of wrongful trading and the disqualification of directors.

[2] Section 122(1).

[3] Sections 89 and 90.

to an insolvent liquidation is essentially a difference of form rather than substance since present inability to pay debts is determinative in both cases. An administrator can only be appointed by the court, the directors, or the company, if the company is or is likely to become unable to pay its debts.[4] This slightly looser test, expressly importing the ability to anticipate inability to pay debts, is consistent with administration being a reorganizational procedure designed to facilitate the rescue of viable enterprises. (The requirement is different where the appointment is made by the holder of a qualifying floating charge where, instead of demonstrating actual or anticipated inability to pay debts, the test is whether the floating charge is enforceable—which reflects the special position of such administrations as a substitute for administrative receivership.[5]) There is no formal requirement to demonstrate inability to pay debts when proposing a company voluntary arrangement (although the company may already be in liquidation or administration) but, given that, even where the proposal is that of the company's directors, it is a proposal to the company and its creditors for a composition in satisfaction of its debts or a scheme of arrangement of its affairs, it would follow that there would be at least anticipated insolvency.[6]

The meaning of inability to pay debts is explained in section 123.[7] Subsections **4.03** (1) and (2), excluding paragraphs which apply only to Scotland and Northern Ireland, provide:

123 Definition of inability to pay debts

(1) A company is deemed unable to pay its debts –
 (a) if a creditor (by assignment or otherwise) to whom the company is indebted in a sum exceeding £750 then due has served on the company, by leaving it at the company's registered office, a written demand (in the prescribed form) requiring the company to pay the sum so due and the company has for 3 weeks thereafter neglected to pay the sum or to secure or compound for it to the reasonable satisfaction of the creditor, or
 (b) if, in England and Wales, execution or other process issued on a judgment, decree or order of any court in favour of a creditor of the company is returned unsatisfied in whole or in part, or ...
 (e) if it is proved to the satisfaction of the court that the company is unable to pay its debts as they fall due.
(2) A company is also deemed unable to pay its debts if it is proved to the satisfaction of the court that the value of the company's assets is less than the amount of its liabilities, taking into account its contingent and prospective liabilities.

'Debt' and 'liability' are defined in very wide terms in rule 14.1. In order to establish inability to pay debts, it is sufficient to demonstrate either inability to pay

---

[4] Schedule B1 paras 11 and 27.
[5] Schedule B1 para 18. See further Chapter 8.
[6] The various threshold tests of insolvency to be satisfied when commencing insolvency proceedings are not, of course, the only requirements of the legislation. See further Chapters 7, 8, and 9.
[7] Section 123 applies to liquidations and to administrations by virtue of Schedule B1 para 111.

debts as they fall due or an asset deficiency; both may be present but one is possible without the other.[8]

4.04 Both subsections (1) and (2) are expressed to be deeming provisions but in reality only paragraphs (a) and (b) of subsection (1) can properly be so described. They are both instances of particular events being treated as determinative of inability to pay debts but the distinction between those cases and the more general proof of inability to pay for the purposes of subsection (1)(e) is illusory. The courts may treat the failure of even an ostensibly well-funded company to pay an undisputed liability as evidence of its inability to pay for the purposes of subsection (1)(e), whether or not a statutory demand has been served.[9]

4.05 There are two broad issues about the application of both the cash-flow and balance sheet tests of insolvency under section 123. The first, which is a question of interpretation, concerns futurity—the extent to which the courts should take into account what may happen in the future in deciding whether they are satisfied that there is a present inability to pay debts. The second, which is a more practical question, concerns the valuation of assets and liabilities when striking the necessary balance between them. These issues are explored in subsequent sections of this chapter.

4.06 The legal test of insolvency is not to be confused with the accounting test to be applied in determining whether a company's accounts should be prepared on a going concern basis. The accounting test is directed to whether a company will be able to discharge its liabilities as they fall due in the foreseeable future (which, in practice means a minimum period of twelve months).[10] This is ostensibly similar to the legal cash-flow test but, for accounting purposes, directors are expected to take all available information about the future into account. That includes, for example, non-binding letters of comfort from parent companies and the prospects of further capitalization—neither of which constitute assets for the purposes of section 123. Accounts should only be prepared on a liquidation basis if management either

[8] *Re Cheyne Finance Plc (No 2)* [2007] EWHC 2402 (Ch), [2008] Bus LR 1562 [55]; *BNY Corporate Trustee Services Ltd v Eurosail-UK 2007-3BL Plc* [2013] UKSC 28, [2013] 1 WLR 1408 [42].
[9] *Cornhill Insurance Plc v Improvement Services Ltd* [1986] 1 WLR 114 (Ch); *Taylors Industrial Flooring Ltd v M&H Plant Hire (Manchester) Ltd* [1990] BCLC 216 (CA) but see also *Eurosail* ibid at [25].
[10] See further Schedule 1 para 11 to each of the Small Companies and Groups (Accounts and Directors' Report) Regulations 2008 (SI 2008/409) and the Large and Medium Sized Companies and Groups (Accounts and Reports) Regulations 2008 (SI 2008/410); Financial Reporting Council, *Guidance on Risk Management, Internal Control and Related Financial and Business Reporting* (September 2014) <https://www.frc.org.uk/Our-Work/Publications/Corporate-Governance/Guidance-on-Risk-Management,-Internal-Control-and.pdf> and *Guidance on the Going Concern Basis of Accounting and Reporting on Solvency and Liquidity Risks – Guidance for directors of companies that do not apply The UK Corporate Governance Code* (April 2016) <https://www.frc.org.uk/Our-Work/Publications/Accounting-and-Reporting-Policy/Guidance-on-the-Going-Concern-Basis-of-Accounting.pdf> both accessed 31 August 2016.

intends to liquidate the company or to cease trading (or has no realistic alternative but to do so). There is therefore a mismatch between the legal and accounting tests which can be misleading and companies with current liabilities which comfortably exceed their assets may nonetheless prepare going concern accounts because they have adequate working capital for the foreseeable future and do not envisage liquidation.

2. Interpretation of section 123

It is possible to advance the following general propositions about the way in which **4.07** subsections 123(1)(e) and (2) are interpreted:

a) Although presented as two separate tests, they are more properly regarded as two aspects of a single test with the distinction turning on when the debts will fall due.

b) 'Taking into account' contingent and prospective liabilities does not involve treating such liabilities as if they were due and payable; a proper allowance must be made for uncertainties and deferment.

c) Cash-flow insolvency may (but not necessarily will) be averted by the availability of new borrowing to discharge liabilities.

d) Balance sheet insolvency is less likely to be affected by new borrowing but altering the maturity of future liabilities may make it more difficult to prove that the company will be unable to pay its debts in the future.

e) Future assets can only be taken into account if based on present rights as opposed to hopes or expectations but the prospects of acquiring further assets, or of restructuring liabilities, may be taken into account when considering whether it has been proved that a company will be unable to pay prospective liabilities when they fall due.

f) In a finely balanced case, the outcome will depend on the burden of proof, thus admitting the possibility that different conclusions on solvency could be reached on the same facts for different purposes.

The most obvious starting point on the interpretation of section 123 is the decision **4.08** of the Supreme Court in *BNY Corporate Trustee Services Ltd v Eurosail-UK 2007-3BL Plc*. The leading judgment, delivered by Lord Walker, conveniently traces the history of the legislation. He noted substantial changes during the evolution of the statutory test but concluded:[11]

> The changes in form served, in my view, to underline that the 'cash-flow' test is concerned not simply with the petitioner's own presently due debt, nor only with other presently-due debt owed by the company, but also with debts falling due

---

[11] [2013] UKSC 28, [2013] 1 WLR 1408 [37].

from time to time in the reasonably near future. What is reasonably near future, for this purpose, will depend on all the circumstances, but especially on the nature of the company's business ... The express reference to assets and liabilities is in my view a practical recognition that once the court has to move beyond the reasonably near future (the length of which depends, again, on all the circumstances) any attempt to apply a cash-flow test will become completely speculative, and a comparison of present assets with future liabilities (discounted for contingencies and deferment) becomes the only sensible test. But it is still very far from an exact test, and the burden of proof must be on the party which asserts balance-sheet insolvency.

Later he quoted and approved the following passage from the judgment of Toulson LJ in *Eurosail* in the Court of Appeal:[12]

> Essentially, section 123(2) requires the court to make a judgment whether it has been established that, looking at the company's assets and making proper allowance for its prospective and contingent liabilities, it cannot reasonably be expected to be able to meet those liabilities. If so, it will be deemed insolvent although it is currently able to pay its debts as they fall due. The more distant the liabilities, the harder this will be to establish.

The practical effect of this approach to futurity is substantially to assimilate the liquidation test with that mandated by the legislation for administration (which refers to a company which 'is or is likely to become unable to pay its debts').[13]

4.09 *Re Casa Estates (UK) Ltd*[14] was a case where the issue of solvency arose in the context of transaction avoidance claims and the burden of proof was reversed so that the onus was on the recipient of certain payments to prove that the company had not been insolvent when the payments were made and the company was in fact paying its debts to its creditors when they required them to be paid. The case was the subject of two successive appeals, first to Warren J and, secondly, to the Court of Appeal where Lewison LJ gave a judgment (with which the other members of the court agreed) upholding Warren J's decision that the transaction avoidance claims had been made out. The judgment of Warren J is of continuing interest, not least for a particular observation concerning the effect of reversing the burden of proof. Having referred to the observation of Toulson LJ in *Eurosail* quoted above, about the more distant the liabilities making it harder to establish insolvency, he said:[15]

> ... where the burden is on a person ... to rebut the presumption of insolvency, the further into the future one needs to go the harder it will be to prove that the company can reasonably be expected to meet its liabilities.

---

[12] Ibid at [42].

[13] Where 'likely' means more probable than not: *Re AA Mutual International Insurance Co Ltd* [2004] EWHC 2430 (Ch), [2005] 2 BCLC 8.

[14] [2014] EWCA Civ 383, [2014] 2 BCLC 49.

[15] [2013] EWHC 2371 (Ch), [2014] 2 BCLC 49 [86].

Lewison LJ said of the relationship of the tests:[16]

> I agree with Warren J at [34] that the two tests feature as part of a single exercise, namely to determine whether a company is unable to pay its debts.

and went on to make the following observation about funding the payment of current liabilities:[17]

> It certainly seems counter-intuitive (to me at least) that a company that manages to stave off cash-flow insolvency by going deeper and deeper into long-term debt is not insolvent. It may be able to trade its way out of insolvency, and thus avoid going into insolvent liquidation, but that is a different matter. Equally if (as Warren J held) Casa UK was only able to pay its debts as they fell due by taking new deposits, and using them to pay off old debts, in any commercial sense the company was insolvent, whether on a cash-flow basis or a balance-sheet basis.

Nourse J had earlier considered the question of borrowing to discharge liabilities in *Re* **4.10**
a Company. As regards the cash-flow test, he first said:[18]

> One thing that is perfectly clear in this case is that the company is being propped up by loans made to it by associated companies and possibly by others. Counsel for the petitioner's first submission is that in those circumstances the company is unable to pay its debts, since it can only pay them by recourse to loans made to it by others … I think that if a company can pay its debts only with the help of loans made by others, it is nevertheless prima facie able to pay its debts for the purposes of that subsection. However, that is by no means an end of the case.

He then went on to consider the implications for the balance sheet test:[19]

> That is not an end of the matter, because I must now consider the second part [of the relevant provision of the Companies Act 1948], which requires me to take into account the contingent and prospective liabilities of the company. Counsel for the petitioner submits, correctly, that every time the company borrows money from somebody else to pay off the petitioner or the supporting creditor, or whoever, that borrowing increases its prospective liabilities, because it incurs a further debt prospectively due to the lender. Counsel says that if I take into account the contingent and prospective liabilities of the company, it is clearly insolvent in balance sheet terms. So indeed it is if I treat the loans made by the associated companies as loans which are currently repayable. However, what I am required to do is to 'take into account' the contingent and prospective liabilities. That cannot mean that I must simply add them up and strike a balance against assets. In regard to prospective liabilities I must principally consider whether, and if so when, they are likely to become present liabilities.

The possibility that the calculation of a company's present ability to pay its debts **4.11**
might take into account any hope or expectation of future assets was succinctly

---

[16] Ibid at [29].
[17] Ibid at [31].
[18] [1986] BCLC 261 (Ch) 262e. The presence of immediately realizable assets may also be taken into account: *Re Capital Annuities Ltd* [1979] 1 WLR 170 (Ch) 188A.
[19] At 263b. See also *Casa Estates* (n 14), in particular Warren J at [35].

rejected by the Court of Appeal in *Byblos Bank SAL v Al-Khudhairy* where Nicholls LJ (with whom the other members of the court agreed) said:[20]

> ... it is not correct to take into account, in addition to assets presently owned by it, any hope or expectation [the company] then had that it would acquire further assets in the future without any accompanying right to such further assets.
>
> ... I can see no justification for importing into [the relevant provision of the Companies Act 1948], from the requirement to take into account prospective and future liabilities, any obligation or entitlement to treat the assets of the company as being, at the material date, other than they truly are.

Prospective assets were relevant to the exercise of the court's discretion but not to the calculation of solvency on which the jurisdiction to exercise its discretion is based.

4.12 However, in assessing the balance sheet solvency of a company that is presently meeting its liabilities as they fall due but has liabilities which increasingly exceed its assets, it may be possible to take into account the prospects of a future restructuring when considering the balance of probabilities. This was one of the issues in *Myers v Kestrel Acquisitions Ltd*[21] where it was treated as a matter of evidence but, on the facts, it was found that the intention to effect a restructuring was no more than an aspiration. The rigidity of the Court of Appeal's exclusion of future assets in *Byblos Bank* now requires reconsideration in the light of the more nuanced approach of the Supreme Court in *Eurosail* to balance sheet insolvency. If it is appropriate to consider the possibility of a future restructuring, it should also be possible to have regard to the prospects of acquiring further assets when assessing the likelihood of a future default—provided that prospect is supported by appropriate evidence. Indeed, Lord Walker appeared to contemplate something of the sort in *Eurosail* when he pointed out that the issue before the court in that case was simplified by the fact that Eurosail itself was not an ordinary trading company which might, for example, raise new capital.[22]

3. Valuation

4.13 Not only are the legal tests of inability to pay debts such that the court must exercise judgment over futurity issues, the data upon which its conclusions will be based also raises valuation issues. Such issues can affect the computation of both assets and liabilities and give rise to considerable uncertainty in the practical application of the balance sheet test. In this, the company's own accounts are of little

---

[20] [1987] BCLC 232 (CA) 246h, 247g. See also *Evans v Jones* [2016] EWCA Civ 660.
[21] [2015] EWHC 916 (Ch), [2016] 1 BCLC 719.
[22] *Eurosail* (n 11) at [38].

use. First, they will inevitably be historic and, secondly, they will have been pre-pared in accordance with accounting standards which are different from the legal tests. For example, an asset must be owned[23] in order to be brought into account and the relevant value of an asset is its realizable value when the computation of net balance sheet worth is made. Certain contingent liabilities which merely required noting in the company's own accounts must be evaluated and taken into account.

Asset valuations may be established by evidence which falls short of formal valu-ations.[24] A threshold question arises as to the basis of the valuation. The value of a company's assets as a going concern may exceed the aggregate value of the same assets on a break-up basis. If the question is whether a company will be able to pay its debts at some time in the future and the company is both generating operating profits and has sufficient working capital to avert any question of current cash-flow insolvency, it may be appropriate to value its assets on a going concern basis if that is more favourable to it. If, on the other hand, its current trading is unprofitable (regardless of its longer term liabilities) a piecemeal valuation of its assets on a break-up basis would be indicated. (If the company is cash-flow insolvent, the question of balance sheet insolvency is unlikely to need to be resolved.) Even when the correct basis of valuation is established, there is considerable scope for disagree-ment as to actual values. **4.14**

It has already been seen that contingent and prospective liabilities fall to be taken into account. A contingent liability is one which may or may not materialize depending upon future events. The amount for which it should be brought into account could therefore vary from something nominal to almost 100 per cent.[25] By contrast, a prospective liability is a liability which has materialized but which is not yet payable and may not have been quantified.[26] The valuation issues can over-lap in that it is necessary for the court to reach a conclusion, in respect of a given contingent or prospective liability, both on the amount and when it will fall due for payment. This is essentially a question of fact to be determined on the evidence before the court. **4.15**

The Rules make provision for the discounting of future debts for dividend purposes in liquidation and administration.[27] However, although Lord Walker in *Eurosail* referred to the need to discount for deferment, it is thought that it would be wrong to apply the formula in the Rules for the purposes of determining inability to pay debts. The whole point of the balance sheet test is to reach a conclusion as to the **4.16**

---

[23] As opposed to an economic interest being enjoyed—for example in goods held under a finance lease.

[24] *Re Capital Annuities Ltd* [1979] 1 WLR 170 (Ch) 188D.

[25] *Re HLC Environmental Projects Ltd* [2013] EWHC 2876 (Ch), [2014] BCC 337 is an example of a case where full provision was required.

[26] *Re Dollar Land Holdings Plc* [1994] 1 BCLC 404 (Ch).

[27] Rule 14.44.

likelihood of the company discharging its prospective liability in the future when it has matured into a liability which is due and payable. To treat it as a present liability for a discounted amount is inconsistent with the statutory test and the application of the relevant rules should therefore be confined to their expressed purpose, namely the computation of dividends. There may be a distinction in this respect between contingent and prospective liabilities. The Rules require a liquidator or administrator to estimate the value of contingent liabilities for the purposes of admission as provable debts but are silent as to the methodology to be employed.[28] The practical results of a court evaluating a contingent liability for the purposes of taking it into account in an assessment of inability to pay debts may be nearer to those that would result from an office-holder's determination; in both cases it is necessary for the conclusion to reflect both probabilities and the potential quantum (although in determining inability to pay debts, the court will also need to have regard to when the contingent liability may mature into an actual liability).

4. Contractual tests of insolvency

4.17   Section 123 is frequently adopted as the test of insolvency for the purposes of stipulating events of default in finance documents and in other contractual arrangements as a trigger for additional rights on the part of the counterparty. Here a distinction must again be drawn between subsection (1)(a) and (b) and both subsections (1)(e) and (2) because the latter both refer to proof to the satisfaction of the court. The dangers of uncritical transposition of the statutory formulation are illustrated by contrasting the decisions in *Fraser v Oystertec Plc*[29] and *Invertec Ltd v De Mol Holding BV*.[30] In the former, the court was strongly attracted to the proposition that:

> If you choose to incorporate s.123 of the Insolvency Act you take it warts and all. You take it with the provision that nothing final can happen until the court finds insolvency.[31]

but was reluctantly persuaded that it was not right to decide the point on an application for summary judgment. In the *Invertec* case, the court refused to construe a warranty that a company was not unable to pay its debts within the meaning of section 123 as merely meaning that there had been no court order to the contrary.[32] Any contract will be construed with reference to its context; ultimately its meaning is a matter of drafting and those who intend that a court ruling should not be necessary should say so.

---

[28] Rule 14.14.
[29] [2003] EWHC 2787 (Ch), [2004] BCC 233.
[30] [2009] EWHC 2471 (Ch).
[31] *Fraser* (n 29) at [107].
[32] *Invertec* (n 30) at [298].

5. Conclusions

The tests of inability to pay debts are not based on a snapshot. The ability to have **4.18** regard to futurity undoubtedly enables the court to reach conclusions which are more grounded in commercial reality than would otherwise be the case. The advantages of this more flexible approach are clear when the court is considering whether or not to open insolvency proceedings under the Act on the hostile application of an individual creditor. However, the tests of inability to pay debts are not only determinative in that context and the very flexibility which enables the court to have regard to commercial reality also promotes uncertainty. When directors are considering their duties in respect of a company in financial difficulty or advisers are seeking to apply the same tests as transposed into commercial contracts, the willingness of the courts to have regard to futurity according to the facts of the case can make it difficult to predict whether a company would or would not be found to be unable to pay its debts. Arguably, the courts could have achieved the same ability to reflect commercial reality through the exercise of their residual discretion as to the opening of proceedings without any need to rely on futurity.

In one particular respect, the present state of the law is potentially unjust. That con- **4.19** cerns the position of the respondent in transaction avoidance proceedings where the transaction is safe unless there was contemporaneous insolvency. If the burden of proof is reversed, it may often be too difficult to satisfy a court on the balance of probabilities that a company would have been able to pay its future and contingent liabilities when due, such that the insolvency ingredient of such claims may be little more than a formality—a result which does not appear consistent with the ostensible balance of the legislation.

5

SOURCES OF ENGLISH CORPORATE INSOLVENCY LAW

1. Introduction

5.01 Reference is quite frequently made to the 'insolvency code' but this is misleading; there is no codification of English insolvency law which would bear comparison with a civil law code. The term is used colloquially to refer to the general body of insolvency law, covering both personal and corporate insolvency, which derives from a number of different sources. The term is also sometimes used more specifically to refer to the rules dealing with the ranking and priority of creditors.

5.02 In 1982, the Cork Report observed:[1]

> No comprehensive statement of insolvency law in England and Wales exists. Instead, there is a patchwork of materials dealing with the subject consisting of legislation such as … ; all this has to be supplemented by the principles of common law and equity, as illustrated by case law and discussed in the text books.

This observation remains equally true today despite the major overhaul of the law which the Report heralded and the subsequent enactment of the Act.

5.03 The modern patchwork of English corporate insolvency law comprises:

---

[1] Report of the Review Committee, *Insolvency Law and Practice* (Cm 8558, June 1982) para 26.

a) the Act, the Company Directors Disqualification Act 1986 and their associated secondary legislation;
b) other domestic legislation;
c) common law;
d) equitable principles; and
e) European law.

What follows is intended to illustrate the interaction of those different sources (without attempting to be definitive as to their various contributions to the whole).

2. The Act, the Company Directors Disqualification Act 1986, and their associated secondary legislation

The history of legislation dealing with personal insolvency dates back to the six- **5.04** teenth century but legislation dealing with corporate insolvency law as it is now known began with the enactment of the Companies Act 1862.

The Act and the Rules are now the principal source of English corporate insol- **5.05** vency law but there is a considerable body of other secondary legislation in addition to the Rules.[2] The Cork Report led to enactment of the Insolvency Act 1985 which was only partially brought into force before the consolidation of that Act with the insolvency provisions of the Companies Act 1985 and the Bankruptcy Act 1914, in the Insolvency Act 1986. The consolidation also involved the separation of the law on the disqualification of directors into the Company Directors Disqualification Act 1986 (CDDA). Both 1986 Acts came into force on 29 December 1986 and both have been substantially amended by subsequent legislation.

The Act and the CDDA are regarded as two parts of the same statutory scheme.[3] **5.06**

3. Other domestic legislation

The extent to which English corporate insolvency law was consolidated in the Act **5.07** has always been illusory because of other legislation affecting its operation which exists outside the Act and because, latterly, of carve-outs and the proliferation of special regimes. It is also necessary to take the Human Rights Act 1998 into account.

---

[2] The Rules (SI 2016/1024) are the result of a recently completed project of consolidation and reformulation.
[3] *Re Pantmaenog Timber Co Ltd* [2003] UKHL 49, [2004] 1 AC 158 [60].

a. Special regimes

5.08 The detail of the various special regimes lies outside the scope of this book but broadly they divide into five different groups:

a) procedures under which the orthodox procedures under the Act are adapted for business structures which are not registered companies (examples are friendly societies, co-operative societies, and collective investment schemes);

b) insurance insolvency;

c) executive intervention in NHS foundation trusts;

d) procedures dealing with a range of essential service providers (examples are utilities and transport service providers); and

e) the special resolution regime for financial institutions.[4]

(The impact of the procedures applicable to essential service providers on the concept of insolvency proceedings has already been considered in Section 5 of Chapter 3.)

5.09 There is no uniform approach to legislation in this area. Ordinary insolvency law can include special provisions which only apply in specified circumstances, or the general law applicable to the entity in question (for example, the applicable regulatory law) can include special provisions to apply in the event of insolvency. A third approach is that insolvency can be the subject of discrete legislation. English law affords examples of all these approaches but one very common characteristic of these special regimes is that they incorporate provisions of the Act by reference, with or without modifications. It follows that decided cases on the operation of these special regimes can be directly relevant to the operation of the Act in respect of registered companies.

b. Carve-outs

5.10 Carve-outs are provisions of other enactments which selectively disapply significant parts of the Act as regards particular classes of transaction so that they can take effect according to their own terms. The details of these carve-outs are also outside the scope of this book but they fall into two broad categories:

a) Those flowing from financial markets legislation contained in the Companies Act 1989 and regulations made pursuant to it, which deal with market contracts, market charges, and system charges in favour of settlement banks. These will not be encountered outside the financial markets.

b) Those dealing with financial collateral, where the regulations are made pursuant to the European Communities Act 1972. Some of these regulations

---

[4] See further Hamish Anderson, 'What is the Purpose of Insolvency Proceedings?' [2016] JBL 670.

are concerned with settlement finality through designated systems and, as above, will not be encountered outside the financial markets. However, the Financial Collateral Arrangements (No 2) Regulations 2003[5] are of more general application because they apply to financial collateral arrangements (ie arrangements relating to cash or financial instruments) between companies. *Re Lehman Brothers International (Europe) (No 5)* provides a practical example of some of the issues which can arise.[6]

c. Other legislation making special provision for insolvencies

General law questions arise in every insolvency proceeding. However, in some cases the ordinary rules of general law are modified in their application to companies which are the subject of insolvency proceedings or in relation to the position of office-holders. The following are examples of legislation of this sort which are commonly encountered: **5.11**

a) Under the Employment Rights Act 1996, certain liabilities to a company's employees are paid out of the National Insurance Fund in the event of an employer company entering insolvency proceedings and the Secretary of State is subrogated to the employee's claims in the proceeding.
b) Insolvency exceptions are made in the Transfer of Undertakings (Protection of Employment) Regulations 2006[7] which modify the ordinary rules whereby the transferee assumes liability on contracts of employment.
c) The commencement of insolvency proceedings triggers a debt under the Pensions Act 1995 in respect of certain pension schemes based on the value by which the scheme's liabilities exceed the value of the scheme assets.
d) Under the Environmental Protection Act 1990, office-holders in insolvency proceedings have a qualified exemption from personal liability for remediation costs which do not result from their own unreasonable acts or omissions.
e) The Third Party (Rights Against Insurers) Act 2010 provides that, where a company which is subject to insolvency proceedings has a liability in respect of which it is insured, the creditor is subrogated to the company's rights against its insurer and the insurance money does not form part of the company's estate.

The foregoing list deals with legislation within which some provisions dealing with insolvency might reasonably be anticipated by practitioners. Unfortunately that is not true of all the relevant sources—some are much more obscure. The Partnership Act 1890 affords a good example. According to its terms, sums due in respect of loans **5.12**

---

[5] SI 2003/3226.
[6] [2012] EWHC 2997 (Ch), [2014] 2 BCLC 295.
[7] SI 2006/246.

made at a rate of interest which varies according to a debtor's profits and consideration for the acquisition of goodwill which takes the form of a profit share, are deferred debts in the event of bankruptcy. The Partnership Act is not where one would expect to find a provision dealing with the ranking and priority of debt in corporate insolvency proceedings which do not involve either bankruptcy (as such) or a partnership, but it applies because it is incorporated by an oblique reference in the Rules.[8]

d. Human Rights Act 1998

5.13 Companies have 'Convention rights' and the office-holder in insolvency proceedings may be a 'public authority' for the purposes of the 1998 Act. All other legislation must, as far as possible, be interpreted in a way which is compatible with the European Convention on Human Rights. Other legislation for these purposes naturally includes the Act and Rules but the reported cases show Convention rights as having been raised more often in the field of personal insolvency than in corporate insolvency.

4. Common law

5.14 Common law rules apply alongside the insolvency legislation. Sometimes the operation of the rules is consistent with the express terms of the Act but other rules have never been reflected in the terms of the legislation. Much of this law has its origins in older bankruptcy cases.

5.15 Examples of extant common law rules are as follows:

a) The Act provides for pari passu distribution but it is a common law rule which strikes down agreements which purport to contract out of that scheme.[9]

b) A closely aligned common law rule is the anti-deprivation rule which strikes down arrangements which take assets out of the insolvent estate in the event of insolvency proceedings.[10]

c) The rule against double proof (which receives no mention in the Act or Rules) precludes the admission of more than one proof of debt in respect of what is, in substance, one liability of the company. The most usual situation in which the rule is encountered concerns guarantees. Where the company's liability has been guaranteed, the creditor has an ordinary claim against the company but the surety will also have an indemnity claim. The rule prevents dividends being paid on both claims to the detriment of other creditors.[11]

---

[8] Rule 14.2(4)(b).
[9] See further Chapter 21.
[10] See also Chapter 21.
[11] *Re Oriental Commercial Bank, ex parte European Bank* (1871) 7 Ch App 99 (CA); *Barclays Bank Ltd v TOSG Trust Fund Ltd* [1984] AC 626 (HL).

d) The rule in *Ex parte James* which means that an office-holder acting as an officer of the court will not be allowed to pursue a course of conduct, or take advantage of a technical position in law, where it would be dishonourable to do so.[12]

e) The power of the court to treat the English liquidation of a foreign registered company which is also subject to insolvency proceedings in its home jurisdiction, as being an 'ancillary liquidation'.[13]

f) The common law jurisdiction to recognize and grant assistance to foreign insolvency proceedings.[14]

5.16 By contrast it is thought that, to the extent that common law rules on transaction avoidance have been superseded by the very detailed provisions of the Act, there is no room for the operation of the original common law rules which previously addressed the same mischief and that they no longer even serve any useful purpose as a guide to the interpretation of the Act.[15]

5. Equitable principles

5.17 Equity and equitable principles permeate insolvency law. Thus, for example, equity helps to define the insolvent estate through the exclusion of trust property and the scheme for pari passu distribution in insolvencies may be said to be founded on the maxim that 'equality is equity'.

5.18 In other respects, equity supplements the legislation in ways that are comparable with the effect of the common law rules referred to above. Examples of this are as follows:

a) In the event of winding-up, the company ceases to be the beneficial owner of its property which is held on trust for the purposes of the statutory scheme.[16]

b) Directors of a company in the zone of insolvency have a fiduciary duty to act with regard to the interests of the creditors of the company.[17]

c) An office-holder has a fiduciary duty to avoid both conflicts of duty and conflicts of interest with duty.[18]

---

[12] *Re Condon, ex parte James* (1874) LR 9 Ch App 609 (CA). See further Chapter 11.

[13] *Re Bank of Credit and Commerce International SA (No 10)* [1997] Ch 213 (Ch); *Re HIH Casualty and General Insurance Ltd* [2008] UKHL 21, [2008] 1 WLR 852. See further Chapter 22.

[14] *Rubin v Eurofinance SA* [2012] UKSC 46, [2013] 1 AC 236; *Singularis Holdings Ltd v PricewaterhouseCoopers* [2014] UKPC 36, [2015] AC 1675. See further Chapter 22.

[15] See further Chapter 15.

[16] *Ayerst v C&K (Construction Ltd)* [1976] AC 167 (HL). See further Chapter 7.

[17] *West Mercia Safetywear Ltd v Dodd* [1988] BCLC 250 (CA); *Colin Gwyer & Associates Ltd v London Wharf (Limehouse) Ltd* [2002] EWHC 2748 (Ch), [2003] 2 BCLC 153.

[18] *Re Corbenstoke Ltd (No 2)* [1990] BCLC 60 (Ch).

d) In an appropriate case the court will permit the office-holder in insolvency proceedings to draw upon trust property for his own remuneration and expenses.[19]

e) The rule in *Cherry v Boultbee*,[20] which provides that a person who is liable to contribute to a fund cannot participate in its distribution without first making the fund whole and which may therefore fill the gap where set-off does not apply.[21]

f) The court will issue anti-suit injunctions against creditors amenable to its personal jurisdiction to prevent proceedings being brought in foreign courts which will interfere with the statutory trusts resulting from an English liquidation.[22]

g) Where a company is being wound up in England and in another jurisdiction, a creditor who receives a dividend in the foreign proceedings may not receive a dividend in the English proceeding without bringing the foreign dividend into hotchpot.[23]

5.19 The equitable principles under discussion in the preceding paragraph are not to be confused with the 'equity of a statute' under which the courts were in fairly distant legal history prepared to enlarge the wording of a statute by disregarding its own terms so as to apply it to analogous cases. This was never an aspect of the equitable jurisdiction of the Court of Chancery. Latterly the term means no more than that the courts will give a statute a purposive interpretation. Whilst this is unquestionably the approach adopted by the courts to the interpretation of the Act, it stops well short of the application of the Act (or any other applicable legislation) on an 'as if' basis, as was roundly rejected by Lord Collins in *Singularis Holdings Ltd v PricewaterhouseCoopers*.[24]

6. European law

5.20 It may appear a little odd to treat European law as one of the sources of *English* corporate insolvency law but the treatment is justified because, where they apply, the European Regulations on insolvency proceedings[25] have overriding effect (subject to the exception mentioned below). The Regulations deal with the jurisdiction to

---

[19] *Re Berkeley Applegate (Investment Consultants) Ltd (No 2)* (1988) 4 BCC 279 (Ch).

[20] (1839) 4 My & Cr 442 (Ch).

[21] *Re Kaupthing Singer & Friedlander Ltd (No 2)* [2011] UKSC 48, [2012] 1 AC 804.

[22] *Stichting Shell Pensioenfonds v Krys* [2014] UKPC 41, [2015] AC 616.

[23] *Cleaver v Delta American Reinsurance Co* [2001] UKPC 6, [2001] 2 AC 328; *Re HIH Casualty and General Insurance Ltd* [2008] UKHL 21, [2008] 1 WLR 852.

[24] [2014] UKPC 36, [2015] AC 1675 [78]–[83].

[25] Council Regulation (EC) No 1346/2000 of 29 May 2000 on Insolvency Proceedings [2000] OJ L 160/1 to be replaced by Regulation (EU) 2015/848 of the European Parliament and of the Council of 20 May 2015 on Insolvency Proceedings [2015] OJ L 141/19 (RR).

open insolvency proceedings within the European Union (excluding Denmark) where a company has its 'centre of main interests' in a member state, and the consequential recognition and effects of such proceedings in the other member states. This has, for example, the consequence of curtailing the historic jurisdiction of the English courts to wind up foreign registered companies.

The exception to the overriding effect of the Regulations concerns section 426 **5.21** which provides for the English courts to act in aid of the courts of a list of designated countries and territories (with which Great Britain has or had constitutional ties). The Regulations provide that they shall not apply in so far as they are irreconcilable with obligations under section 426.[26]

7. Conclusions

This patchwork of sources is difficult to assimilate and, in any event, is the subject **5.22** of constant change. A sensible methodology when answering a question of insolvency law is to consider the application of special regimes and, subject thereto, begin with the Act and Rules before pausing to consider whether there is a cross-border element on which the European Regulations will have an impact because of their overriding effect. Next it is a question of identifying whether there is any issue with transactions which are the subject of carve-outs and whether there are relevant insolvency provisions in the general laws affecting the company's business and relationships. Finally, it is necessary to consider whether there are common law rules or equitable principles which will affect what might otherwise appear to be the applicable law or whether Convention rights protected by the Human Rights Act are involved.

---

[26] See further Chapter 22.

6

ENGLISH CORPORATE
INSOLVENCY PROCEEDINGS

1. Introduction

6.01 There are currently three forms of corporate insolvency proceeding in English law. Liquidation (whether compulsory or voluntary) is a terminal proceeding designed to realize the assets of the debtor company and distribute the realized value amongst creditors according to their respective priorities, following which the company is dissolved. Administration and company voluntary arrangements (CVA) (not mutually exclusive and sometimes used together) are two different forms of proceeding which are primarily designed to preserve going concerns. Although the three procedures are constituted as standalone procedures under the Act, there is considerable room for movement from one procedure into another in order to achieve an optimal outcome for creditors.

6.02 The law relating to all these procedures, which are discussed in more detail in the next three chapters, is principally to be found in the Act and Rules. All three procedures have one characteristic in common, namely that none can properly be regarded as a 'debtor in possession' procedure, that is to say an insolvency procedure to which the management of a distressed company can subject it without ceding control to an office-holder—the liquidator, administrator or, in the case of a CVA, the supervisor.

6.03 This book is concerned with modern corporate insolvency law but a brief historical introduction nevertheless serves two useful purposes: first, it explains how the proceedings have come to exist in their distinct forms within a single act of parliament and, secondly, because it helps to identify the underlying trend which is playing a dominant part in the continuing development of the law. That trend is an increasing emphasis on reorganizational procedures and the promotion of a 'rescue culture'.

The historical development of English corporate insolvency law was significantly **6.04** affected by the rise, and eventual fall, of what came to be labelled by the Act as 'administrative receivership'. During the second half of the twentieth century this form of security enforcement was the principal means by which distressed businesses were sold as going concerns.

2. The historical development of English corporate insolvency law

Early insolvency law was concerned only with personal insolvency because com- **6.05** panies did not exist. Even as between individuals, bankruptcy was only applicable to traders. It was recognized that trade could not be carried on without credit and that incurring debts for commercial purposes was therefore justifiable. By contrast, non-traders were not expected to live on credit and it was not until the Bankruptcy Act 1861 that bankruptcy law was extended to non-traders.

Against the background of personal insolvency law just referred to, came the rise of **6.06** corporate trading and the development of a separate body of corporate insolvency law to deal with its attendant problems. Commercial corporations first emerged at the end of the sixteenth and the beginning of the seventeenth centuries through the exercise of the common law right of the Crown to grant charters of incorporation, and companies such as the East India Company and the Hudson's Bay Company were incorporated. Towards the end of the seventeenth century the joint stock company emerged. Limited liability began with the Bubble Companies etc. Act 1825 but it was not until the Limited Liability Act 1855 that it was possible to incorporate, simply by registration, companies whose members enjoyed limited liability. The next milestone was the Companies Act 1862 which repealed and consolidated previous legislation and became the foundation of modern company law.

With the rise of limited liability companies enjoying a distinct legal personality, **6.07** it became necessary to formulate special insolvency procedures. The 1862 Act provided for both voluntary and compulsory liquidation of companies according to procedures which are recognizable precursors of the winding-up procedures currently in force. Although there have been innumerable refinements of detail, the only overarching change in structure was the separation of solvent and insolvent voluntary liquidations (members' and creditors' voluntary liquidations respectively) which was introduced by section 67 of the Companies Act 1928. The details of this history are not important for present purposes. What is important is the central point that the Act represents the culmination of a very long legislative history during which legislators have provided for the resolution of insolvent trading enterprises. As the substance of trade moved away from sole traders and partnerships into companies, so the law applicable to the latter developed, in particular to address the problem of abuse of the privilege of limited liability.

6.08 Liquidation nonetheless remained the only corporate insolvency procedure until the Insolvency Act 1986 replaced the insolvency provisions of the Companies Act 1985 and introduced administration and CVAs as rescue procedures. Subsequent major developments have been directed to making the new procedures more accessible. Thus the Insolvency Act 2000 amended the Act to make a moratorium available where directors of small companies are proposing a CVA and the Enterprise Act 2002 further amended the Act by radically changing administration into its current form—most notably by providing out of court entry routes to encourage its use.

3. The rise and fall of administrative receivership

6.09 The background of administrative receivership explains why the development of formal reorganizational procedures only came relatively recently in English law and why the holder of a qualifying floating charge enjoys the powers that it now has in administration.[1]

6.10 Receivership is not, and never was, a collective insolvency procedure; it is the means by which a secured creditor can enforce security on its own behalf. Administrative receivership is a particular form of receivership where the security held covers the whole or substantially the whole of the company's property and includes a floating charge.[2] Administrative receivership is now prohibited by section 72A except in relation to the enforcement of the dwindling number of extant floating charges created before 15 September 2003 and a series of special cases relating to the capital and financial markets, social landlords, railways, and certain forms of project financing.[3]

6.11 Receivership was developed in the nineteenth century as the means whereby a mortgagee could enforce security without exposure to the risk of liability as a mortgagee in possession.[4] The receiver, chosen and appointed by the mortgagee

---

[1] See further Chapter 8.
[2] Sections 29 and 251.
[3] Sections 72B–72H.
[4] *Gaskell v Gosling* [1896] 1 QB 669 (CA), [1898] AC 575 (HL).

pursuant to powers granted by the security, acted as the agent of the borrower. The mortgagee was not liable for the acts or omissions of the receiver unless it interfered with the conduct of the receivership. In its original form, the function of the receiver was to collect the income of the mortgaged property. Statutory powers in this respect were first contained in Lord Cranworth's Act[5] and are now to be found in the provisions of the Law of Property Act 1925. By section 101 of the 1925 Act, a mortgage by deed confers an implied power on the mortgagee to appoint a receiver of income when the mortgage money is due. Section 109 provides for the manner of appointment and removal, remuneration, and agency. Crucially, these provisions are capable of being extended by the provisions of the security. It was the facility to extend the powers of a receivership coupled with the development of the floating charge which gave receivership its commercial potency.

6.12 The floating charge was another product of inventive Victorian lawyers fashioning security to meet the needs of a rapidly developing commercial environment. Having first established that it was possible to create a fixed charge over future property,[6] the floating charge was developed as a form of ambulatory security, granted by a company, covering all property falling within the description of the property being charged but leaving the borrower free to deal in the ordinary course of business pending the occurrence of some 'crystallizing' event, the result of which was to make the floating charge a fixed charge on the property then within its scope. The concept has eluded precise definition but, according to the classic formulation, a charge will be a floating charge if it exhibits the following characteristics: it is a charge on a class of assets of a company present and future; the assets are of a nature which will change from time to time in the ordinary course of business; and, the terms of the charge contemplate that the charger will be free to deal with the assets in the ordinary course of business until some step is taken by the chargee.[7]

6.13 The practice developed of banks taking debentures from companies under which, by a combination of fixed and floating charges, all the assets and undertaking of the company, present and future, were charged to the debenture-holder. The debenture would typically give its holder the power to appoint a receiver with extensive powers to manage and sell the charged property. Since in the latter part of the twentieth century large parts of British commerce and industry were financed by facilities repayable on demand, the banks in question were in a very powerful position. Throughout most of the twentieth century, receivership nonetheless met the need for a procedure whereby a business could be sold as a going concern. Whilst it

---

[5] Powers of Trustees, Mortgagees, etc. Act 1860.
[6] *Holroyd v Marshall* (1862) HL Cas 191 (HL).
[7] *Re Yorkshire Woolcombers Association Ltd* [1903] 2 Ch 284 (CA), affirmed *sub nom Illingworth v Houldsworth* [1904] AC 355 (HL).

was never a procedure for the rescue of the company itself, it could rescue a business because the effect of a receivership sale was to divorce the ownership of assets from the burden of historic debt. Ironically, in view of the subsequent prohibition of administrative receivership, administration was, when first proposed, perceived as making the *advantages* of receivership available to companies who had not granted debentures conferring on the debenture-holder the power to appoint receivers over all their assets and undertakings.[8] The high-water mark of receivership came with the 1985/86 reforms which introduced the concept of administrative receivership. Under the Act, administrative receivership was invested with some of the trappings of an insolvency procedure even though it remained resolutely a method of security enforcement. That said, in practice, the position of administrative receivers and administrators was very similar even though they were ultimately serving different interests.

6.14 During the period between the 1985/86 reforms and the passage of the Enterprise Act 2002, receivership ceased to be regarded as having a useful role to play in facilitating the survival of businesses and came to be viewed by government as an obstacle to the rescue culture:[9]

> The Government's view is that, on the grounds of both equity and efficiency, the time has come to make changes which will tip the balance firmly in favour of collective insolvency proceedings – proceedings in which all creditors participate, under which a duty is owed to all creditors and in which all creditors may look to an office holder for an account of his dealings with a company's assets. It follows that we believe that administrative receivership should cease to be a major insolvency procedure ...

> In taking this step we recognise that in order to ensure the position of secured creditors within collective insolvency procedures there will need to be substantial reform to the process of administration so as to make it more effective and accessible. Whilst our aim is to guarantee unsecured creditors a greater say in the process and its outcome, secured creditors should not feel at any risk from our proposals. We see no reason why, given the changes we propose to make to the administration procedure ... their interests should not be protected equally well by an administrator as by an administrative receiver. Indeed we are confident that, over time, secured creditors will come to see administration as their remedy of choice for maximising value.

These proposals led not only to the prohibition of administrative receivership but also to the entrenched rights and powers of the holder of a qualifying floating charge in administration.[10] Although the government was overstating its case in claiming that administration would become the 'remedy of choice' for

---

[8] Cork Report, Chapter 9; Department of Trade and Industry, *A Revised Framework for Insolvency Law* (White Paper, Cm 9175, February 1984) Chapter 6.

[9] Department of Trade and Industry, *Insolvency – A Second Chance* (White Paper, Cm 5234, July 2001) paras 2.5 and 2.6.

[10] As to which, see Chapter 8.

secured creditors, the ability of a bank holding a qualifying floating charge to influence the conduct of administration has made the procedure generally acceptable.

4. No debtor in possession procedures

All the formal insolvency procedures available under the Act require the appoint-**6.15** ment of an independent office-holder with responsibility for the conduct of the procedure. These procedures are therefore not debtor in possession procedures which companies can impose on their creditors without ceding control of the process to an insolvency practitioner.

Contrary to the proposition just advanced, it is sometimes suggested that a CVA **6.16** is a form of debtor in possession procedure because it can be invoked by the directors of the company making a proposal for an arrangement which, if accepted, can result in the company continuing to trade under its own management. However, it is not a true debtor in possession procedure because the directors cannot advance their proposal without the services of an insolvency practitioner acting first as the nominee for the purposes of reporting to the court as to whether the proposal should be considered by the company and its creditors and then, if the proposal is approved, acting as supervisor as regards its implementation. The fact that the procedure can be started by the directors of their own volition does not distinguish voluntary arrangements from either liquidation or administration.

Although none of the procedures can be conducted without the appointment of an **6.17** office-holder, administration involves an interim stay while the procedure is pending.[11] This is only likely to be for a very short period.

As originally enacted, the Act made no provision for any stay whilst a company vol-**6.18** untary arrangement was being proposed—the assumption being that an administration order would be obtained if needed for that purpose. Almost from inception, critics of the procedure suggested that the absence of a stay was the obvious reason why the procedure was being little used.[12] The Insolvency Act 2000 set out to fill this perceived lacuna by amending the 1986 Act to permit the directors of 'small' companies to invoke a short administration-style moratorium without seeking the appointment of an administrator.[13] The result is still not a true debtor in possession procedure because it requires the support of a nominee who has a monitoring role and, if the arrangement is approved, it still requires the appointment of a

---

[11] Schedule B1 para 44.
[12] The absence of a moratorium was, in fact, only one reason for the limited appeal of the procedure. Another important disadvantage is the lack of finality because of the right of aggrieved creditors to apply to the court to have the approval of an arrangement set aside.
[13] Schedule A1.

supervisor. Although the interim moratorium was a significant conceptual development, its use in practice has been negligible.[14]

6.19 Despite these limited qualifications, it remains the case that (as yet) English insolvency proceedings cannot be conducted without the appointment of an independent insolvency practitioner to act as the office-holder. It is not thought that the limited facility to impose a stay whilst a proceeding is pending, which is any event subject to the power of the court to relieve the stay, amounts to anything which can properly be regarded as analogous to the debtor in possession procedures available in some other jurisdictions (notably the USA). Future reform of English insolvency law may, however, go further in that direction.[15]

5. Demarcation of procedures

6.20 Although liquidation, administration, and CVAs are discrete procedures serving different purposes, the distinctions are more apparent than real because directly or indirectly, all the procedures can be either voluntary or compulsory and, due to the comparative ease with which a company can move from one procedure to another, can lead to the same outcomes.

6.21 Pared down to essentials, there can only be one of two outcomes to an insolvency procedure: survival or dissolution. This dichotomy is sometimes characterized as the distinction between the results of reorganizational and terminal procedures but it is more elemental than that; when a company becomes insolvent it either survives or it does not. Anything else, typically some form of reconstruction, is a refinement. Administration and CVAs can result in either survival or dissolution, depending upon the purposes for which they are used in any given case. Liquidation is ostensibly a dedicated procedure for a single outcome—dissolution following completion of the winding-up—but even liquidation is more versatile than might be supposed because it is possible to move out of liquidation into either administration or a voluntary arrangement. On this basis, all three existing procedures can lead to either outcome.

6.22 Liquidation is available as either a voluntary procedure, started by a shareholders' resolution, or a compulsory procedure where a creditor can petition for a winding-up order. A company (or its directors) can appoint an administrator as can a creditor holding a qualifying floating charge. A creditor can apply to the court for an administration order. A CVA can only be proposed by the company's directors (unless the company is already in liquidation or administration) but a creditor who wishes to promote a voluntary arrangement can do so indirectly by first

---

[14] See further Chapter 9.
[15] See further Chapter 9 Section 6.

procuring the appointment of an administrator. Although there are differences in how a company enters an insolvency proceeding of its own volition (for example, as to whether a shareholder resolution is required), the common theme is that, one way or another, the company can always take the initiative. So too can a creditor, with the refinement that the creditor must act indirectly in the case of a voluntary arrangement.

The initial choice of procedure is not determinative of the outcome. A liquidator can apply to the court for an administration order. If granted, the court will discharge any winding-up order and, if the liquidation is a voluntary liquidation, may stay the proceedings.[16] A liquidator can also propose a voluntary arrangement. If approved, the court can again stay the proceedings.[17] Liquidation therefore lacks the inevitable finality that might be expected. An administrator can cause a company to go into either voluntary or compulsory liquidation.[18] An administrator can also propose a voluntary arrangement, with consequences for the administration which are directly comparable with the consequences of a liquidator's approved proposal.[19] The supervisor of a CVA can apply to the court for a winding-up order or an administration order.[20] The office-holder must always consider possible conflicts of interest but will ordinarily be free to accept the sequential appointment when the company moves from one procedure to another.[21] **6.23**

6. Conclusions

The Cork Report described insolvency law before the 1985/86 reforms as having been 'replete with anomalies, inconsistencies and deficiencies'.[22] Although the law is now much modernized and improved, the description nonetheless remains disturbingly apt for a variety of reasons. First, the consolidation of the law into the Act was not accompanied by consolidation of the procedures; secondly, the legislation has been the subject of too much piecemeal amendment; and, thirdly, because of the proliferation of special procedures and exceptions to the ordinary rules. (The latter fall outside the scope of this book because they cast no light on the fundamentals of the subject except, perhaps, to demonstrate some shortcomings in the general procedures.[23]) **6.24**

---

[16] Schedule B1 para 38 and section 147.

[17] Sections 1(3) and 5(3).

[18] Schedule 1 para 21 and Schedule B1 para 83. (A company can also proceed directly from administration to dissolution under Schedule B1 para 84.)

[19] Sections 1(3) and 5(3).

[20] Section 7(4)(b).

[21] See further The Insolvency Service, *Insolvency practitioner code of ethics* (7 April 2014) <https://www.gov.uk/government/publications/insolvency-practitioner-code-of-ethics> accessed 24 October 2016.

[22] Report of the Review Committee, *Insolvency Law and Practice* (Cm 8558, June 1982) para 9.

[23] See further Chapters 3 and 5.

6.25 The 1977 terms of reference of the Cork Committee included a requirement that they:[24]

> … examine the possibility of formulating a comprehensive insolvency system and the extent to which existing procedures might, with advantage, be harmonised and integrated.

The Committee's report included proposals for a new unified procedure but those proposals were not followed and the practical effect of the subsequent reforms was to increase rather than to reduce diversity.

6.26 The idea of integration briefly surfaced again in 1999 with the government's review of business rescue procedures which canvassed views on full integration through a single gateway. The Review Group subsequently reported that the proposal had received little support and advanced a more modest proposal (which was also not pursued).[25]

6.27 Following the amendments resulting from the Insolvency Act 2000 and the Enterprise Act 2002, the landscape changed again and the procedures are now even more unnecessarily Byzantine than they were before. To put the case for some rationalization at its lowest, there are more procedures than outcomes.

---

[24] As recorded in the Cork Report (n 22) at (iii).

[25] The Insolvency Service, *A Review of Company Rescue and Business Reconstruction Mechanisms* (Consultation Paper, 1999) see para 10(f) and (g); The Insolvency Service, *Report by the Review Group* (May 2000) at 22 and 59. Subsequent consultations, The Insolvency Service, *Encouraging Company Rescue* (June 2009) and The Insolvency Service, *Proposals for a Restructuring Moratorium* (July 2010) were focused on the possibility of a moratorium being allowed in order to facilitate rescue through a CVA or, in the latter case, also by other means. Those proposals were also not pursued.

7

LIQUIDATION

1. The function of liquidation

As Nicholls LJ said in *Re Atlantic Computer Systems Plc*:[1]   **7.01**

> The basic object of the winding up process, in the case of an insolvent company, is to achieve an equal distribution of the company's assets among the unsecured creditors.

Liquidation is the only meaningful option for insolvent companies that have no realizable value as a going concern.

Liquidation is a process of collective enforcement. It is the corporate insolvency **7.02** equivalent of bankruptcy for individuals. Liquidation was described in the following terms by Brightman LJ in *Re Lines Bros Ltd*:[2]

> The liquidation of an insolvent company is a process of collective enforcement of debts for the benefit of the general body of creditors. Although it is not a process of execution, because it is not for the benefit of a particular creditor, it is nevertheless akin to execution because its purpose is to enforce, on a pari passu basis, the payment of the admitted or proved debts of the company. When, therefore, a company goes into liquidation a process is initiated which, for all creditors, is similar to the process which is initiated, for one creditor, by execution.

---

[1] [1992] Ch 505 (CA) 527H.
[2] [1983] Ch 1 (CA) 20E.

and to like effect by Lord Hoffmann in *Cambridge Gas Transportation Corpn v Official Committee of Unsecured Creditors of Navigator Holdings Plc*:[3]

> The purpose of bankruptcy proceedings … is not to determine or establish the existence of rights, but to provide a mechanism of collective execution against the property of the debtor by creditors whose rights are admitted or established. That mechanism may vary in its details … In the case of personal bankruptcy, the bankrupt may afterwards be discharged from liability for his pre-bankruptcy debts. In the case of corporate insolvency, there is no provision for discharge. The company remains liable but when all its assets have been distributed, there is nothing more against which the liability can be enforced … At that point, the company is usually dissolved.

7.03 The proper administration of such a process of collective execution is the function of a liquidator and not a task to be undertaken by directors. Scott J observed in *Re Perfectair Holdings Ltd*, when making a winding-up order on a contested petition:[4]

> The directors were not put into office and cannot claim to be maintained in office for the purpose of liquidating the company. That is not the function of managers. That is the function of a liquidator.

Shortly afterwards in *Re Ipcon Fashions Ltd*, a directors' disqualification case, Hoffmann J (as he then was) said:[5]

> [The director] suggested that he was in effect acting as a liquidator at lower rates than a professional liquidator would have charged. But the law, for good reason, requires a liquidator to be an independent and qualified insolvency practitioner and I do not think [the director] was entitled to take into his own hands the liquidation of an insolvent company.

2. Outline of the procedures

7.04 Liquidation can either result from a winding-up order made by the court, in which case it is called a 'compulsory liquidation', or a shareholder resolution, in which case it is a 'voluntary liquidation'. A voluntary liquidation is called a 'members' voluntary liquidation' if the company is solvent or a 'creditors' voluntary liquidation' if the company is insolvent.[6] Creditors' voluntary liquidations are by far the most common form of insolvency proceeding.

---

[3] [2006] UKPC 26, [2007] 1 AC 508 [14]. See also *Parmalat Capital Finance Ltd v Food Holdings Ltd* [2008] UKPC 23, [2009] 1 BCLC 274.

[4] (1989) 5 BCC 837 (Ch) 849G.

[5] (1989) 5 BCC 773 (Ch) 775F.

[6] Although members' voluntary liquidations are a procedure under the Insolvency Act 1986 which must be conducted by a liquidator who is an insolvency practitioner, they are outside the scope of this book.

In *Ayerst v C&K (Construction) Ltd*, Lord Diplock summarized the processes for **7.05** winding up a company by reference to the provisions of the Companies Act 1948 then in force, saying:[7]

> My Lords, the making of a winding-up order brings into operation a statutory scheme for dealing with the assets of the company that is ordered to be wound up. The scheme is now contained in Part V of the Companies Act 1948 and extends to voluntary as well as to compulsory winding up; but in so far as it deals with compulsory winding up its essential characteristics have remained the same since it was first enacted by the Companies Act 1862. The procedure to be followed when a company is being wound up varies in detail according to whether this is done compulsorily under an order of the court or voluntarily pursuant to a resolution of the company in general meeting, and, in the latter case, whether it is a members' voluntary winding up or a creditors' voluntary winding up; but the essential characteristics of the scheme for dealing with the assets of the company do not differ whichever of these procedures is applicable. They remain the same as those of the original statutory scheme in the Companies Act 1862 …
>
> Upon the making of a winding-up order:
>
> (1) The custody and control of all the property and choses in action of the company are transferred from those persons who were entitled under the memorandum and articles to manage its affairs on its behalf, to a liquidator charged with the statutory duty of dealing with the company's assets in accordance with the statutory scheme. Any disposition of the property of the company otherwise than by the liquidator is void.
>
> (2) The statutory duty of the liquidator is to collect the assets of the company and to apply them in discharge of its liabilities. If there is any surplus he must distribute it among the members of the company in accordance with their respective rights under the memorandum and articles of association. In performing these duties in a compulsory winding up the liquidator acts as an officer of the court, and if the company is insolvent the rules applicable in the law of bankruptcy must be followed.
>
> (3) All powers of dealing with the company's assets, including the power to carry on its business so far as may be necessary for its beneficial winding up, are exercisable by the liquidator for the benefit of those persons only who are entitled to share in the proceeds of realisation of the assets under the statutory scheme. The company itself as a legal person, distinct from its members, can never be entitled to any part of the proceeds. Upon completion of the winding up, it is dissolved.
>
> The functions of the liquidator are thus similar to those of a trustee (formerly official assignee) in bankruptcy or an executor in the administration of an estate of a deceased person. There is, however, this difference: that whereas the legal title in the property of the bankrupt vests in the trustee and the legal title to property of the deceased vests in the executor, a winding-up order does not of itself divest the company of the legal title to any of its assets. Though this is not expressly stated in the Act it is implicit in the language used throughout Part V, particularly in

---

[7] [1976] AC 167 (HL) 176F (references to sections of the 1948 Act omitted).

sections ... which relate to the powers of liquidators and refer to 'property ... to which the company is ... entitled,' to 'property ... belonging to the company,' to 'assets ... of the company' and to acts to be done by the liquidator 'in the name and on behalf of the company.'

Lord Diplock's summary of the essential characteristics of liquidation under the 1948 Act is equally applicable to liquidation under the 1986 Act.

7.06 Directors who recognize that their company should be put into liquidation will usually prefer a creditors' voluntary liquidation (provided they can procure the necessary shareholder resolution) because it is quicker and cheaper to pass a resolution than to apply for and obtain a winding-up order and because the shareholders (who in an SME are likely to be the directors or their associates) have an opportunity to nominate the liquidator. Creditors who cannot persuade an insolvent company to put itself into liquidation can only force the issue by means of a winding-up petition. The presentation of a petition can of itself cause irreparable harm to a company and the court will grant an injunction to restrain the presentation of a petition where there is reason to anticipate proceedings being wrongly commenced. The petitioning creditor must have a petition debt which is not genuinely disputed and must satisfy the court of the company's insolvency. A common way in which insolvency is established for these purposes is through service of a statutory demand pursuant to section 123. The making of a winding-up order remains a matter for the court's discretion but an order will only be refused in exceptional circumstances where jurisdiction and grounds have been established.

7.07 On the making of a winding-up order, the official receiver becomes the liquidator and remains in office unless or until he is replaced by a private sector insolvency practitioner.[8] In a creditors' voluntary liquidation, the liquidator nominated by the members is in office from the passing of the resolution for his appointment but his powers are restricted until the creditors have either nominated or had the opportunity (in accordance with the Rules) to nominate another insolvency practitioner to act in his place. The creditors' nomination prevails over the members' choice.[9]

7.08 The liquidator's powers are provided by the Act. The powers are sufficiently wide to cover all normal methods of realizing the value of the company's assets including the commencement of such proceedings against third parties as may be necessary for that purpose but a liquidator only has power to carry on the company's business so far as may be necessary for it to be wound up.[10] In an exceptional case, that power might be used to complete a pending contract but,

---

[8] Section 136.
[9] Sections 100 and 166.
[10] Schedule 4. See further Chapter 19.

in most cases, the commencement of liquidation brings any continued trading to an abrupt halt.

The other side of a liquidator's functions is the distribution of the realized estate, **7.09** net of the costs and expenses of the liquidation (which include the liquidator's own remuneration) amongst the creditors. For this purpose, the liquidator will call for the submission of proofs of debt from the creditors. Secured creditors need only prove to the extent that their security is not sufficient to cover their claims but all creditors who wish to participate in the liquidator's distributions must submit proofs upon which the liquidator then adjudicates. A creditor who is aggrieved by the liquidator's decision on his proof can appeal to the court.[11]

In keeping with the nature of liquidation as a terminal insolvency proceeding, the **7.10** process ends with the dissolution of the company. Upon dissolution, any remaining property of the company is deemed to be *bona vacantia* which belongs to the Crown pursuant to section 1012 of the Companies Act 2006. It is important to note, in this respect, that section 1012 does not engage the definition of property in section 436 of the Act.[12] Neuberger J drew this distinction in *Re Wilmott Trading Ltd (Nos 1 and 2)* when he held that a waste management licence issued to the company would not vest, saying:[13]

> … it does seem to me that in considering whether or not something is property, for the purposes of a particular statute, one should be entitled to take into account the consequences of it being property … it would seem to me extraordinary that a waste management licence could become vested in the Crown, with all the obligations that the waste management licence might involve, without the Crown having any control over its vesting.

It follows that upon dissolution some of the company's property may, exceptionally, simply cease to exist.

3. The effect on directors' powers

Section 103 makes express provision as to the continuation of the directors' pow- **7.11** ers in a creditors' voluntary liquidation: their powers cease except in so far as the liquidation committee, or the creditors if there is no committee, sanction their continuation. This provision presupposes that the directors remain in office with the power to act as such, subject to the necessary consent having been given.[14]

There is no equivalent provision in the Act dealing with the effect of compulsory **7.12** liquidation but there is some case law. It is not open to doubt that the powers of the

---

[11] See generally Chapters 19, 20, and 21.
[12] See further Chapter 14.
[13] [1999] 2 BCLC 541 (Ch) 554b.
[14] See also *Midland Counties District Bank Ltd v Attwood* [1905] 1 Ch 357 (Ch).

directors cease upon the making of a winding-up order. As Lord Sterndale MR said in *Re Farrow's Bank Ltd*:[15]

> There is no express provision in the [Companies (Consolidation) Act 1908] in the case of a compulsory liquidation as there is in the case of a voluntary liquidation, that the powers of the directors shall cease on the appointment of a liquidator ... but they do in fact cease on the appointment of a liquidator in a compulsory liquidation.

However, there are conflicting authorities on whether the office itself survives. In *The Madrid Bank Ltd v Bayley*, Blackburn J said in the context of ordering sanctions against directors who had failed to answer to answer interrogatories:[16]

> ... these gentlemen were directors at the time the order for winding up the company was made, and I see nothing in the Companies Act which made them then cease to be directors. I quite concede they had no control over the affairs of the company after the winding-up commenced, but that does not prevent their continuing to be officers of the company.

The point arose again in *Re Ebsworth and Tidy's Contract*, a conveyancing case concerning defects in title where Lord Esher MR said obiter:[17]

> If a registered company goes into liquidation the Court has power to appoint an official liquidator; and if it does so, what is the position of the persons who were directors? To my mind they have ceased to exist.

In *Measures Brothers Ltd v Measures*, the Court of Appeal refused to grant an injunction to enforce a restrictive covenant given by a director as part of a service agreement. The company got into financial difficulty, a receiver was appointed, and a winding-up order was made. The receiver gave the director notice that his services were no longer required. The ratio of the case is that the company could not enforce the covenant in its favour because it was in breach of its own obligations. There were three members of the court. Cozens-Hardy MR referred to the company's breaches of its obligations without alluding to the effect of the winding-up order as such. Buckley LJ who, despite delivering a dissenting judgment as to the consequences, was in agreement with the other members of the court that the company could not perform its own obligations, said:[18]

> ... by the operation of the winding-up order made on October 13, 1909, the office [ie the directorship] itself came to an end.

Kennedy LJ also referred to the order as having determined the office and to the director's 'displacement' from that office.

7.13 *Madrid Bank* is the only one of these cases in which submissions appear to have been made to the court directly on the cessation of office point and it is the only

---

15 [1921] 2 Ch 164 (CA) 173.
16 (1866–67) LR 2 QB 37 (QB) 40.
17 (1889) 42 Ch D 23 (CA) 43.
18 [1910] 2 Ch 248 (CA) 256.

one where the court's conclusion was a reasoned part of the ratio of its decision. Unfortunately, neither the court in *Ebsworth* nor that in *Measures* referred to *Madrid Bank*. It would have been sufficient for the court's reasoning in *Ebsworth* to conclude that the making of the order had resulted in a cessation of powers and, in *Measures*, that the company was in breach of its obligations to remunerate the director.[19] Having regard to provisions of the Act which appear to assume that directors remain in office,[20] albeit not in power, it is suggested that the conclusion in *Madrid Bank* is to be preferred.

4. The effect on the assets and liabilities of a company in liquidation

a. Assets

Upon liquidation, a company ceases to be the beneficial owner of its property. In **7.14** *Ayerst*, the House of Lords was invited to hold that decisions to that effect going back over a hundred years had been wrongly decided because the supposed trust did not conform in all respects to a conventional trust. Lord Diplock dismissed this submission in the following terms:[21]

> My Lords, it is not to be supposed that in using the expression 'trust' and 'trust property' in reference to the assets of a company in liquidation the distinguished Chancery judges whose judgments I have cited and those who followed them were oblivious to the fact that the statutory scheme for dealing with the assets of a company in the course of winding up its affairs differed in several aspects from a trust of specific property created by the voluntary act of the settlor. Some respects in which it differed were similar to those which distinguished the administration of estates of deceased persons and of bankrupts from an ordinary trust, another peculiar to the winding up of a company is that the actual custody, control, realisation and distribution of the proceeds of the property which is subject to the statutory scheme are taken out of the hands of the legal owner of the property, the company, and vested in a third party, the liquidator, over whom the company has no control. His status, as was held by Romer J. in *Knowles v. Scott* differs from that of a trustee 'in the strict sense' for the individual creditors and members of the company who are entitled to share in the proceeds of realisation. He does not owe to them all the duties that a trustee in equity owes to his cestui que trust. All that was intended to be conveyed by the use of the expression 'trust property' and 'trust' in these and subsequent cases (of which the most recent is *Pritchard v. MH Builders (Wilmslow) Ltd*) was that the effect of the statute was to give to the property of a company in liquidation that essential characteristic which distinguished trust property from other property, viz., that it could not be used or disposed of

---

[19] *Ebsworth* and *Measures* were applied without critical consideration in *Park Associated Developments Ltd v Kinnear* [2013] EWHC 3617 (Ch) [2], as to which see Chapter 15.

[20] For example, section 133 (public examination in a compulsory liquidation).

[21] [1976] AC 167 (HL) 180C.

by the legal owner for his own benefit, but must be used or disposed of for the benefit of other persons.

In *Mitchell v Carter*, Millett LJ highlighted the very important point that this is a special form of trust where the beneficiaries, the creditors, have no beneficial interests in the trust property:[22]

> The making of a winding-up order divests the company of the beneficial ownership of its assets which cease to be applicable for its own benefit. They become instead subject to a statutory scheme for distribution among the creditors and members of the company. The responsibility for collecting the assets and implementing the statutory scheme is vested in the liquidator subject to the ultimate control of the court. The creditors do not themselves acquire a beneficial interest in any of the assets, but only a right to have them administered in accordance with the statutory scheme.

7.15   One consequence of this change in the nature of the company's interest in its own property is that even a voluntary liquidation is not readily reversible. It is not open to the members of the company to rescind a winding-up resolution. Once a company has gone into liquidation, and the statutory scheme for the application of its property has therefore been engaged, the only way to halt the process is to apply to the court to exercise its power under section 147 to stay the proceedings.[23]

b. Liabilities

7.16   In *Wight v Eckhardt Marine GmbH*, Lord Hoffmann explained that the debts of a company survive its liquidation. Creditors participate in the distributions made by a liquidator by virtue of their surviving claims as creditors; liquidation does not change the juridical nature of the creditors' rights by replacing their debt claims with new rights under the statutory scheme. Lord Hoffmann said:[24]

> The winding up leaves the debts of the creditors untouched. It only affects the way in which they can be enforced. When the order is made, ordinary proceedings against the company are stayed (although the stay can be enforced only against creditors subject to the personal jurisdiction of the court). The creditors are confined to a collective enforcement procedure that results in pari passu distribution of the company's assets. The winding up does not either create new substantive rights in the creditors or destroy the old ones. Their debts, if they are owing, remain debts throughout. They are discharged by the winding up only to the extent that they are paid out of dividends. But when the process of distribution is complete, there

---

[22] [1997] 1 BCLC 673 (CA) 686f.

[23] There appears to be no English authority directly on this point but it is supported by *Ross v PJ Heeringa Pty Ltd* [1970] NZLR 170 (High Court of New Zealand). See also *Thomson v Henderson's Transvaal Estates Ltd* [1908] 1 Ch 765 (CA) per Buckley LJ where the necessity for a stay appears to have been assumed.

[24] [2003] UKPC 37, [2004] 1 AC 147 [27].

are no further assets against which they can be enforced. There is no equivalent of the discharge of a personal bankrupt which extinguishes his debts. When the company is dissolved, there is no longer an entity which the creditor can sue. But even then, discovery of an asset can result in the company being restored for the process to continue.

This analysis was followed by the Court of Appeal in *Financial Services Compensation* **7.17** *Scheme Ltd v Larnell (Insurances) Ltd* where Lloyd LJ said:[25]

> In so far as it is necessary to ascertain what the creditor's rights are, they have to be established in contract, tort, or otherwise as the case may be. The creditor's cause of action remains as it was before … It is only as regards giving effect to those rights in the insolvency that the rights are subjected to the statutory trust resulting from the duty of distribution imposed on the liquidator or trustee in bankruptcy.

5. The cut-off date and the hindsight principle

The scheme of distribution in a liquidation proceeds on the basis of a fiction that **7.18** everything occurs immediately upon the procedure taking effect. Thus, liabilities are quantified as at the outset—the cut-off date—but the potential rigidity of the fiction is substantially mitigated because the court will apply hindsight to take account of any material developments occurring before an actual distribution is made. In *Re Humber Ironworks and Shipbuilding Company*, Selwyn LJ referred to the fiction in the context of explaining why post-commencement interest should not be a provable debt, saying:[26]

> I think the tree must lie as it falls; that it must be ascertained what are the debts as they exist at the date of the winding-up, and that all dividends in the case of an insolvent estate must be declared in respect of the debts so ascertained.

Without a cut-off date, as at which the liabilities of the company are quantified, it would be impossible to arrange for a pari passu distribution amongst the creditors. Thus the underlying objective is to achieve fairness between creditors even though the more specific rationale for this approach is essentially one of practicality. As Giffard LJ said in the same case:[27]

> … if we are to consider convenience, it is quite clear that, where an estate is insolvent, convenience is in favour of stopping all the computations at the date of the winding-up … I am of the opinion that dividends ought to be paid on the debts as they stand at the date of the winding up; for when the estate is insolvent this rule distributes the assets in the fairest way …

---

[25] [2005] EWCA Civ 1408, [2006] QB 808 [18].
[26] (1869) LR 4 Ch App 643 (CA) 647.
[27] Ibid.

7.19 Some of the more significant results of imposing a cut-off date for the purposes of making distributions are now enshrined in the Rules but the principle of there being a cut-off date was first established by the judges. The following citations explain the nature and purpose of the cut-off date:

a) In *Re British American Continental Bank Ltd*, PO Lawrence J said:[28]

> In a winding up, this Court has to ascertain all the liabilities of the company being wound up for the purpose of effecting the proper distribution of its assets amongst its creditors. A date has necessarily to be fixed on which all debts and other liabilities are to be treated as definitely ascertained, both for the purpose of placing all creditors on an equality and for the purpose of properly conducting the winding up of the affairs of the company. According to the rules and practice now prevailing, the date so fixed is the date of the winding-up order.

b) On the question of identifying the correct date to be the cut-off date, Lord Westbury had earlier said in *Re European Assurance Society Arbitration (Wallberg's Case)*:[29]

> ... when is the property of the debtor company subjected to equal distribution among the creditors? At the date of the winding up order. Then, and not till then, is the company divested of its property ... Well, then, it follows immediately that the valuation must be made when the necessity for a valuation arises. The necessity arises, as I have said, when the order to wind up is made; and that, therefore, becomes necessarily the date of valuation.

c) Later, in *Re Dynamics Corporation of America*, Oliver J provided the following useful summary when considering the conversion of foreign currency claims:[30]

> The provisions of both the Companies Act 1948 and the Bankruptcy Act 1914 with regard to the submission of proof are I think all directed to this end, that is to say, to ascertaining what, at the relevant date, were the liabilities of the company or the bankrupt as the case may be, in order to determine what at that date is the denominator in the fraction of which the numerator will be the net realised value of the property available for distribution. It is only in this way that a rateable, or pari passu, distribution of the available property can be achieved, and it is, as I see it, axiomatic that the claims of the creditors amongst whom the division is to be effected must all be crystallised at the same date, even though the actual ascertainment may not be possible at that date, for otherwise one is not comparing like with like ...
>
> Now the moment that you start introducing into this scheme of things different dates for the ascertainment of the value of the claims of individual creditors or

---

28 [1922] 2 Ch 575 (Ch) 582. PO Lawrence J's judgment was upheld on appeal to the Court of Appeal where no comparable statement of general principle was repeated.
29 (1872) 17 SJ 69, 70.
30 [1976] 1 WLR 757 (Ch) 764E and H.

classes of creditors, you introduce, as it seems to me, potential inequalities and thus the possibility of that which the Act impliedly prohibits, that is to say a distribution of the property of the company otherwise than pari passu.

d) More recently, in *Lockston Group Inc v Wood*, David Richards J said:[31]

> As has frequently been observed, the distribution of an insolvent estate among the general body of creditors on a pari passu basis is, as it has always been, a fundamental feature of our insolvency law. It applies to distributions across all the various forms of insolvency proceedings: the bankruptcy of individuals and the administration and liquidation of companies.
>
> A pari passu distribution among creditors requires a common date and a common currency for the ascertainment and quantification of debts.

The cut-off date is generally the date on which the order is made in compulsory **7.20** liquidation and the date of the winding-up resolution in a voluntary liquidation. This now applies to determine the following questions:

a) Provable debts are debts and liabilities to which the company is subject on the cut-off date (unless liquidation is preceded by administration, in which case the relevant date is that when the company entered administration).[32]
b) Liabilities incurred after the cut-off date will usually be expenses of the liquidation and, as such, paid in priority.[33]
c) Contingent claims are valued as at the cut-off date for proof of debt.[34]
d) Insolvency set-off occurs on the cut-off date for proof of debt.[35] As Lord Hoffmann said in *Stein v Blake*:[36]

> Bankruptcy set-off therefore requires an account to be taken of liabilities which, at the time of bankruptcy, may be due but not yet payable or may be unascertained in amount or subject to contingency. Nevertheless, the law says that the account shall be deemed to have been taken and the sums due from one party set off against the other as at the date of the bankruptcy.

e) Claims denominated in a foreign currency must be converted into sterling on the cut-off date for proof of debt.[37]
f) Payments of a periodical nature falling due before the cut-off date for proof of debt are provable.[38]

---

[31] [2015] EWHC 2962 (Ch), [2016] 1 WLR 2091 [24]–[25].
[32] Rules 14.1 and 14.2. See further Chapter 21 paras 21.16 to 21.18.
[33] Rules 6.42 and 7.108. See further Chapter 20.
[34] Rule 14.14; *Stein v Blake* [1996] 1 AC 243 (HL) 252H.
[35] Rule 14.25 (with refinements relating to excluded debts).
[36] *Stein v Blake* (n 34) 252B.
[37] Rule 14.21.
[38] Rule 14.22.

g) Interest payable in respect of the period before the cut-off date for proof of debt is provable; interest in respect of the subsequent period is not.[39]

h) Debts which are not due until after the cut-off date for proof of debt are provable but subject to discounting for acceleration.[40]

i) As regards claims pursued in the liquidation, time ceases to run for the purposes of the Limitation Act 1980. James LJ said in *Re General Rolling Stock Company, Joint Stock Discount Company's Claim*:[41]

> A duty and a trust are thus imposed upon the Court, to take care that the assets of the company shall be applied in discharge of its liabilities. What liabilities? All the liabilities of the company existing at the time when the winding-up order was made which gives the right. It appears to me that it would be most unjust if any other construction were put upon the section. After a winding-up order has been made, no action is to be brought by a creditor except by the special leave of the Court, and it cannot have been the intention of the Legislature that special leave to bring an action should be given merely in order to get rid of the Statute of Limitations.

As is apparent, the case concerned compulsory liquidation but the reasoning applies with equal force to a voluntary liquidation (in which case the relevant date is that of the winding-up resolution).[42]

7.21 As already stated, the rigidity of the rule that the liabilities of a company in liquidation are determined at the outset is mitigated by the application of the hindsight principle. The application of that principle will inform the correct quantification of the company's liabilities and, exceptionally, may even eliminate them.

7.22 The most obvious situation in which the hindsight principle will lead to a reappraisal of the quantum of a creditor's claim is where the claim is made in respect of a contingent liability. So long as the liability remains contingent, rule 14.14 provides for it to be quantified by an estimate made by the liquidator (against which an aggrieved creditor can appeal under rule 14.8). If, however, the contingency occurs before a distribution is made then the actual liability is treated as having been due at the cut-off date. In *Stein v Blake*, Lord Hoffmann explained this process in the context of insolvency set-off in the following terms:[43]

---

[39] Rule 14.23.

[40] Rule 14.44.

[41] (1872) 7 Ch App 646 (CA) 648. (The petitioning creditor is treated more favourably in that the presentation of a petition stops time running against him: *Re Cases of Taff Wells Ltd* [1992] BCLC 11 (Ch).) See also *Financial Services Compensation Scheme Ltd v Larnell (Insurances) Ltd* [2005] EWCA Civ 1408, [2006] QB 808.

[42] *Re Art Reproduction Co Ltd* [1952] Ch 89 (Ch) 94.

[43] [1996] 1 AC 243 (HL) 252E. See also *Re Northern Counties of England Fire Insurance Co, Macfarlane's Claim* (1880) 17 Ch D 337 (CA); *Sovereign Life Assurance Co v Dodd* [1892] 2 QB 573 (CA).

How does the law deal with the conundrum of having to set off, as of the bankruptcy date, 'sums due' which may not yet be due or which may become owing upon contingencies which have not yet occurred? It employs two techniques. The first[44] is to take into account everything which has actually happened between the bankruptcy date and the moment when it becomes necessary to ascertain what, on that date, was the state of account between the creditor and the bankrupt. If by that time the contingency has occurred and the claim has been quantified, then that is the amount which is treated as having been due at the bankruptcy date.

In *Wight v Eckhardt Marine GmbH*, he added:[45]

The cases on the use of hindsight to value debts which were contingent at the date of the winding up order show that the scene does not freeze at the date of the winding up order. Adjustments are made to give effect to the underlying principle of pari passu distribution between creditors. Hindsight is used because it is not considered fair to a creditor to value a contingent debt at what it might have been worth at the date of the winding up order when one now knows that prescience would have shown it to be worth more.

Something similar occurs, in substance if not in form, where a secured creditor **7.23** realizes its security for something insufficient to discharge the secured indebtedness in full. In that situation, rule 14.19 allows the creditor to prove for the balance of the debt after deducting the amount realized.

In both those cases, application of the hindsight principle will usually serve to **7.24** increase the quantum of the company's liabilities but the reverse is also possible. In *Eckhardt Marine* the issue concerned a creditor's claim in respect of a debt which had been discharged according to its own proper law during the course of the liquidation. The claim was rejected with Lord Hoffmann saying: [46]

The image of collecting and uno flatu distributing the assets of the company on the day of the winding-up order is a vivid one, but the courts apply it to give effect to the underlying purpose of fair distribution between creditors pari passu and not as a rigid rule ... The principle of valuation at the date of winding up ensures that distribution among creditors is truly pari passu. It would, however, be pure conceptualism to apply [the principle of valuation at the date of winding up] so as to require payment of a dividend to someone who, at the time of the distribution, is not a creditor at all.

---

[44] The second being the process of estimation already described.

[45] [2003] UKPC 37, [2004] 1 AC 147 [32]. See also *Re Federal-Mogul Aftermarket UK Ltd* [2008] EWHC 1099 (Ch), [2008] Bus LR 1443.

[46] Ibid at [29], see also [32].

8

ADMINISTRATION

1. The function of administration

8.01 The defining characteristic of administration is the imposition of a temporary stay on creditor remedies—usually referred to as the 'moratorium'. As originally conceived the procedure was merely a means to an end and not an end in itself. However, administration was radically recast by amendments made to the Act by the Enterprise Act 2002 which enabled administrators to make distributions to creditors and for the company to be dissolved following administration without the need for a liquidation.[1] In consequence of those changes, administration can take one of two forms. First, and as before, it may be used simply to protect the insolvent estate whilst a rescue or a more advantageous realization of assets takes place, following which the company will either survive or it will be wound up in accordance with the procedures considered in the previous chapter. In this form, the following description of administration given by Nicholls LJ in *Re Atlantic Computer Systems Plc*, remains apt:[2]

> … an administration is intended to be only an interim and temporary regime. There is to be a breathing space while the company, under new management in the person of the administrator, seeks to achieve one or more of the purposes set out in section 8(3).[3] There is a moratorium on the enforcement of debts and rights,

---

[1] See further *Re Lune Metal Products Ltd* [2006] EWCA Civ 1720, [2007] Bus LR 589.
[2] [1992] Ch 505 (CA) 528B.
[3] Now reformulated in Schedule B1 para 3.

proprietary and otherwise, against the company, so as to give the administrator time to formulate proposals and lay them before the creditors, and then implement any proposals approved by the creditors. In some cases winding up will follow, in others it will not.

In its second form, sometimes known as a 'liquidating' or 'distributing' administration, administration effectively replaces liquidation as a terminal procedure but one which is better suited to the preservation and realization of a company's business as a going concern.

8.02 Two points should be noted in this connection: first, it will not invariably be necessary to put a company into administration in order to gain a short respite from creditor pressure but, secondly, administration is only available to resolve creditor issues and not for other purposes.

8.03 The general rule, in dealing with competing creditors outside the context of insolvency proceedings, is that it is a race of diligence. As Cooke J observed in *FG Hemisphere Associates LLC v The Republic of Congo*:[4]

> Where no compulsory statutory regime of apportionment can apply, the historic first past the post rule applies on enforcement of judgments, and the effect of a charging order or third party debt order is that a defeasible charge is obtained which gives priority over other creditors, if it is then confirmed and made final at the later stage.

Although there is no statutory power to order a stay under the Act or Rules outside the context of insolvency proceedings, the courts have been prepared to exercise discretion or case management powers to protect the collective interests of creditors. Thus, whilst it is well established that the court will usually refuse to make an interim charging order into a final order where a judgment debtor has gone into liquidation, the court may also refuse to do so on the ground that insolvency proceedings are imminent.[5] More generally, the courts have been willing to stay proceedings or the enforcement of a judgment in order to hold the ring while a scheme of arrangement is proposed, provided that it has a reasonable prospect of success.[6] In principle, there seems no good reason why the exercise of such a jurisdiction should be confined to the protection of prospective schemes of arrangement if the nature and prospects of some other form of rescue or reconstruction can be established with comparable clarity. It follows that the role of administration is

---

[4] [2005] EWHC 3103 (Comm) [14].

[5] *Roberts Petroleum Ltd v Kenny Ltd* [1983] 2 AC 192 (HL); *Sandhu v Sidhu* [2011] EWHC 3675 (Ch), [2012] BPIR 456.

[6] *Roberts Petroleum Ltd v Kenny Ltd* [1982] 1 WLR 301 (CA) 307H, on appeal above at 212C; *BlueCrest Mercantile BV v Vietnam Shipbuilding Industry Group* [2013] EWHC 1146 (Comm) [37]; *Novoship (UK) Ltd v Mikhaylyuk* [2014] EWCA Civ 252, [2014] BPIR 698 but see also *Dewji v Banwaitt* [2013] EWHC 3746 (QB), [2014] BPIR 63 as to the potential relevance of the precise terms of what is being proposed.

to provide more formal and generalized protection than is achievable through the exercise of discretion and case management powers.

8.04 Administration is an insolvency procedure which is not available for other purposes. In an early administration case, *Re Business Properties Ltd*, the court was asked to make an administration order in respect of an illiquid company whose shareholders were deadlocked. Harman J declined to do so saying:[7]

> An administration order is not, in my view, a suitable route to adopt when it is plain that at the end members must be paid out and the business of the company completely brought to an end with a distribution to members. Thus, although I accept that it is possible, where a company is asset solvent but cash insolvent, to appoint an administrator, yet I do not believe the court would frequently wish so to do or to exercise its discretion in favour of that remedy.

> It seems to me that in a situation where there is, as here, a deadlock and where there is, as here, sadly, a total breakdown of trust and confidence between the two corporators, the only answer must be a winding up, whether by members' voluntary, creditors' voluntary or, in the last resort, compulsory winding up; and, to my mind ... it was an error to proceed by way of administration petitions.

Part of Harman J's reasoning was that an administrator (under the law as it then was) had no power to make distributions. That is no longer the case but it is suggested that his conclusions nonetheless remain valid. The objective of administration and the statutory duty of an administrator are to serve creditors' interests. It is difficult to see how those interests are served by suspending creditors' remedies simply in order to facilitate the resolution of issues between members.

2. Outline of the procedure

8.05 Administration is an insolvency procedure which involves the appointment of an office-holder, the administrator, to fulfil the prescribed purpose of the proceeding. That purpose is defined by a waterfall of objectives:

a) rescuing the company as a going concern;
b) achieving a better result for the company's creditors generally than would be likely to result from immediate liquidation; and
c) making realizations in order to make distributions to secured or preferential creditors.

The administrator must pursue objective (a) unless he thinks that is not reasonably practicable or that objective (b) would be better for creditors. In the pursuit of either of those objectives, he must perform his functions in the interests of the creditors as a whole. He may only pursue objective (c) if he thinks that neither

---

[7] (1988) 4 BCC 684 (Ch) 686.

objectives (a) or (b) are achievable and he does not unnecessarily harm the interests of the general body of creditors.[8] In practice, the rescue of the company as a going concern is rare and most administrations result in the pursuit of either objective (b) or (c).

An administrator may be appointed by the court (on the application of the com- **8.06** pany, its directors, its liquidator, the supervisor of a voluntary arrangement or one or more creditors), the holder of a qualifying floating charge, or by the company or its directors.[9] Appointments by holders of qualifying floating charges, the company or its directors are 'out of court' appointments but a court appointment is likely to be preferred where questions of international recognition are anticipated.

The holder of a qualifying floating charge is a creditor holding security over the **8.07** whole or substantially the whole of the company's property resulting from a charge which is, or a number of charges which include, a floating charge. The charge must either state that it qualifies for these purposes or purport to confer a power to appoint an administrator or a person who would be an administrative receiver.[10] The reason why the holder of a qualifying floating charge enjoys this privileged position is explained in Chapter 6.

The provisions of Schedule B1 dealing with these different appointment routes are **8.08** very detailed but the following commonalities emerge:

a) Unless the appointment is being made by the holder of a qualifying floating charge, the company must be, or be likely to become, unable to pay its debts. Where the appointment is being made by the holder of a qualifying floating charge, the requirement is that the charge must be enforceable—which, in practice, will often amount to the same thing.[11]
b) It must be reasonably likely that the purpose of administration can be achieved.[12]
c) The qualifying floating charge-holder's choice of administrator will usually prevail.[13]

Where it is necessary to establish that the company 'is or is likely to become unable **8.09** to pay its debts', the tests under section 123 are engaged.[14] In *Re Colt Telecom Group*

---

[8] Schedule B1 para 3.
[9] Schedule B1 paras 2, 12(5), and 38 and section 7(4)(b). The court retains a discretion even where the conditions for making an order are satisfied: *Rowntree Ventures Ltd v Oaktree Property Partners Ltd* [2016] EWHC 1523 (Ch).
[10] Schedule B1 paras 14 and 111(1).
[11] Schedule B1 paras 11(a), 16 (see also paras 35 and 27(2)(a)).
[12] Schedule B1 paras 11(b), 18(3)(b) and 29(3)(b).
[13] Schedule B1 paras 14(1), 26(1) (indirectly, because notice of the intention to appoint given by the company or its directors affords the charge-holder the opportunity to intervene), and 36.
[14] Schedule B1 para 111(1). See further Chapter 3.

Plc (No 2), Jacob J considered the meaning of 'likely' in this context, when dismissing a hostile creditor application for an administration order, and held:[15]

> To put a company into administration is a serious matter. Creditors, as well as the company itself, can apply. To expose the company to all the expense, danger, and problems associated with administration is a serious matter. It is most unlikely that Parliament intended this when there was only a real prospect of insolvency rather than where insolvency was more probable than not.
>
> The experience of this case fortifies my view that it is not enough to merely to show a 'real prospect' of insolvency as opposed to insolvency being more likely than not. I cannot think Parliament intended that companies should be exposed to this kind of hostile proceeding where it is more likely than not that the company is not insolvent. Administration is a rescue procedure — it must be shown that rescue is probably needed before asking for a rescue team.

8.10   In general, liquidation and administration are mutually exclusive. Administration triggers a moratorium to protect the company whilst the purpose of the administration is being pursued and a qualified form of the same moratorium applies while an administration is pending.[16] The scope of the moratorium is considered later in this chapter.

8.11   Upon appointment, an administrator has a duty to take custody or control of all property to which he thinks the company is entitled.[17] In theory, he then manages the company while putting proposals to the company's creditors for achieving the purpose of administration. After approval of his proposals by the creditors, he then proceeds to implement his proposals subject to any approved revisions and any directions from the court.[18] In practice, this model is often pre-empted by the process of 'pre-packing' which is examined in Chapter 18.

8.12   An administrator's powers to manage the company's affairs, business, and property are much more extensive than those of a liquidator and this will often be determinative when the choice of procedure is being made. It is, however, important to recognize that administration does not, of itself, necessarily produce better results for creditors and a prospective administrator who is considering whether he can properly opine that the purpose of administration is achievable (because of prospective results for creditors) must carefully identify what it is that he would do as administrator that a liquidator could not do. This may be difficult if there is no going concern.

8.13   In principle, an administrator enjoys all the powers of the directors to deal with the company's affairs, business, and property.[19] In *Denny v Yeldon*, Jacob J said, while

---

15 [2002] EWHC 2815 (Ch), [2003] BPIR 324 [25], [26].
16 Schedule B1 paras 40 to 44.
17 Schedule B1 para 67.
18 Schedule B1 para 68.
19 Schedule B1 paras 59, and 60 and Schedule 1.

reflecting on the significance of an administrator's statutory power to change the composition of the board:[20]

> I think that leads to the conclusion that any power of the directors before an administration order is made is within the powers of the administrators after the order is made. Any other conclusion would be pointless.

However, there is an implicit restriction in that the administrator is bound by any limits to the company's own powers. That issue arose in *Re Home Treat Ltd* where Harman J said:[21]

> The powers of the administrator are, of course, set out in sec. 14 of the Act of 1986 and they include in sec. 14(1)(a) to 'do all such things as may be necessary for the management of the affairs, business and property of the company'. [Counsel] submitted that must mean for the 'lawful' management of the affairs of the company which must mean in accordance with the objects of the company as laid out in its memorandum. The powers in Sch. 1 to the Act of 1986 which are given to administrators by sec. 14(1)(b) must also be powers to carry on a lawful business and the same submission plainly applies. Further, by sec. 14(5) the administrator is deemed to act as the company's agent. An agent has no greater power than his principal and the administrator must therefore act in accordance with the company's powers. Finally, submitted [counsel], subsec. (4) of sec. 14 would be an unnecessary provision if the administrator had powers greater than those provided by the memorandum of association. I accept [counsel's] submissions on these points.

In addition to those general powers, the administrator has power to deal with **8.14** property which is subject to a floating charge as if it was not charged and can apply to the court for orders permitting him to dispose of goods which the company possesses under a hire-purchase agreement[22] and property subject to a fixed charge. If the court authorizes sale under these provisions, the owner or chargee (as the case may be) must be paid the net proceeds plus any additional sum required to bring the payment up to market value. Orders authorizing the disposal of hire-purchase goods and fixed charge security can only be made where the court thinks disposal would promote the purpose of administration. The purpose of these special powers is obviously to enable an administrator to preserve a going concern by preventing fragmentation of the necessary assets. Richard Snowden QC, sitting as a deputy judge of the High Court, examined

---

[20] [1995] 1 BCLC 560 (Ch) 564e.

[21] [1991] BCC 165 (Ch) 166E. As is apparent, this was an old law case and, instead of reference to section 14, reference should now be made to Schedule B1 paras 59, 60, 64, and 69. The new wording is different but not so as to cast doubt on the validity of Harman J's conclusion. Note also that changes resulting from the Companies Act 2006 mean that any restrictions will now be found in the company's articles.

[22] Despite the ordinary meaning of a 'hire-purchase agreement' being clear, the term has a confusingly extended meaning for these purposes whereby it includes conditional sale agreements, chattel leasing agreements and, crucially, retention of title agreements: Schedule B1 paras 70 to 72, and 111(1).

the nature of the jurisdiction to authorize the sale of fixed charge security in *Re Capitol Films Ltd* where he said:[23]

> In a typical case, an application might be made by an administrator under para 71 in order to achieve a sale of a company's business as a going concern, thereby fulfilling the purpose of achieving a better result for creditors as a whole than would be likely if the company was wound up. If, for example, a company operates from premises which are subject to a fixed charge, the administrator may wish to sell the business as a going concern and in situ, and will need to be able to convey the premises free of the fixed charge in order to do so. In such a case, an order of the court necessarily involves a balancing exercise. On the one side are the interests of the holder of the fixed charge, who has rights to seek a sale of the charged property for himself and may, for example, prefer a deferred sale with vacant possession. On the other side are the interests of the holders of floating security and the unsecured creditors, who are likely to benefit from an immediate sale of the business as a going concern. The administrator seeking an order under para 71, and the court in considering whether to make it, will be required to balance the prejudice that will be felt by the secured creditor if the order is made, against the prejudice that will be felt by those interested in the promotion of the purposes specified in the administration order if it is not: see *Re ARV Aviation Ltd*.

8.15 An administration ends automatically after twelve months unless it has been extended in the meantime. Extension can be the result of a court order or by consent.[24] The legislative policy is clear, that administration should ordinarily be an expeditious procedure,[25] but the policy is hopelessly impractical for cases of any serious complexity.[26] If an administration has inadvertently been allowed to expire, the court has no jurisdiction to extend it. This has significant implications not only for the consequences of any purported conduct of the administration in the meantime but also for other matters, for example claw-back actions, where the date of the commencement of proceedings may determine whether a claim can be made.[27] When the administration ends, the company reverts to management by its directors unless administration is followed by liquidation or dissolution.

8.16 Apart from expiry by the effluxion of time, an administration may end:

a) by court order on the application of the administrator;[28]
b) by the administrator filing a notice if he thinks that the purpose of the administration has been 'sufficiently achieved';[29]

---

[23] [2010] EWHC 3223 (Ch), [2011] 2 BCLC 359 [36] (internal citation omitted).
[24] Schedule B1 paras 76 to 78.
[25] Schedule B1 para 4.
[26] In *Re Maxwell Communication Corporation Plc* [2016] EWHC 2200 (Ch) an order was made for the discharge of an administration order made some twenty-five years earlier.
[27] See further Schedule B1 paras 77(1) and 78(4); *Re Frontsouth (Witham) Ltd* [2011] EWHC 1668 (Ch), [2011] BCC 635; Dear IP, October 2008, Chapter 1.12 <https://www.insolvencydirect.bis.gov.uk/insolvencyprofessionandlegislation/dearip/dearipindex.htm> accessed 16 January 2017.
[28] Schedule B1 para 79.
[29] Schedule B1 para 80.

c) by court order on the application of a creditor;[30]

d) upon the making of a winding-up order pursuant to the administrator's petition;[31]

e) by the administrator giving and filing a notice to move the company into creditors' voluntary liquidation;[32] and

f) by the administrator giving and filing a notice that he thinks that the company has no property to enable a distribution to be made to creditors (which leads to dissolution three months later).[33]

Determination of whether the purpose of administration has been 'sufficiently **8.17** achieved', thereby enabling the administrator to bring the administration to an end by notice, involves a judgment on the part of the administrator. This may be straightforward if the administrator is opining on whether a better result for creditors has been achieved or whether he has made realizations enabling distributions to be made to secured or preferential creditors, but a conclusion that the rescue of a company as a going concern has been achieved is potentially much more problematic. The question was considered by Lord Hodge, in *Joint Administrators of Station Properties, Petitioners*, a Scottish case, where he said in a passage of his judgment which also informs the nature of the primary objective of administration: [34]

> In the context of a rescue as a going concern, I do not think that much is added by the word 'sufficiently'. The adverb, for which 'adequately' might be a synonym in this context, does not dilute the test of the restoration of the company as a going concern. It may serve as recognition that an assessment of whether a company has become or remains a going concern is a matter of looking into the uncertain future and making an informed judgement … The concept involves the idea of remaining in business and of paying one's debts as they fall due.
>
> The exercise which an administrator carries out in making his assessment for the purposes of para 80 of Schedule B1 is not identical to that of the company director or auditor. The latter is usually making a judgement about whether a company, which is trading, will continue to trade in the future. The administrator is making a judgement about a company which has been insolvent and is asking himself whether it will be able to trade in future. Both exercises are principally an assessment of cash flow solvency. A company can be treated as a going concern if it has secured the continued financial support from another person to meet its debts as they fall due, even if it is balance sheet insolvent.
>
> Before one can treat a company as a going concern one must look into the foreseeable future and decide whether it is probable that the company will be able to pay its debts as they fall due.

---

[30] Schedule B1 para 81.
[31] Schedule B1 para 79 and rule 4.7 (but see also Schedule B1 para 82).
[32] Schedule B1 para 83.
[33] Schedule B1 para 84.
[34] [2013] CSOH 120 (Court of Session, Outer House) [17]–[19]; see also *Re Olympia & York Canary Wharf Holdings Ltd* [1993] BCC 866 (Ch).

3. The position of the directors

8.18 The directors are likely to play a more important role in administration than in liquidation. They have the power to put the company into administration (as opposed to petitioning the court) and, if the company continues to trade during the period it is in administration, their services are likely to be required by the administrator.

8.19 The power of the directors to appoint an administrator out of court, or to apply to the court for an administration order, was designed to overcome the difficulty exposed by the decision in *Re Emmadart Ltd*[35] where it was held that a company could not present its own winding-up petition unless its directors were acting pursuant to a resolution of the shareholders. The directors must be acting unanimously unless a formal board resolution has been passed which binds any dissenters.[36]

8.20 The directors remain in office following the appointment of an administrator. They have a duty to co-operate with the administrator and are the persons most likely to be required to provide him with a statement of affairs.[37] Two other special provisions apply:

a) The administrator has the power to appoint and remove directors. This power, which has no parallel in liquidation, appears to have been considered necessary for the purposes of rescue or reconstruction. It has attracted little judicial attention but was relied upon by Jacob J in *Denny v Yeldon* as part of his reasoning that an administrator must be able to exercise all the powers of the directors.[38]

b) Whilst the company is in administration, officers of the company may not exercise management powers without the administrator's consent. A management power is curiously defined for these purposes as being a power which could be exercised so as to interfere with the exercise of the administrator's own powers.[39] In this respect there is a parallel with section 103, which provides for the cesser of directors' powers upon the appointment of a liquidator

---

[35] [1979] Ch 540 (Ch). The much more recent decision in *Re Frontsouth (Witham) Ltd* [2011] EWHC 1668 (Ch), [2011] BCC 635, in which it was held that the making of an application for an administration order by the company was a matter for the directors where the company's articles entrusted management to them, casts doubt on the decision in *Emmadart* (which was not referred to) but see further *Re Eiffel Steelworks Ltd* [2015] EWHC 511 (Ch), [2015] 2 BCLC 57 which followed *Emmadart*.

[36] *Re Instrumentation Electrical Services Ltd* (1988) 4 BCC 301 (Ch); *Re Equiticorp International Plc* [1989] 1 WLR 1010 (Ch); *Minmar (929) Ltd v Khalatschi* [2011] EWHC 1159 (Ch), [2012] 1 BCLC 798; *Re Melodious Corpn* [2015] EWHC 621 (Ch), [2016] Bus LR 101; see also *Re Information Governance Ltd* [2013] EWHC 2611 (Ch), [2015] BCC 277.

[37] Section 235 and Schedule B1 paras 47 and 48.

[38] [1995] 1 BCLC 560 (Ch) 564e, see para 8.13.

[39] Schedule B1 para 64.

in a creditors' voluntary liquidation, but the administration provision is more nuanced—no doubt again reflecting anticipation of a continuing role for directors in at least some administrations.

4. The moratorium

Although referred to in the Act and in judgments as being a moratorium, the **8.21** stay which results from a company being in administration is not a moratorium properly so-called because it is a suspension of creditor remedies rather a legal authorization to postpone payment of debt. Millett J identified the true nature of the moratorium in *Barclays Mercantile Business Finance Ltd v Sibec Developments Ltd* when he said:[40]

> The administrators submit that the claim is doomed to fail because by virtue of section 11(3)(c) of the Act the immediate right to possession of the goods was no longer vested in the applicants after the making of the administration order. That submission treats section 11 as affecting substantive rights. In my judgment it does not have that effect. The section is couched in purely procedural terms: '(c) no other steps may be taken to enforce any security ... or to repossess goods ...' Similarly paragraph (d): 'no other proceedings ... may be commenced or continued ...'
>
> Those paragraphs presuppose that both the legal right to enforce the security or repossess the goods and the cause of action remain vested in the party seeking leave. By giving leave the court does not alter the parties' legal rights. It merely grants the person having a legal right liberty to enforce it by proceedings if necessary. The section imposes a moratorium on the enforcement of the creditor's rights but does not destroy those rights.

and very shortly afterwards, in *Re Olympia & York Canary Wharf Holdings Ltd*, he added:[41]

> [The moratorium provisions] are intended to impose a moratorium upon the creditors of the company in order to assist the administrator in his attempts to achieve the statutory purpose for which he was appointed. They are couched in procedural terms and are designed to prevent creditors from depriving the administrator of the possession of property which may be required by him for the purpose of the administration.
>
> [Provisions now located in Schedule B1 paragraph 42] operate to prevent the replacement of the administration by an alternative insolvency procedure before the statutory purpose for which the administrator was appointed has been achieved. Paragraphs (c) and (d) impose the moratorium. Their construction should be approached with that legislative purpose in mind. They are not intended to interfere with the rights of creditors further than is required to enable the administrators to

---

[40] [1992] 1 WLR 1253 (Ch) 1257D. This was an old law case. Old section 11(3) corresponds with new Schedule B1 para 43.

[41] [1993] BCC 154 (Ch) 157H.

carry out their functions, and in particular they are not intended to interfere with the creditors' contractual rights to crystallise their rights or discharge their own contractual liabilities.

a. The formal scope of the moratorium

8.22   As indicated by the quoted passage from Millett J's judgment in *Olympia & York*, the moratorium has two components. First, it prevents administration being circumvented by liquidation and, secondly, actions by individual creditors are restrained.

8.23   Paragraph 42 of Schedule B1 is concerned with the prevention of liquidation. The terms are clear: no winding-up resolution can be passed while a company is in administration and, subject to specified public interest exceptions, no winding-up order can be made by the court.

8.24   Paragraph 43 of Schedule B1 deals with other forms of adverse creditor action. This is the constraint of individual creditor remedies and the drafting raises a number of interpretation issues. In principle, the following forms of creditor action are prohibited unless the administrator consents or the court grants permission:

a) security enforcement;
b) repossession of hire-purchase goods;[42]
c) peaceable re-entry by landlords;[43]
d) appointment of an administrative receiver;[44] and
e) 'legal process' including legal proceedings, execution, and distress against the company or its property.

b. Interpretation of the moratorium provisions

8.25   The courts have adopted a strongly purposive approach to the interpretation of paragraph 43 of Schedule B1 (and its analogue in section 11(3)). In *Bristol Airport Plc v Powdrill*, Sir Nicolas Browne-Wilkinson V-C said:[45]

> ... it may be helpful to state what, in my opinion, is the correct approach to the construction of the provisions dealing with administrators contained in Part II of the Act. The judge was very much influenced in his construction by the manifest statutory purpose of Part II of the Act. I agree with this approach. The provisions of Part II themselves, coupled with the mischief identified in the Cork Report, show that the statutory purpose is to install an administrator, as an officer of the

---

[42]   See footnote 22 as to the extended meaning of this term.
[43]   This was not part of the moratorium as originally enacted in section 11(3). Its introduction reversed the decision in *Re Lomax Leisure Ltd* [2000] Ch 502 (Ch) and the earlier authorities to like effect reviewed by Neuberger J in his judgment.
[44]   This covers the permitted exceptions to section 72A, see sections 72B to 72H.
[45]   [1990] 1 Ch 744 (CA) 758F.

court, to carry on the business of the company as a going concern with a view to achieving one or other of the statutory objectives ... It is of the essence of administration under Part II of the Act that the business will continue to be carried on by the administrator. Such continuation of the business by the administrator requires that there should be available to him the right to use the property of the company, free from interference by creditors and others during the, usually short, period during which such administration continues. Hence the restrictions on the rights of creditors and others ... In my judgment in construing Part II of the Act it is legitimate and necessary to bear in mind the statutory objective with a view to ensuring, if the words permit, that the administrator has the powers necessary to carry out the statutory objectives, including the power to use the company's property.

On the other hand, however desirable it may be to construe the Act in a way calculated to carry out the parliamentary purpose, it is not legitimate to distort the meaning of the words Parliament has chosen to use in order to achieve that result. Only if the words used by Parliament are fairly capable of bearing more than one meaning is it legitimate to adopt the meaning which gives effect to, rather than frustrates, the statutory purpose.

Generally speaking, attempts by creditors to evade the effects of the moratorium by drawing fine distinctions based on the language of the Act have failed and become instead issues about whether permission should be granted.

The following applications of the moratorium relate to wildly different factual **8.26** cases but, together, they illustrate the purposive approach taken towards the interpretation of the legislation:

a) The exercise of a statutory right of detention by an airport over aircraft leased to a company in administration was held to amount not only to the perfection but also the enforcement of security over the company's property.[46]

b) The moratorium was held to apply to a repairer's lien over an aircraft which had been delivered to the repairer by receivers after the commencement of administration (in the course of permitted security enforcement) and which had never been in the possession of the company which owned it during administration.[47]

c) Goods which remain in the possession of the company in administration following the pre-administration termination of a hire-purchase agreement remain in its possession 'under' that agreement for the purposes of the moratorium even if pre-administration repossession has been wrongfully resisted.[48]

d) Goods which have been sub-leased to end-users remain in the possession of a company in administration for the purposes of the moratorium.[49]

---

[46] *Bristol Airport Plc v Powdrill* [1990] Ch 744 (CA).
[47] *London Flight Centre (Stansted) Ltd v Osprey Aviation Ltd* [2002] BPIR 1115 (Ch).
[48] *Re David Meek Access Ltd* [1993] BCC 175 (Ch).
[49] *Re Atlantic Computer Systems Plc* [1992] Ch 505 (CA).

e) It has been suggested that, where goods supplied subject to retention of title have been re-sold and delivered by administrators to a third party on terms that the purchaser will honour any valid claims advanced within a reasonable period, it is arguable that the goods remain in the constructive possession of the company in administration during that period so as to engage the moratorium.[50]

f) Proceedings brought by a competitor in the Patents Court for the revocation of a patent are covered.[51]

g) The adjudication procedure under section 108 of the Housing Grants, Construction and Regeneration Act 1996 is covered.[52]

h) An application to an employment tribunal is covered whether initiated by an individual or an organization. In *Carr v British International Helicopters Ltd*, Lord Coulsfield elaborated on the scope of 'proceedings':[53]

> In our opinion, the starting point for consideration of this case is that a complaint or other application before an industrial tribunal must be regarded as falling within the description 'proceedings' in the ordinary sense of that term. As *Quazi v. Quazi* shows, the word 'proceedings' may encompass procedures which fall outwith formal legal, or court, procedures, or proceedings analogous to formal legal proceedings. For the purposes of the present case, however, it is not necessary to extend the meaning of the term so far. It is quite clear that the term 'proceedings' covers not only court procedures but also analogous procedures such as arbitrations. There is, in our view, no reason why procedures before an industrial tribunal, whether initiated by individuals or by organisations, should not fall within the meaning of the term.

i) The moratorium applies to criminal proceedings.[54]

j) A review hearing before a regulatory panel of the Gambling Commission in order to consider the revocation or suspension of gaming licences (which could be the subject of an appeal process) has been held to be covered.[55]

k) Service of a statutory demand is covered.[56]

8.27 In contrast, the following points demonstrate the limitations of the wording and Browne-Wilkinson V-C's warning in *Bristol Airport* that the moratorium can only be applied consistently with the language of the provisions:

a) The moratorium does not prevent the exercise of contractual rights, for example the service of termination notices, which do not engage other limbs of the

---

[50] *Fashoff (UK) Ltd v Linton* [2008] EWHC 537 (Ch), [2008] 2 BCLC 362.
[51] *Re Axis Genetics Plc* [2000] BCC 943 (Ch).
[52] *A Straume (UK) Ltd v Bradlor Developments Ltd* [2000] BCC 333 (Ch).
[53] [1994] ICR 18 (EAT: Scotland) 26H (internal citation omitted).
[54] *Re Rhondda Waste Disposal Company Ltd* [2001] Ch 57 (CA).
[55] *Re Frankice (Golders Green) Ltd* [2010] EWHC 1229 (Ch), [2010] Bus LR 1608.
[56] *Fulton v AIB Group (UK) Plc* [2014] NICh 8 (High Court of Northern Ireland).

provisions.[57] (In practice, this is a highly significant limitation although its effects are moderated by sections 233 and 233A where they apply.)

b) The moratorium does not preclude the exercise of contractual rights of set-off before insolvency set-off is triggered by giving notice of a proposed distribution pursuant to rule 14.29.[58]

c) The power of a regulator to give directions to a company in administration on the application of a third party is not a judicial or quasi-judicial role involving 'legal process' even though the actual procedure may have some similarities with legal proceedings in order to ensure fairness.[59]

8.28 The moratorium will also not be applied by the courts where an application is required to be made to the court in any event in order for the court to exercise some power vested in it. This point arose in *Re Barrow Borough Transport Ltd* in connection with the late registration of a charge where Millett J said:[60]

> One procedural point was raised before me: whether, before making the application, the council ought to have obtained the consent of the administrators or the leave of the court …

> In my judgment, an application for an extension of time under the Companies Act 1985 for the registration of a charge cannot be described as 'proceedings against the company or its property.' It is an application which can equally well be made by the company, and which normally is made by the company while it is a going concern. I would not unless compelled to do so construe the Act as imposing an obligation upon a creditor to apply to the court for leave in order to make an application to the court for leave to register out of time. A double-barrelled application for leave is an absurdity. In my judgment, the Insolvency Act 1986 does not require it.

c. Permission to proceed

8.29 The purpose of the moratorium is to facilitate the achievement of the purpose of the administration in the interests of the creditors as a whole; it is not to afford the administrator commercial leverage in negotiations with individual creditors.

8.30 The onus is on the creditor seeking permission to make out its case. In the first instance, a request for permission will naturally be made to the administrator who must consider it objectively. As Nicholls LJ said in *Re Atlantic Computer Systems Plc* when delivering the judgment of the court:[61]

---

[57] *Re Olympia & York Canary Wharf Ltd* [1993] BCC 154 (Ch); *Re Pan Ocean Ltd* [2014] EWHC 2124 (Ch), [2014] Bus LR 1041.

[58] *Electro Magnetic(s) Ltd v Development Board of Singapore Ltd* [1994] 1 SLR 734 (Court of Appeal of Singapore).

[59] *Re Railtrack Plc (No 2)* [2002] EWCA Civ 955, [2002] 1 WLR 3002. There are fine distinctions to be drawn between such cases and those which are analogous to the decision referred to in para 8.26(j) above.

[60] [1990] Ch 227 (Ch) 232D.

[61] [1992] Ch 505 (CA) 529F.

An administrator is an officer of the court. He can be expected to make his decision speedily, so far as he can do so ... The administrator should also make his decision responsibly. His power to give or withhold consent was not intended to be used as a bargaining counter in a negotiation in which the administrator has regard only to the interests of the unsecured creditors.

An administrator who fails to observe these precepts risks incurring a personal liability.[62]

8.31 Having regard to the purpose of the moratorium, the first question is whether the proposed action will interfere with the conduct of the administration. If the action would have no adverse consequences for the company in administration or relates to the recovery of property (not being hire-purchase goods) which does not belong to the company, permission should be granted.[63] Such cases should not be unduly difficult for an administrator to decide because he is the person best placed to determine what will impede the administration.

8.32 If, however, there will (or may) be a negative impact on the administration, the competing interests of the general body of creditors and those of the creditor seeking to perform some act which would offend the terms of the stay have to be balanced.[64] It is clearly more difficult for an administrator, who is charged with a duty to act in the interests of the general body of creditors, to determine objectively whether those interests are outweighed by the interests of an individual creditor. In *Re Atlantic Computer Systems Plc*, the Court of Appeal gave general guidelines as to when administrators should consent or the court should give permission (to which reference should be made for a fuller discussion of the relevant factors).[65]

8.33 The court will attach great weight to upholding proprietary rights. Nicholls LJ said of this in *Atlantic Computer Systems*:[66]

The underlying principle here is that an administration for the benefit of unsecured creditors should not be conducted at the expense of those who have proprietary rights which they are seeking to exercise, save to the extent that this may be unavoidable and even then this will usually be acceptable only to a strictly limited extent.

It is often necessary to consider the magnitude and probability of the prospective losses of both the creditor seeking leave and the company in administration. In an appropriate case either the grant or refusal of permission may be made conditional upon imposed terms. The Court of Appeal's guidelines were given in the context of

---

[62] *Barclays Mercantile Business Finance Ltd v Sibec Developments Ltd* [1992] 1 WLR 1253 (Ch).
[63] *Lazari GP Ltd v Jervis* [2012] EWHC 1466 (Ch), [2013] BCC 294; *Re UK Housing Alliance (North West) Ltd* [2013] EWHC 2553 (Ch), [2013] BCC 752; *Re A/Wear Ltd* [2013] EWCA Civ 1626.
[64] *Re Atlantic Computer Systems Plc* [1992] Ch 505 (CA); *Lazari GP Ltd v Jervis* ibid.
[65] Ibid at 541–544.
[66] Ibid at 542G.

its decision that the court enjoyed a discretion as to the payment of administration expenses. That part of its decision is no longer good law (see generally Chapter 20) but the guidelines remain valid.

d. Limitation issues

A potential trap for the unwary is that, according to present authority, time does **8.34** not stop running for the purposes of the Limitation Act 1980 because the company is in administration. In *Re Maxwell Fleet and Facilities Management Ltd*, Jules Sher QC (sitting as a deputy judge of the High Court) said:[67]

> The Insolvency Act 1986 is silent in relation to limitation. There is no reference to limitation in relation to administration in the Report of the Review Committee on Insolvency Law and Practice (1982) (Cmnd 8558) (the Cork Report). There appears to be no specific provision which arrests the running of a limitation period under the Limitation Act 1980 during the course of an administration. The whole idea of an administration was included in legislation for the first time in the Insolvency Act 1986. If there had been an intention to stop the running of the limitation periods during the tenure of an administrator, Parliament could have easily done so. No matter how much one can see sense and reason behind a provision freezing the running of time during the administration moratorium the fact is that such a provision is not there.

This question is revisited in the next section of this chapter.

5. Transition to a liquidating administration

a. Power to distribute

The administrator's power to make distributions to creditors, introduced as part of **8.35** the reforms of the procedure made by the Enterprise Act 2002, is a qualified power. Paragraph 65 of Schedule B1 provides that the administrator may not make a distribution (other than a distribution to a secured or preferential creditor or a distribution of the prescribed part) unless the court gives its permission. The discretion of the court is entirely at large and is to be exercised in the interests of the creditors as a whole.[68] Norris J elaborated on this in *Re MG Rover Belux SA/NV* saying:[69]

> I doubt however that it is possible to draw up a definitive list of considerations relevant to all cases (given the width of the discretion), and the considerations

---

[67] *Re Maxwell Fleet and Facilities Management Ltd* [2001] 1 WLR 323 (Ch) 327E. See also *Re Cases of Taffs Well Ltd* [1992] Ch 179 (Ch); *Re Cosslett Contractors Ltd* [2004] EWHC 658 (Ch); *Re Leyland Printing Co Ltd* [2010] EWHC 2105 (Ch), [2011] BCC 358.

[68] *Re GHE Realisations Ltd* [2005] EWHC 2400 (Ch), [2006] 1 WLR 287; *Re MG Rover Belux SA/NV* [2005] EWHC 1296 (Ch), [2007] BCC 446.

[69] Ibid at [7].

will obviously vary from case the [sic] case ... The following considerations have appeared to me material in this case:

(a) The matter is to be judged at the time when permission is sought.
(b) The court must at that time be satisfied that the proposed distribution is conducive to the achievement of the then current objectives of the administration.
(c) The court must be satisfied that the distribution is in the interests of the company's creditors as a whole (because para.3(2) of Sch.B1 says that the administrator must perform his functions in that manner).
(d) The court must be satisfied that proper provision has been made for secured and preferential creditors (for the requirement to obtain the permission of the court seems to be directed at their protection).
(e) The court must consider what are the realistic alternatives to the proposed distribution sought by the administrators, consider the merits and demerits of adopting a course other than that proposed by the administrators and assess whether the proposed distribution adversely affects the entitlement of others (when compared with their entitlement if one of the other realistic alternatives were to be adopted).
(f) The court must take into account the basis on which the administration has been conducted so far as the creditors are concerned (under the original proposals, any modification to those original proposals, or any indications given in any reports to creditors), and in particular whether the creditors have approved (or not objected to) any proposal concerning the relevant distribution.
(g) The court must consider the nature and terms of the distribution.
(h) The court must consider the impact of the distribution upon any proposed exit route from the administration.

Norris J was careful to link his statement of the relevant considerations to the rather unusual circumstances of the case before him but they nonetheless appear to be of general application and were treated as such by Snowden J in *Re Nortel Networks UK Ltd*.[70]

8.36 Administrators, intending to make a distribution for which the court has granted permission, must next give notice of the proposed distribution to creditors in accordance with rule 14.29. The giving of a rule 14.29 notice has two incidental consequences apart from its role in the mechanics of distribution:

a) It sets the date as at which the account of mutual dealings must be taken for the purposes of insolvency set-off pursuant to rule 14.24.[71]
b) It engages the pari passu rule which renders ineffective agreements which purport to displace the statutory scheme for distribution.[72] In *Revenue and Customs Commissioners v Football League Ltd*, David Richards J said:[73]

---

[70] [2015] EWHC 2506 (Ch) [20].
[71] Rule 14.24(2). See further Chapter 21.
[72] See further Chapter 21.
[73] [2012] EWHC 1372 (Ch), [2012] Bus LR 1539 [89], [90].

In my judgment, the pari passu principle serves a purpose and should come into play only if the purpose of the insolvency procedure is to effect a distribution. In the case of liquidation or bankruptcy, this is when the company enters liquidation or the debtor is declared bankrupt. In the case of administration, this is when the administrator gives notice of the proposed distribution.

It is, in my judgement, significant that insolvency set-off applies in an administration to debts as at the date of such notice, and not earlier. It indicates that it is at that date and not before that the pari passu regime is to operate.

The methodology of proof of debt and the scheme of distribution is the same as **8.37** that applicable in liquidation. Provable debts are debts or liabilities to which the company is subject to when it went into administration unless administration was preceded by liquidation, in which case the liquidation date applies.[74]

b. Statutory trust and limitation issues further considered

Two related questions arise when an administration becomes a liquidating or dis- **8.38** tributing administration: first, whether the assets of the company become subject to a statutory trust and, secondly, whether time should continue to run for the purposes of the Limitation Act 1980.

It is settled law that liquidation gives rise to a statutory trust with the consequence **8.39** that the company ceases to be the beneficial owner of its assets.[75] In the course of his definitive judgment on this subject in *Ayerst v C&K (Construction) Ltd*, Lord Diplock explained the nature of the trust by comparing the position of a trustee in bankruptcy:[76]

> Another example, which owes its origin to statute, is to be found in the law of bankruptcy. The legal ownership of the bankrupt's property becomes vested in the trustee in bankruptcy. Here, while the property is still being administered, not only is there a similar absence of specific subjects identifiable as the trust fund but also the fact that the right to share in the proceeds of realisation of the property is dependent upon the creditor making a claim to prove in the bankruptcy makes it impossible until the time for proof has expired to identify those persons for whose benefit the trustee is administering the property. Both these factors would, in equity, have prevented that property possessing those characteristics of trust properties which have the consequence of vesting the beneficial ownership of any part of the undistributed property in those persons who will eventually become entitled to share in the proceeds of realisation. Nevertheless, as the very word 'trustee' used in the statute implies, the beneficial ownership is not vested in him. He cannot enjoy the fruits of it himself or dispose of it for his own benefit. He is under a duty to deal with it as directed by the statute for the benefit of all the creditors who come in to prove a valid claim. It is no misuse of language to describe the property as being held by the trustee on a statutory trust if the qualifying adjective 'statutory'

---

[74] Rules 14.1 and 14.2.
[75] See further Chapter 7.
[76] [1976] AC 167 (HL) 178C.

is understood as indicating that the trust does not bear all the indicia which characterise a trust as it was recognised by the Court of Chancery apart from statute.

Lord Diplock held that the position of a liquidator was the same and that the fact that the property of the company did not vest in the liquidator (as a bankrupt's property vests in his trustee in bankruptcy) was immaterial.

8.40 In decisions on limitation issues which were decided by reference to the pre-Enterprise Act version of the law where an administrator had no power to make distributions, it was either held or assumed that there was no comparable statutory trust in respect of a company in administration.[77] The question remains an open question following the Enterprise Act reforms facilitating liquidating administrations. In *Revenue and Customs Commissioners v Football League Ltd*, David Richards J said:[78]

> I think [counsel] is probably right when he says that the statutory trust, as discussed in *Ayerst*, does not apply to the assets of a company in administration, at least before notice of a proposed distribution is given and even then difficulties may arise if only some of the assets are to be distributed.

Where there is to be a general distribution of all the company's assets, it is suggested that, following notice being given of the proposed distribution, the situation is indistinguishable from that described by Lord Diplock where a company goes into liquidation. There is no reason, in principle, why a statutory trust should not arise at that point in the same way that the insolvency set-off account falls to be taken as at that date and the pari passu rule bites. The (less common) case of a partial distribution is more problematic but could be resolved by recognizing the trust as applying only to such part of the company's assets as were to be the subject of the statutory scheme for distribution.

8.41 The question then arises as to whether this calls for a reappraisal of the position in respect of time running for limitation purposes because the existence of the statutory trust is the foundation of the rule that time ceases to run against a creditor of a company in liquidation. In *Re General Rolling Stock Company, Joint Stock Discount Company's Claim*, Mellish LJ said:[79]

> … I think we must consider that the Legislature intended us to follow the analogy of other cases where the assets of a debtor are to be divided amongst his creditors, whether in bankruptcy or insolvency, or under a trust for creditors, or under a decree of the Court of Chancery, in an administration suit. In these cases the rule is that everybody who had a subsisting claim at the time of the adjudication, the insolvency, the creation of the trust for creditors, or the administration decree,

---

[77] *Re Cases of Taffs Well Ltd* [1992] Ch 179 (Ch) 195D; *Re Maxwell Fleet and Facilities Management Ltd* [2001] 1 WLR 323 (Ch) 328F; *Re Leyland Printing Co Ltd* [2010] EWHC 2105 (Ch), [2011] BCC 358 [11].

[78] [2012] EWHC 1372 (Ch), [2012] Bus LR 1539 [102].

[79] (1872) 7 Ch App 646 (CA) 649 and 650.

as the case may be, is entitled to participate in the assets, and that the Statute of Limitations does not run against this claim ...

The analogy between liquidation and a liquidating administration is that in both cases the assets are subject to a trust (as argued above), the liabilities to be discharged are those existing at the outset of the proceeding, and creditor action has been stayed during the proceeding.[80] On the other hand, the fundamental distinction between a liquidation and a liquidating administration (for these purposes) is that there is certainty from the outset in a liquidation and none in a liquidating administration until notice of a proposed distribution is given.

There is no satisfactory answer to this. If time continues to run during adminis-   **8.42** tration, it is possible that an applicable limitation period would expire during the administration but after the date when the company went into administration and by reference to which provable debts must be quantified. If time ceases to run, then a choice would have to be made between time ceasing to run at the outset or only when the rule 14.29 notice is given. The former would entail time ceasing to run before it was known whether the administration was to be a liquidating administration; the latter would entail the same problem as that applying if time did not cease running at all. It is plainly a matter which ought to have been addressed by legislation and not left to the courts to resolve.

---

[80] See also *Re Polly Peck International Plc (No 4)* [1998] 2 BCLC 185 (CA) 201; *Bloom v Harms Offshore AHT Taurus GmbH & Co KG* [2009] EWCA Civ 632, [2010] Ch 187 [22]–[26]; *Re Lehman Brothers International (Europe) (No 2)* [2009] EWHC 3228 (Ch), [2010] 2 BCLC 301 [204], the decision was reversed in part on appeal but not so as to affect the cited dictum.

9

COMPANY VOLUNTARY
ARRANGEMENTS

1. Introduction

9.01 A company voluntary arrangement (CVA) is a procedure under the Act whereby a company and a sufficient majority of its creditors can reach an agreement and thereby contract out of the insolvency rules which would otherwise apply.

9.02 The social dimensions of insolvency law are not such that it is contrary to principle for a debtor company to reach a consensual solution with its creditors. It would not be thought questionable for a debtor to reach agreement with a single creditor outside insolvency proceedings and a collective procedure merely provides the framework for such agreement to be reached with the creditors generally, without either the debtor or the willing creditors being held to ransom by a minority of dissenting creditors. The fact that the usual insolvency rules may be disapplied by such an agreement reached by the company outside insolvency proceedings is consistent with the ability of a liquidator to make a compromise, in the exercise of his statutory powers in the course of an insolvency proceeding, which departs from the statutory scheme.[1]

---

[1] *Taylor, Noter* [1992] BCC 440 (Court of Session, Inner House); *Re Bank of Credit and Commerce International SA (No 2)* [1992] BCC 715 (CA).

CVAs were a new procedure introduced by the Act to meet perceived shortcomings **9.03** in Companies Act schemes of arrangement. The proposal in this respect emanated from the Cork Report which stated:[2]

> We have concluded that there is no means of substantially improving the present scheme of arrangement process for insolvent companies. However, whilst the [Companies Act] procedure should remain available for insolvent companies, where it may be necessary in the case of a complicated scheme by a large company, we propose two alternative procedures for arrangements by corporate debtors which we consider will facilitate the effecting of fair and reasonable schemes.

As will be seen later in this chapter, the suggestion that schemes should be retained for larger and more complicated cases was a prescient recommendation.

The two alternatives postulated by the Cork Report were the proposed introduc- **9.04** tion of administration and CVAs, the latter being an adaptation of the Report's proposal for individual voluntary arrangements enabling debtors to avoid bankruptcy. More specifically, the Report said of its proposed CVA procedure:[3]

> In our a view a Voluntary Arrangement for a company on these lines is only likely to be used, first, where for some reason it is not appropriate to appoint an Administrator and, secondly, where the scheme is a simple one involving a composition or moratorium or both for the general body of creditors which can be formulated and presented speedily. However, we are convinced that the facility to promote such arrangements without the obligation to go to the Court will prove of value to small companies urgently seeking a straightforward composition or moratorium.

The thinking which underlies the legislation on both schemes of arrangement and CVAs is that there is a need to facilitate voluntary debt resolution agreements and that, for that purpose, it is necessary for a majority to be able to bind a dissenting minority.

2. Outline of CVAs

There are two versions of the CVA procedure: the original version introduced **9.05** in response to the Cork Report recommendations (as subsequently much amended) and a variant of that procedure which is only available for small companies and which provides for a moratorium where directors propose a CVA. Neither is formally predicated upon actual or even anticipated insolvency but the concept of a debt solution with creditors in any other circumstances makes no commercial sense.

---

[2] Report of the Review Committee, *Insolvency Law and Practice* (Cm 8558, June 1982) para 422.
[3] Cork Report ibid at para 430.

a. Standard CVAs

9.06 A CVA can be proposed by a company's directors, or its liquidator or administrator. The proposal must be for something which amounts to a composition in satisfaction of the company's debts or a scheme of arrangement of its affairs. It must provide for an insolvency practitioner to act as the 'nominee' for the purpose of supervising its implementation.[4]

9.07 Where the directors propose a CVA, the Act provides for them to give notice of their proposal to the nominee who then reports to the court on whether he considers the proposal has a reasonable prospect of being approved and implemented and whether, in his opinion, the proposal should be considered by a meeting of the company and by the company's creditors.[5] The reality is that this will almost inevitably be a fiction. A CVA proposal is a complicated document and the associated procedural requirements are so detailed that it is almost inconceivable that directors would attempt to formulate their proposal without the assistance of an insolvency practitioner.[6] That practitioner will usually assume the role of the nominee and his favourable opinion of any proposal which results from their joint endeavours is therefore likely to be a foregone conclusion.

9.08 Where the nominee has reported to the court that a directors' proposal should be considered by the company and its creditors, he proceeds to convene the company meeting and to seek a decision from the creditors unless the court directs otherwise (but there is no hearing to consider the nominee's report unless an application is made). Where the proposal is being made by a liquidator or administrator the procedure differs if the office-holder is himself/herself acting as the nominee because there is no report to the court; the office-holder simply proceeds to convene the company meeting and to seek the creditors' decision.[7]

9.09 The nominee will usually be the chairman of the company meeting and, as the convener for the purposes of the creditors' decision procedure, will have to resolve the questions which can arise over the eligibility to vote of persons with disputed or uncertain claims against the company.[8] Members vote according to their rights under the company's articles and, subject to the articles, a resolution is passed if a majority (in value) of those voting have voted in favour of it.[9] A creditors' decision approving a proposed CVA is made when three-quarters or more in value

---

[4] Section 1.
[5] Section 2.
[6] See Part 2 of the Rules and SIP 3.2 <https://www.r3.org.uk/what-we-do/publications/professional/statements-of-insolvency-practice> accessed 16 January 2017.
[7] Section 3. The former requirement for a meeting of the company's creditors no longer applies. The creditors' decision will ordinarily be taken in accordance with another 'qualifying decision procedure': section 246ZE and rules 2.25 and 15.3.
[8] Rules 15.31(3) and 15.33.
[9] Rules 2.35 and 2.36.

of those responding vote in favour of it.[10] A proposal may be approved with or without modifications but the rights of secured and preferential creditors cannot be affected without their consent. If the creditors approve a proposal which the company rejects, the creditors' decision prevails.[11] This is most likely to occur where the creditors have insisted on modifications to a directors' proposal or where a liquidator or administrator is putting forward a proposal which offers shareholders no benefits. The chairman must report the results of the voting to the court.

If the company has voted against a proposal which has been approved by the creditors, an aggrieved member of the company can apply to the court for relief. This protects members from oppression by creditors but there are also safeguards to protect creditors from misuse of the procedure by other creditors. Even if supported by a three-quarters majority of those voting in favour of a CVA proposal, a resolution is invalid if more than half of the total value of the unconnected creditors vote against it.[12] This is intended to ensure that a proposal is not forced on the creditors of the company through the support of those who may have an ulterior purpose. **9.10**

Upon the approval of the proposal, the nominee becomes the 'supervisor' of the CVA (unless the nominee has been replaced by the court or the proposal has been modified to provide for a different insolvency practitioner to be the supervisor). An aggrieved person may apply to the court on the grounds that an approved arrangement is unfairly prejudicial or that there was a material irregularity in the procedures to obtain approval.[13] Those qualified to make such an application are those entitled to vote on the proposal, those who would have been entitled to vote as creditors if they had had notice, the nominee (or his replacement), and any liquidator or administrator. There is a time limit of twenty-eight days starting with the first day on which reports on the outcome of the voting have been made to the court, unless the application is by a creditor who was not given notice of the decision procedure, in which case the twenty-eight-day period only begins to run when he becomes aware that the creditors' decision procedure has taken place. If the court is satisfied that the application is well-founded, it may revoke or suspend the approval and can direct that a further company meeting be held or that a further decision be sought from the creditors.[14] **9.11**

Any person who is dissatisfied with the supervisor's conduct of the CVA can apply to the court which can confirm, reverse, or modify his decisions and give him **9.12**

---

[10] Rule 15.34.

[11] Sections 4 and 4A.

[12] Rule 15.34.

[13] In order to constitute a good ground for challenge, the unfair prejudice must have been caused by the terms of the arrangement: *SISU Capital Fund Ltd v Tucker* [2006] EWHC 2170 (Ch), [2006] BCC 463 [69]–[70].

[14] Section 6.

directions. The supervisor himself can also apply for directions. If necessary, the court can replace the supervisor.[15]

9.13 The procedure is merely a framework; the substance of the arrangement and its intended duration (including provisions for termination) depend on the terms of the proposal which has been approved. The court has no power to modify a CVA on an application for directions.[16]

9.14 There has only been modest use of CVAs since the introduction of the procedure. Even such modest figures may exaggerate the true levels of use because of the instances of CVAs being used to effect distributions following administration before administrators acquired distribution powers under the Enterprise Act reforms of that procedure, and because of the instances of a group of companies entering into linked CVAs as part of a group solution. Unfavourable comparisons are sometimes made with individual voluntary arrangements which, introduced at the same time, have had a major impact on personal insolvency statistics. However, such comparisons are misleading because the vast majority of individual voluntary arrangements are not concerned with the more challenging task of structuring a proposal which allows for the survival of a continuing business. Two reasons for the comparative lack of success of CVAs as a rescue or reconstruction procedure are commonly advanced: first, the lack of a moratorium and, secondly, the lack of finality achieved by the approval of a CVA because of the twenty-eight-day challenge period (which may not even commence until a creditor which was overlooked is on notice that a creditors' decision procedure has taken place). The first of these issues was addressed by the procedure next considered.

b. Small company CVAs with a moratorium

9.15 Formal proposals for the introduction of a new form of CVA which allowed the directors of a small company to impose a moratorium on its creditors in order to enable them to advance and secure approval of a proposal, were advanced by the Insolvency Service as early as 1993.[17] However, it was not until the Insolvency Act 2000 was enacted and brought into force on 1 January 2003 that what are now section 1A and Schedule A1 of the Act took effect.[18] (The brief explanation which follows concentrates on the aspects of the small company CVA procedure which distinguish it from the standard CVA procedure.)

---

[15] Section 7.
[16] *Re Alpa Lighting Ltd* [1997] BPIR 341 (CA).
[17] The Insolvency Service, *Company Voluntary Arrangements and Administration Orders* (Consultation Paper, October 1993).
[18] Insolvency Act 2000 (Commencement No 3 and Transitional Provisions) Order 2002 (SI 2002/2711).

Subject to the exclusion of certain types of company (for example, insurance and **9.16** capital markets companies) a 'small' company for these purposes is a company which satisfies two or more of the Companies Act tests namely that it has:

a) a turnover of not more than £6.5 million;
b) a balance sheet total of not more than £3.26 million; and
c) not more than fifty employees.

The procedure starts with the submission of a proposal by the directors to a nominee **9.17** with supporting information. The nominee must then opine as to whether there is a reasonable prospect of the proposed CVA being approved and implemented and whether it should be considered by a meeting of the company and by the company's creditors. In an important departure from the requirements in respect of a standard CVA, the nominee must also opine as to whether the company is likely to have the funds that it needs to carry on its business during the moratorium. Assuming that the nominee's opinion is favourable, the directors then obtain a moratorium by filing their papers in court with the opinion. The moratorium lasts until the later of the days on which a company meeting takes place and the creditors decide whether to approve the proposal, which must be within twenty-eight days of the moratorium taking effect, but, subject to conditions, the moratorium can be extended for another two months by either the company or the creditors. No court order is needed.

The terms of a small company CVA moratorium are modelled on the terms of **9.18** the moratorium which applies when a company is in administration. The fact of the moratorium must be disclosed to those dealing with the company and there are also constraints on obtaining credit without disclosure, on disposals outside the ordinary course of business, and on payments to pre-moratorium creditors. The administration provisions for the disposal of charged property and goods in the possession of the company under hire-purchase agreements (which covers retention of title goods) are adapted to apply during the moratorium but it is not necessary to obtain the leave of the court if the secured creditor or owner consents to the disposal.

Aggrieved persons can challenge the directors' acts and omissions during the mor- **9.19** atorium and the court can make such order as it thinks fit including an order bringing the moratorium to an end.

During the moratorium, the nominee is required to monitor the company's affairs. **9.20** If he considers that the proposal no longer has a reasonable prospect of being approved or implemented, or that the company will not have sufficient funds for its continued trading, he must withdraw his consent to act and the moratorium comes to an end. Any creditor, member, director, or other person affected by the moratorium can apply to the court if dissatisfied with the nominee's discharge of his functions. Such an application can result in the court giving the nominee directions and the termination of the moratorium. If there are grounds for believing that the company has suffered loss as a result of the nominee's conduct during the moratorium, claims can be brought against him.

9.21 Criminal sanctions apply to fraudulent conduct on the part of officers of the company during the moratorium and in the preceding twelve months. In particular, it is an offence to obtain a moratorium (or extension of a moratorium) on the basis of a false representation. Those offences are supported by reporting obligations on the part of nominees and supervisors.[19]

9.22 Neither the Insolvency Service nor Companies House keep any records of the use of the Schedule A1 procedure as such (the available statistics treat all CVAs as a single procedure). However, anecdotal evidence suggests that the use of Schedule A1 since its introduction in 2003 has been negligible. One reason may be concerns which were expressed during the enactment of the Insolvency Act 2000 about the potential civil, and even criminal, liability of nominees performing a role where they would be substantially reliant upon information provided by the officers of the company and where they would not be in control of the company's ongoing trading activity. Another reason may be that the (proper) requirements for disclosure of the application of the Schedule A1 moratorium would have substantially the same reputational effects as those resulting from a company going into administration and the ability of a company to go into administration without a court order (which took effect only months later in 2003) removed the incentive to experiment with a novel procedure carrying the risks for the office-holder already identified. For whatever reason, the small company CVA procedure has been a failure.

3. The effect of approval

9.23 The Act provides that an approved CVA takes effect as if made by the company at the time that the creditors decide to approve it and binds every person who was entitled to vote in the decision procedure, or would have been entitled to vote if he had had notice of it, as if he were a party to the arrangement.[20] The legal basis on which a creditor is bound has been examined in a number of cases. It is important because it may determine the wider consequences of any discharge from liability, for example the rights of a creditor against a co-debtor or surety.

9.24 *Johnson v Davies* was an individual voluntary arrangement case but the relevant provisions as to the binding of creditors are the same. Chadwick LJ, with whom

---

[19] Section 7A.
[20] Section 5 and Schedule A1 para 37.

the other members of the court agreed, first identified the issue in the following terms:[21]

> There is nothing in that subsection, or elsewhere, which saves a party who is bound 'as if he were a party to the arrangement' from the consequences which would follow as a matter of law if he were indeed a party to the arrangement. The statutory hypothesis is that the person who has notice of and was entitled to vote at the meeting is party to an arrangement to which he has given his consent. It is important to keep in mind that, where B and C are co-debtors of A, the reason why C is released as a result of an arrangement or bargain between A and B is that the effect of that bargain is to extinguish the debt; alternatively, that the effect of that bargain is that A has agreed with B that A will not sue C on a debt which, if paid by C, will give C rights of contribution against B and so negate the release from any further liability in respect of that debt which is the basis of B's arrangement with A.

He later concluded:[22]

> ... the Act of 1986 does not purport, directly, to impose the arrangement on a dissenting creditor whether or not he has agreed to its terms; rather, he is bound by the arrangement as the result of a statutory hypothesis. The statutory hypothesis requires him to be treated as if he had consented to the arrangement. The consequence, as it seems to me, is that the legislature must be taken to have intended that both the question whether the debtor is discharged by the arrangement and the question whether co-debtors and sureties are discharged by the arrangement were to be answered by treating the arrangement as consensual; that is to say, by construing its terms as if they were the terms of a consensual agreement between the debtor and all those creditors who, under the statutory hypothesis, must be treated as being consenting parties.

In *Re NT Gallagher & Son Ltd*, Peter Gibson LJ, giving the judgment of the court, **9.25** referred to an approved CVA as being a 'statutory contract'.[23] Such a contract is to be contrasted with a composition or arrangement which is imposed by operation of law, for example a Companies Act scheme of arrangement. Crossman J said of such a scheme in *Re Garner's Motors Ltd*:[24]

---

[21] [1999] Ch 117 (CA) 129H. Note that Chadwick LJ is referring to an earlier form of the relevant provisions, whereby only a creditor who had had notice of a creditors' meeting was bound, but the principles here discussed are equally applicable to current provisions whereby an arrangement also binds those who would have been entitled to vote if they had received notice of the qualifying decision procedure.

[22] Ibid at 138B. Applied in *Raja v Rubin* [2000] Ch 274 (CA). It is important to note that this general rule can be ousted by the express terms of the co-debtor or surety's liability: *Lombard Natwest Factors Ltd v Koutrouzas* [2002] EWHC 1084 (QB), [2003] BPIR 444; *Prudential Assurance Co Ltd v Powerhouse Ltd* [2007] EWHC 1002 (Ch), [2007] Bus LR 1771 [41].

[23] [2002] EWCA Civ 404, [2002] 1 WLR 2380 [4]. (See also *Lloyds Bank Plc v Ellicott* [2002] EWCA Civ 1333, [2003] BPIR 632 [51]; *Narandas-Girdhar v Bradstock* [2016] EWCA Civ 88, [2016] 1 WLR 2366 [34]; and *Fehily v Atkinson* [2016] EWHC 3069 (Ch) [121].) However it does not necessarily follow that the contract is an agreement for the purposes of other legislation, which must be construed as such: *Re Britannia Heat Transfer Ltd* [2007] BCC 470 (Ch).

[24] [1937] Ch 594 (Ch) 599.

The scheme when sanctioned by the Court becomes something quite different from a mere agreement signed by the parties. It becomes a statutory scheme … It is settled law that a discharge of one of several judgment-debtors by operation of law does not release the other debtors.

Lord Hoffmann further explained the distinction in *Kempe v Ambassador Insurance Co* when referring to a scheme proposed by the liquidators under the equivalent Bermudian company law:[25]

It is true that the sanction of the court is necessary for the scheme to become binding and that it takes effect when the order expressing that sanction is delivered to the registrar. But this is not enough to enable one to say that the court (rather than the liquidators who proposed the scheme or the creditors who agreed to it) has by its order made the scheme … it is for the liquidators to propose the scheme, for the creditors by the necessary majority to agree to it and for the court to sanction it. It is the statute which gives binding force to the scheme when there has been a combination of these three acts …

4. Schemes of arrangement

9.26 Companies Act schemes of arrangement are not an insolvency proceeding: they do not necessarily involve actual or even anticipated insolvency and, even when taking the form of a creditor scheme, they may only affect some of a company's creditors. However, like CVAs, they can also be used by an insolvent company and its creditors to displace the insolvency rules.[26]

9.27 The history of schemes of arrangement under the Companies Acts is instructive. The origins of modern schemes lie in the Joint Stock Companies Arrangement Act 1870, which only applied to companies which were already in liquidation. The 1870 Act was passed for the purpose of preventing individual creditors obstructing schemes against the wishes of the majority.[27] Schemes remained creditor schemes until the Companies Act 1900 applied the 1870 Act to arrangements between a company and its members but it was not until the Companies Act 1907 was passed that the requirement for the company to be in liquidation was removed. Since that time, a procedure which was conceived and introduced as an adjunct to insolvency proceedings has operated as a free-standing procedure for arrangements and

---

[25] [1998] 1 WLR 271 (PC) 276C.

[26] Where a scheme is proposed as an alternative to liquidation, the court will consider the rights of creditors by reference to their rights in a liquidation but that does not mean that the scheme cannot disapply the distribution principles applicable in liquidation: *Re Hawk Insurance Co Ltd* [2001] EWCA Civ 241, [2001] 2 BCLC 480 [42]; *Re Telewest Communications Plc (No 2)* [2004] EWHC 1466 (Ch), [2005] 1 BCLC 772 [15], [36].

[27] *Re Dominion of Canada Freehold Estate and Timber Co Ltd* (1886) 55 LT 347 (Ch). (This overcame deficiencies in provisions to facilitate arrangements with creditors in the Companies Act 1862.)

reconstructions. The provisions now in force are those contained in Part 26 of the Companies Act 2006.

In summary, the scheme procedure is as follows.[28] The scheme must be for a compromise or arrangement between the company and its members or creditors or any class of either of them.[29] It can be proposed by the company (or its liquidator or administrator) or any member or creditor of the company. The party proposing the scheme applies to the court for an order convening meetings of the members, creditors, or class, as the case may be, who would be affected by the scheme. If the court orders that meetings be convened, the meetings notice must be accompanied by an explanatory statement. Meetings are then held at which members and creditors vote according to classes reflecting their different rights.[30] If the scheme is approved by a majority in number representing 75 per cent in value of the different classes of affected members and creditors, the court may sanction the scheme at a further hearing of the application (the outcome is not a foregone conclusion because this is a genuine exercise of judicial discretion). When the scheme becomes effective it binds all the members and creditors of each class that voted on it. The court has wide-ranging ancillary powers to make orders, for example for the transfer of property or liabilities, for the purpose of facilitating any reconstruction or amalgamation.

9.28

Alongside the statutory genesis recorded above, the commercial use of schemes of arrangement has undergone profound changes. When considering the needs for CVAs, the Cork Report noted that:[31]

9.29

> The modern practice is that schemes ... are frequently placed before the Court in the case of solvent companies, but only rarely in the case of insolvent companies.

The Report identified the lack of a moratorium, the formality and complexity of the procedure, issues over classes and ongoing management as all being factors contributing to this desuetude. These were all issues ostensibly addressed by the alternative of CVAs (coupled with administration in cases where a moratorium was needed). The unpopularity of creditor schemes persisted until relatively recently[32] when schemes began to be used as the means of restructuring the claims of finance creditors of both English and foreign companies. In such cases the absence of

---

[28] See further: *Practice Statement (Companies: Schemes of Arrangement)* [2002] 1 WLR 1345 and *Practice Direction 49A: Applications under the Companies Acts and Related Legislation* supplementing CPR Part 49.

[29] See further *Re Savoy Hotel Ltd* [1981] Ch 351 (Ch).

[30] Rights, not interests, are the governing factor: *Re Telewest Communications Plc (No 1)* [2004] EWHC 924 (Ch), [2005] 1 BCLC 752 (Ch) permission to appeal refused [2004] EWCA Civ 728, [2005] BCC 29; *Re Metinvest BV* [2016] EWHC 79 (Ch).

[31] Cork Report (n 2) at para 404.

[32] See, for example, the joint report of the Department of Trade and Industry and HM Treasury, *A Review of Company Rescue and Business Reconstruction Mechanisms* (May 2000) para 43, noting essentially the same reasons for disuse as had been identified in the Cork Report.

a moratorium is often of less practical importance because the company being restructured either has no trade creditors (as when it is a finance vehicle within a group structure and the underlying businesses are carried on by separate operating companies) or the finance parties accept that trade creditors need to be kept whole.

5. Schemes and CVAs contrasted

9.30 For companies with solvency issues, CVAs and Companies Act schemes of arrangement serve similar purposes. Section 1 of the Act provides that a CVA is either 'a composition in satisfaction of its debts' or 'a scheme of arrangement of its affairs'. Section 895 of the Companies Act 2006 provides that a Companies Act scheme is 'a compromise or arrangement' between a company and its creditors. Subject to two general exceptions, there is little that a company is likely to wish to effect by way of a consensual debt solution which would fall outside these parameters. In *Re Contal Radio Ltd*[33] it was held that a composition with creditors intended to make a company solvent was not an 'arrangement' as opposed to a compromise (and it would clearly also be a 'composition in satisfaction' for the purposes of section 1) but, subject to that 'arrangement', has a very wide meaning. In *March Estates Plc v Gunmark Ltd*, Lightman J held:[34]

> In [section 1] a scheme of arrangement (a scheme) is plainly something different from a composition and involves something less than the release or discharge of creditors' debts, eg a moratorium ... A scheme does not, or does not necessarily, involve any compromise or release.

9.31 The two general limitations are:

a) A Companies Act scheme cannot affect a beneficiary's rights in respect of property held on trust by the company. As Patten LJ held in *Re Lehman Brothers International (Europe)*:[35]

> It seems to me that an arrangement between a company and its creditors must mean an arrangement which deals with their rights inter se as debtor and creditor. That formulation does not prevent the inclusion in the scheme of the release of contractual rights or rights of action against related third parties necessary in order to give effect to the arrangement proposed for the disposition of the debts and liabilities of the company to its own creditors. But it does exclude from the jurisdiction rights of creditors over their own property which is held by the company for their benefit as opposed to their rights in the company's own property held by them merely as security.

---

[33] [1932] 2 Ch 66 (Ch). Maughan J was construing the meaning of 'arrangement' in the analogous context of section 251 Companies Act 1929.

[34] [1996] 2 BCLC 1 (Ch); approved in *Commissioners of Inland Revenue v Adam & Partners Ltd* [2001] 1 BCLC 222 (CA).

[35] [2009] EWCA Civ 1161, [2010] Bus LR 489 [65].

This conclusion is equally applicable to a CVA (except as regards the position of secured creditors whose rights cannot be affected by a CVA without their consent).

b) It has also been held that 'compromise or arrangement' for the purposes of Companies Act schemes requires some element of reciprocity. The authority for this proposition is the following statement of Brightman J in *Re NFU Development Trust Ltd*:[36]

> ... the Act is dealing with what is described as a 'compromise or arrangement between a company and its creditors or a company and its members.' The word 'compromise' implies some element of accommodation on each side. It is not apt to describe total surrender. A claimant who abandons his claim is not compromising it. Similarly, I think that the word 'arrangement' in this section implies some element of give and take. Confiscation is not my idea of an arrangement. A member whose rights are expropriated without any compensating advantage is not, in my view, having his rights rearranged in any legitimate sense of that expression.

So far as the meaning of 'arrangement' is concerned, this too appears equally applicable to CVAs but the practical effect is lessened for both purposes by the willingness of modern courts to have regard to full context in which a proposal is advanced.[37] As regards the meaning of 'compromise' as explained by Brightman J, it is arguable that 'composition in satisfaction' is wide enough to describe a release without a countervailing benefit (in the unlikely event that an approved CVA, viewed in its full context, was found to have offered no countervailing benefits).

CVAs and schemes also have in common a governing principle of good faith **9.32** in relation to securing their approval, and protections against the abuse of the procedures by majorities acting in pursuit of extraneous interests.

Despite their ostensibly overlapping scope, in modern practice schemes and **9.33** CVAs are used in different situations. Some features of the two procedures which may be taken into account when choices are being made between them are:

a) Jurisdiction and recognition in relation to foreign companies. Any company liable to be wound up under the Act is a company for the purposes of a Companies Act scheme. The courts have interpreted this to include foreign companies with a sufficient connection to England even though, under European law, there may be no jurisdiction to open winding-up proceedings.[38] This has proved to be attractive to foreign companies whose domestic laws have no equivalent procedure—particularly where the object

---

[36] [1972] 1 WLR 1548 (Ch) 1555C.

[37] As in *Re Bluebrook Ltd* [2009] EWHC 2114 (Ch), [2010] BCC 209 and *Re Uniq Plc* [2011] 1 BCLC 749 (Ch), [2012] 1 BCLC 783.

[38] *Re Rodenstock GmbH* [2011] EWHC 1104 (Ch), [2011] Bus LR 1245. As to the jurisdiction of the English courts to wind up foreign companies generally, see Chapter 22.

of the scheme use is to restructure liabilities governed by English law.[39] In *Re Apcoa Parking Holdings GmbH*, the governing law of the company's facilities was changed from German to English law by a majority vote in order to enable a debt restructuring to be effected using an English scheme.[40] The fact that such steps have been taken is not regarded as an objection to exercising jurisdiction if it is done in the interests of creditors. As Newey J said in *Re Codere Finance (UK) Ltd* of the (different) steps that had been taken in that case to bring a proposed restructuring within the scheme jurisdiction:[41]

> In a sense, of course ... what is sought to be achieved in the present case, is forum shopping. Debtors are seeking to give the English court jurisdiction so that they can take advantage of the scheme jurisdiction available here and which is not widely available, if available at all, elsewhere. Plainly forum shopping can be undesirable. That can potentially be so, for example, where a debtor seeks to move his COMI with a view to taking advantage of a more favourable bankruptcy regime and so escaping his debts. In cases such as the present, however, what is being attempted is to achieve a position where resort can be had to the law of a particular jurisdiction, not in order to evade debts but rather with a view to achieving the best possible outcome for creditors. If in those circumstances it is appropriate to speak of forum shopping at all, it must be on the basis that there can sometimes be good forum shopping.

Further on jurisdiction, it has also been held that (subject to satisfying a test of expediency) the domicile of one creditor in England is sufficient to satisfy any applicable requirements of the European Parliament and Council Regulation 1215/2012/EU (usually referred to as the 'Judgments Regulation') as to jurisdiction.[42] The use of Companies Act schemes by foreign companies is very controversial and some questions as to jurisdiction (and, consequentially, recognition of English schemes abroad) are far from settled.[43] By comparison, the position in respect of CVAs is more straightforward. A foreign company is only a 'company' for CVA purposes if it is incorporated in an EEA state, or, if incorporated elsewhere, it has its 'centre of main interests' in an EU member state other than Denmark. This jurisdiction is subject to the overriding effects of European law (which dictates where insolvency proceedings can be opened and which also deals with recognition) where a company has its centre of main interests within the EU (again other than Denmark).[44]

---

[39] English law does not recognize a discharge of indebtedness resulting from proceedings in a foreign country if the applicable law of the relevant contract is that of another country: *Antony Gibbs & Sons v La Société Industrielle et Commerciale des Métaux* (1890) 25 QBD 399 (CA).

[40] [2014] EWHC 997 (Ch) and [2014] EWHC 1867 (Ch), [2014] BCC 538 (convening) and [2014] EWHC 3849 (Ch), [2015] Bus LR 374 (sanction).

[41] [2015] EWHC 3778 (Ch) [18].

[42] *Re Van Gansewinkel Groep BV* [2015] EWHC 2151 (Ch), [2015] Bus LR 1046.

[43] See also *Codere* above; *Re CBR Fashion GmbH* [2016] EWHC 2808 (Ch).

[44] See further Chapter 22.

b) Formality, expense, and control. The basic choice to be made is between a process that need not involve any court applications but does require the appointment of an insolvency practitioner as office-holder and another that necessarily involves at least two hearings and the attendant expense.

c) Creditor voting. The requisite creditor majorities for approvals are similar in that both require a majority in value of 75 per cent but the voting rules for schemes also require a majority in number[45] and the rules for CVAs are more complicated because of the safeguards concerning connected creditor votes which can override the majority decision. The practical effect of these particular differences is lessened by the need to obtain the court's sanction of a scheme which enables the underlying issues to be ventilated (if necessary). More significantly, CVAs treat the creditors as a single class for voting purposes but schemes involve the division of creditors into classes—which can be a troublesome aspect of the procedure. An important limitation of schemes is that they cannot be used to 'cram down' an entire class, as opposed to a minority within a class.[46] On the other hand, CVAs cannot affect the rights of secured or preferential creditors without their consent but, subject to achieving the necessary majorities and court sanction, schemes can do so. (It may also be relevant, from a practical point of view, that creditors' decisions in respect of CVAs will usually be made in accordance with a qualifying decision procedure instead of a physical meeting.)

d) Leasehold property. Leases are a special category of liability because, typically, the landlord will not only be a creditor for arrears of rent which have already accrued due but will also have rights in respect of the unexpired term of the lease. This presents formidable complications for a scheme of arrangement because of the inability to cram down an entire class but may be more amenable to resolution through a CVA. In *Prudential Assurance Co Ltd v Powerhouse Ltd*, Etherton J said:[47]

> In my judgment, depending on the circumstances, a comparison with what the position would have been on a scheme of arrangement under section 425 of the 1985 Act may be of assistance on the issue of unfair prejudice in a CVA. I agree with [counsel], nevertheless, that caution must be exercised in carrying out that comparative exercise. The fact that a particular class of creditors could and might have blocked a scheme under section 425 of the 1985 Act, while

---

[45] Numerosity, as a safeguard, is a blunt instrument because of the risk of votes being split (but see *Re PCCW Ltd* [2009] 3 HKC 292 (Hong Kong Court of Appeal)). It previously applied to creditor voting in liquidations but was abandoned as a feature of formal insolvency proceedings when the Act took effect (vote splitting is expressly permitted by rule 15.31(9)(b)).

[46] Complicated techniques have been developed to address this difficulty, see, for example, *Re Bluebrook Ltd* [2009] EWHC 2114 (Ch), [2010] BCC 209.

[47] [2007] EWHC 1002 (Ch), [2007] Bus LR 1771 [95]. (Section 425 was the relevant scheme provision in the Companies Act 1985.)

relevant and potentially important, does not necessarily mean that they have been unfairly prejudiced within section 6 of the 1986 Act.

CVAs have been used successfully for the purpose of restructuring leasehold liabilities and associated guaranties. Landlords do not have a veto due to class voting but must rely instead on unfair prejudice. Not all prejudice is unfair. Unfair prejudice involves 'vertical' comparisons, comparing a creditor's rights with the rights that it would have in a hypothetical liquidation, and 'horizontal' comparisons, comparing the treatment of creditors with like claims and rights. Differential treatment of the leases of performing and non-performing business outlets may be justifiable.[48]

e) Rights against third parties. Reference has already been made to the distinction between the statutory contract which results from a CVA and the statutory binding which results from a Companies Act scheme, in that the former (subject to the express terms of the third party liabilities) has the effect of discharging sureties and co-debtors whereas this is not an automatic consequence of the latter. It is, however, possible to make provision for third party releases in a scheme provided such releases are essential for the operation of the scheme and ancillary to the arrangement between the company and its own creditors.[49]

f) Obtaining creditor consent. Insolvency practitioners and professional advisers promoting both schemes and CVAs are likely to engage in informal discussions with key stakeholders in order to anticipate and accommodate difficulties and, preferably, to obtain assurances that support will be forthcoming. A question then arises as to how far these overtures can properly go. It is now market practice to procure 'lock-up' agreements whereby creditors bind themselves to support schemes and such agreements may even include payment of a modest fee in return for support.[50] It is probably right to regard this as a developing aspect of the procedure where the touchstone is whether the agreement and fee would have had a material effect on voting.[51] For example, materiality may have to have regard to the price paid for acquired debt. David Richards J added the following cautionary words to his judgment when sanctioning a scheme in *Re Public Joint-Stock Company Commercial Bank Privatbank*:[52]

---

[48] The potential difficulties of such CVAs are well illustrated by *Mourant & Co Trustees Ltd v Sixty UK Ltd* [2010] EWHC 1890 (Ch), [2010] BCC 882.

[49] *Re T&N Ltd* [2006] EWHC 1447, [2007] Bus LR 1411; *Re La Seda de Barcelona SA* [2010] EWHC 1364 (Ch), [2011] 1 BCLC 555.

[50] *Re Telewest Communications Plc (No 1)* [2004] EWHC 924 (Ch), [2005] 1 BCLC 752 (Ch) permission to appeal refused [2004] EWCA Civ 728, [2005] BCC 29; *Re McCarthy & Stone Plc* [2009] EWHC 712 (Ch); *Re DX Holdings Ltd* [2010] EWHC 1513 (Ch); *Re Seat Pagine Gialle SpA* [2012] EWHC 3686 (Ch); *Primacom Holding GmbH v A Group of the Senior Lenders & Crédit Agricole* [2011] EWHC 3746 (Ch), [2013] BCC 201.

[51] As in *Re Garden Products Italy SpA* [2016] EWHC 1884 (Ch).

[52] [2015] EWHC 3299 (Ch) [26].

One test for considering the relevance of this type of agreement is whether the fee is sufficiently small as to be very unlikely to have a material effect on the decision of a creditor to support the scheme. While [counsel], appearing for the Bank, pointed to the fact that the fee was only 2% of the principal amount outstanding on the Notes held by a Noteholder entering into such agreement, he readily accepted that materiality might more appropriately be judged by reference to the price at which Notes had been acquired by a Noteholder. If, for example, Notes were acquired at a price of 25 cents per US $1 nominal of Notes, a fee of 2% of the nominal value might well be considered material. However, I need not explore this further in the circumstances of the present case, given the factors to which I have already referred.

Other issues have arisen in relation to predetermining the outcome of voting on voluntary arrangements—perhaps reflecting the rather different creditor constituencies likely to be encountered in the practical application of these alternative forms of proceeding.[53] The relevant authorities concern individual voluntary arrangements but may be taken to be equally applicable to CVAs. *Cadbury Schweppes Plc v Somji*[54] and *Kapoor v National Westminster Bank Plc*[55] both involved the acquisition of debts by friendly parties who then voted in favour of the arrangements to procure their approval. In *Somji* the assignments, which offered substantially better terms to certain opposing creditors, were secret and the court made a bankruptcy order on the basis that there had been a material omission in the information provided to creditors. In *Kapoor* the relevant assignment was known to the debtor's other creditors but the approval of the voluntary arrangement was set aside on the ground of material irregularity in that the assignor had been a connected person and the assignee's vote should therefore have been left out of account. The detail of these cases is less important than the emerging principles, which are that the long-standing authorities to the effect that there is a duty of good faith in negotiating arrangements with creditors apply to voluntary arrangements under the Act and that a breach of that obligation can amount to a material irregularity leading to an arrangement being set aside. As Etherton LJ said in *Kapoor*:[56]

> The good faith principle articulated in the authorities considered by the deputy judge in *Somji*, and acknowledged by the Court of Appeal in that case, is not restricted to the non-disclosure of secret deals benefiting one or some of the creditors. Although the facts in all those authorities did concern such a situation, the good faith principle, as articulated by the deputy judge and approved by the Court of Appeal, encapsulated 'the fundamental rule that there should be complete good faith between the debtor and his creditors, and between the creditors inter se'. In *Dauglish v Tennent*, for example, in which the court declared void a deed by which the defendant assigned all his estate to trustees on trust for distribution equally amongst all his creditors, Cockburn CJ said:

---

[53] But see *SISU Capital Fund Ltd v Tucker* [2006] EWHC 2170 (Ch), [2006] BCC 463 for an example of lock-up agreements being used in connection with CVAs.

[54] [2001] 1 WLR 615 (CA).

[55] [2011] EWCA Civ 1083, [2011] BPIR 1680.

[56] Ibid at [65]–[69] (internal citations omitted).

'In order that such a deed should be binding on the creditors, it is essential that there should be the most perfect good faith between the debtor and all his creditors.' ...

The arrangement given effect by the Assignment in the present case was patently intended, and intended only, for the purpose of subverting [the policy of the Act] ...

The expression 'material irregularity' is not defined. I agree with [counsel] that the well established good faith principle applicable to agreements between a debtor and creditors is capable of colouring, and should colour, the meaning of that expression.

The important question is whether, despite these significant differences in the way in which such questions may come before the court, there is or should be any material difference in the approach to be adopted by the court to arrangements which seek to elicit pre-voting consents. It is suggested that the cases exemplify opposite ends of a spectrum and that it is perfectly possible to draw a principled distinction between, on the one hand, open agreements, offered even-handedly, which serve a genuine commercial purpose in facilitating the expeditious approval of an arrangement and, on the other hand, agreements, whether open or secret, which have as their object the manipulation of the voting rights of creditors. It is difficult to imagine that if anything of the sort that occurred in *Somji* or *Kapoor* were to occur in the context of a Companies Act scheme, it would attract any more favourable treatment from the court. The more prevalent market practice of entering into lock-up agreements in the context of schemes may nonetheless be a factor in their favour where it is necessary to obtain more formal commitments in advance of voting.

g) Minority protection. The safeguards for minority interests are structurally quite different but the differences may again be more apparent than real. Quite apart from the likely commonality of approach in relation to the specific issues just discussed concerning obtaining pre-meeting creditor consent, it appears that the generality of issues likely to be considered material to fairness at a sanction hearing will be substantially the same as those which the court will consider on an application to set aside a CVA on the ground of unfairness. David Richards J commented on this in *Re T&N Ltd*:[57]

There is no statutory guidance on the criteria for judging fairness either for a scheme of arrangement under [the Companies Act] or for a CVA under s 6 of the 1986 Act. There is a difference in the onus. Under [the Companies Act], it is for the proponents to satisfy the court that it should be sanctioned, whereas under s 6 it is the objector who must establish unfair prejudice. I do not, however,

---

[57] [2004] EWHC 2361 (Ch), [2005] 2 BCLC 488 [81], [82] (internal citations omitted). (The passage quoted refers to a meeting of creditors to approve a CVA but, following amendment of the Act, any such approval is now likely to be obtained by means of a qualifying decision procedure.) See also *Carruth v Imperial Chemical Industries Ltd* [1937] AC 707 (HL) 769 (Lord Maughan) considering fairness in the context of votes being cast to further extraneous interests.

consider that there is any difference in the substance of the underlying test of fairness which must be applied. It is deliberately a broad test to be applied on a case by case basis, and courts have struggled to do better than the approach adopted by the Court of Appeal in *Re Alabama, New Orleans, Texas and Pacific Junction Railway Co* and summarised in the often-cited passage from a leading textbook, *Buckley on the Companies Acts*:

> 'In exercising its power of sanction the court will see, first, that the provisions of the statute have been complied with, second, that the class was fairly rep-resented by those who attended the meeting and that the statutory majority are acting bona fide and are not coercing the minority in order to promote interests adverse to those of the class whom they purport to represent, and thirdly, that the arrangement is such as an intelligent and honest man, a member of the class concerned and acting in respect of his interest, might reasonably approve. The court does not sit merely to see that the majority are acting bona fide and thereupon to register the decision of the meeting, but, at the same time, the court will be slow to differ from the meeting, unless either the class has not been properly consulted or the meeting has not considered the matter with a view to the interests of the class which it is empowered to bind or some blot is found in the scheme.'

That paragraph is directed to schemes of arrangement. The crucial difference with a CVA is that there is just one meeting of creditors, so that necessarily means that there may be sub-groups who would constitute separate classes for a scheme. In consider-ing unfair prejudice, the court will have regard to the different position of different groups of creditor. This, too, will be the case with a scheme of arrangement where groups of creditors with different interests or even rights none the less have been included in the same class for the purpose of considering and voting on the scheme.

While I am wary of laying down in advance of a hearing on the merits of any scheme or CVA any particular rule, there is one element which can be mentioned at this stage. I find it very difficult to envisage a case where the court would sanction a scheme of arrangement, or not interfere with a CVA, which was an alternative to a winding up but which was likely to result in creditors, or some of them, receiving less than they would in a winding up of the company, assuming that the return in a winding up would in reality be achieved and within an acceptable time-scale: see *Re English, Scottish and Australian Chartered Bank*.

h) Finality. There are highly material differences between schemes and CVAs in relation to the degree of finality achieved by the process. These differences may be determinative when choices are being made and are considered to be a substantial reason for the relatively low usage of CVAs since their introduc-tion. Absent considerations of fraud[58] or an appeal, the sanction order pro-vides complete finality for a Companies Act scheme. By contrast, the approval of a CVA leaves a twenty-eight-day window during which an aggrieved credi-tor or office-holder can apply for the CVA to be set aside on the grounds of unfair prejudice or material irregularity, following which the timing of a

---

[58] See further *Fletcher v Royal Automobile Club Ltd* [2000] 1 BCLC 331 (CA).

final decision will be determined by court procedure. Even more seriously, the twenty-eight-day period does not begin to run against a creditor who was not given notice of the creditors' decision procedure until the creditor becomes aware that the procedure has taken place. This is a severe practical impediment to the conclusion of new supply and financial arrangements which may be indispensable for continued trading.

Current market practice confines Companies Act schemes to larger cases involving the restructuring of liabilities to financial creditors. CVAs tend to be used only for smaller cases apart from those instances where they have been used to address leasehold obligations. The actual numbers of cases using either procedure are low by comparison with administrations and, particularly, liquidations. As will be apparent from the last section of this chapter, there is a perceived need for further measures to facilitate the rescue of viable businesses.

6. The future

9.34 In May 2016, the Insolvency Service launched a further consultation on options for reform entitled *A Review of the Corporate Insolvency Framework*. The consultation advanced proposals to introduce:

a) A new procedure to enable 'out of the money' creditors to be crammed down without their consent.

b) A new pre-insolvency moratorium lasting up to three months which would be available to companies of all sizes in order to enable a restructuring to take place.

c) Provisions enabling insolvent companies to designate some contracts as essential supplies (in addition to existing provisions relating to IT contracts and utilities) which could not be varied or terminated during a moratorium (or subsequent CVA or administration).

Rather more tentatively, the consultation also examined the question of rescue finance and invited views on how the provision of such finance could be encouraged.

9.35 The consultation document casts some light on the Insolvency Service's view of the principal limitation of CVAs and Companies Act schemes (in addition to the lack of a moratorium):[59]

> The cram-down of a rescue plan onto 'out of the money' creditors is currently possible in the UK only through a costly mix of using a scheme of arrangement and an administration. The Government believes that developing a more sophisticated restructuring process with the ability to 'cram-down' may facilitate more

---

[59] At para 9.9.

restructurings, and the subsequent survival of the corporate entity as a going concern.

It suggested that such a procedure could be developed as a variant of the CVA procedure or as a discrete restructuring procedure but the proposals drew significantly on existing scheme of arrangement features in adopting class voting, scheme majorities, and court involvement.

In September 2016, the Insolvency Service published its *Summary of Responses* to the consultation. The Service reported broad support for its proposals in respect of a cram down procedure, a new moratorium, and essential supplies but a need to consult further on detail.[60] It is clear that the revision or augmentation of the procedures discussed in this chapter is the Insolvency Service's immediate priority for legislative reform and that this is therefore a developing field. **9.36**

There is also a European dimension to the future of these proposals. Part of the background to the Insolvency Service consultation was the publication in 2014 of an EC Recommendation on a new approach to business failure and insolvency.[61] The Insolvency Service proposals were designed to ensure compliance at the same time as according with the government's domestic agenda to promote the United Kingdom as a business-friendly jurisdiction and to improve the United Kingdom's standing in World Bank rankings of insolvency laws. Since the publication of the *Summary of Responses* by the Insolvency Service, the European Commission has reinforced its earlier Recommendation by bringing forward a proposed directive on the same subject.[62] Inevitably, the proposal for a directive is much more detailed than the earlier Recommendation. The direct relevance of the proposed directive for the UK depends on the progress of the Brexit negotiations and it remains to be seen whether it will lead to any modification of the existing Insolvency Service proposals. **9.37**

---

[60] The Insolvency Service also reported that a majority of respondents had thought additional measures to facilitate rescue finance unnecessary.

[61] European Commission Recommendation of 12.3.2014.

[62] European Commission, *Proposal for a Directive of the European Parliament and of the Council on preventive restructuring frameworks, second chance and measures to increase the efficiency of restructuring, insolvency and discharge procedures and amending Directive 2012/30/EU*, COM(2016) 723 final <http://ec.europa.eu/information_society/newsroom/image/document/2016-48/proposal_40046.pdf> accessed 23 November 2016.

10

CREDITORS' RIGHTS AS A CLASS REMEDY

1. Introduction

10.01 The concept of insolvency proceedings as a class remedy is one consequence of the collective nature of insolvency proceedings under the Act. It explains the need for creditors' rights to be exercised in accordance with the purposes of the legislation. The concept is a judicial construct which, although a logical progression from the statutory rules, is not mentioned in the legislation itself. Harman J gave a useful summary of the concept in *Re a company (No 001573 of 1983)* where he said in the context of a winding-up petition:[1]

> On a petition in the Companies Court in contrast with an ordinary action there is not a true lis between the petitioner and the company which they can deal with as they will. The true position is that a creditor petitioning the Companies Court is invoking a class right ... and his petition must be governed by whether he is truly invoking that right on behalf of himself and all others of his class rateably, or whether he has some private purpose in view.

The concept therefore informs the court's exercise of its own powers in insolvency proceedings.

---

[1] [1983] BCLC 492 (Ch) 495b. See also *Re Southbourne Sheet Metal Co Ltd* [1992] BCLC 361 (Ch) 364f.

The characterization of proceedings under the Act as a class remedy is also consist- **10.02**
ent with prioritization of the collective interests of the company's creditors over the
interests of members and third parties during those proceedings, and with the various mechanisms by which the creditors can together influence or even control the
process through meetings and other decision-making powers.[2] In liquidation, the
importance of creditors' interests is implicit in the liquidator's duty being to realize
the company's assets and use the proceeds to discharge its liabilities. Although a
liquidator no longer requires sanction before exercising any of his general powers
under Schedule 4, creditors control the proceeding by choosing the liquidator and,
if necessary, removing him.[3] The Act also provides that the court may have regard
to the wishes of creditors in all matters relating to a liquidation.[4] In administration,
an administrator appointed by the company or its directors can also be replaced by
a resolution of the creditors. An administrator has an explicit duty to perform his
functions for the benefit of the company's creditors as a whole and is required to
put a statement of his proposals for achieving the purpose of the administration to
the company's creditors. The administrator must thereafter manage the company's
affairs in accordance with his proposals as modified and approved by the creditors.[5]
In a company voluntary arrangement (CVA), creditors' interests prevail because
the decision of the creditors on the proposal overrides any contrary decision of the
members.[6] The voting rules in respect of creditors' decisions in proceedings under
the Act are complicated by provisions to prevent abuse (and an enlarged majority
is required for approval of a CVA), but the basic rule is that creditors' decisions are
taken by a majority in value of the voting debts.[7] All this ensures that the creditors'
interests which are protected are their collective interests.

Whilst creditors' collective interests may be prioritized over those of individual **10.03**
creditors in proceedings under the Act, those interests are identified with those of
the insolvent estate so that the wishes of even a majority of the creditors will not
necessarily prevail in every situation. This resonates with the general principle of
company law (and, indeed of law and equity more generally) that, where rights
are conferred upon a class, there is an implicit restriction on the power of a majority to bind the minority. Of this Viscount Haldane said in *British America Nickel
Corporation Ltd v MJ O'Brien Ltd*:[8]

---

[2] See further section 246ZE.
[3] Appointment: sections 100 and 139. Removal: sections 171 and 172. (Subject to safeguards in
both cases.)
[4] Section 195, originally sections 91 and 149 Companies Act 1862. The court has a residuary
discretion as to whether to give effect to the wishes of the creditors: *Re Bank of Credit and Commerce
International SA (No 3)* [1993] BCLC 1490 (CA).
[5] Schedule B1 paras 3, 49, 68, and 97.
[6] Section 4A (again subject to safeguards).
[7] Rule 15.34.
[8] [1927] AC 369 (PC) 371. See also *Re Holders Investment Trust Ltd* [1971] 1 WLR 583 (Ch);
Assénagon Asset Management SA v Irish Bank Resolution Corpn Ltd [2012] EWHC 2090 (Ch), [2013]
Bus LR 266.

> [Such power] must be exercised subject to a general principle, which is applicable to all authorities conferred on majorities of classes enabling them to bind minorities; namely, that the power given must be exercised for the purpose of benefitting the class as a whole, and not merely individual members only.

The analogous approach in the context of creditors' rights in insolvency proceedings is to require a creditor to be acting for the purposes of the proceeding and for the court to intervene where necessary to regulate the wishes of a majority prevailing where that too would be contrary to the purposes of the proceeding.

10.04 The concept of a class remedy also resonates with the principle that those seeking to participate in insolvency proceedings must not only have the standing required for that purpose but also be seeking relief for proper reasons. *Deloitte & Touche AG v Johnson* was a case where the defendants in other proceedings brought by liquidators applied for the removal of the liquidators, as to which Lord Millett said:[9]

> The company is insolvent. The liquidation is continuing under the supervision of the court. The only persons who could have any legitimate interest of their own in having the liquidators removed from office as liquidators are the persons entitled to participate in the ultimate distribution of the company's assets, that is to say the creditors. The liquidators are willing and able to continue to act, and the creditors have taken no step to remove them. The plaintiff is not merely a stranger to the liquidation; its interests are adverse to the liquidation and the interests of the creditors. In their Lordships' opinion, it has no legitimate interest in the identity of the liquidators, and is not a proper person to invoke the statutory jurisdiction of the court to remove the incumbent liquidators.

2. The concept applied in practice

10.05 A number of more specific propositions derive from the concept of insolvency proceedings as a class remedy:

a) Even an undisputed creditor's application to commence insolvency proceedings must be made for a proper purpose. Conversely, an application which is made for a collateral purpose unrelated to the applicant's rights as a prospective participant in the proceedings will fail.

b) Although the court will ordinarily give effect to the wishes of the majority of unconnected creditors, the court will not do so if the result would subvert the purpose of the insolvency proceedings.

c) An application for relief made by a creditor in the course of insolvency proceedings must be made for the purposes of those proceedings.

d) The court may refuse to enforce creditors' rights in insolvency proceedings where enforcement would be contrary to the interests of creditors more generally.

---

[9] [1999] 1 WLR 1605 (PC) 1611H. See also *Walker Morris v Khalastchi* [2001] 1 BCLC 1 (Ch).

The unifying principle underlying all these propositions is that the rights and interests of individual creditors are subordinate to the interests of the estate. Although the operation of that principle can be illustrated by reference to a number of different specific situations, it should not be taken to be narrowly confined; on the contrary it is capable of general application.

a. Duplicative proceedings

The concept of insolvency proceedings as a class remedy impacts quite generally on the commencement of insolvency proceedings in court. This is particularly striking in the case of winding-up proceedings where a second petition should not be issued whilst a prior petition is pending.[10] There is ordinarily no need for a second petition because the first will already have established an earlier commencement date for the winding-up (assuming that an order is made) and the Rules both prevent the withdrawal of the prior petition without the leave of the court and enable the court to permit substitution of another petitioner.[11]

10.06

Substitution neatly illustrates the evolution of the concept of a class remedy being derived from the legislation. A winding-up petition was originally considered amenable to withdrawal in the same way as ordinary proceedings notwithstanding the objection of another creditor appearing on it. In *Re Home Assurance Association*, Wickens V-C held:[12]

10.07

> … I must assume that a Petitioner who has presented a Petition to wind up a company, is dominus litis

However from 1893 onwards,[13] the rules have made provision for substitution thereby providing that such proceedings result in the fair treatment of all creditors. As Needham J said in *DMK Building Materials Pty Ltd v Baker Timbers Pty Ltd*:[14]

> The purpose of substitution, in my opinion, is to ensure that once a prima facie right to the winding up of a company has arisen, the company should not escape from that position except upon the basis of fair dealing with all its creditors, not merely by paying off the particular plaintiff.

There is no provision for substitution as such on an administration application (where creditor applications are much less likely) but the application cannot be withdrawn without leave and any creditor is entitled to ask the court for permission to appear on its hearing as a person with an interest in its outcome.[15] This ensures that a similar result is possible. In both liquidation and administration, the rules

---

[10] Practice Direction: Insolvency Proceedings, 29 July 2014, para 11.
[11] Section 129(2) and rules 7.13 and 7.17.
[12] (1871) LR 12 Eq 59 (Court of Chancery) 60.
[13] General Rules Made Pursuant to Section 26 of the Companies (Winding-up) Act 1890 (29 March 1893).
[14] (1985) 3 ACLC 729 (Supreme Court of New South Wales) 732.
[15] Schedule B1 para 12(3) and rule 3.12.

are incompatible with treating the petition or application as a private matter to the exclusion of other creditors' interests.

10.08   Insolvency orders are orders made in the court's discretion. Just as with substitution so too in determining whether a winding-up order should be made, the approach of the courts has matured with the development of the concept of a class remedy. In earlier cases, a petitioning creditor with an undisputed claim was regarded as being entitled to an order as of right. Lord Cranworth said in *Bowes v The Hope Life Insurance and Guarantee Company*:[16]

> ... it is not a discretionary matter with the Court when a debt is established, and not satisfied, to say whether the company shall be wound up or not; that is to say, if there be a valid debt established, valid both at law and in equity. One does not like to say positively that no case could occur in which it would be right to refuse it; but, ordinarily speaking, it is the duty of the Court to direct the winding up.

As between the petitioner and the company, an order remains the legitimate expectation of a petitioning creditor,[17] but the position is different when the making of an order is opposed by other creditors (even though the legislation gives the majority no right to bind a minority as to the commencement of insolvency proceedings). In such circumstances the nature of the proceedings as a class remedy may dictate a different outcome. In *Re Chapel House Colliery Company*, the court refused to make a winding-up order where the petitioner would not benefit because of the absence of any assets for a liquidator to realize and the petition was opposed by an overwhelming majority of other creditors who might benefit from continued trading. Bowen LJ said:[18]

> The power of winding-up was given for the benefit of a particular class, and is entrusted to the Court for their benefit.

In *Re ABC Coupler and Engineering Co Ltd*, Pennycuick J said when dismissing the petition of an unpaid judgment creditor which was opposed by other creditors:[19]

> ... it seems to me that where the wishes of the majority of the creditors are on the face of them reasonable the court ought to follow those wishes in the absence of any special circumstances.

10.09   A similar issue arises when a petition is presented against a company which is already in voluntary liquidation. In *Re JD Swain Ltd*, Diplock LJ drew a distinction between opposition to any form of winding-up and disagreements as to the

---

[16]   (1865) 11 HL Cas 389 (HL) 402.

[17]   *Re Lummus Agricultural Services Ltd* [2001] BCC 953 (Ch).

[18]   (1883) 24 Ch D 259 (CA) 270.

[19]   [1960] 1 WLR 243 (Ch) 246. See also *Re P & J Macrae Ltd* [1961] 1 WLR 229 (CA); *Re Bank of Credit and Commerce International SA (No 3)* [1993] BCLC 1490 (CA) and *Re Demaglass Holdings Ltd* [2001] 2 BCLC 633 (Ch)—the court will make a qualitative assessment of the majority's opposition.

form of the liquidation—where the views of a majority of the outside creditors will ordinarily prevail. As to this he said:[20]

> The difference or the distinction seems to me to be an obvious one, namely, in the former case, what is being resisted is any winding up at all, so that the petitioning creditor, if he fails, will be denied the class remedy which he would otherwise have if the winding up took place; whereas, in the latter case, he will obtain the class remedy anyway under the voluntary winding up, and the matter then turns upon his being able to show some reason why the remedy under the voluntary winding up is not an adequate remedy for him.

although, ultimately, the issue will be decided in accordance with the dictates of fairness and commercial morality.[21]

b. Collateral purpose

Another relevant line of authority concerns those circumstances in which insolvency orders will be refused on the ground that the applicant has a collateral purpose.[22] Abuse of process arises in a variety of contexts. Thus, for example, winding-up petitions are routinely dismissed when the petition debt is a disputed debt; in those cases the petitioner fails to establish that they are a creditor. Where the debt is not disputed (so the petitioner undoubtedly has standing to petition), the issue concerns purpose. There are two broad categories of case: in the first, the applicant does not want the insolvency order to be made but sees the application as the means of achieving some other end and, in the second, the applicant does desire the making of the order but because of benefits which are anticipated outside the proceeding. An example of the former is a petition presented for the purpose of coercing the resolution of other demands and an example of the latter is a proceeding to trigger contractual termination rights which become exercisable in the event of an order being made. **10.10**

Purpose, in this context, must be distinguished from motive. Motives lead to purpose but are themselves irrelevant.[23] The starting point is that the court will not readily interfere with proceedings which are otherwise regular even if the motivation of the applicant is unattractive. Ungoed-Thomas J said in *Mann v Goldstein*:[24] **10.11**

---

[20] [1965] 1 WLR 909 (CA) 915C. The judgment of Snowden J in *Maud v Aabar Block Sarl* [2016] EWHC 2175 (Ch) contains a review of further authorities at [77]–[82].

[21] *Re Gordon & Breach Science Publishers Ltd* [1995] BCC 261 (Ch); *Re Zirceram Ltd* [2000] BCC 1048 (Ch).

[22] There are some fine distinctions to be drawn here. In the more extreme cases, not only will the application fail because of the collateral purpose but the making of the application will itself constitute a tort: *Partizan Ltd v OJ Kilkenny & Co Ltd* [1998] BCC 912 (Ch) (see also *Land Securities Plc v Fladgate Fielder* [2010] Ch 467 (CA)).

[23] *Ebbvale Ltd v Hosking* [2013] UKPC 1, [2013] 2 BCLC 204 (PC) [28]. See also: *Maud v Aabar Block Sarl* [2016] EWHC 2175 (Ch) [93].

[24] [1968] 1 WLR 1091 (Ch) 1095G.

> It seems to me that to pursue a substantial claim in accordance with the procedure provided and in the normal manner, even though with personal hostility or even venom, and from some ulterior motive, such as the hope of compromise or some indirect advantage, is not an abuse of the process of the court or acting mala fide but acting bona fide in accordance with the process.

but it is otherwise if the applicant has some purpose other than the inception and subsequent conduct of the insolvency proceeding.

10.12 As Harman J said in *Re a company (No 001573 of 1983)*:[25]

> In my judgment the true question is 'for what purpose does the petitioner wish to wind up this company'. A judge has to decide whether the petition is for the benefit of the class of which the petitioner forms a part or is for some purpose of his own, If the latter, then it is not properly brought.

The case is a good example of an impermissible collateral purpose. The petitioner had unsuccessfully negotiated with the company to acquire a lease which was the company's major asset. When those negotiations broke down, the petitioner negotiated directly with the landlord and entered into an agreement to take a new lease in the event of the company's lease being terminated. The winding-up proceedings were brought with a view to triggering the rights of the company's landlord to terminate the company's lease, thereby enabling the petitioner to enter into the anticipated new lease with the landlord.

10.13 *Re Leigh Estates (UK) Ltd*[26] was another case of a petitioner seeking a winding-up order to the potential detriment of the general body of creditors. In that case the petitioner was a local authority seeking to recover rates and it was found that the authority was not seeking to swell the estate of the company but rather to gain a preference for itself over the company's secured and unsecured creditors. The petition was again dismissed.

10.14 Some decisions which might otherwise be thought to be inconsistent with this approach can be reconciled by applying a test as to whether the collateral purpose will have a negative impact on the estate. Thus, in *Re Eloc Electro-Optieck and Communicatie BV*[27] a winding-up order was made against a company incorporated in the Netherlands for the purpose of enabling its employees to make a claim on the redundancy fund administered under the Employment Protection (Consolidation) Act 1978. The case concerned the jurisdiction to wind up foreign companies and the question of the benefit to the petitioners where there were no assets in England. It was held that the prospective benefits need not be channelled through the liquidator and there appears to have been no objection to what might otherwise be thought to have been a collateral purpose.

---

[25] [1983] BCLC 492 (Ch) 495h.
[26] [1994] BCC 292 (Ch).
[27] [1982] 1 Ch 43 (Ch).

Re a company (No 001573 of 1983),[28] where the collateral purpose was to acquire **10.15**
a lease at the expense of the respondent company, can be contrasted with *Maud v*
Aabar Block Sarl[29] where it was held that a bankruptcy petition brought to trigger pre-emption rights relating to property owned by the debtor would not be an
abuse of process because there was no reason to suppose that the property would
be acquired for less than a proper price. The pre-emption rights therefore did not
threaten the interests of the general body of creditors.

The test of abuse of process is a low one because the mere presence of a collateral **10.16**
purpose does not make a petition an abuse. The presence of a proper purpose will
be sufficient to save the proceedings even if it is a secondary purpose. The test is
whether it is any part of the petitioner's purpose to obtain its ordinary rights as
a creditor in the liquidation.[30] However an ulterior objective, which falls short
of being an abuse of process, will nonetheless be relevant to the discretion of the
court as to whether to make an order on the basis of such a petition.[31] This is again
because of the concept of the proceeding as a class remedy and, as in cases where no
issue of collateral purpose arises, the consequential need to consider the interests
of the class.

c. Influencing other proceedings

A number of cases concern winding-up petitions brought in the context of **10.17**
other proceedings between the parties where the collateral purpose is to influence the conduct of those other proceedings. Here the approach taken by the
courts is that it is legitimate to seek the appointment of a liquidator who can
be expected to take a more objective view of the merits of those proceedings
(something which is in the interests of the creditors generally) but that it is
not legitimate to bring winding-up proceedings for the purpose of stifling
proceedings or the defence of proceedings. *Re Wallace Smith & Co Ltd*[32] and *Re*
Wallace Smith Group Ltd[33] illustrate the latter point. As the names of the cases
suggest, the respondent companies were part of the same group. The petitioner
was another company in the same group which was already in liquidation and
which had already brought proceedings against the respondent companies in
Canada. Both winding-up petitions were dismissed for a number of different
reasons amongst which was the desire of the petitioner's liquidators to procure
the appointment of themselves (or persons connected with them) as liquidators

---

[28] [1983] BCLC 492 (Ch).
[29] [2015] EWHC 1626 (Ch), [2015] BPIR 845 (but for further developments in the same case,
see *Maud v Aabar Block Sarl* [2016] EWHC 2175 (Ch)).
[30] *Re Millennium Advanced Technology Ltd* [2004] EWHC 711 (Ch), [2004] 1 WLR 2177;
Ebbvale Ltd v Hosking [2013] UKPC 1, [2013] 2 BCLC 204.
[31] *Maud v Aabar Block Sarl* [2016] EWHC 2175 (Ch) [98].
[32] [1992] BCLC 970 (Ch).
[33] [1992] BCLC 989 (Ch).

of the respondent companies and thereby control the defence of the Canadian proceedings.

10.18   *Carman v The Cronos Group SA*[34] affords a more recent example of the same approach in a different context. In that case, the respondents in fraudulent trading proceedings brought by a liquidator took assignments of the debts owed by the companies in liquidation as a result of which one of the respondents became the only creditor of the companies in liquidation and took various steps with a view to stifling the fraudulent trading proceedings. One such step was to requisition a creditors' meeting with a view to passing a resolution for the removal of the liquidator. Despite holding that the assignments had been valid, the court directed the liquidator not to hold the meeting. It was held that the fraudulent trading proceedings should be allowed to continue with a view to the liquidator generating a sufficient fund to cover the costs of the liquidation—an instance of the interests of the estate transcending the interests of creditors.

10.19   On the other hand, the court has made winding-up orders where the collateral purpose was to promote an objective view of the merits. In *Re Lummus Agricultural Services Ltd* the court made a winding-up order on the petition of a creditor which was involved in litigation with the respondent company. It was suggested that the petition should be dismissed because it was an attempt to stifle the respondent's participation in the litigation. Park J rejected this submission saying: [35]

> [Counsel] says that [the petitioner's] purpose is, or might be, to stifle [the respondent's] appeal to the Zambian Supreme Court. Again, I do not accept that that is correct. I do accept that, if the petition succeeds and a liquidator is appointed, he will probably wish to review the Zambian proceedings and reach his own decision on whether [the respondent] should persevere with them. But in my judgment there is nothing wrong with that. On the contrary, it may be a very good thing in the interests of creditors of [the respondent] that someone should take a dispassionate look at the Zambian appeal before [the respondent] finally goes ahead with it.

Although the *Wallace Smith* cases are not mentioned in the judgment, it would appear that the distinguishing feature of the *Lummus* case was the absence of any intention to control the respondent's case in the pending litigation. In *Ebbvale Ltd v Hosking*[36] the Privy Council upheld a winding-up order made on a petition presented by the claimant in pending proceedings against the respondent company for the purpose of having the respondent's defence directed by a liquidator. Although this was an advantage to the petitioner creditor as claimant, it was also in his interests as a creditor of the respondent company. As with *Lummus* there was no suggestion that the petitioner would interfere in the liquidator's conduct of the defence.

---

[34]   [2006] EWHC 1390 (Ch).
[35]   [1999] BCC 953 (Ch) 957.
[36]   [2013] UKPC 1, [2013] 2 BCLC 204.

The litigation need not have been brought by the petitioner against the respondent. **10.20** In *Bell Group Finance (Pty) Ltd v Bell Group (UK) Holdings Ltd*, the petitioning creditor (which was itself in liquidation in Australia) was contemplating proceedings against third parties. The winding-up petition was presented in the hope that a liquidator would conclude that it was in the interests of the respondent's creditors to co-operate in the provision of information which might enable claims to be brought against the third parties. Chadwick J held: [37]

> ... I am satisfied that it is just and equitable to make a winding-up order in this case so that a liquidator of BG (UK) can consider whether there is any advantage to the creditors in his or her liquidation in co-operation with the Australian liquidators. As I have already indicated, in reaching a decision on that point the liquidator will have regard only to the interests of the creditors in the liquidation of BG (UK) and will be at liberty to seek directions from the court in case of difficulty.

d. Promoting restructuring

Some of these cases may appear to draw a distinction between constructive and **10.21** negative collateral purpose. This is, in substance, correct but not because of a view that one collateral purpose is intrinsically more meritorious than another. The true distinction is that what might otherwise be characterized as a proper or constructive collateral purpose is in fact as much for the benefit of the insolvent estate as for the applicant. A more recent case shows that what may be in the interests of the estate can go beyond the completion of the formal insolvency proceedings. In *Astra Resources Plc v Credit Veritas USA LLC* a debtor company applied for an injunction to restrain presentation of a winding-up petition. David Richards J held: [38]

> ... it is submitted that the true purpose of CV in presenting a winding-up petition would not be to obtain payment of the amount due to it, to the extent that the assets of the company permitted it, but would be to obtain control of the company through the 'submission of a reorganisation plan in the London Courts' ... it is possible to replicate in English proceedings the effect of a plan or reorganisation through the means of either a scheme or arrangement or a company voluntary arrangement. The critical point, though, is that any such reorganisation could be achieved only through the proper processes of the liquidation. It would require in practice the support of the liquidator and, on any footing, the support of a majority of the creditors and, if a scheme of arrangement were used, the approval of the court on the basis of the fairness of the proposals. In short, a scheme of arrangement or company voluntary arrangement would take effect only if it were beneficial to the unsecured creditors as a whole, of whom CV is one.

The court rejected comparison with the abuse of process cases and refused to restrain the presentation of a petition.

---

[37] [1996] BCC 505 (Ch) 514.
[38] [2015] EWHC 1830 (Ch) [38].

e. Inspection of books and records

10.22 Creditors (and contributories) have no automatic right to inspect the books and records of a company in liquidation but may be allowed to do so by order of the court.[39] It has long been established that the court's powers in this respect are exercisable for the purposes of the liquidation and not for the private advantage of the applicant. In *Re North Brazilian Sugar Factories*, Cotton LJ held:[40]

> ... the powers given by [the corresponding provision of the Companies Act 1862] are prima facie to be exercised for the purposes of the winding-up, and for the benefit of those who are interested in the winding-up. I do not say that in no case can inspection be ordered where it is not for the general benefit of the contributories, but prima facie it is only to be ordered with a view to their general benefit.

The court rejected an application made for the purpose of gathering evidence in support of actions by individual shareholders for their own benefit and not for the more beneficial winding-up of the company. However, an order may be justified as being for the purposes of the liquidation even if the prospective benefits are indirect, as in the case where a successful action against third parties will lead to reduction in claims against the company.[41] (The same approach of restricting the use of statutory powers to situations where the power was being invoked for the purposes of the liquidation was illustrated by cases dealing with examination powers under the legislation which preceded the 1986 Act. However changes introduced in the Act mean that the same point will not arise in that context in the future.[42])

f. Requisitioning meetings

10.23 Under various provisions of the Act creditors have the power to requisition meetings but the courts have asserted a general jurisdiction to direct office-holders to disregard such requisitions where compliance would not be in the interests of the creditors as a whole. A number of the cases involved attempts to remove office-holders where the applicant was pursuing a private objective. Thus, in *Re Mansel, ex parte Sayer*[43] the court held that it had power to restrain a trustee in bankruptcy from holding a creditors' meeting to consider his removal until after the question of expunging a disputed proof of debt had been resolved in circumstances where it was clear to the court that the purpose of removal was to impede investigation of the debt. In *Re Burn, ex parte Dawson*,[44] another bankruptcy case, the court held more generally that it could restrain the holding of a meeting where it would serve

---

[39] Section 155 (for compulsory liquidation, but capable of being indirectly applied in voluntary liquidation by section 112).
[40] (1837) 37 Ch D 83 (CA) 87.
[41] *Sunwing Vacation Inc v E-Clear (UK) Plc* [2011] EWHC 1544 (Ch), [2011] BCC 889.
[42] *Re Imperial Continental Water Corporation* (1886) 33 Ch D 314 (CA); *Re Embassy Art Products Ltd* [1988] BCLC 1 (Ch); *Re James McHale Automobiles Ltd* [1997] BCC 202 (Ch).
[43] (1887) 19 QBD 679 (CA).
[44] [1932] 1 Ch 247 (Ch).

no useful purpose because the court exercised overall control for the benefit of all persons interested in the estate.[45] These cases are equally applicable to corporate insolvency proceedings because existence of the jurisdiction does not turn on any peculiarity of bankruptcy proceedings.[46] The leading case is now *Re Barings Plc (No 6)* where Sir Andrew Morritt V-C directed the liquidators of Barings, pending further order, not to convene a meeting requisitioned for the purposes of their own removal. He held that: [47]

> ... I must consider whether if the meeting requisitioned by the 1986 trustee is held it will be conducive to both the proper operation of the process of liquidation and to justice as between all those interested in the liquidation.

On the facts, he concluded that the 1986 trustee was acting only in the interests of itself as representing a class of noteholders and not in the interests of the creditors as a whole whose interests would, on the contrary, be damaged by interference with the conduct of pending litigation if the liquidators were to be replaced.[48]

g. Pursuing realizations

In *Re Longmeade Ltd*[49] liquidators applied for directions as to whether they should **10.24** convene a creditors' meeting and as to whether they should bring proceedings against a third party. The claim was substantial and the liquidators were advised that it had good prospects of success but the circumstances were unusual. Although arrangements had already been made for the litigation to be pursued with the support of a funder which eliminated the risk of an adverse result for the estate, the prospective litigation was opposed by over 99 per cent in value of Longmeade's creditors for reasons which had nothing to do with their status as creditors of the company. Snowden J held that the liquidators were not obliged to convene a creditors' meeting and, in any event, would not be bound by the outcome. Only if all the company's creditors opposed proceedings being taken would the wishes of the creditors be decisive. So long as any of the company's creditors were in favour of the proceedings being brought, or were even neutral on the question, it was for the liquidators to decide what was in the interests of the estate.

h. Unfair harm

The concept also informs the court's exercise of its jurisdiction to give relief to **10.25** creditors who are unfairly harmed by an administrator's actions.[50] In *Re Zegna III*

---

[45] See also *Re Young* [2014] EWHC 4315 (Ch).
[46] *Donaldson v O'Sullivan* [2008] EWCA Civ 879, [2009] 1 WLR 924; *Re Overfinch Ltd* [2015] EWHC 2691 (Admin).
[47] [2001] 2 BCLC 159 (Ch) [47].
[48] See also *Carman v The Cronos Group SA* [2006] EWHC 1390 (Ch).
[49] [2016] EWHC 356 (Ch), [2016] Bus LR 506.
[50] Schedule B1 para 74.

Holdings Inc, the relevant complaint was that an agreement for the provision of services by a project manager had been terminated following the appointment of administrators to the counterparty company. In the course of rejecting the project manager's application, Norris J said:[51]

> … administration is a form of class remedy. The obligation of the administrators is to perform their functions in the interests of 'the creditors as a whole'.

and

> BLV's true complaint is not that its interests *as a creditor* have been harmed but that its interests *as a contractor* after the date of the administration have been treated less favourably than other contractors, because the other contractors have been kept on whereas BLV has not. I agree with Leading Counsel for the administrators that it is well established in other company and insolvency contexts that where an application may be made as 'a creditor' then it must be made by that creditor in his capacity as such (and not in any other capacity).

3. Conclusions

10.26 Ultimately, upholding the concept of insolvency proceedings under the Act as a form of class remedy is about maintaining the integrity of the proceedings. Such proceedings exist for the benefit of the creditors collectively. It follows that no individual creditor (or group of creditors) should be able to institute insolvency proceedings or thereafter influence their conduct for private advantage—at least not where to do so would be to the detriment of the estate. The decided cases show this approach being followed in a variety of different situations but they do not define its limits; it remains open to the courts to apply the same approach in other contexts as new issues present themselves. There is, however, an overriding limitation in that the concept of a class remedy is essentially a constraint on the exercise of rights to prevent their misuse. Its deployment restrains acts which offend against it but it does not compel positive action on the part of individual creditors to protect the interests of the creditors as a whole. The latter is the province of sanctions provided by the law, for example the various rules which incentivize directors to institute insolvency proceedings in a timely manner when they become unavoidable and otherwise to act in a manner which protects creditors' interests.

---

[51] [2009] EWHC 2994 (Ch), [2010] BPIR 277 [20], [24].

11

OFFICE-HOLDERS

1. Introduction

At one level the title 'office-holder' is merely a convenient way generically to refer **11.01** to the person (liquidator, administrator, or supervisor) who has the conduct of the insolvency proceeding in question.[1] However, there is a burgeoning concept of the office-holder being a person to whom a number of privileges and responsibilities attach regardless of the form of the proceedings in which the appointment has been made.

Liquidators and administrators have much in common as office-holders. Although **11.02** the fundamentals also apply to supervisors of voluntary arrangements, there are material differences. Even as regards the fundamentals, the position of a supervisor could differ in some respects because of the express terms of the company voluntary arrangement (CVA) although this is unlikely to be encountered in practice.

---

[1] This is the meaning ascribed to the term in rule 1.2 but it does not have a universal meaning in the Act—see sections 233, 234, 238, 246, 246ZD, and 246B. (A nominee in respect of a CVA is also an office-holder within the meaning of rule 1.2 but the role of a nominee is different and references to office-holders in this chapter are not references to nominees.)

Elsewhere, the variances can be ascribed to the fact that a voluntary arrangement is a way of contracting out of the other insolvency procedures, which the creditors have chosen instead, making it inappropriate to invest the supervisor with the full range of powers and privileges enjoyed by other office-holders.[2] However, this is not a complete explanation because it does not explain why, for example, a supervisor is an office-holder for the purposes of compelling the continued provision of essential supplies but does not have the statutory right to co-operation from the company's directors. The differentiation between different office-holders for different purposes gives rise to some anomalies.

11.03 In summary, the core distinguishing characteristics of office-holders in insolvency proceedings (which are, in some cases, subject to the unlikely possibility of contrary provision in a voluntary arrangement) are:

a) the appointment is a personal appointment;
b) the office-holder is a fiduciary;
c) the office-holder acts as the agent of the company;
d) the office-holder does not generally owe duties to individual creditors;
e) the office-holder can compel the continued provision of essential supplies; and
f) the office-holder can be removed and replaced by the court.

11.04 In addition liquidators and administrators, both of whom are charged with responsibility for the execution of a statutory scheme, have the following additional characteristics in common:

a) persons dealing with the office-holder are protected from defects in his appointment;
b) directors and others have a legal duty to co-operate with the office-holder;
c) the office-holder has powers to compel the disclosure of information relating to the affairs, business, and property of the company;
d) a lien cannot be used to deny the office-holder access to the books, documents, and records belonging to the company;
e) the office-holder may enjoy immunity from suit by third parties;
f) the office-holder has transaction avoidance powers; and
g) following the conclusion of the proceedings the office-holder will be discharged from liability for his acts whilst in office.

11.05 An administrative receiver is also an office-holder in the generic sense and it should be noted that under the Act the position of an administrative receiver is, in some respects, directly comparable with that of an office-holder in liquidation and administration. This is because the Act (as originally enacted) was drafted on the

---

[2] If the ability of the office-holder to utilize such powers and privileges is a material consideration, then that is a reason for the creditors to prefer liquidation or administration.

basis that administrative receivership, although a security enforcement mechanism, was a constructive procedure for the rescue of businesses and that it is was therefore appropriate for administrative receivers to share some of the powers and privileges of office-holders appointed in collective insolvency proceedings. These parallels do not inform the concept of the office-holder in true insolvency proceedings any more than they make administrative receivership into such a proceeding. In the remainder of this chapter, references to 'office-holders' are references only to liquidators, administrators, and supervisors.

2. Factors common to all office-holders

a. The personal nature of an office-holder's appointment

Only an individual can be an insolvency practitioner and qualified to act as an office-holder.[3] There is, therefore, a tension between the way the legislation is framed and the commercial reality of the market for insolvency services where office-holders are frequently chosen on the basis of the firms to which they belong and then rely on their firm's resources in order to perform their functions. The firms in turn regard the office-holder's work in progress as belonging to the firm and this is likely to be reflected in the partnership agreements or other constitutional documents of the firms.[4] In *Re Sankey Furniture Ltd, ex parte Harding*, Chadwick J described the position of the office-holder in the following terms:[5]

11.06

> ... the practice in relation to the administration of insolvency, at least in the case of large firms with many skilled and experienced employees, may not fit easily into the current legislative framework. The 1986 Act provides that a person who is not an individual cannot be qualified to act as an insolvency practitioner (see s 390(1)). A person who acts as an insolvency practitioner at a time when he is not qualified to do so commits an offence (see s 389(1)). The effect is that, in law, appointment as a liquidator or trustee in bankruptcy is an appointment which is personal to the individual who accepts it. It is not an appointment to the firm of which he or she happens, for the time being, to be a member. But in large firms containing a number of partners and employees who are qualified as insolvency practitioners it is not unlikely that the work comes to the firm rather than to the individual. It is the collective expertise of the firm which attracts the appointment ... the day-to-day administration is carried out by employees of the firm.

---

[3] Section 230 (liquidation), Schedule B1 para 6 (administration), sections 1(2), 2(4), 4(2), and 7(5) (CVAs) and see generally Chapter 13 as to insolvency practitioners.

[4] In *Casson Beckman & Partners v Papi* [1991] BCLC 299 (CA) the court held that the office-holder had an equitable obligation to account to the firm for which he had worked. See also *Wood v Priestley* [2016] EWHC 2986 (Ch).

[5] [1995] 2 BCLC 594 (Ch) 600f–601a. See also *Re A&C Supplies Ltd* [1998] 1 BCLC 603 (Ch) 606f; *HM Customs and Excise v Allen* [2003] BPIR 830 (Ch) [4]. In *A&J Fabrications Ltd v Grant Thornton* [1998] 2 BCLC 227 (Ch), the court refused to strike out a claim in contract against a liquidator's firm arising out of the conduct of the liquidation.

In these circumstances it may well be that the firm, and perhaps also the creditors, regard the identity of the individual in whose name the appointment is held as relatively unimportant. The appointment 'belongs' to the firm, and if the individual leaves the firm he should not take the appointment with him.

The view which I have described in the preceding paragraph may or may not be widely held ... It is likely to accord with commercial reality. But it does not accord with the relevant provisions in the 1986 Act.

The personal nature of an office-holder's appointment can give rise to succession issues—a question which is considered later in this chapter.

11.07   Even though the appointment is personal to the office-holder, his firm is not treated as an independent contractor and the cost of the firm's services forms part of the office-holder's own remuneration claim.[6] This reflects the fact that, in contrast to the office-holder's professional advisers, his staff are performing his own functions in his name and on his behalf. Indeed, if called upon to assess the office-holder's remuneration, the court will have regard to whether those tasks have been undertaken at an appropriate level of seniority.[7]

b. The office-holder as fiduciary and agent

11.08   In *Bristol & West Building Society v Mothew*, Millett LJ described the position of a fiduciary in the following terms:[8]

A fiduciary is someone who has undertaken to act for or on behalf of another in a particular matter in circumstances which give rise to a relationship of trust and confidence. The distinguishing obligation of a fiduciary is the obligation of loyalty. The principal is entitled to the single-minded loyalty of his fiduciary. This core liability has several facets. A fiduciary must act in good faith; he must not make a profit out of his trust; he must not place himself in a position where his duty and his interest may conflict; he may not act for his own benefit or the benefit of a third person without the informed consent of his principal. This is not intended to be an exhaustive list, but it is sufficient to indicate the nature of fiduciary obligations. They are the defining characteristics of the fiduciary.

It is clear that an office-holder satisfies this definition because he administers the insolvent estate for the benefit of others and not for himself. The recognition of the office-holder as a fiduciary underpins the approach of the courts to remuneration questions.[9]

---

[6] Rule 18.16; Practice Direction: Insolvency Proceedings, Part Six: Applications relating to the remuneration of appointees [2014] BCC 502 (see also *Brook v Reed (Practice Note)* [2011] EWCA Civ 331, [2012] 1 WLR 419); SIP 9: Payments to Insolvency Office Holders and their Associates <https://www.r3.org.uk/what-we-do/publications/professional/statements-of-insolvency-practice> accessed 16 January 2017.

[7] *Re Cabletel Installations Ltd* [2005] BPIR 28 (Ch) [20], [24], and [36]. See also *Institute of Chartered Accountants in England Wales v Webb* [2009] EWHC 3461 (Ch), [2010] Bus LR Digest D37 [11].

[8] [1998] Ch 1 (CA) 18A.

[9] *Mirror Group Newspapers Plc v Maxwell (No 2)* [1998] 1 BCLC 638 (Ch) 648d; *Brook v Reed (Practice Note)* [2011] EWCA Civ 331, [2012] 1 WLR 419 [52].

A further ground for concluding that an office-holder is a fiduciary is that he acts **11.09** as the agent of the company. The basis of the agency depends on the procedure in question:

a) In liquidation, the agency is established at common law. In *Knowles v Scott*, Romer J said:

> In my view a voluntary liquidator is more rightly described as the agent of the company—an agent who has, no doubt, cast upon him by statute and other- wise special duties, amongst which may be mentioned the duty of applying the company's assets in paying creditors and distributing the surplus among the shareholders ... I think at any rate agency more nearly defines his true position than trusteeship ...

As is apparent, the case concerned a liquidator in a voluntary liquidation but the same is true of a compulsory liquidation.

b) In administration, the agency is statutory. Paragraph 69 of Schedule B1 pro- vides that in exercising his functions under that schedule, the administrator acts as the company's agent.
c) There is no equivalent provision in the Act dealing with the agency status of the supervisor of a voluntary arrangement; it is yet another matter which is left to be determined by the terms of the arrangement. However, a well drawn arrangement will include an express provision for the supervisor to act as the company's agent where necessary for the purposes of the CVA and the result- ing agency is therefore contractual. In addition (or, exceptionally, instead) the supervisor may act as a trustee. Where the CVA provides for money or other assets to be paid, transferred, or held for the benefit of CVA creditors, a trust will ordinarily arise.[10] Whether it is the company or the supervisor who is the trustee will depend upon the terms of the CVA and the facts of the case but the possibility of the supervisor being a trustee is expressly contemplated by section 1(2).

The office-holder's agency for the company differs from an ordinary agency in a **11.10** number of respects:

a) the agent controls the principal (the company);
b) it is more accurate to say that the office-holder has the power to deal with the company's affairs and property as its agent since his statutory powers and duties are not powers and duties of the company; and
c) further, in a liquidation, the property of the company would be vested in the liquidator in the unlikely event of a vesting order being made pursuant to section 145.[11]

---

[10] *Re NT Gallagher & Son Ltd* [2002] EWCA Civ 404, [2002] 1 WLR 2380.
[11] See also the preceding paragraph as to the possibility of a supervisor being a trustee.

11.11 A consequence of the office-holder's agency is that he may benefit from the rule in *Said v Butt* which provides that an agent acting in good faith and within the scope of his authority is not liable to the injured counterparty if he procures or causes a breach of contract by his principal.[12]

11.12 Office-holders, like other fiduciaries, have a duty to avoid conflicts of interest (and conflicts of duties). Harman J observed in *Re Corbenstoke Ltd (No 2)*:[13]

> It is the oldest rule of all in equity that a man should not place himself in a position where his duty and his interest conflict, without the fullest disclosure of the conflict and the approval of his continuing to hold that position despite the conflict. It is a proposition which applies across many fields to anyone holding a fiduciary office. Here the office of liquidator is well set out by *Swinfen Eady* J. in *Re Charterland Goldfields Ltd*, and it is plain that a liquidator, although not strictly speaking a trustee, is nonetheless a fiduciary, holding an office with statutory duties analogous to the duties of a trustee to his beneficiaries, being the duties of a liquidator to his creditors.

Conflicts inevitably arise from time to time and the court approaches such issues pragmatically.[14] In an appropriate case, the courts will manage potential conflicts of interest by dividing functions between office-holders.[15]

c. Absence of liability to individual creditors

11.13 In general, the duties of an office-holder as to the proper performance of his functions are duties owed to the company, and possibly to the creditors as a class, but not to individual creditors. The leading authority on the point is the decision of the Court of Appeal in *Kyrris v Oldham* where Jonathan Parker LJ (with whom the other members of the court agreed) said:[16]

> It has not been suggested (nor could it be, in my judgment) that there is any relevant distinction for present purposes between a fiduciary duty and a common law duty of care. Further, I accept [counsel's] submission that the position of an administrator appointed under the 1986 Act vis-à-vis creditors is directly analogous to that of a director vis-à-vis shareholders ...

> Given the nature and scope of an administrator's powers and duties, I can for my part see no basis for concluding that an administrator owes a duty of care to creditors in circumstances where a director would not owe a duty to shareholders. In

---

[12] [1920] 3 KB 497 (KB); but see also *Welsh Development Agency v Export Finance Co Ltd* [1992] BCLC 148 (CA) and *Lictor Anstalt MIR Steel UK Ltd* [2011] EWHC 3310 (Ch), [2012] Bus LR Digest D84.

[13] [1990] BCLC 60 (Ch) 62d (internal citation omitted).

[14] *Re Arrows Ltd* [1992] BCC 121 (Ch); *Parmalat Capital Finance Ltd v Food Holdings Ltd* [2008] UKPC 23, [2009] 1 BCLC 274.

[15] See further para 11.36.

[16] [2003] EWCA Civ 1506, [2004] 1 BCLC 305 [143], [146]. See also *Leon v York-O-Matic Ltd* [1966] 1 WLR 1450 (Ch) and *Charalambous v B&C Associates* [2009] EWHC 2601 (Ch), [2013] BCC 491.

each case the relevant duties are, absent special circumstances, owed exclusively to the company.

The decision was cited with approval by the Privy Council, and treated as being applicable to liquidators, in *Hague v Nam Tai Electronics Inc*.[17]

It had earlier been held by the Court of Appeal in *King v Anthony* that the supervisor **11.14** of an individual voluntary arrangement (and therefore by analogy the supervisor of a company voluntary arrangement) also had no liability to individual creditors. Brooke LJ (with whom the other members of the court also agreed) said:[18]

> Part VIII of the Act contains a self-contained statutory scheme which includes express powers of the court to give appropriate directions if complaint is made to the court of the conduct of a supervisor ... I can see no hint in the language of Pt VIII that Parliament intended individual creditors to have a private law right of action for breach of statutory duty against a supervisor ...

There are two established qualifications to the proposition that individual creditors **11.15** have no individual rights of action against office-holders and a possible, but as yet unresolved, third:

a) In special circumstances, the office-holder may have assumed duties to one or more individual creditors. This is the exception identified in the passage from Jonathan Parker LJ's judgment in *Kyrris* which is quoted above, when he referred to the circumstances in which a director would be liable to shareholders. The exception had already been applied in the slightly earlier decision of the Court of Appeal in *Prosser v Castle Sanderson Solicitors* where the nominee of a voluntary arrangement and chairman of a creditors' meeting to consider the proposal assumed an advisory role, and thus a duty of care, during a short adjournment of the meeting.[19] However, the exception is not necessarily predicated upon the assumption of a distinct capacity. In *Kyrris*, Jonathan Parker LJ said that the special circumstances required to give rise to a duality of duties could simply be the result of an assumption of fiduciary obligations to persons other than the company.[20] All such cases will turn on their own facts but, in practice, the *Prosser* example of misplaced advice is likely to be more typical.

b) Where a liquidator fails to apply the company's assets in accordance with the statutory scheme, creditors have a direct claim following the dissolution of the company.[21] The significance of dissolution, for these purposes, is that upon

---

[17] [2008] UKPC 13, [2008] BCC 295 [14]. See also [13] where Lord Scott said: 'It is well arguable that the duties owed by a liquidator in an insolvent liquidation are owed also to the creditors as a class.'

[18] [1998] 2 BCLC 517 (CA) 523f.

[19] [2002] EWCA Civ 1140, [2003] BCC 440 but the resultant claim failed on a causation issue.

[20] See also *Peskin v Anderson* [2001] 1 BCLC 372 (CA).

[21] *Pulsford v Devenish* [1903] 2 Ch 625 (Ch); *James Smith & Sons (Norwood) Ltd v Goodman* [1936] Ch 216 (CA); *Kyrris v Oldham* (n 16) [153]–[163].

dissolution the remedies of creditors under the Act cease to exist. The liquidator's duty as to the application of the estate is an absolute duty which survives dissolution and thereupon becomes a duty to the creditors. There is no reason why the same reasoning should not apply to an administrator.

c) The open question is whether secured and preferential creditors are in a different position and have individually enforceable rights. The question was identified but not answered in *Lomax Leisure Ltd v Miller*.[22] There is little difficulty in the proposition that an office-holder may be liable to a secured creditor. Secured creditors have proprietary rights and, if the office-holder acts in a way which injures those rights, it would be perverse if the secured creditor were to be deprived of any remedy that he would have had as a stranger simply because he is a creditor of the company.[23] The position of preferential creditors is less obvious. The court in *Lomax Leisure* referred to the earlier decision in *Inland Revenue Commissioners v Goldblatt*, a pre-1986 receivership case in which a receiver was held to be liable to the plaintiffs as preferential creditors for breach of statutory duty in releasing floating charge assets to the company for onward transfer to the debenture-holder without paying the plaintiffs.[24] The reasoning sits uncomfortably with the subsequent authorities to the effect that, in insolvency proceedings, individual creditors have no enforceable rights unless and until the company is dissolved, and it is submitted that *Goldblatt* should be confined to receivership cases. Although an administrative receiver is an office-holder for many of the purposes of the Act, the fundamental difference is that a receiver or (where permitted) an administrative receiver is enforcing security on behalf of a secured creditor and there is no equivalence with a true insolvency procedure where there is a self-contained statutory scheme including specified creditor remedies (the existence of which was regarded by the Court of Appeal in *King v Anthony* as precluding parallel private law rights).

11.16 Even though individual creditors are not owed personal duties they can nonetheless pursue remedies for a breach of the office-holder's duties to the company by means of misfeasance proceedings in a liquidation or administration and by means of a challenge to the supervisor's conduct of a voluntary arrangement.[25]

11.17 A potential divergence of approach is emerging between legal liability and disciplinary process. In a report into the handling of complaints against insolvency practitioners, the Insolvency Service stated:[26]

---

[22] [2007] EWHC 2508 (Ch), [2008] 1 BCLC 262 [34].

[23] See also *Kyrris v Oldham* (n 16) where claims *qua* secured creditor were allowed to proceed whilst claims *qua* unsecured creditor were struck out.

[24] [1972] 1 Ch 498 (Ch).

[25] Section 212 (liquidation), Schedule B1 para 75 (administration) and section 7 (CVAs).

[26] The Insolvency Service, *Review of handling of complaints about Insolvency Practitioners* (September 2016) para 5.3. See further Chapter 13.

There is currently no formal or agreed regulatory mechanism for compensation across the insolvency profession either from insolvency practitioners directly or through the RPBs [recognized professional bodies]. This in part is explained by the fact that insolvency practitioners are part of a unique profession whereby individuals act under the general supervision and powers of the Court. Any such mechanism would not be a substitute for any legal remedies available to individual complainants through the Courts.

and went on to recommend:

The RPBs should enter into discussions with the Insolvency Service to consider the feasibility of a regulatory mechanism whereby compensation can be paid by the insolvency practitioner to the complainant where they have suffered inconvenience, loss, or distress as a result of their actions.

Although the recommendation is carefully prefaced by a clear statement that compensation would not be a substitute for legal redress, it is difficult to see how the availability of direct compensation in one avenue and not the other could do other than result in perverse incentives unless there is the clearest possible demarcation between the proper purview of disciplinary action and legal remedies.

d. Essential supplies

At common law, no unwilling supplier can be compelled to trade with an insolvent **11.18** counterparty. However, this exposes the office-holder to ransom demands from suppliers who make payment for past supplies a precondition of further supplies and may therefore undermine his efforts to preserve a going concern.[27] The problem was identified in the Cork Report:[28]

There is one type of creditor who, although unsecured and non-preferential, is often able to insist upon and obtain payment of his debt in full from a company in liquidation or receivership in priority to other creditors. This is the monopoly supplier of goods or services, such as gas, electricity or water, which are essential to the carrying on of the company's business. It is the common practice for each public utility, on the insolvency of a customer, to threaten to cut off supplies unless the outstanding account is paid in full …

To a lesser extent, the situation is not confined to public utilities. It may arise whenever there is an outstanding account with a private supplier, and there is no practicable alternative supplier. In such a case, the creditor is doing no more than exploit the commercial advantages of his position.

---

[27] *Wellworth Cash & Carry (North Shields) Ltd v North Eastern Electricity Board* (1986) 2 BCC 99, 265 (Ch) is an example of the mischief which the measures considered in this part of the commentary are now intended to address.

[28] Report of the Review Committee, *Insolvency Law and Practice* (Cm 8558, June 1982) at paras 1451 and 1453.

As is apparent, the Review Committee perceived this as a problem which required special provision in the case of public utilities because of their (then) statutory monopolies.

11.19 Pursuant to a recommendation in the Cork Report,[29] section 233, as originally enacted, prevented utilities from demanding payment of outstanding charges as a condition of continuing supply but allowed them to make it a condition of providing the supply that the office-holder personally guaranteed payment of the charge for the new supply. However, subsequent (commercial and legal) developments made this initial provision inadequate and the government took powers to amend the Act in sections 92 and 93 of the Enterprise and Regulatory Reform Act 2013. In the ensuing consultation on the exercise of those powers, the government summarized the need for changes to be made in the following terms:[30]

> The debates during passage of the ERR Act recognised that commercial practice and supplier behaviour has moved on considerably since 1986 following the deregulation of the utilities sector, and that the existing provisions may not effectively ensure continuity of supply of utilities, particularly where supply is through an intermediate provider (known as an 'on-seller'). It was recognised that it was important for an insolvent business to be able to continue to obtain essential supplies and these extended to IT as well as utility supplies. Such services cannot readily be sourced from alternative suppliers and will be essential to the survival of most businesses.

The changes were effected by the Insolvency (Protection of Essential Supplies) Order 2015 which both amended section 233 and added section 233A.[31]

11.20 Under the amended section 233 the range of protected supplies is considerably expanded but the essential framework remains the same, in particular by permitting the supplier to require a personal guarantee from the office-holder. Arguably, this aspect of the provisions dealing with essential supplies is inconsistent with the principle that an office-holder acts as a fiduciary and agent whose liabilities are determined by the terms of the scheme which he is administering.[32] In summary and subject to conditions, section 233A now also prevents suppliers from exercising contractual termination rights in the event of administration and/or a voluntary arrangement but does not apply in liquidation. The rationale for distinguishing between the procedures in this way was explained in the consultation document in the following terms:[33]

---

[29] Ibid at para 1462.
[30] The Insolvency Service, *Continuity of supply of essential services to insolvent businesses* (July 2014) para 17.
[31] SI 2015/989.
[32] Contrast, for example, the alternative approach to the provision of IT services in the Investment Bank Special Administration Regulations 2011 (SI 2011/245) and the Financial Services (Banking Reform) Act 2013.
[33] At para 37.

The Government recognises that preventing utility and IT suppliers from relying on termination clauses will interfere with the right to freedom of contract, and believes that such interference is only justified where absolutely necessary. These powers are therefore restricted to the main business rescue procedures, that is; administration, company voluntary arrangements and individual voluntary arrangements in cases where the individual has been carrying on a business.

This is no longer considered to go far enough and further measures are proposed.[34]

e. Removal and replacement

The power of the court to remove and replace office-holders is an aspect of the residual supervisory jurisdiction which the court exercises in respect of insolvency proceedings.[35] The power is set out in different provisions of the Act and is stated in differing terms.[36] Due to the fact that it is a much older procedure, there is a greater weight of authority on the subject of removing liquidators from office but the court can be expected to approach the question of removing administrators and supervisors in the same way.[37] **11.21**

The court will not remove a liquidator simply 'if it thinks fit', the applicant must show due cause.[38] In *Re Adam Eyton Ltd, ex parte Charlesworth*, Bowen LJ said:[39] **11.22**

> ... due cause is to be measured by reference to the real, substantial, honest interests of the liquidation, and to the purpose for which the liquidator is appointed. Of course, fair play to the liquidator himself is not to be left out of sight, but the measure of due cause is the substantial and real interest of the liquidation.

Due cause will cover, but is not confined to, misconduct and personal unfitness. Malins V-C said in *Re Marseilles Extension Railway and Land Co*:[40]

> On one side it is contended that 'due cause' must be something amounting to misconduct or personal unfitness; on the other side it is contended ... that the Court may take all the circumstances into consideration, and if it finds that it is, upon the whole, desirable that a liquidator should be removed, it may remove him. I do not feel much doubt that the latter is the true construction, and that I have the power to remove these gentlemen.

Conversely, however, the possibility of the office-holder having exposed himself to liability will found an application for removal. In *Shepheard v Lamey*, Jacob J said:[41]

---

[34] See The Insolvency Service, *A Review of the Corporate Insolvency Framework* (Consultation Paper, May 2016) and *Summary of Responses* (September 2016).
[35] See more generally Chapter 12.
[36] Sections 108 and 171 (voluntary liquidation), section 172 (compulsory liquidation), Schedule B1 paras 88 and 91 (administration) and section 7 (voluntary arrangements).
[37] As the court did in *SISU Capital Fund Ltd v Tucker* [2005] EWHC 2170 (Ch), [2006] BCC 463 [88] when dealing with an application for the removal of administrators.
[38] *Re Keypak Homecare Ltd* [1987] BCLC 409 (Ch) 415e.
[39] (1887) LR 36 Ch D 299 (CA) 306.
[40] (1867) LR 4 Eq 692 (Court of Chancery) 694.
[41] [2001] BPIR 939 (Ch) 940C.

… all that one has to find is some good cause why a person should not continue as liquidator. You do not have to prove everything in sight; you do not have to prove, for example, misfeasance as such; you do not have to show more than there may well be a case of misfeasance or, indeed, incompetence.

11.23 In *SISU Capital Fund Ltd v Tucker*, Warren J identified the need to strike a balance:[42]

There is a, sometimes difficult, balance to be held. On the one hand, the court expects any liquidator to be efficient, vigorous, and unbiased in his conduct of the liquidation and should have no hesitation in removing him if satisfied that he has failed to live up to those standards unless it can reasonably confidently be said that he will live up to those requirements in the future. On the other hand, the court must think carefully before removing him, otherwise similar applications by disgruntled creditors in other cases would be encouraged; and there would, of course, be likely to be cost implications …

Perhaps one can say that this is another area of the law where one's flexible friend, proportionality, is to be found at work and the matter should simply be approached on a proportionate basis.

3. Additional factors applicable to liquidators and administrators

a. Defective appointments

11.24 Section 232 provides that the acts of a liquidator 'are valid notwithstanding any defect in his appointment, nomination or qualifications'. Although differently worded, paragraph 104 of Schedule B1 is to like effect in administration. In order for these provisions to apply there must have been some purported appointment.[43] There are conflicting first instance authorities on whether these provisions can be relied upon where the purported appointment is a nullity.[44] Detailed consideration of that issue is outside the scope of this book but it is submitted that the better view is that the provisions can be relied on where there is a proceeding and the purported appointment is made by someone who has the power to appoint. As Norris J said in *Re Care Matters Partnership Ltd*:[45]

---

[42] [2005] EWHC 2170 (Ch), [2006] BCC 463 [85].

[43] *Morris v Kanssen* [1946] AC 459 (HL) 471–472 (dealing with an analogous provision of the Companies Act 1929 concerning directors).

[44] There is a useful review of the authorities and the divergence of conclusions in the judgment of Arnold J in *Re Ceart Risk Services Ltd* [2012] EWHC 1178 (Ch), [2013] Bus LR 116. In the context of administration, the issue of the scope of para 104 has become linked with the question whether failure to give the required notices invalidates the proceeding but that question is logically anterior to that of the scope of para 104.

[45] [2011] EWHC 2543 (Ch), [2011] BCC 957 [8].

It may well be that para.104 is of no assistance where there is no power to make an appointment (for example because there is no valid charge in respect of which the power under para.14 of Sch.B1 could be exercised, or the persons purporting to appoint an administrator under para.22 are not themselves directors). But it may well be that para.104 is of assistance where there is a power to make an appointment but that power has been defectively exercised through some irregularity in procedure.

b. Co-operation of directors

Directors and other insiders are required by section 235 to co-operate with liquidators and administrators. This is discussed in more detail in Section 2 of Chapter 16. **11.25**

c. Examination powers

Both liquidators and administrators have examination powers. For most purposes, the more important examination powers are those relating to private examination under section 236 which liquidators and administrators can use against anyone capable of giving information about the affairs, business, and property of the company. This is discussed in more detail in Section 3 of Chapter 16. **11.26**

d. Liens

A lien on the company's books, papers, and records is unenforceable against a liquidator or administrator. This is discussed in more detail in Section 4 of Chapter 16. **11.27**

e. Immunity from suit

Even the most careful office-holder may find that he has taken possession of property in the belief that it belongs to the company which subsequently proves to be the property of another. Indeed, the statutory duty of a liquidator in a compulsory liquidation to take into his/her custody or control all the property to which the company 'appears' to be entitled, and the similar duty on the part of an administrator, anticipate that contingency.[46] **11.28**

Section 234 provides the office-holder with a qualified immunity in this respect. Where the office-holder seizes or disposes of third party property in the reasonable belief that he is entitled to do so, he is not liable in respect of any resultant damage except to the extent that it is caused by his own negligence (and he has a lien on the property or its proceeds for the expenses of the seizure or disposal). In *Welsh Development Agency v Export Finance Co Ltd*, the Court of Appeal held that this **11.29**

---

[46] Section 144 (liquidation) and Schedule B1 para 67 (administration), see further Chapter 14.

immunity applied only to action taken in respect of tangible property, essentially because intangibles could not be seized.[47]

f. Transaction avoidance

11.30 Liquidators and administrators enjoy a wide range of transaction avoidance powers and remedies which are discussed in Chapter 15. As an exception to the generality of the provisions under consideration in this section of this chapter, supervisors share the powers of other office-holders to take action in respect of transactions defrauding creditors. This is consistent with the remedy under section 423 also being available to a victim of the impugned transaction without the necessity for there to be any insolvency proceedings. In such circumstances, the exclusion of supervisors from the range of permitted applicants would be illogical.

g. Discharge from liability

11.31 A conundrum for an office-holder approaching the conclusion of an insolvency proceeding is the prospective loss of the right to indemnity from the insolvent estate for any liabilities which may have been properly incurred in the performance of his duties. In the case of known and quantifiable liabilities, he will ensure that the liability is discharged before closure but the possibility of other late claims being advanced is more problematic. The Act addresses this by providing that a liquidator or administrator who has ceased to hold office shall be discharged from liability incurred in that capacity.[48]

11.32 Although releases for office-holders have a long history in English law, they have attracted little judicial comment. The following statements serve to explain the general purpose and effect of releases. In *Re Munro, ex parte Singer*, Walton J said:[49]

> ... it appears to me that the intention ... and it is a very right, proper and wholesome intention, is to wipe the slate completely clean so far as the trustee is concerned, so that he may thereafter pay no thought to the previous course of his actions as the trustee in bankruptcy.

and in *Re Hellas Telecommunications (Luxembourg) II SCA*, Sales J said:[50]

> The reason that it will usually be right to order such a discharge is that the administrator will no longer retain in his hands the assets of the company out of which

---

[47] [1992] BCLC 148 (CA), but note the disagreement of Lord Nicholls in *OBG Ltd v Allan* [2007] UKHL 21, [2008] 1 AC 1 [236]. See also Chapter 14.

[48] Sections 173 and 174 (liquidators, where the discharge is called the liquidator's 'release') and Schedule B1 para 98 (administrators). Note that these provisions include detailed rules on when the discharge takes effect.

[49] [1981] 1 WLR 1358 (Ch) 1362G—the position of a trustee in bankruptcy is analogous in this respect.

[50] [2011] EWHC 3176 (Ch), [2013] 1 BCLC 426 [96].

he is entitled to meet any liability properly incurred by him, so that it is unfair to leave him on risk generally.

The release of the office-holder may be postponed if there are or may be known **11.33** claims to be brought against him/her or there are matters to be investigated.[51]

Despite the breadth of the discharge wording of the Act and the description of its **11.34** effects in *Munro*, the protection afforded is illusory. A liquidator's release does not prevent the exercise of the court's powers on a misfeasance summons issued pursuant to section 212 and, similarly, an administrator's discharge does not prevent the exercise of the court's powers under paragraph 75 of Schedule B1. Since these are procedural provisions enabling a very wide range of proceedings for breach of duty to be pursued, it follows that the scope of the absolute discharge which is obtained by the office-holder is correspondingly limited. The more real protection is that, in both cases, misfeasance proceedings can only be brought against an office-holder who has been discharged from liability with the leave of the court. In *Re Angel Group Ltd*, Rose J regarded this as a salutary means of ensuring that unmeritorious claims are not pursued.[52]

4. Joint appointments, succession issues, and block transfers

The personal nature of an office-holder's appointment can result in some practical **11.35** problems if the office-holder is unavailable and some succession issues if the office-holder retires, dies, or ceases to be qualified to act as an insolvency practitioner at a time when he has current cases. [53]

The first of these questions is easily resolved by joint appointments unless the **11.36** office-holder is a sole practitioner. Section 231 provides that the appointment of joint liquidators must declare whether they are empowered to act only jointly or whether they can also act severally. Paragraph 100 of Schedule B1 is to like effect in the case of administrators.[54] (There is no equivalent provision in relation to supervisors, where the matter is left to be determined by the terms of the CVA.) In all but the largest cases, it is likely that one office-holder will act as the lead office-holder and, in practice, discharge all the office-holders' functions with the other appointee(s) providing cover in case of absence. Joint appointments can also

---

[51] *Re Sibec Developments Ltd* [1992] 1 WLR 1253 (Ch); *Re Angel Group Ltd* [2015] EWHC 3624 (Ch), [2016] BPIR 260.

[52] Ibid at [48].

[53] See further The Insolvency Service, *Insolvency Guidance Paper – succession planning*, 7 April 2014 <https://www.gov.uk/government/publications/succession-planning-insolvency-practitioner-guidance-paper/insolvency-guidance-paper-succession-planning> accessed 23 January 2017.

[54] Note also Schedule B1 paras 101–103 for further provisions on the joint appointment of administrators.

be made, or functions divided between existing appointees, in order to manage conflicts of interest.[55]

11.37 If an office-holder vacates office before the conclusion of a particular case, the procedures under the Act and Rules for the appointment of a successor will naturally be followed. The issues arising from vacation of office covering the practitioner's entire current caseload or from a practice move are potentially more difficult to manage. In *Re Sankey Furniture Ltd, ex parte Harding*, Chadwick J considered the options which would be available in the not uncommon situation of an insolvency practitioner moving from one firm to another:[56]

> There are three courses which can be adopted when an insolvency practitioner leaves one firm to join another: (i) transferring the work to the new firm – so that the work follows the individual who is the office holder; or (ii) leaving the work with the old firm but retaining the existing individual office holder – so that the office holder becomes divorced from the day-to-day work; or (iii) calling meetings of creditors or contributories to approve the transfer of office to a new individual in the old firm – so retaining both work and office where they 'belong'. Each of those courses is likely to give rise to inconvenience and expense.

The courts developed the jurisdiction to make 'block transfer orders' in order to address this question.

11.38 The jurisdiction was explained by the Court of Appeal in *Donaldson v O'Sullivan* where Lloyd LJ said:[57]

> Block transfer orders were developed, starting in about 1993, in order to cope with a variety of situations in which a licensed insolvency practitioner had ceased to hold office, or wished to do so, or it was desired that he or she should do so, in respect of a number of insolvent estates, and it was sought to achieve this by a court order rather than by the holding of a series of creditors' meetings in each estate. In some cases there was a need for urgent action, but in most cases the predominant motive was to save time and money.

The jurisdiction and the associated procedure is now contained in Chapter 6 Subdivision B of Part 12 of the Rules.

11.39 Those entitled to apply for a block transfer order include the recognized professional body that authorized the outgoing office-holder to act as an insolvency practitioner. *Institute of Chartered Accountants in England Wales v Webb* was a case in

---

[55] See: *SISU Capital Fund Ltd v Tucker* above; *Re York Gas Ltd* [2010] EWHC 2275 (Ch), [2011] BCC 447; *Re MF Global UK Ltd* [2014] EWHC 2222 (Ch), [2014] Bus LR 1156; *Re Angel Group Ltd* above and *Re BHS Ltd* [2016] EWHC 1965 (Ch). The nature and gravity of the conflict of interest will determine whether it can be managed by the joint appointment of another practitioner from the same firm or whether an appointment from a different firm is required.

[56] [1995] 2 BCLC 594 (Ch) 601c.

[57] [2008] EWCA Civ 879, [2009] 1 WLR 924 [7]. (Note that this case and *Sankey Furniture* preceded changes which introduced qualifying decision and deemed consent procedures to take the place of meetings.)

which the outgoing office-holder opposed his RPB's nomination of new practitioners and put forward an alternative. Norris J said:[58]

> … appointment as office holder is not to be regarded as an income stream, where the existing office holder may dispose of the benefit of the offices to a chosen assignee. It must be clearly understood that an office holder is someone upon whom duties are imposed by the court and who is supervised by the court, and whose duties are to be discharged in the interests of creditors. On an application for the transfer of offices from a former office holder to new office holders the court's concern must primarily be to protect the interests of the creditors in the various estates, and to the extent that there may be a surplus in any of the insolvencies, the company or individual whose affairs are being administered by the office holder. The loss of an insolvency licence also brings an end to the source of income for the office holder concerned; but it will be a very rare case where the interests of the office holder have any weight in the exercise of the court's power to appoint new office holders.

5. Conclusions

The concept of the insolvency office-holder transcends the purposes of specific procedures and establishes an underlying commonality of approach. There are three different aspects to the concept: **11.40**

a) The office-holder is perceived to be an independent fiduciary whose personal interest in the insolvent estate is confined to the remuneration to which he is entitled. This underpins the requirement for the office-holder to be an individual and informs the approach of the courts to block transfer orders.

b) Provided that he acts properly, the office-holder's tenure of his office is safeguarded and he will have the benefit of various protections from liability to aggrieved creditors and third parties.

c) The office-holder has a number of special powers to assist him in the proper performance of his functions.

---

[58] [2009] EWHC 3461 (Ch), [2010] Bus LR Digest D37 [6]; see also *Association of Chartered Certified Accountants v Koumettou* [2012] EWHC 1265 (Ch).

12

JURISDICTION OF THE COURT

1. Introduction

12.01   The 'court', for the purposes of the Act and Rules, means the court with jurisdiction to wind up a company. The High Court has jurisdiction to wind up any company registered in England and Wales. The county court has concurrent jurisdiction in respect of any company whose paid up share capital does not exceed £120,000, unless the place which has longest been the registered office of the company during the previous six months is in the London insolvency district.[1]

12.02   The court exercises a wide-ranging jurisdiction over insolvency proceedings relating to companies although the extent of its involvement naturally varies according to the nature of the proceeding. In that respect, the most significant distinction is between insolvency proceedings which result from court orders and out of court proceedings. In *Re Phoenix Oil and Transport Co Ltd*, Wynn-Parry J said of an earlier era of insolvency legislation:[2]

---

[1] Sections 117 and 251 (see also rule 12.3) and the London Insolvency District (County Court at Central London) Order 2014 (SI 2014/818). Insolvency business is handled in accordance with Practice Direction: Insolvency Proceedings [2014] BCC 502; Practice Direction: Order under section 127 of the Insolvency Act 1986 [2007] BCC 839; and Practice Direction: Directors' Disqualification Proceedings [2015] BCC 224.

[2] [1958] 1 Ch 565 (Ch) 570. See also *Donaldson v O'Sullivan* [2008] EWCA Civ 879, [2009] 1 WLR 924.

A study of the relevant sections of the Companies Act, 1948, dealing with winding up shows clearly that as regards voluntary winding up the legislature has followed (in pursuance of the policy of previous Companies Acts) a different policy from that laid down in the case of compulsory winding up. The reason is not far to seek. In the case of voluntary winding up, the jurisdiction of the court is not invoked in order to place a company in liquidation. In the case of a creditors' liquidation, the creditors, through their committee of inspection, are in control as against the contributories; while in the case of a members' voluntary winding up it is the members who are in control. In both cases the court is given a certain degree of jurisdiction, but I think it can be accurately, though shortly, said that in both forms of voluntary winding up the court is in the background to be referred to if the necessity should arise. In the case of a winding up by the court, however, different considerations arise. In this case the court is conducting an administration, and so, as in the case of an ordinary administration action in the Chancery Division, it retains, under the express provisions of the statute, a much greater degree of control.

Two points need to be borne in mind in connection with this analysis:

a) The insolvency procedures which can now be conducted without there necessarily being any recourse to the court include administration and company voluntary arrangements (CVAs). In practice, out of court proceedings greatly outnumber court proceedings.
b) The consolidation of insolvency legislation in the Act has tended to reduce the difference between court and out of court proceedings after the initial order has been made which, in the case of the former, is necessary in order to open the proceedings.

In addition to the many provisions of the Act and Rules which expressly require an order of the court, the court has a general supervisory role which arises in a number of different ways: **12.03**

a) it has jurisdiction to wind up companies of its own motion;
b) it exercises an inherent jurisdiction to regulate the conduct of office-holders who are officers of the court;
c) office-holders can seek directions from the court; and
d) aggrieved persons can challenge the office-holder's conduct of the proceeding by application to the court.

2. The jurisdiction to wind up companies

Section 122 states the grounds on which a company may be wound up and sections 124 and 124A make provision for who may petition for a winding-up order, but these provisions are not of the same character. The former confers jurisdiction but the latter deal with procedural requirements which do not preclude the court from **12.04** acting of its own motion. The authorities in this respect start with the judgment of Neuberger J in *Lancefield v Lancefield* where he said:[3]

> If one looks at the commonest case, that of registered companies, s122 of the 1986 Act empowers the court to wind up a company if one or more of the circumstances set out in s122(1) applies. Section 124 then provides how an application for the winding-up of a company can be made by certain categories of person. It seems to me, therefore, that two propositions are clear. First, if one or more of the circumstances in s122 exists, the court has the power – not an obligation; note the word 'may' in s122(1) – to make a winding-up order. Secondly, if a person seeks a winding-up, then by virtue of s124, he has to apply by petition, and has to be within the ambit of that section.
>
> However, I do not see why that should mean that, where a matter concerning the company is before the court and the court is quite satisfied that there is jurisdiction to make a winding-up order because one or more of the circumstances in s122(1) applies, the court is in every case powerless to act simply because nobody has petitioned for a winding-up under s124(1). I do not see why, in the case of a registered company, the court should not, in an appropriate case, of its own motion, decide on the facts before it that it has the power to make a winding-up order under s122(1) and that it should make such an order.

He then went on to stress that it was a jurisdiction which the court would only exercise in very exceptional circumstances.

12.05 Although the exercise of the court's jurisdiction to wind up of its own motion will only rarely be encountered in practice, it provides a salutary backdrop to the court's more general supervision and control of insolvency proceedings relating to companies.

3. The inherent jurisdiction over officers of the court

12.06 In *Deloitte & Touche AG v Johnson*, Lord Millett said:[4]

> The court's inherent jurisdiction to control the conduct of its own officers is beyond dispute.

So much is clear, but distinguishing between office-holders who are officers of the court and those who are not, and identifying the consequences of the distinction, is more difficult.

12.07 It is settled law that liquidators in compulsory liquidations and administrators are officers of the court but that liquidators in voluntary liquidations are not. The

---

[3] [2002] BPIR 1108 (Ch) 1111F. The decision concerned an insolvent partnership but the quoted passage of the judgment is dealing expressly with companies and the principle is the same. See further *Secretary of State for Business, Innovation and Skills v PLT Anti-Marketing Ltd* [2015] EWHC 3981 (Ch).

[4] [1999] 1 WLR 1605 (PC) 1612C.

position of liquidators in compulsory liquidations is uncontroversial and replicates the treatment of trustees in bankruptcy as officers of the court. An example of the ready acceptance of their comparable status is *Donaldson v O'Sullivan* where Lloyd LJ said:[5]

> ... a trustee in bankruptcy, like a liquidator under a compulsory winding up, is an officer of the court.

Administrators were recognized to be officers of the court by the Court of Appeal in *Re Atlantic Computer Systems Plc*.[6] That case was decided under Part II of the Act as originally enacted (which made no express reference to the administrator's status as an officer of the court). Paragraph 5 of Schedule B1 now provides that an administrator is an officer of the court, whether or not appointed by the court.

The status of voluntary liquidators was settled by the Court of Appeal in *Re TH Knitwear (Wholesale) Ltd* where Slade LJ (with whom the other members of the court agreed) said:[7] **12.08**

> ... in my judgment... a liquidator in a voluntary winding up is not an officer of the court within the principle. As [counsel] pointed out on behalf of the liquidator in the present case, he is not appointed by the court and the exercise of his powers is not subject to the control of the court, unless and until he or some other interested party chooses to bring questions relating to such exercise before the court for its directions or other relief.

The authorities on the status of supervisors in voluntary arrangements are con-**12.09** fused. In *King v Anthony* the Court of Appeal held that aggrieved creditors had no private law cause of action against the supervisor of an individual voluntary arrangement on the basis that he was an officer of the court and amenable to its control through the self-contained statutory scheme which included the power to give directions.[8] The decision was cited by Clarke LJ with apparent approval when a similar issue arose in *Prosser v Castle Sanderson Solicitors*.[9] On the other hand, in *Firth v Everitt*, Ian Croxford QC, sitting as a deputy judge of the High Court, rejected the proposition that the supervisor of a partnership voluntary arrangement was an officer of the court on the ground that he was not in office by virtue of any order of the court, without alluding to the earlier decisions of the Court of Appeal to the contrary.[10] The deputy judge instead drew support from what he took to be the same conclusion of Neuberger J in *Clements v Udal*. However, Neuberger J

---

[5] [2008] EWCA Civ 879, [2009] 1 WLR 924 [39]. The quoted statement was made in the course of stating that being an officer of the court was not, as such, determinative of the point before the court but it is nonetheless a convenient recognition and restatement of the liquidator's status.

[6] [1992] Ch 505 (CA) 529F, 543G.

[7] [1988] 1 Ch 275 (CA) 288E. The principle referred to is that in *Ex parte James*, as to which see below.

[8] [1998] 2 BCLC 517 (CA) 523.

[9] [2002] EWCA Civ 1140, [2003] BCC 440 [61].

[10] [2007] EWHC 1979 (Ch) [67].

in that case had merely observed, of an insolvency practitioner holding a large number of different appointments, that:[11]

> In relation to many of his offices, Mr Udal has been appointed by the court and is indeed an officer of the court.

This was, at best, a negative implication and there is no indication that Neuberger J was addressing the status of supervisors as such. In *Appleyard Ltd v Ritecrown Ltd*,[12] on an application by the supervisor of a CVA for a declaration as to his powers under the terms of the arrangement, Lewison J treated the supervisor as an officer of the court but no authorities are considered in the judgment and it had been common ground between the parties that, as an officer of the court, the supervisor was required to act reasonably (which might be expected of any office-holder).[13]

12.10   A recurrent theme in these decisions is that the status of the office-holder as an officer of the court turns on whether the appointment is made by the court or not. However, this cannot be the true test because, even disregarding the status of an out of court appointed administrator as an officer of the court, this does not distinguish sufficiently clearly between the procedures; the liquidator in a compulsory liquidation may have been appointed by the creditors or the Secretary of State and the liquidator in a voluntary liquidation and the supervisor of a company voluntary arrangement could have been appointed by the court. It is suggested that the office-holder is an officer of the court if either:

a) the procedure is being conducted by the court; or
b) the governing legislation so provides (as in the case of administration).

The liquidator in a compulsory liquidation is an officer of the court because the company is being wound up *by the court*; section 160 provides a power to make rules for the delegation of some of the functions of the court to the liquidator 'as an officer of the court' and section 167(3) says that the Schedule 4 powers of a liquidator are subject to the control of the court.

12.11   The analogy of pre-Enterprise Act administration with compulsory liquidation was clear enough (even though the language of Part II of the Act was different) and it was only necessary to make express provision for the status of administrators when the Enterprise Act reforms introduced out of court appointments (thereby avoiding anomalies which would arise as a result of the choice of entry route). Precisely the same test shows why a voluntary liquidator is not an officer of the court: a

---

[11] [2001] BCC 658 (Ch) 659.

[12] [2007] EWHC 3515 (Ch), [2009] BPIR 235 [38], [55]. See also *Re Pinson Wholesale Ltd* [2008] BCC 112 (Ch) where the status of supervisors as officers of the court was one of the premises on which the court approached a remuneration claim.

[13] There is a potential inconsistency between treating an officer of the court as having a duty to act reasonably and the perversity which must be established before the court will interfere with a liquidator's acts and decisions under section 168(5) (discussed below).

voluntary liquidation can be conducted without any reference to the court. That leaves the question of CVAs where the court's involvement in the procedure may be confined to receipt of the nominee's report and some filed documents. A CVA cannot properly be characterized as a proceeding being conducted by the court. Indeed, its title 'company *voluntary* arrangement' demonstrates the contrary intention. It is suggested that, even allowing for the greater potential involvement of the court in individual voluntary arrangements where an interim order is obtained, the decisions treating supervisors as officers of the court are inconsistent with the true test to establish that status.[14]

Status as an officer of the court has two broad consequences so far as the jurisdiction of the court is concerned: **12.12**

a) the so-called 'rule' in *Re Condon, ex parte James*[15] will apply; and
b) interference with the performance of the office-holder's functions will be a contempt of court.

a. *Ex parte James*

The rule, which is better regarded rather as a principle because of its uncertain scope, is derived from the following passage in the judgment of James LJ:[16]   **12.13**

> The Court, then, finding that [the trustee in bankruptcy] has in his hands money which in equity belongs to someone else, ought to set an example to the world by paying it to the person really entitled to it. In my opinion, the Court of Bankruptcy ought to be as honest as other people.

David Richards J said of the principle in *Re Lehman Brothers International (Europe); Lomas v Burlington Loan Management Ltd*:[17]   **12.14**

> The principle in *Ex parte James* has been described as anomalous but it is a well-established principle providing a means by which the court can control the conduct of its officers. Administrators, liquidators in a compulsory winding-up and trustees in bankruptcy are all officers of the court and subject to this jurisdiction. The case to which the principle owes its name, like a number of cases immediately following it, concerned the retention by a liquidator or trustee in bankruptcy of money paid under a mistake of law. At that time, money paid under a mistake of law was not recoverable, but the court directed that its officer should not stand on his strict legal rights but should return the funds, notwithstanding that the effect was to

---

[14] It may be significant in that respect that the Court of Appeal in both *King* and *Prosser* was dealing with the ability to bring claims against supervisors without using the statutory scheme and not addressing the consequences described below of treating an office-holder as an officer of the court. It is suggested that a conclusion that the statutory scheme was definitive thereby precluding parallel private law remedies could have been reached without any need to treat supervisors as officers of the court.

[15] (1874) LR 9 Ch App 609 (CA).

[16] Ibid at 614.

[17] [2015] EWHC 2270 (Ch), [2015] BPIR 1162 [174].

deprive the creditors of funds which would otherwise be available for distribution among them. The rationale for the principle was that, although irrecoverable at law, the officer of the court could not in all conscience retain the money, given the circumstances in which it had been paid. It would amount to an unjust enrichment of the estate. Although the principle was first developed and exercised in these circumstances, subsequent cases applied it in other circumstances and it cannot now be said to be confined to particular categories of case.

12.15 The idea of fair dealing is central to the application of the principle. In *Re Nortel GmbH*, Lord Neuberger PSC said:[18]

> As to the common law, there are a number of cases, starting with *Ex p James; In Re Condon*, in which a principle has been developed and applied to the effect that 'where it would be unfair' for a trustee in bankruptcy 'to take full advantage of his legal rights as such, the court will order him not to do so', to quote Walton J in *In Re Clark (a bankrupt), Ex p The Trustee v Texaco Ltd*. The same point was made by Slade LJ in *Re TH Knitwear (Wholesale) Ltd*, quoting Salter J in *In Re Wigzell, Ex p Hart*: 'where a bankrupt's estate is being administered ... under the supervision of a court, that court has a discretionary jurisdiction to disregard legal right', which 'should be exercised wherever the enforcement of legal right would ... be contrary to natural justice'. The principle obviously applies to administrators and liquidators: see *In Re Lune Metal Products Ltd*.

David Richards J said of this aspect of the principle in *Lehman*:[19]

> I take it that unfairness is a sufficient ground for the application of the principle in *Ex Parte James* if the court thinks that, in all the circumstances, it is right to apply the principle. This is not a surprising development. While in some of the earlier cases the judges refer to the difficulty in applying the principle in *Ex parte James* because it involved moral rather than legal judgments, unfairness as a substantive legal concept is now well embedded in our law ... What constitutes unfairness will, just like what constitutes dishonourable conduct, depend on the circumstances of the case.

12.16 The anomalies attending the principle operate at two levels. First, there is the anomalous distinction between those office-holders who are officers of the court and those that are not and, secondly, there is the anomalous distinction between officers of the court and other persons administering funds. As regards the latter of these points, Harman J said in *Re (John) Bateson & Co Ltd*:[20]

> The concept is to some minds a surprising one, since in other jurisdictions this court insists that persons before it should act in what might be called an unethical way: eg if trustees have agreed, subject to contract, to sell a house, part of the trust estate, and the contract is almost ready for exchange, but then a higher offer comes in from some prospective new purchaser, it is the trustee's duty, as I understand

---

[18] [2013] UKSC 52, [2014] AC 209 [122] (internal citations omitted).
[19] *Lehman* (n 17) [183]. See also *PricewaterhouseCoopers v SAAD Investments Company Ltd* [2016] UKPC 33 [10], [32] where reference is made to officers of the court not being permitted to benefit from their own errors.
[20] [1985] BCLC 259 (Ch) 262.

the law, to throw over the existing proposed contract which they have assented to and which one might say they were morally obliged to carry out and to accept the higher offer. That is because, the court says, they should not be generous with other people's money; they have a duty to get all they can for their beneficiaries. Such an attitude does not appear to be the attitude of the bankruptcy court which says the money of the creditors, who are in a sense the beneficiaries of the trustee in bankruptcy, should be disposed of and that the rights of the creditors through the trustee in bankruptcy should not be enforced to their full extent.

These double standards are not adequately explained by the fact that the office-holder (where the principle applies) is acting as an officer of the court. It might be said, on the one hand, that the court should be promoting standards of honourable conduct and fair dealing in all issues coming before it and, on the other hand, that of all people an officer of the court should apply the law. If the application of the law produces an unfair result, the fault lies in the law itself and not the conduct of the office-holder in applying it as he finds it.

The distinction between office-holders who are officers of the court and those who are not appears to owe more to history than logic. It should be borne in mind that formal out of court insolvency procedures were in their infancy when *Ex parte James* was decided and the court did not have to consider the implications of the application of the principle which it was enunciating depending on the happenchance of the chosen form of insolvency proceeding. An even more striking anomaly arises out of the possibility of a creditors' voluntary liquidation following administration. This was addressed by Lewison J in *Re Agrimarche Ltd* where he said (obiter):[21]   **12.17**

> The Court of Appeal has decided that the principle does not apply to a liquidator in a creditors' voluntary liquidation on the ground that he is not an officer of the court: *Re TH Knitwear (Wholesale) Ltd*. The liquidation in the present case is such a liquidation. On the other hand the events which, at least potentially, bring the principle into play took place during the currency of the administration; and the administrators were officers of the court ... In *Re TH Knitwear (Wholesale) Ltd* Slade LJ said that in view of the uncertainty inherent in the principle, it should not be extended. Nevertheless, it would be odd if moving from administration to creditors' voluntary liquidation radically altered the standard of conduct to be expected of the office-holder, particularly where there is no change in the identity of the office-holder.

Given that the principle confers no substantive rights on the office-holder and will only operate to restrain the exercise or enforcement of rights by the office-holder, it has been suggested that the principle is, or should be, part of the law of restitution. If that were so, it would remove the anomalies arising between different types of office-holder because the law of restitution would draw no such distinction. In any event, wherever the court has a discretion in giving directions   **12.18**

---

21 [2010] EWHC 1655 (Ch), [2011] 1 BCLC 1 [25].

to an office-holder, it is to be hoped that a uniform approach will be developed in determining what is and what is not appropriate conduct on the part of an insolvency office-holder.

b. Contempt of court

12.19 Interference with the performance of an officer of the court's functions constitutes contempt of court. In this case, the distinction drawn between office-holders who are officers of the court and those who are not is more rationally grounded.

12.20 The court's protection of its officers was well established before the development of modern insolvency procedures. Thus, in *Ames v Birkenhead Docks Trustees*, Lord Romilly MR said of court appointed receivers:[22]

> There is no question but that this Court will not permit a receiver, appointed by its authority, and who is therefore its officer, to be interfered with or dispossessed of the property he is directed to receive, by anyone, although the order appointing him may be perfectly erroneous; this Court requires and insists that application should be made to the Court, for permission to take possession of any property of which the receiver either has taken or is directed to take possession ...

12.21 The application of the same approach to liquidators in a compulsory liquidation is demonstrated by the decision on the Court of Appeal in *Re Henry Pound, Son, & Hutchins*, a case in which it was held that a receiver appointed by debenture-holders required leave to take possession of the security following the making of a winding-up order. Cotton LJ said:[23]

> ... nothing has been said ... to lead to the suggestion that ... they would [not] be guilty of contempt of Court if a receiver had been appointed under this deed and if, after the appointment of the liquidator, and after the liquidator was in possession, he had taken possession of that which the liquidator, as officer of the Court, held. That is the reason why they must apply to the Court to enable them, notwithstanding the possession of the officer of the Court, to exercise the rights they have under their own deed.

The same approach is followed in respect of administrators where a breach of the moratorium constitutes a contempt.[24]

4. Office-holders' applications for directions

12.22 All office-holders, whether or not officers of the court, can apply to the court for directions as to the performance of their functions. There is no universal provision

---

[22] (1855) 20 Beav 322 (Court of Chancery) 353.
[23] (1889) 42 Ch D 402 (CA) 420.
[24] *Re Atlantic Computer Systems Plc* [1992] Ch 505 (CA) 532C; *Re Sabre International Products Ltd* [1991] BCC 694 (Ch).

of the Act to this effect but each procedure includes such a power.[25] The power to apply for directions is slightly differently worded in each case, but this merely reflects the piecemeal assemblage of the Act; there is no difference of substance.

The jurisdiction to give directions to an office-holder is analogous to the jurisdiction exercised in respect of trustees and the courts have regard to the trust jurisdiction in determining questions of both procedure and substance when dealing with office-holders' applications. Thus, for example, in *Craig v Humberclyde Industrial Finance Ltd and Ors*[26] a liquidator applied to the court seeking directions as to whether he should assign causes of action to the company's directors or to the defendants against whom the actions existed and who were also creditors of the company. At first instance, Chadwick J, whose decision the Court of Appeal upheld, adopted the procedure of the Chancery Division on hearing an action by a trustee for directions. On that basis, he excluded the defendants from that part of the hearing dealing with the evidence and merits of the company's case against the defendants. In the Court of Appeal, Morritt LJ (with whom the other members of the court agreed) said:[27]   **12.23**

> The purpose of the procedure is in an essentially administrative jurisdiction, as described by Wilberforce J in *In Re Eaton, decd*, to ensure so far as practicable the proper exercise of fiduciary powers or obligations. It is true that the directions sought in this case are essentially how and to whom the asset of the company should be sold rather than whether the company should itself sue. But that distinction lacks substance. In each case the problem is how best to realise an asset of the fund, be it a trust fund or the property of a company in liquidation divisible amongst its creditors, which consists of a chose in action. Such an asset may be realised by suing on it or selling it. The *In Re Moritz* procedure plainly applies to the former alternative and I can see no reason why it should not similarly apply to the latter. In my view it is appropriate to apply the practice and procedure applicable to applications by trustees ... to comparable applications by a liquidator under section 168(3) save in so far as the Act of 1986 or Rules of 1986 make other provision.

An application for directions can be used to resolve a wide range of different questions arising during the course of insolvency proceedings. One common use is to resolve questions of law and to determine the extent of the office-holder's powers. In *Gleave v Pension Protection Fund*,[28] the supervisors of CVAs obtained directions as to the correct quantification of pension fund deficit liabilities for the purposes of the arrangements and, in *Re Home Treat Ltd*,[29] an administrator was given directions to carry on the company's business notwithstanding doubts which had arisen as to whether that business was permitted by the company's memorandum   **12.24**

---

[25] Sections 112 and 168(3) (liquidation), Schedule B1 para 63 (administration) and section 7(4) (CVAs).
[26] [1999] 1 WLR 129 (CA).
[27] Ibid at [19] (internal citation omitted).
[28] [2008] EWHC 1099 (Ch), [2008] Bus LR 1443.
[29] [1991] BCC 165 (Ch).

of association. In *Re Pinson Wholesale Ltd*,[30] directions to supervisors of a CVA permitted them to recover remuneration which had not been provided for by the express terms of the arrangement.

12.25   There are, however, limits to the proper use of the procedure:

a) The procedure is not appropriate for the resolution of substantive issues as to the ownership of assets where the facts are unclear. In *Re Stetzel Thomson & Co Ltd*, liquidators applied for directions as to the ownership of a fund in just such circumstances. Harman J said:[31]

> It is quite clear that the Companies Court has jurisdiction to allow liquidators to apply to the court for directions as to funds in their hands and in suitable cases to allow them, as it were, to act as trustees and simply ask the court for assistance, even though the result may be that the direction is that the liquidator should retain the fund for the benefit of the company and its creditors generally …
>
> Although there is plainly, in my view, jurisdiction to allow that form of proceeding, it by no means follows that the court should always permit it. In this case I am faced with voluntary liquidators appointed in a case where they assumed the office of their own will, where there are funds in hand, although not very large funds, and claimants to the syndicate fund who are very well able to fight their own corner …
>
> As it seems to me, as a matter of discretion, this is a case which is wholly unsuitable to be dealt with by any form of proceedings such as normal trustee proceedings.

b) An application for directions cannot be used to bypass other provisions of the Act and Rules which provide bespoke provisions for determining particular questions or issues.[32]

c) The office-holder must make and accept responsibility for his own commercial judgments. In *Re T&D Industries Plc*, Neuberger J considered the circumstances in which it would and would not be appropriate for an administrator to apply for directions, saying:[33]

> … a person appointed to act as an administrator may be called upon to make important and urgent decisions. He has a responsible and potentially demanding role. Commercial and administrative decisions are for him, and the court is not there to act as a sort of bomb shelter for him.

He went on to say that an application might be appropriate if an administrator wished to pursue a different course or there was a disagreement with the creditors.

---

[30] [2008] BCC 112 (Ch).
[31] (1988) 4 BCC 74 (Ch) 78.
[32] *Re McHale (James) Automobiles Ltd* [1997] 1 BCLC 273 (Ch); *Re Chinn* [2016] BPIR 346 (Ch).
[33] [2000] 1 WLR 646 (Ch) 657G. See also *Re Mirror Group (Holdings) Ltd* [1992] BCC 972 (Ch) 976, where Sir Donald Nicholls V-C noted that the court had not been asked for directions on a point and 'That being so, it is not for me to interfere with the exercise by them of discretions entrusted to them.'

Any office-holder applying to the court for guidance in the performance of his functions must make full and frank disclosure of all relevant circumstances.[34] Even so, Neuberger J in *T&D Industries* warned that:[35]

> ... while it may well be appropriate for an administrator to make an application where there is a point of principle at stake or where there is a dispute as to the appropriate course and it is possible for there to be an inter partes hearing, it would require a very unusual case before the court could give any real assistance in circumstances where there cannot be a proper hearing inter partes and where the decision is essentially an administrative or commercial one for the administrator.

12.26 The power of the court to give directions has sometimes been invoked by administrators in the context of settlement agreements notwithstanding the office-holder's statutory power to enter into such agreements. Just such an application was made to David Richards J in *Re Lehman Brothers International (Europe)*.[36] The court was not asked to approve the settlement as such but instead to direct administrators to exercise their powers so as to cause the company to perform its obligations under the settlement agreement in accordance with its terms. The settlement agreement contained the usual exclusion of personal liability on the part of the administrators and the purpose of the direction, which was given as sought, was to provide the counterparty with assurance as to its performance notwithstanding that lack of personal responsibility. In *Re MF Global UK Ltd (No 5)*,[37] the same judge considered a settlement agreement resolving issues between a trust estate and the general estate where the administrators (despite having taken appropriate steps to manage the inevitable conflict) were on both sides. The court directed that the administrators be at liberty to enter into the agreement, which they had concluded was in the best interests of both estates. In *Re Nortel Networks UK Ltd & Ors*, sanction was sought for the execution and performance of a settlement agreement because of the momentous consequences for the administrations of the subject companies. Again, the court was careful to emphasize that it was not approving the settlement agreement as such; the court's role was to satisfy itself that the administrators' own decision to enter into the agreement was a reasonable decision, taken on proper grounds, in which all relevant considerations had been taken into account. His Honour Judge Hodge QC (sitting as a deputy judge of the High Court) added the following warning before proceeding to give the direction for which the administrators had applied:[38]

> The court is not a rubber stamp, and the parties and their advisers must be astute not to appear to treat the court as such.

---

34 See further *Re Nortel Networks UK Ltd & Ors* [2014] EWHC 2614 (Ch).
35 *T&D Industries* (n 33) 658D.
36 [2013] EWHC 1664 (Ch), [2014] BCC 132.
37 [2014] EWHC 2222 (Ch), [2014] Bus LR 1156.
38 [2014] EWHC 2614 (Ch) [38]. See also *Re Nortel Networks UK Ltd* [2016] EWHC 2769 (Ch).

5. Challenging the office-holder's conduct of the proceeding

12.27 Unsurprisingly, office-holders are liable for any breaches of their various duties. Thus, for example, misfeasance proceedings could be taken against a liquidator or supervisor under section 212 and against an administrator under paragraph 75 of Schedule B1. The more novel feature of the court's supervisory jurisdiction over office-holders lies in its ability (on application) to intervene to reverse or modify the office-holder's acts and decisions.

12.28 As with the power to apply for directions, there is no universal provision dealing with applications of this nature. Instead there are differently worded provisions in respect of each procedure and, in contrast to the directions provisions, some of the differences in wording are material to the relief which is available.[39]

12.29 Consistently with the general principle applicable to all insolvency proceedings, these provisions are only available to persons with a sufficient interest and to ensure the proper conduct of the proceeding for its proper purposes.[40] These provisions do not exist to support extraneous interests or to facilitate officious interference by busybodies.

a. Liquidation

12.30 Section 168(5) provides that any person who is aggrieved by an act or decision of a liquidator in a compulsory liquidation may apply to the court and the court may confirm, modify, or reverse that act or decision and make such order as it thinks fit. A creditor or contributory can invoke the same jurisdiction in a voluntary liquidation by an application under section 112. Such an application raises two questions: first, whether the applicant is an aggrieved person and, secondly, the test to be satisfied in order to warrant interference by the court.

12.31 The locus standi of the applicant was addressed by Peter Gibson LJ in *Mahomed v Morris (No 2)* where he said in the context of an application by sureties:[41]

> The words 'any person ... aggrieved' are very wide at first sight and are not on their face limited to creditors and contributories. The provision goes back a long way. It first appeared as s.24 of the Companies (Winding up) Act 1890. It was borrowed from s.90 of the Bankruptcy Act 1883 which was enacted in part to remedy the injustice created by the disability of the bankrupt to sue, even where he had been gravely wronged by his assignee ... With a solitary exception no authority has been cited to us where a person not being a creditor or contributory has been allowed to apply under the subsection. That exception is *Re Hans Place Ltd.* In that case a

---

[39] *Re London & Westcountry Estates Ltd* [2014] EWHC 763 (Ch), [2014] Bus LR 441 [16].
[40] As to the general principle, see *Deloitte & Touche AG v Johnson* [1999] 1 WLR 1605 (PC) 1611B.
[41] [2001] BCC 233 (CA) [24]–[26] (internal citations omitted).

landlord was held able to challenge under s.168(5) the exercise by a liquidator of the power conferred on liquidators by s.178 of the Insolvency Act 1986 to disclaim onerous property such as a lease. But there must be some limit to the class of persons who can complain under s.168(5). An example is provided in *Re Edennote Ltd*. Nourse LJ (with whom Millett LJ agreed) said of applicants under s.168(5) who were both unsecured creditors and persons denied an opportunity to purchase an asset of a company in compulsory liquidation sold by the liquidators:

'In the latter capacity alone, like any other outsider to the liquidation, they would not have had the locus standi to apply under s.168(5).'

… In general I respectfully agree with the sentence which I have cited from *Edennote*. It could not have been the intention of Parliament that any outsider to the liquidation, dissatisfied with some act or decision of the liquidator, could attack that act or decision by the special procedure of s.168(5). However, I would accept that someone, like the landlord in *Hans Place Ltd*, who is directly affected by the exercise of a power given specifically to liquidators, and who would not otherwise have any right to challenge the exercise of that power, can utilise s.168(5). It may be that other persons can properly bring themselves within the subsection. But the mere fact that the act or decision is that of a liquidator in respect of an asset of the company the proceeds of which would be available for unsecured creditors is not enough, as can be seen from the example of the persons denied an opportunity to buy an asset of the company from the liquidators in *Edennote*. Nor in my view is it enough that the person claiming to be aggrieved by the act or decision of the liquidator in respect of assets of the company is a surety when his subrogation rights do not in any way depend on the company being in liquidation.

A person who can show that the liquidator's decision affects the amount of the distribution that they stand to receive in the liquidation will always have locus standi to apply under section 168(5).[42]

It is well established that the test to be satisfied by the applicant before the **12.32** court will reverse or modify the act or decision of the liquidator is a very high one. In the absence of fraud or bad faith, the court will not interfere unless the liquidator has done something so completely unreasonable and absurd that no reasonable person would have done it. This approach is wholly consistent with the approach to applications for directions where the court eschews any assumption of the office-holder's responsibility to take commercial and administrative decisions.[43]

b. Administration

Paragraph 74 of Schedule B1 provides for challenges to an administrator's conduct **12.33** of the company. This is the most elaborate formulation of the type of relief under consideration in this section of this chapter. A creditor or member of a company in

---

[42] *Re Edennote Ltd* [1996] BCC 718 (CA) 721.

[43] *Re A Debtor, ex parte the Debtor v Dodwell* [1949] 1 Ch 236 (Ch) 241; *Leon v York-O-Matic Ltd* [1966] 1 WLR 1450 (Ch); *Re Edennote Ltd* ibid at 722.

administration may apply to the court on the ground that the administrator has acted, is acting, or is proposing to act so as to unfairly harm the interests of the applicant (alone or with others). It does not matter for these purposes whether or not the administrator is acting within his statutory powers or even whether the administrator is acting in reliance upon an order permitting him to sell charged or hire-purchase property. Alternatively, an application can be made on the ground that the administrator is not performing his functions as quickly or as efficiently as is reasonably possible. The court has an unfettered discretion as to the order which it may make, which may regulate the administrator's exercise of his functions, require him to do or not do something, require a creditors' decision to be sought, and provide for his appointment to cease to have effect. There are, however, constraints in that an order under paragraph 74 may not impede or prevent the implementation of a company voluntary arrangement, a scheme of arrangement, or the administrator's proposals (or revised proposals) if approved more than twenty-eight days before the paragraph 75 application was made.

12.34 In contrast to section 168(5) (the provenance of which lies in the Bankruptcy Acts) paragraph 74 derives from the unfair prejudice provisions of the Companies Acts[44] but comparisons with the latter can be misleading:

a) The Companies Act provisions are only available to members whereas paragraph 74 is available to both members and creditors. In practice, it is much more likely to be used by creditors.

b) The concept of unfair prejudice affecting a member of a company relates to relationships between members whereas unfair harm, in the context of administration, must be judged by reference to the object of administration and the administrator's Schedule B1 duties.[45]

12.35 The scope of paragraph 74 has been clarified in the following respects:

a) The applicant must establish unfair harm in his capacity as a member or creditor.[46]

b) Interests are wider than rights.[47]

c) There must be a causative link between the alleged unfairness and harm relied on to make the application.[48]

---

[44] Now found in Part 30 of the Companies Act 2006.

[45] *Re Lehman Brothers International (Europe)* [2008] EWHC 2869 (Ch), [2009] 1 BCLC 161 [39].

[46] *Re New Oxford Street Property Ltd (in administration), Somethin' Outta Nothing Ent Ltd & Ors v Andronikou & Ors* [2012] EWHC 2462 (Ch) [102]; *Re Zegna III Holdings Inc* [2009] EWHC 2994 (Ch), [2010] BPIR 277 [24]; *Re London & Westcountry Estates Ltd* [2014] EWHC 763 (Ch), [2014] Bus LR 441[14].

[47] *Re Sam Weller Ltd* [1990] Ch 682 (Ch) 690B; *Re Charnley Davies Ltd (No 2)* [1990] BCC 605 (Ch) 624.

[48] *Re Kilnoore Ltd* [2005] EWHC 1410 (Ch), [2006] Ch 489 [66]; *Re Lehman Brothers International (Europe)* (n 17).

d) Harm will not be unfair if it is merely the product of the administrator seeking in good faith to perform his functions in the interests of the creditors as a whole.[49]

e) Unfairness will usually, but not invariably, involve differential treatment of persons with the same class of interests.[50]

f) However, differential treatment will not, of itself, necessarily be unfair.[51]

g) In contrast to section 168(5), there is no need to establish that the administrator's conduct was perverse.[52]

Paragraph 74 provides a much more refined and sophisticated jurisdiction to inter-   **12.36**
fere with the conduct of an administrator than section 168(5) provides in the case of a liquidation. However, the cumulative effect of the foregoing propositions is also to put a heavy onus on the applicant to justify interference. The same reluctance on the part of the courts to usurp the commercial decision-making of the office-holder is again exhibited. As Neuberger J said in *Re CE King Ltd* on a counterparty's application for directions to be given to administrators to perform a contract:[53]

> First, prima facie, what the administrators should do about the Kodak contract is a commercial decision. Secondly, at least in principle and in general, it is not for the court to interfere with such commercial decisions: those are to be left to the administrator. Thirdly, if the administrators are proposing to take a course which is based on a wrong appreciation of the law and/or is conspicuously unfair to a particular creditor or contractor of the company, then the court can and, in an appropriate case, should be prepared to interfere. I put it in that somewhat neutral way because even if it is appropriate for the court to interfere, the actual course the court should take must depend inevitably on the actual facts and circumstances of the case.

c. Company voluntary arrangements

Section 7(3) provides that any creditor or other person who is dissatisfied by an   **12.37**
act, omission, or decision of a supervisor may apply to the court and the court may confirm, modify, or reverse that act or decision, give the supervisor directions, or make such other order as it thinks fit. (It should be noted that this jurisdiction is distinct from that conferred on the court under section 6 to set aside the approval of a voluntary arrangement when challenged on the grounds of unfair prejudice or material irregularity.) In *Holdenhurst Securities Plc v Cohen*, Laddie J observed:[54]

---

[49] *Re Lehman Brothers International (Europe)* (n 17).

[50] *Re Coniston Hotel (Kent) LLP* [2013] EWHC 93 (Ch), [2013] 2 BCLC 405 [36]; *Re London & Westcountry Estates Ltd* (n 46).

[51] *Re Zegna III Holdings Inc* (n 46) [22].

[52] *Re New Oxford Street Property Ltd (in administration), Somethin' Outta Nothing Ent Ltd & Ors v Andronikou & Ors* above at [96]; *Re London & Westcountry Estates Ltd* (n 46) [16].

[53] [2000] 2 BCLC 297 (Ch) 302i.

[54] [2001] 1 BCLC 460 (Ch) [17].

No doubt it is true that the courts should be careful not to allow the wide words of s7(3) to be used as a means for allowing the expensive and time consuming ventilation of claims which are likely to be fruitless.

12.38 In *County Bookshops Ltd v Grove*,[55] Neuberger J made an order under section 7(3) determining that a claimant was entitled to prove in a CVA but the judgment does not include any analysis of the scope of the section.

12.39 Although the language of section 7(3) is not the same as that of section 168(5) (for example, the omission of the reference to an 'aggrieved' person), it is difficult to discern any substantive difference. It is thought that section 7(3) replicates the jurisdiction under section 168(5), albeit in modernized language.[56] If that is correct, the perversity test applies.

---

[55] [2002] EWHC 1160 (Ch), [2002] BPIR 772.
[56] See further *Stericker v Horner* [2012] BPIR 645 (Ch) [38] where HHJ Langan QC appeared minded to favour the 'aggrieved person' test for locus standi.

13

REGULATION OF INSOLVENCY PRACTICE

Insolvency practice is highly regulated. Regulation is needed because, as described **13.01** in earlier chapters, the day-to-day conduct of insolvency proceedings is entrusted to office-holders and the supervisory jurisdiction exercised by the court is both selective and triggered by application.

Regulation is achieved through a combination of government control and the **13.02** licensing of insolvency practitioners by a small number of 'recognized professional bodies' (RPBs) which are then responsible for ensuring their respective practitioners' compliance with both the law and practice standards. Within government, insolvency law and practice is primarily the responsibility of the Department of Business, Energy & Industrial Strategy (BEIS) which acts through the Insolvency Service, an executive agency of BEIS.[1]

---

[1] The general background to the current system of regulation was described in The Insolvency Service, *Oversight regulation and monitoring in the insolvency profession* (June 2014) <https://www.gov.uk/government/publications/insolvency-practitioner-regulation-oversight-and-monitoring-of-authorising-bodies> accessed 28 October 2016.

1. The regulators and the regulated

a. The Insolvency Service

13.03 The Insolvency Service (which deals with both corporate and personal insolvency) has a number of distinct strands of activity: policy, regulatory oversight, investigation, and enforcement in connection with corporate malpractice (disqualification and prosecution), some case administration, and paying statutory redundancy payments when employers default.

13.04 As part of its policy functions, the Insolvency Service initiates the secondary legislation which is made pursuant to the rule-making powers contained in the Act. Those rule-making powers expressly cover making regulations for the purposes of Part XIII of the Act (Insolvency Practitioners and their Qualification).[2] An unusual feature of the process for making secondary legislation is the existence of the Insolvency Rules Committee which must be consulted before rules are made.[3] The committee is chaired by a High Court judge and its other members are a circuit judge, a registrar in bankruptcy, a district judge, a practising barrister, a practising solicitor, and a practising accountant (the absence of any requirement for the Committee to include an authorized insolvency practitioner from this list is unfortunate but can be overcome if one or more of the practitioner members holds a licence). The Insolvency Service provides the secretariat for the committee.

13.05 Direct case administration by the Insolvency Service is undertaken through a network of twenty-three official receivers' offices serving different courts.[4] With limited exceptions, the appropriate official receiver becomes the first liquidator when a winding-up order is made and will thereafter continue to administer the estate if no private sector liquidator is appointed or if a vacancy arises. By this means, English law ensures that a terminal insolvency procedure is always an available option notwithstanding any difficulty in securing the services of a private sector insolvency practitioner. If the circumstances of a case warrant it, the official receiver can be appointed as provisional liquidator before a winding-up order is made.

13.06 In the context of the regulation of insolvency practice, the Insolvency Service acts as the regulator of regulators. It finances its functions in this respect by charging a levy on the RPBs according to the numbers they have each authorized.

---

[2] Section 419.
[3] Section 413. The courts occasionally suggest matters warranting consideration by the Insolvency Rules Committee, see, for example, *Re Austintel Ltd* [1997] 1 WLR 616 (CA).
[4] Section 400.

b. Recognized professional bodies

A body can be designated as an RPB for the purposes of authorizing its insolvency **13.07** specialist members to act as insolvency practitioners if it regulates the practice of a profession and it has rules for securing that those members are fit and proper persons who meet required standards of education, training, and experience.[5] Its rules and practices must also be designed to ensure that the insolvency regulatory objectives are met (see below).[6]

The legislation does not specify what makes a practitioner a fit and proper person or **13.08** what is required in respect of education, training, and experience. These matters are instead dealt with in a Memorandum of Understanding between the Insolvency Service and the RPBs.[7] A key requirement is that an applicant for authorization (who has not previously held an authorization) should have passed examinations set by the Joint Insolvency Examination Board.

There are currently five RPBs: the Chartered Association of Certified Accountants, **13.09** the Institute of Chartered Accountants in Ireland, the Insolvency Practitioners Association, the Institute of Chartered Accountants in England & Wales, and the Institute of Chartered Accountants of Scotland.[8] However, by sections 144 to 146 of the Small Business, Enterprise and Employment Act 2015, the Secretary of State took a reserved power to establish a single regulator. The Insolvency Service said of this in its 2015 Annual Review:[9]

> A power has been taken to enable a single regulator to be introduced in place of the current system. This would need to be used by October 2022 and any such move would be subject to consultation and further changes to the law. This power will significantly shape the work that the Insolvency Service carries out in the next few years to evaluate the effectiveness of the current regulatory system.

---

[5] 'Members' has an expanded meaning for these purposes which includes persons who are subject to the RPB's insolvency practice rules: section 391(7).

[6] Section 391. The Act permits recognition limited to the grant of partial authorization (see below under 'Insolvency practitioners') but all the current recognized professional bodies are recognized for the purposes of both full and partial authorization.

[7] See <https://www.gov.uk/government/uploads/system/uploads/attachment_data/file/301579/MoU_between_RPBs_and_SoS_October_2011.doc> accessed 28 October 2016. (The need for the Memorandum of Understanding, following the introduction of the regulatory objectives described below, is under review.)

[8] Insolvency Practitioners (Recognised Professional Bodies) Order 1986 (SI 1986/1764) as amended by the Insolvency Practitioners (Recognised Professional Bodies) (Revocation of Recognition) Orders 2015 and 2016 (SI 2015/2067 and SI 2016/403). The Chartered Accountants Regulatory Board acts on behalf of the Institute of Chartered Accountants in Ireland.

[9] The Insolvency Service, *2015 Annual Review of Insolvency Practitioner Regulation* (March 2016) 4 <https://www.gov.uk/government/publications/insolvency-practitioner-regulation-process-review-2015> accessed 28 October 2016.

c. Joint Insolvency Committee

13.10 The Joint Insolvency Committee was formed in 1999 to provide a forum for the development of a co-ordinated approach to insolvency regulation. Its membership includes representatives of the RPBs and the Insolvency Service and others. The committee was responsible for the development of the Code of Ethics and settles the Statements of Insolvency Practice, both of which are referred to in more detail below.

d. Insolvency practitioners

13.11 Insolvency practitioners are to be distinguished from office-holders. To be an insolvency practitioner is to hold a qualification; to be an office-holder is to hold an appointment. Prior to the Act taking effect, when the only relevant corporate insolvency appointment was that of liquidator, there were only two restrictions: first, there was an outright prohibition on the appointment of a body corporate (any purported appointment being void) and, secondly, it was an offence for an undischarged bankrupt to act as a liquidator.[10] Although the majority of cases were properly conducted, there was clearly scope for abuse.

13.12 The Cork Report noted:[11]

> The success of any insolvency system, however, is very largely dependent upon those who administer it. If they do not have the confidence and respect, not only of the courts and creditors and debtors, but also of the general public, then complaints will multiply and, if remedial action is not taken, the system will fall into disrepute and disuse.

and advanced proposals for office-holders to hold a qualification to act as such. Those proposals were taken up by the government, which said in the White Paper which preceded the 1985/86 reforms:[12]

> It is desirable that the public should have trust in those who handle insolvencies and the Government recognises that the present law which allows persons with no

---

[10] Sections 187 and 335 Companies Act 1948 (see also rule 168 Companies (Winding-Up) Rules 1949 (SI 1949/330)). Before the decision in *Re Gertzenstein Ltd* [1937] 1 Ch 115 (Ch), appointments in insolvent liquidations were usually taken by solicitors or accountants. However, in *Gertzenstein*, it was held that a solicitor liquidator could not be paid for his professional legal services in addition to his remuneration as liquidator and solicitors largely withdrew from the market. Rules 2.106(8) and 4.128(3) of the Insolvency Rules 1986 (SI 1986/1925) made express provision for approval of the payment of profit costs where a solicitor office-holder employed his own firm but those rules are not replicated in the 2016 Rules and it is thought that such costs are now to be treated in the same way as other remuneration and expenses.

[11] Report of the Review Committee, *Insolvency Law and Practice* (Cm 8558, June 1982) para 732.

[12] Department of Trade and Industry, *A Revised Framework for Insolvency Law* (White Paper, Cm 9175, February 1984) para 8.

practical experience or relevant professional qualification to act as ... liquidator ... is unsatisfactory.

It is now an offence to act as the office-holder in English insolvency proceedings when not qualified to do so. In order to be so qualified, an individual has, amongst other things, to have been authorized to act as an insolvency practitioner.[13]

Amendments to the Act by the Deregulation Act 2015 enable RPBs to grant either full or partial authorization. Full authorization permits the practitioner to act as office-holder in respect of both companies and individuals whereas partial authorization is limited to one or the other.[14] **13.13**

There are approximately 1650 insolvency practitioners authorized pursuant to the Act. Active appointment-taking insolvency practitioners are subject to monitoring by the RPBs to ensure that their cases are conducted in accordance with the law and good practice. **13.14**

2. Regulatory functions and regulatory objectives

The regulatory functions of an RPB are its functions in relation to the authorization and regulation of insolvency practitioners. An RPB must, as far as is reasonably practicable, discharge those functions in a way which is both compatible with the regulatory objectives and which it considers most appropriate for meeting those objectives.[15] **13.15**

The 'regulatory objectives' are defined in section 391C: **13.16**

> (3) *'Regulatory objectives'* means the objectives of—
>   (a) having a system of regulating persons acting as insolvency practitioners that—
>   (i) secures fair treatment for persons affected by their acts and omissions,
>   (ii) reflects the regulatory principles, and
>   (iii) ensures consistent outcomes,
>   (b) encouraging an independent and competitive insolvency-practitioner profession whose members—
>   (i) provide high quality services at a cost to the recipient which is fair and reasonable,
>   (ii) act transparently and with integrity, and
>   (iii) consider the interests of all creditors in any particular case,

---

[13] The prohibition of companies and undischarged bankrupts now applies to administrators and supervisors of voluntary arrangements as well as liquidators. Persons subject to disqualification orders under the Company Directors Disqualification Act 1986 and persons who lack capacity within the meaning of the Mental Capacity Act 2005 are also disqualified. See generally section 390(1) and (4).

[14] Section 390A.

[15] Section 391B(1).

(c) promoting the maximisation of the value of returns to creditors and promptness in making those returns, and

(d) protecting and promoting the public interest.

'Regulatory principles', for these purposes, means that activities should be transparent, accountable, proportionate, consistent, and targeted only at cases which warrant action, and also any other principle appearing to lead to best regulatory practice.[16]

13.17 In discharging functions in relation to insolvency practitioners and their qualification, the Secretary of State must also have regard to the regulatory objectives.[17]

3. Bonding

13.18 In addition to holding authorization from an RPB, an insolvency practitioner may not accept appointment as an office-holder unless there is security in force for the proper performance of his obligations.[18] The required form of security is a bond whereby the surety accepts joint and several liability for losses resulting from fraud or dishonesty. The requirements are detailed but, in summary, the amount of the cover is the combination of a specific penalty sum which is referable to the value of the estate (up to a maximum of £5,000,000) and a general penalty sum of a further £250,000. The surety's total liability for the practitioner under all bonds relating to him can be limited to an aggregate sum of not less than £25,000,000. The practitioner's bond is the only statutory requirement but insolvency practitioners also have to comply with the requirements of their respective RPBs as regards professional indemnity cover.

13.19 The bonding requirements are the subject of ongoing review by the Insolvency Service.[19] There are various perceived weaknesses in the present system which derives from requirements originally introduced in 1986.[20] Amongst other deficiencies noted by the Insolvency Service, the present system relies on the honesty of a potentially dishonest insolvency practitioner to obtain cover. There is also no hypothecation of the proceeds of claims; the proceeds are paid into the estate instead of being used to provide redress for the creditors who have been adversely

---

[16] Section 391C(4).

[17] Section 391B(2).

[18] Section 390(3); Insolvency Practitioners Regulations 2005 (SI 2005/524) Part 3 and Schedule 2 (alternative requirements for practitioners already established in another EEA state are outside the scope of this work).

[19] The Insolvency Service, *2015 Annual Review of Insolvency Practitioner Regulation* (March 2016) (n 9) 12.

[20] The Insolvency Service, *Bonding arrangements for insolvency practitioners: Call for Evidence* (15 September 2016) <https://www.gov.uk/government/consultations/bonding-arrangements-for-insolvency-practitioners-call-for-evidence> accessed 28 October 2016.

affected by the practitioner's fraud—an outcome which looks anomalous when contrasted with the effects of the Third Parties (Rights against Insurers) Act 2010.

4. Regulatory tools

The requirements of good practice are represented by the common Code of Ethics **13.20** and a series of Statements of Insolvency Practice (SIPs), all promulgated by the Joint Insolvency Committee (JIC).[21] The Code sets out fundamental principles of integrity, objectivity, professional competence and due care, confidentiality, and professional behaviour. It specifies the requirements of practitioners in respect of the identification and evaluation of threats and possible safeguards before illustrating the application of the fundamental principles to a number of commonly encountered issues. The issues include consideration of the circumstances in which previous relationships may make it improper for an insolvency practitioner to accept appointment as an office-holder.

The drafting and content of the SIPs are markedly different. SIPs deal with the **13.21** requirements of best practice in a number of different respects all of which serve to supplement the governing legislation. Examples of the subjects covered are office-holders' remuneration, disposals to directors, and pre-packing. The approach to drafting has changed and is now based on the expression of generally worded principles. This alternative to secondary legislation has the dual advantages, from a regulatory point of view, of encouraging practitioners to follow the spirit of best practice and enabling best practice to be developed in a more timely and flexible manner than might otherwise be the case.

Breaches of the Code and the SIPs expose the errant insolvency practitioner to **13.22** disciplinary action.

In addition, the Insolvency Service periodically issues Insolvency Guidance Papers **13.23** and sends 'Dear IP' letters to all insolvency practitioners which contain a mixture of alerts and indications of the Service's view on current issues. The Guidance Papers and the consolidated Dear IP letters can be accessed through the Service's website.[22]

---

[21] The Code of Ethics can be found on the Insolvency Service website <https://www.gov.uk/government/publications/insolvency-practitioner-code-of-ethics> but the most convenient way to access the Statements of Insolvency Practice is via the website of R3, the trade association of insolvency practitioners <https://www.r3.org.uk/what-we-do/publications/professional/statements-of-insolvency-practice> both accessed 28 October 2016.

[22] See <https://www.gov.uk/government/organisations/insolvency-service accessed 23 January 2017.

5. The regulatory waterfall

13.24 As already said, the Insolvency Service acts as the regulator of regulators; it is responsible for the oversight of the RPBs and its more detailed requirements in this respect are contained in the Memorandum of Understanding referred to above.

13.25 The regulation of individual insolvency practitioners is primarily the responsibility of the RPBs but the Insolvency Service has residual powers of direct regulatory intervention. All these powers result from recent amendments to the Act made by the Small Business, Enterprise and Employment Act 2015 and their overall effect therefore remains to be seen.

13.26 The regulatory powers which are exercisable by the Secretary of State (through the Insolvency Service) in respect of RPBs are powers to:

a) give directions (which can include directions as to regulatory proceedings to be taken by the RPB);
b) impose financial penalties;
c) publish a reprimand; and
d) revoke recognition.[23]

In introducing these powers, the Insolvency Service made it clear that they would normally expect to resolve matters without the need for recourse to sanctions:[24]

> The expectation is that these sanctions would not be used frequently and, in general, the Insolvency Service would seek to resolve matters directly with an RPB before commencing these procedures.

13.27 If an RPB fails to comply with any requirement imposed on it by or by virtue of the provisions of the Act dealing with insolvency practitioners and their qualification, the Secretary of State can apply to the court for a compliance order, that is to say an order that it take such steps as the court considers will secure compliance with the relevant requirement.[25]

13.28 The RPBs' regulatory control of the insolvency practitioners they have authorized is undertaken through their ability to set their own professional rules and, where necessary, to resort to their own disciplinary procedures. One of the problems of having five different RPBs is that someone wishing to make a complaint may not readily identify which is the relevant RPB to which they should address their

---

[23] Sections 391D to 391M.
[24] The Insolvency Service, *Insolvency practitioner regulation – regulatory objectives and oversight powers, Legislative changes introduced on 1 October 2015* (December 2015) 10 <https://www.gov.uk/government/publications/insolvency-practitioner-regulation-regulatory-objectives-and-oversight-powers> accessed 28 October 2016.
[25] Section 391T.

complaint. This potential difficulty is met by the Complaints Gateway operated by the Insolvency Service. Complaints submitted through the Complaints Gateway are filtered by the Service. Although the unmeritorious go no further, a majority of the complaints are referred on to the relevant RPB and the Service thereafter monitors progression and outcomes.[26]

Notwithstanding the primary responsibility of the RPBs for the regulation of their **13.29** own insolvency practitioners, if it is in the public interest to do so, the Secretary of State has the power to apply to the High Court for a direct sanctions order, that is to say an order that:

a) declares that a person is no longer authorized (or no longer fully authorized) to act as insolvency practitioner;
b) declares that a practitioner's authorization is suspended;
c) requires a practitioner to comply with specified requirements; or
d) requires a practitioner to make a contribution to one or more creditors of the company. (The amount of any such contribution must not exceed the practitioner's remuneration in the relevant case.)

Amongst other pre-conditions, such an order can only be made if the practitioner has failed to comply with the rules of his RPB or any standards, or code of ethics, adopted by the RPB. Where a direct sanctions order is made, the RPB must take all necessary steps to give effect to it.[27] The Insolvency Service has made it clear that, although it will generally leave it to the RPB to take appropriate action, there could be cases of egregious or generalized misconduct in which it will consider that action by the RPB will not be sufficient.[28]

If the pre-conditions for the making of a direct sanctions order are satisfied and if it **13.30** is in the public interest to do so, the Secretary of State may issue a direct sanctions direction to the relevant RPB instead of making or pursuing an application for an order. A direct sanctions direction covers the same range of sanctions as an order. It cannot be made without the consent of the practitioner concerned but, if made, also requires the RPB to take all necessary steps to secure its effect. A direct sanctions direction is therefore a mechanism for the consensual disposal of cases which has some parallels with director disqualification undertakings.[29]

---

[26] See further: The Insolvency Service, *Review of handling of complaints about Insolvency Practitioners* (September 2016) <https://www.gov.uk/government/uploads/system/uploads/attachment_data/file/554113/Review_of_handling_of_complaints_about_insolvency_practitioners.pdf>, and *Insolvency practitioners: guidance on how to complain about an insolvency practitioner* (updated 19 May 2016) <https://www.gov.uk/government/publications/insolvency-practitioners-guidance-for-those-who-want-to-complain/insolvency-practitioners-guidance-on-how-to-complain-about-an-insolvency-practitioner> both accessed 23 January 2017.
[27] Sections 391O to 391Q.
[28] The Insolvency Service, *Insolvency practitioner regulation – regulatory objectives and oversight powers, Legislative changes introduced on 1 October 2015* (December 2015) (n 24) 17, 18.
[29] Section 391R.

14

THE INSOLVENT ESTATE

1. Introduction

14.01 The insolvent estate is comprised of the property which is the subject matter of an insolvency proceeding. It is important that there is clarity in this respect. If the proceeding is distributive, the estate is the property which will be realized for the benefit of the creditors; if it is reorganizational, the estate is the property which will be protected by any stay and which may be the subject of the reorganization. The Act does not define the insolvent estate for the purposes of its corporate insolvency provisions; the crucial term used by the Act is 'property'.[1]

14.02 Section 143 provides that the functions of the liquidator, in a compulsory liquidation, are '… to secure that the assets of the company are got in, realised and distributed …'. The term 'assets' is also undefined but the meaning becomes clear from section 144 which provides that the liquidator '… shall take into his custody or under his control all the property and things in action to which the company is or appears to be entitled'.[2] 'Assets' in section 143 means property to which the company is actually entitled; the wider duty to take into his custody property to which the company *appears* to be entitled is consistent with his function of securing and

---

[1] There is a definition in rule 1.2 for the purposes of the Rules.
[2] The reference to 'things in action' is superfluous—see section 436 below.

protecting the estate (as a precautionary or protective measure), but it is no part of the liquidator's functions to realize and distribute property to which the company is not in fact entitled. The position in voluntary liquidation is more straightforward: section 107 provides that in a voluntary liquidation the company's property shall be applied in satisfaction of its liabilities.

Paragraph 67 of Schedule B1 provides that an administrator shall take custody **14.03** or control of all the property to which he thinks the company is entitled. This is the same protective function as that for which section 144 provides in the case of a compulsory liquidation. Thereafter, paragraph 68 provides for him to manage the company's affairs, business, and property in accordance with any approved proposals and any directions of the court. Meanwhile, paragraphs 42 to 44 apply the moratorium in administration which, amongst other things, protects the company's property from security enforcement and legal process.

A company voluntary arrangement (CVA) is either a composition in satisfaction **14.04** of its debts or a scheme of arrangement of its affairs. Although many arrangements will be concerned with the realization and distribution of an insolvent estate, the flexibility of the procedure is such that the content of the insolvent estate does not have the same inevitable relevance to voluntary arrangements as it does to liquidations and administrations. The starting point must always be the terms of the arrangement itself. Where the arrangement is concerned with realization and distribution, the estate for the purposes of the procedure is likely to be the same as it would be in a liquidation or administration but it is conceivable that an arrangement may be dealing with something less than the totality of a company's property—for example where non-core assets are to be realized immediately and the company is to be left with the assets which are essential for the future conduct of its business.

2. The meaning of 'property'

'Property' is amongst the 'expressions generally used' whose meanings are explained **14.05** in section 436. That section provides that, except in so far as the context may otherwise require, 'property':

> includes money, goods, things in action, land and every description of property wherever situated and also obligations and every description of interest, whether present or future or vested or contingent, arising out of, or incidental to, property.

Strictly speaking, section 436 does not provide a definition (although it is often referred to as such):

a) the word 'includes' instead of 'means' shows that it is not intended to be exhaustive; and

b) the use of the word 'property' to elucidate the statutory meaning of 'property' demonstrates that any examination of the scope of the term begins with the ordinary or dictionary meaning of property.

As a matter of ordinary usage 'property' can have a number of meanings (for example, it can mean the attributes of a thing or phenomenon) but, in the case of section 436, the word is being used in its most common sense of something which is owned.

14.06 The breadth of the meaning of 'property' reflects a long established principle of insolvency law. In *Hollinshead v Hazleton*, Lord Atkinson referred to the:[3]

> ... principle of public policy, which has found expression in the provisions of the Bankruptcy Codes of both England and Ireland for close on half a century, as estimable and as conducive to the welfare of the community as any. It is this, that in bankruptcy the entire property of the bankrupt, of whatever kind or nature it be, whether alienable or inalienable, subject to be taken in execution, legal or equitable, or not so subject, shall, with the exception of some compassionate allowances for his maintenance, be appropriated and made available for the payment of his creditors.

The modern concept of the insolvent estate differs between corporate and personal insolvency law. Thus:

a) section 283 defines a bankrupt's estate by reference to the property of the bankrupt at the commencement of the bankruptcy thereby necessitating the rules on after-acquired property which form part of the bankruptcy regime;

b) some personal effects and personal injury compensation are excluded from the bankrupt's estate (what Lord Atkinson called 'compassionate allowances'); and

c) section 306 provides that it is the bankrupt's estate (as so defined) which vests in the trustee in bankruptcy with the consequence that property which does not vest continues to belong to the debtor.[4]

By contrast, the insolvent estate of a company is not limited to property belonging to the company at the commencement of its liquidation or administration.[5] Another important consideration is that, apart from the very rare cases in which a vesting order is made pursuant to section 145, there is no vesting of the company's property in its liquidator or administrator. The office-holder exercises his powers over the company's property as an agent thereby excluding the potential issues which can arise between the debtor and his/her trustee in a bankruptcy case. This makes the concept of the insolvent estate in corporate insolvency more straightforward. (A number of the bankruptcy cases are nonetheless relevant to questions

---

[3] [1916] 1 AC 428 (HL) 436.

[4] See further *Re Oasis Merchandising Ltd* [1998] Ch 170 (CA) 180E.

[5] *The Connaught Income Fund, Series 1 v Capita Financial Managers Ltd* [2014] EWHC 3619 (Comm) [50].

arising on the margins of the section 436 formulation, but the underlying differences between the regimes need to be borne in mind.)

The nature of the rights and interests which make up the insolvent estate of a company is not changed by the advent of insolvency proceedings.[6] The general principle is that an insolvency office-holder takes the property comprising the insolvent estate 'subject to all equities'. In *Re Scheibler, ex parte Holthausen*, James LJ said:[7]   **14.07**

> ... with certain exceptions, the trustee in bankruptcy is bound by all the equities which affect a bankrupt or liquidating debtor; that is to say, if a bankrupt or liquidating debtor, under circumstances which are not impeachable under any particular provision connected with his bankruptcy or insolvency, enters into a contract with respect to his real estate for a valuable consideration, that contract binds his trustee in bankruptcy as much as it binds himself.

Although James LJ referred to contracts binding the debtor, it is important to note that equities are proprietary rights which are enforceable against property and that the principle does not apply to purely personal obligations.

Browne-Wilkson V-C observed of section 436 in *Bristol Airport Plc v Powdrill*[8] that   **14.08**
'It is hard to think of a wider definition of property.' and went on to hold that the specifically enforceable rights of the lessee under a lease of an aircraft constituted property. Questions nonetheless have arisen as to whether the apparent breadth of the meaning of the term is restricted by reference to whether rights and interests need to be:

a) such as confer a benefit on the company;
b) legally enforceable;
c) transferrable; or
d) of realizable value

in order to qualify as 'property'. It is to be observed, by way of preliminary comment, that none of those characteristics are reflected in the actual wording of section 436 and that, if anything is excluded because it lacks one or more of those characteristics, a question arises as to what consequence that has for the office-holder's powers.

a. Benefit or entitlement

In *Re SSSL Realisations (2002) Ltd*, Lloyd J (whose judgment in this respect was   **14.09**
expressly approved by the Court of Appeal) said:[9]

---

[6] Unless the nature of the right or interest is such that it terminates according to its own terms (without infringing the anti-deprivation principle, as to which see Chapter 21).
[7] (1874) 9 Ch App 722 (CA) 726. See also *Re Anchor Line (Henderson Brothers) Ltd* [1937] 1 Ch 483 (Ch).
[8] [1990] 1 Ch 744 (CA) 759D.
[9] [2004] EWHC 1760 (Ch), [2005] 1 BCLC 1 [60], on appeal [2006] EWCA Civ 7, [2006] Ch 610 [35].

'Property' is defined by section 436 of the 1986 Act as [the words of the section were then quoted]. For present purposes the Deed imposes obligations on Group rather than conferring on it any rights. Although obligations feature in the definition, this is limited to obligations arising out of or incidental to property. Within a definition of property this might seem to be circular, but even taking 'property' in that context at its widest, the obligations under the Deed cannot be said to be to do with property in any way. It seems to me that for something to qualify as 'property', it must involve some element of benefit or entitlement for the person holding it, which is not true of the deed as regards Group or any of the other indemnitors in present circumstances; the indemnitors have already had the benefit for which they entered into the deed. Moreover, even if this is wrong and the obligations under the deed could be regarded as property, it cannot fairly be described as property which is 'unsaleable or not readily saleable'. In itself that phrase seems to confirm the last proposition, that there must be, potentially at least, some benefit or entitlement arising from the thing in question.

Although the requirement for property to involve some element of benefit or entitlement is a gloss on the statutory formulation, it is consonant with 'property' being accorded the meaning of something which is owned. A person is not ordinarily considered to be the owner of his own obligations to others. As is apparent, Lloyd J was considering what constituted onerous property for the purposes of disclaimer under section 178[10] but that does not detract from the more general force of his observations. The requirement for benefit or entitlement does not raise difficult questions about the office-holder's duties and powers in respect of obligations which are not incidental to property because obligations are liabilities and fall to be dealt with as such.

b. Legal enforceability

14.10 The courts have taken an expansive view of the nature of the rights and interests which can constitute property. Thus, in *Webster v Ashcroft*[11] rights by virtue of an equitable proprietary estoppel were held to be property and, in *Re Hemming (dec'd)*,[12] the right of a residuary legatee to compel the due administration of a deceased's estate was also held to be property. The more difficult question is whether some form of legal enforceability is an indispensable feature of property.

14.11 In *Re Rae*, a debtor's 'entitlement' to fishing licences was held to constitute property on the ground that it was an interest which was incidental to the debtor's ownership of fishing vessels. The case is of interest in this context because the debtor's own licences had terminated by virtue of his bankruptcy and he had no legally enforceable rights. However, the licence issuing authority recognized, as a matter of ministerial discretion, an entitlement in respect of the grant of new licences

---

[10] As to which see Chapter 15.
[11] [2011] EWHC 3848 (Ch), [2012] 1 WLR 1309.
[12] [2008] EWHC 2731 (Ch), [2009] Ch 313 [34], [35].

which had a marketable value. Warner J held that the entitlement fell within the words of section 436 but rejected an even wider approach saying:[13]

> I am not persuaded that one can, merely from a consideration of the purposes of the Insolvency Act and the non-exhaustive nature of the definition of 'property' in s436, reach the conclusion that any asset of the bankrupt which can be realised or turned to account is 'property' within the meaning of the Act.

It appears from this authority that a legally enforceable right is not an indispensable characteristic of property. However, it is suggested that Warner J was correct to reject the wider proposition, which failed adequately to distinguish between the nature of property and mere opportunity.

c. Transferability

Notwithstanding Lord Atkinson's reference in *Hollinshead v Hazleton* to property 'whether alienable or inalienable', a number of cases have treated transferability as a necessary quality in order for a right or interest to be regarded as property under the Act. A particularly clear example is *Re Celtic Extraction Ltd* where the Court of Appeal held that waste management licences issued pursuant to the Environmental Protection Act 1990 were property for the purposes of section 436 (and capable of disclaimer pursuant to section 178). Morritt LJ (with whom the other members of the court agreed) reviewed the authorities on the question of whether statutory licences or exemptions were capable of being property and concluded:[14]

14.12

> It seems to me that these cases indicate the salient features which are likely to be found if there is to be conferred on an exemption from some wider statutory prohibition the status of property. First, there must be a statutory framework conferring an entitlement on one who satisfies certain conditions even though there is some element of discretion exercisable within that framework ... Second, the exemption must be transferrable ... Third, the exemption or licence will have value ...

Another such case is *Dear v Reeves* where the Court of Appeal held that a pre-emption right was property for the purposes of section 436. Mummery LJ said:[15]

> A distinguishing feature of a right of property, in contrast to a purely personal right, is that it is transferable: it may be enforced by someone other than the particular person in whom the right was initially vested.

before holding that the pre-emption right in question had that quality because it was expressed to be assignable.

In *Re GP Aviation Group International Ltd* the issue was whether a right of appeal against what would otherwise be a tax liability of a company in liquidation was

14.13

---

[13] [1995] BCC 102 (Ch).
[14] [2001] Ch 475 (CA) [33].
[15] [2001] EWCA Civ 277, [2002] Ch 1 [40].

property within the meaning of section 436. Having carefully reviewed the authorities on rights of appeal, HH Judge Pelling QC said:[16]

> All this leads me to conclude that a bare right to appeal is not property within the meaning of section 436 of the 1986 Act ... a right to appeal available to a company in liquidation can only be exercised by the office-holder once appointed because he she or they then become the only agents of the company entitled to do so. Again, however that is not the result of the right of appeal being treated as a property interest.

The position of an administrator would be the same as that of a liquidator because there is no material difference in their powers in this respect. The issue of transferability arose in *GP Aviation* in reverse order—the argument being that the right of appeal was assignable because it was property (rather than that it was property because it was assignable). This illustrates the potential difficulty in dispensing with the requirement of transferability, namely that it may result in rights and interests which are, by their nature, inalienable becoming so in the hands of an office-holder. The requirement for transferability is consistent with the general principle that the office-holder takes the property in the insolvent estate as he finds it.[17]

14.14 There is a limited incursion to that general principle in that it is well established law that an office-holder can use his statutory power to sell a cause of action which forms part of the insolvent estate without any issues as to maintenance and champerty.[18] The bankruptcy authority on this point is the decision of the Court of Appeal in *Ramsey v Hartley*.[19] The Court of Appeal referred to that decision in *Bang & Olufsen UK Ltd v Ton Systeme Ltd*[20] where Balcombe LJ said:

> ... it was held [in that case] that an assignment made by a trustee in bankruptcy is valid if it is within the powers conferred by statute upon the trustee, notwithstanding that it might otherwise be held void for maintenance and champerty, because one may not automatically bring doctrines from other branches of the law into the statutory code of bankruptcy. There would appear to be no valid distinction on this point between the law of bankruptcy, and the law of insolvent company liquidation. They are both now governed by the Insolvency Act 1986, and there is no relevant difference between the two Schedules, Schedule 4, which deals with the powers of a liquidator in a winding up, and Schedule 5 which deals with the powers of a trustee in bankruptcy.

---

[16] [2013] EWHC 1447 (Ch), [2014] 1 WLR 166 [31].

[17] The decision in *Shlosberg v Avonwick Holdings Ltd* [2016] EWCA Civ 1138, that legal professional privilege is not property within the meaning of section 436 is also consistent with a requirement of transferability.

[18] The practical significance of these common law doctrines is now much reduced by various statutory measures facilitating litigation funding. Such arrangements are outside the scope of this book. The principle that an office-holder's statutory power of sale trumps such considerations remains valid.

[19] [1977] 1 WLR 686 (CA).

[20] (unreported), 16 July 1993 (CA), Transcript No 834 of 1993.

d. Realizable value

In *de Rothschild v Bell*, the Court of Appeal robustly rejected submissions **14.15** that rights in respect of a protected residential tenancy could not be property because they could not turned into money for a bankrupt's creditors. Buxton LJ said:[21]

> ... the issue under section 283 is whether the interest or right is, in juristic terms, 'property'. If the right is, in its legal nature, property, it only falls outside the bankrupt's estate by some specific exclusion. That in practical terms the 'property' when held by a bankrupt may be of no value to the creditors is nothing to the point.

This was another disclaimer case in which it was held that the interest was property because it was not inalienable. *De Rothschild* was followed in *Dear v Reeves* where Mummery LJ said of the relevant pre-emption right:[22]

> It is true that it may be difficult to put a value on it, as the grantor may never decide to sell the property, but it is not necessary for a right to have any present or immediate value for it to be 'property' within section 436. The relevant question is whether it is, in its legal nature, property.

e. Conclusions

All these refinements of the statutory meaning of property as explained in section **14.16** 436 are justifiable:

a) The requirement that, in order to be property, something must confer a benefit or entitlement on the company accords with the notion of property being the subject of ownership.
b) The recognition that property may, exceptionally, be found in the absence of legally enforceable rights preserves the expansive notion of property and gives the Act a purposive interpretation.
c) The requirement for transferability is at first sight unnecessarily restrictive but preserves the true nature of the company's rights and interests.
d) The irrelevance of immediately realizable value properly draws a distinction between the nature of property and what an office-holder may do with it in the exercise of his powers.

As *GP Aviation* demonstrates, the standing of the office-holder to exercise rights **14.17** and interests (or to exploit their commercial value by means other than sale) does not depend upon them being property within the meaning of section 436.

---

[21] [2000] QB 33 (CA) 48H.
[22] *Dear v Reeves* (n 15) [40].

3. Section 234

14.18 Reference has been made, in paragraphs 14.02 and 14.03 above, to the duties of liquidators and administrators to take into their custody property which belongs or appears to belong to the company and the point was made that this does not expand the concept of the insolvent estate. Section 234 contains important provisions in this respect. First, it provides the office-holder with a summary remedy to obtain delivery up of property to which the company appears to be entitled.[23] Secondly, it confers a qualified immunity upon an office-holder who seizes or disposes of property belonging to a third party whilst believing, on reasonable grounds, that he is entitled to do so. The office-holder is not liable for resultant loss or damage, unless it is caused by his own negligence, and he has a lien on the property (or its proceeds of sale) for his expenses.

14.19 It has been held that the court is able to determine the entitlement of the company to property on a section 234 application.[24]

14.20 In *Welsh Development Agency v Export Finance Co Ltd*,[25] the Court of Appeal noted the breadth of the meaning accorded to 'property' in section 436 but nonetheless held that intangibles were not property for the purposes of the qualified immunity under section 234 because intangibles were not capable of being seized. Lord Nicholls referred to this conclusion in the course of his dissenting judgment in *OBG Ltd v Allan* where he said:[26]

> So, the argument runs, this is a legislative recognition that protection was not needed in respect of intangibles. I do not agree. The difficulty I have with this submission lies in the Court of Appeal's restrictive interpretation of 'property'. Contrary to the decision of the Court of Appeal, I see no reason to suppose Parliament intended to exclude the wrongful disposal of contractual rights from the scope of this relieving provision.

Quite apart from this observation, the restrictive interpretation favoured in *Welsh Development Agency* has no application outside the context of section 234—not least because of the express reference to things in action in section 436.

4. Special cases

14.21 This section of this chapter describes classes of interest where a simple correlation between property for the purposes of section 436 and the distribution of

---

[23] As regards compulsory liquidation, see also rule 7.78.
[24] *Re London Iron & Steel Co Ltd* [1990] BCC 159 (Ch) (unless that is a question for a foreign court: *Re Leyland DAF Ltd* [1994] BCC 166 (CA)).
[25] [1992] BCLC 148 (CA).
[26] [2007] UKHL 21, [2008] 1 AC 1 [236].

the insolvent estate is misleading. One such class has already been identified in paragraphs 14.12 to 14.14 above, namely non-transferable interests which are not property but which may nonetheless be used to create value which falls into the insolvent estate.

a. Office-holder recoveries

In principle, neither claims nor the proceeds of claims brought by an office-holder **14.22** in his own right, for example transaction avoidance claims which are not available to the company as such, are property of the company for the purposes of section 436 but they are nonetheless available for distribution as part of the insolvent estate. The issue was addressed by the Court of Appeal in *Re Oasis Merchandising Ltd* in the context of determining whether the fruits of wrongful trading claims could be sold (it was accepted that the claim itself could not be sold under the law then in force[27]). Peter Gibson LJ, delivering the judgment of the court that the fruits could not be sold, referred to:[28]

> … the distinction we would draw between the property of the company at the commencement of the [liquidation] (and property representing the same) and property which is subsequently acquired by the liquidator through the exercise of rights conferred on him alone by statute and which is to be held on the statutory trust for distribution by the liquidator.

It should be noted that the distinction is not a temporal distinction; the crucial difference is the nature of the rights being asserted.

The fact that such claims are not property of the company has two consequences: **14.23**

a) they are outwith the office-holder's power of sale; and
b) they are not caught by a charge created by the company over its assets.[29]

However, the practical importance of the principle is now diminished in both respects by recent statutory intervention. First, section 246ZD now expressly permits assignment of specified office-holder claims. The claims in question are fraudulent and wrongful trading claims, preference and transaction at an undervalue claims, and claims relating to extortionate credit transactions. Secondly, section 176ZB now provides that the proceeds of the same list of office-holder claims (or their assignment) are not part of the company's 'net property' available to the holder of a floating charge.[30]

---

[27] But see now section 246ZD.
[28] [1998] Ch 170 (CA) 182F.
[29] *Re Yagerphone Ltd* [1935] Ch 392 (Ch); *NW Robbie & Co Ltd v Witney Warehouse Co Ltd* [1963] 1 WLR 1324 (CA); *Re MC Bacon Ltd (No 2)* [1991] Ch 127 (Ch).
[30] Section 176ZB can be disapplied by the terms of a scheme of arrangement or CVA—section 176ZB(4).

14.24 It should be noted that the specified claims are not a complete list of the claims to which the principle may apply. For example, the principle was applied to section 127 claims (avoidance of post-commencement dispositions) and claims in respect of unregistered company charges in *Re Ayala Holdings Ltd (No 2)* where Knox J said:[31]

> In my judgment [the assignee's] argument overlooks an important distinction between property of the company, on the one hand, and the rights and powers of a liquidator on the other ... What is to be distinguished in my view are the statutory privileges and liberties conferred upon liquidators as such ... who are officers of the court and act under the court's direction.

and again later referring to:[32]

> ... the fundamental distinction between assets of a company and rights conferred upon a liquidator in relation to the conduct of the liquidation. The former are assignable by sale under para 6 of Sch 4, the latter are not because they are an incident of the office of liquidator.

Although Knox J's judgment in *Ayala* was cited with approval in *Oasis* at first instance and in the Court of Appeal,[33] it is difficult to reconcile it with the later case of *Mond v Hammond Suddards* in which it was held that a debenture-holder was entitled to the benefit of payments which were avoided by section 127.[34] In this respect, it may be necessary to draw a distinction between the assignability of the office-holder's right of action and entitlement to the benefit of the recovery of property which has been the subject of void dispositions.[35]

14.25 The resulting discrepancies are untidy and owe more to historical development than a coherent policy.

b. Retention of title

14.26 In one sense goods purchased subject to retention of title provisions (which have not been satisfied) are a prime example of assets which may be in the possession of the company but which do not belong to it and do not form part of its property within the meaning of section 436.

---

[31] [1996] 1 BCLC 467 (Ch) 480i.

[32] Ibid at 483b.

[33] *Re Oasis Merchandising Services Ltd* [1995] 2 BCLC 493 (Ch) and, on appeal, [1998] Ch 170 (CA).

[34] *Mond v Hammond Suddards* [1996] 2 BCLC 470 (Ch), see also *Mond v Hammond Suddards* [2000] Ch 40 (CA) for further developments in this litigation where the issue was costs and the substantive decision as to the debenture-holder's entitlement was not challenged (*Ayala* is not mentioned in the judgments). See also Chapter 15 para 15.25.

[35] See further *Smith (Administrator of Cosslett (Contractors) Ltd) v Bridgend County Borough Council* [2001] UKHL 58, [2002] 1 AC 336 [24] (Lord Hoffmann).

The reason why goods in the company's possession under a retention of title agree-   **14.27**
ment (or under a hire purchase agreement) require further consideration is that
they are subject to special treatment in administration.[36] Thus, the moratorium
in administration prevents repossession of the goods without the consent of the
administrator or the permission of the court and the administrator can apply to
the court under paragraph 72 of Schedule B1 for an order enabling him to sell the
goods as if the company was the owner. The consequential provisions of paragraph
72 requiring the administrator to account for the net proceeds of disposal (topped
up to market value if necessary) serve to demonstrate that the insolvent estate is not
being augmented by such goods and that any disposal is merely to facilitate achievement of the purpose of administration.

c. Set-off

Insolvency set-off is considered in Chapter 21. Set-off helps to define the insolvent   **14.28**
estate because it is mandatory and self-executing. It strikes a net balance as between
the company and its counterparty. If that balance is in favour of the company, it
constitutes an asset which forms part of the insolvent estate and can be sold by the
office-holder. As Lord Hoffmann said in *Stein v Blake*:[37]

> The next question is whether the trustee can assign the net balance ... the duty of the
> trustee ... is to realise the bankrupt's estate and the right to the net balance is part of
> the property of the bankrupt vested in the trustee. One method of realisation is to
> transfer or assign the individual assets for value.

before going on to hold that the balance could be assigned, as such, without wait-
ing for the taking of the account by which it is quantified.

d. Charged assets

A classic statement of the position of assets which are the subject of security inter-   **14.29**
ests is that of Lord Millett in *Buchler v Talbot* where he said:[38]

> Assets subject to a charge belong to the charge holder to the extent of the
> amounts secured by them; only the equity of redemption remains the prop-
> erty of the chargor and falls within the scope of the chargor's bankruptcy or
> winding up.

This explains how charged assets are treated for the purposes of distribution in
accordance with the statutory scheme,[39] but Lord Millett was not using the word
'property' in its section 436 sense. Thus, for example, where paragraph 43 of

---

[36] Both forms of agreement are defined terms: see section 251 and Schedule B1 para 111(1).
[37] [1996] 1 AC 243 (HL) 257H (the case is a bankruptcy case but the principle is equally applicable to insolvency set-off in a corporate insolvency).
[38] [2004] UKHL 9, [2004] 2 AC 298 [51].
[39] See further Chapter 21.

Schedule B1 precludes the enforcement of 'security over the company's property', it is restricting the action that can be taken in respect of the asset which is charged to the secured creditor as opposed to regulating what action can be taken against the company's equity of redemption in respect of that asset. 'Property' in the section 436 sense means both charged and free assets.

e. Books and records

14.30 The meaning accorded to 'property' by section 436 is broad enough to encompass all the books, papers, and records to which the company is entitled and, in *Re Maxwell Communication Corporation Plc*, Snowden J treated books and records (other than statutory books and records) as simply one form of a company's property.[40] However, in addition to the requirements of general company law as to the maintenance of statutory books and records, the Insolvency Regulations 1994[41] appear to be premised on books, papers, and records being excluded either from the ordinary meaning of property or at least from the application of the office-holder's ordinary powers in respect of property.

14.31 The 1994 Regulations give liquidators in a compulsory liquidation an express power, subject to obtaining permission from the official receiver, to dispose of the company's books, papers, and records. Liquidators in voluntary liquidations and administrators have the power of disposal (without sanction) after the expiration of twelve months from the date of dissolution. *Maxwell* was a case where administrators sought directions as to the destruction of non-statutory books and records in circumstances in which the 1994 Regulations did not apply. The administrators' application was made in conjunction with an application for discharge of the administration, which was to lead to the dissolution of the company without any intervening liquidation, and where the books and records not only had no value or use but were also expensive to preserve (because of their volume). Snowden J resolved the matter by holding that the administrators' ordinary powers to manage the company's property were sufficient to cover destruction of property in such circumstances and, further, that he could properly give directions for its destruction either under the court's general power to give directions to administrators or its extended jurisdiction to make ancillary orders in the context of discharge.

14.32 In view of the doubts raised by the drafting of the 1994 Regulations, it is suggested that an office-holder should not destroy a company's books, papers, and records without directions from the court, unless the Regulations apply.

---

[40] [2016] EWHC 2200 (Ch). Although it should be noted that section 234(2) refers to 'property, books, papers or records'.
[41] SI 1994/2507.

5. Trust assets

Property of the company in the section 436 sense means property to which the **14.33** company is beneficially entitled. It follows that property which is held by the company on trust for third parties forms no part of its insolvent estate.[42] Conversely, where the company has a beneficial interest in property held on trust by another person, that beneficial interest is property belonging to the company which forms part of its insolvent estate.

The liquidation or administration of a company which is a trustee does not termi- **14.34** nate its trusteeship but could trigger an application to the court under section 41 of the Trustee Act 1925 for the appointment of a new trustee. For so long as the company remains a trustee, the office-holder must ensure that any actions which it takes in that capacity are taken in accordance with its fiduciary duties. (The office-holder himself must be careful to avoid conflicts of interest.) The office-holder may be permitted to have recourse to trust assets for the payment of his remuneration and expenses in administering the trust.[43]

---

[42] *Barclays Bank Ltd v Quistclose Investments Ltd* [1970] AC 567 (HL).
[43] *Re Berkeley Applegate (Investment Consultants) Ltd (No 2)* (1988) 4 BCC 279 (Ch); *Re Berkeley Applegate (Investment Consultants) Ltd (No 3)* (1989) 5 BCC 803 (Ch).

15

TRANSACTION AVOIDANCE

1. Introduction

15.01 Laws dealing with the problem of debt avoidance were a feature of English law long before the enactment of laws providing for insolvency proceedings. Thus an enactment in 1376, during the reign of Edward III, provided that property given by debtors to friendly third parties remained available to be taken in execution by the debtor's creditors,[1] whereas the founding statute providing for a bankruptcy law was not enacted until 1542, during the reign of Henry VIII.[2] This illustrates a point which remains equally true today, namely that transaction avoidance overlaps with insolvency law but can go wider. For example section 423, dealing with transactions defrauding creditors, can be invoked by a victim of the transaction even though no insolvency proceedings are taking place.

15.02 Insolvency transaction avoidance rules are rules whereby consensual dealings which would otherwise be binding on a company and its counterparty may be rendered ineffective, set aside, or adjusted by reason of factors which include the actual or anticipated insolvency of the company. The last of these considerations distinguishes insolvency

---

[1] 50 Ed 3 c6 '*Fraudulent assurances of land or goods, to deceive creditors, shall be void*'.
[2] 34 and 35 Hen 8 c4 '*An act against such persons as do make bankrupts*'.

transaction avoidance from rules of general law under which transactions can be attacked, for example, the rules on contracts procured by mistake or misrepresentation and some of the provisions of the Companies Act 2006 regulating transactions by and with directors (although, in any given case, such rules of general law might be invoked by an office-holder simultaneously with the special insolvency rules).

There are eleven transaction avoidance rules in English corporate insolvency law[3] **15.03** which fall into three different classes according to their respective effects. Those rules deal with the following:

Retentive avoidance
a) post-commencement dispositions;
b) transactions offending the anti-deprivation rule;
c) transactions offending the pari passu rule;
d) late floating charges;
e) unregistered charges;
f) liens on books and records;

Restorative avoidance
g) preferences;
h) transactions at an undervalue;
i) extortionate credit transactions;
j) transactions defrauding creditors; and

Dispositive avoidance
k) onerous property.

These are all rules of general application.[4] Taken as a whole, they amount to a significant incursion on the principle that English insolvency law respects pre-proceeding proprietary rights.

The concept of an insolvent estate which is the subject of a collective proceeding **15.04** necessitates the identification of a cut-off date (or dates) by reference to which the composition of the estate and the participating creditors will be identified.

---

[3] It has been suggested that the rules (or at least some of them) could be analysed as part of the law of unjust enrichment (see, for example, Simone Degeling, 'Restitution for Vulnerable Transactions' in John Armour and Howard Bennett (eds), *Vulnerable Transactions in Corporate Insolvency* (Hart Publishing 2003). The purpose of doing so would be to inform the exercise of the court's discretion in granting remedies (as to which, see *Ingram v Ahmed* [2016] EWHC 1536 (Ch)) and to open the door to change of position defences (as to which, see *4Eng Ltd v Harper* [2009] EWHC 2633 (Ch), [2010] 1 BCLC 176) but the utility of this approach seems limited.

[4] In addition, the Pensions Regulator has powers under the Pensions Act 2004 to take action in respect of transactions at an undervalue and transactions defrauding creditors where there are pension scheme deficits, but those powers exist for the benefit of the members of the scheme and are therefore distinguishable from the rules under consideration in this chapter. Conversely, there are exceptions to the application of these rules in the market contracts provisions of the Companies Act 1989, and under the Financial Markets and Insolvency (Settlement Finality) Regulations 1999 (SI 1999/2979) and the Financial Collateral Arrangements (No 2) Regulations 2003 (SI 2003/3226). All those exceptions are outside the scope of this work.

Whatever dates are chosen run the risk of creating anomalies. A principal function of a number of the foregoing transaction avoidance rules is to enforce the cut-off date or ameliorate the potential for injustice which it can cause, and thereby promote fairness as between creditors. As Lord Sumption SCJ said in *Angove's Pty Ltd v Bailey*:[5]

> The statutory rules for the distribution of insolvent estates represent an important public policy designed to achieve a pro rata distribution of the company's estate between its creditors. For that purpose it is necessary to assess claims as at a fixed and common point of time, namely when the company went into liquidation. The arbitrary character of any cut-off date is to some extent mitigated by statutory provisions for adjusting prior transactions prejudicial to creditors, such as preferences and transactions at an undervalue, and imposing liabilities for fraudulent or wrongful trading, but these provisions operate in their current form to restore the insolvent estate for the benefit of creditors as a whole.

15.05 The rules listed above under the heading 'Retentive avoidance' are all concerned with retaining property in the estate. Thus, unauthorized post-commencement dispositions by the company are invalidated as are unregistered charges, and late floating charges are only good security for new credit. Liens on books and records are also rendered unenforceable. In addition, there are two rules which flow from the principle that is not permissible to contract out of the statutory scheme: first, the pari passu rule and, secondly, the anti-deprivation rule which renders void agreements which purport to remove an asset from the insolvent estate in the event of insolvency proceedings.

15.06 Some other rules are concerned with restoring property to the estate which has been the subject of pre-proceeding dispositions. These are grouped together in the list given above under the heading 'Restorative avoidance'. When a debtor company enters into some form of disposition that gives a particular creditor an advantage over others (for example payment or the provision of security) and was influenced by a desire to confer that advantage, then a preference is said to have occurred. If the preference occurred within stipulated time periods prior to insolvency proceedings, the office-holder can apply to the court to have it set aside. Similarly, transactions at an undervalue can be set aside on application to the court provided that they too occurred within a stipulated period. There is harsher treatment for transactions at an undervalue which are entered into for the specific purpose of defrauding creditors. In this case there is no need to prove contemporaneous insolvency and, instead of comparatively short hardening (or 'twilight') periods after which preferences and 'ordinary' transactions at an undervalue are immune from challenge, the only time constraints are the statutory limitation periods for bringing claims. In all these cases, there are protections for equity's darling, the bona fide purchaser for value without notice. Finally, under the heading of 'Restorative

---

[5] [2016] UKSC 47, [2016] 1 WLR 3179 [25].

avoidance', there is also a rarely used power for an office-holder to challenge extortionate credit transactions.

All of the foregoing apply in liquidation and administration but only the rules on **15.07** transactions defrauding creditors also apply to voluntary arrangements. The last form of transaction avoidance, 'Dispositive avoidance', only applies to liquidation and serves an entirely different purpose. A liquidator may, by notice, disclaim any unprofitable contract or unsaleable property—for example an onerous lease. The disclaimer ends the obligations of the company but only affects others to the extent necessary to achieve the release of the company. Anyone suffering loss as a result of the disclaimer can prove in the liquidation. The purpose of this power, which is essentially an administrative power, is to facilitate the closure of the estate and distributions to creditors.

2. Policy objectives

There are difficulties in advancing any coherent analysis of the policy behind the **15.08** insolvency transaction avoidance rules because so many of the statements of policy and purpose, whether in a legislative or judicial context, are dealing with the rules selectively and there are competing policies in play.

In the Cork Report it was said that:[6]   **15.09**

> Most advanced systems of law recognise the need to enable certain transactions between a debtor and other parties to be set aside in appropriate circumstances, so that assets disposed of by the debtor may be recovered and made available to meet the claims of his creditors …
>
> From the earliest attempts to introduce a bankruptcy code in England in the Sixteenth Century, it has been found necessary to provide for the setting aside of certain transactions between the debtor, later made bankrupt, and other parties in the period preceding his bankruptcy. There are two types of case. In the first, the transaction is one in which the initiative is taken by the creditor who, foreseeing the probable insolvency of his debtor, takes active steps to recover the debt or otherwise improve his own position in that event. In the other, the initiative is taken by the debtor himself who, in contemplation of his own imminent insolvency, seeks to preserve his assets for the benefit of his family and friends or favoured creditors …
>
> Cases where the initiative is taken by the creditor are dealt with by various statutory provisions which enable mortgages and charges created over the insolvent's property within a limited period before the insolvency to be set aside in certain circumstances … and incomplete executions over the insolvent's property to be rendered ineffective in an insolvency …

---

[6] Report of the Review Committee, *Insolvency Law and Practice* (Cm 8558, June 1982) paras 1200–1209.

The statutory provisions dealing with [preferences and transactions at an undervalue] are directed at an altogether different objective from that at which [statutes dealing with transactions defrauding creditors] were directed. The latter were designed to protect creditors from fraud; the bankruptcy code, on the other hand, is directed towards achieving a *pari passu* distribution of the bankrupt's estate among his creditors. The justification for setting aside a disposition of the bankrupt's assets made shortly before his bankruptcy is that, by depleting his estate, it unfairly prejudices his creditors; and even where the disposition is in satisfaction of a debt lawfully owing by the bankrupt, by altering the distribution of his estate it makes a *pari passu* distribution among all the creditors impossible.

However, this is an incomplete account of the full range of the transaction avoidance rules.

15.10 Another (equally incomplete) statement of legislative policy can be taken from *A Revised Framework for Insolvency Law*:[7]

The principal purpose of fixing a date prior to that of the relevant order for the commencement of proceedings is to allow the liquidator ... to avoid transactions involving the disposition of the debtor's estate to the detriment of the general body of creditors. There are several different provisions which enable a liquidator ... to do this and, although it is difficult to generalise ... the underlying principle is that transactions in the ordinary course of business and without actual knowledge of the commencement of insolvency proceedings will usually be valid. The provisions are principally aimed at upsetting transactions entered into with the deliberate intention of giving a particular creditor an unfair advantage over others and to preserve the collective nature of the proceedings by preventing individual creditors from retaining the fruits of enforcement action taken by them.

15.11 In *Rubin v Eurofinance SA*, Lord Collins SCJ said of the nature of transaction avoidance proceedings:[8]

In order to achieve a proper and fair distribution of assets between creditors, it will often be necessary to adjust prior transactions and to recover previous dispositions of property so as to constitute the estate which is available for distribution. The principle of equality among creditors which underlies the pari passu principle may require the adjustment of concluded transactions which but for the winding up of the company would have remained binding on the company, and the return to the company of payments made or property transferred under the transactions or the reversal of their effect. Systems of insolvency law use avoidance proceedings as mechanisms for adjusting prior transactions by the debtor and for recovering property disposed of by the debtor prior to the insolvency. Thus under the Insolvency Act 1986 an administrator, or liquidator, or trustee in bankruptcy may, where there has been a transaction at an undervalue, or amounting to an unlawful preference, apply for an order restoring the position to what it would have been had the transaction not taken place: ss238 et seq and 339 et seq. Other systems of law

---

[7] Department of Trade and Industry 1984 (White Paper, Cm 9175, February 1984) para 62.
[8] [2012] UKSC 46, [2013] 1 AC 236 [94], [95].

have similar mechanisms, but they will differ in matters such as the period during which such transactions are at risk of reversal and the role of good faith of the parties to the transaction.

The underlying policy is to protect the general body of creditors against a diminution of the assets by a transaction which confers an unfair or improper advantage on the other party, and it is therefore an essential aspect of the process of liquidation that antecedent transactions whose consequences have been detrimental to the collective interest of the creditors should be amenable to adjustment or avoidance ...

'Fairness' in this context is not synonymous with equality. Creditors only receive **15.12** equal treatment within their respective classes (secured, preferential, and unsecured). The objective of the Retentive and Restorative forms of transaction avoidance is to achieve an appropriate balance between the interests of parties to transactions and the interests of the estate as a whole—which ultimately, in the case of the latter, lie in its timely distribution in accordance with the statutory scheme after the inception of insolvency proceedings. In order to strike that balance, it is necessary to curb certain forms of debtor behaviour and to impose some limits on the extent to which individual creditors can secure advantages through their own diligence.

It would be as unfair to reopen all past transactions as it would be to reopen none. **15.13** Finality in commercial transactions is itself an important policy objective. Some of this tension was reflected in the section of the Cork Report dealing with secured creditors:[9]

> The right of a prospective creditor to stipulate for security and thus, by prudence and foresight, to obtain that priority over other creditors in the event of the debtor's insolvency which the security gives him, is part of the general law of contract. It cannot be curtailed without some erosion of the general freedom of contract. This has been relied upon by some of those who have given evidence to us as an argument for leaving the present law unchanged. We have been referred to Lord Macnaghten's statement in the celebrated case of *Salomon v Salomon & Co*: 'Every creditor is entitled to get and hold the best security the law allows him to take'.
>
> Yet, as the passage itself shows, it is for the law to define the security which a creditor may be permitted to take. Over the years the legislature has intervened by enacting successive provisions curtailing or destroying the effectiveness of certain kinds of security in the event of the debtor's insolvency. Some securities are void if not duly registered; others are invalidated in certain circumstances if the debtor becomes insolvent within a specific time after their creation. Since 1897 the debt secured by a floating charge has been postponed by statute to the claims of unsecured but preferential creditors.
>
> Freedom of contract is thus far from sacrosanct; Parliament has recognised that the right of the creditor to take security needs to be constrained if a fair balance is to be achieved in the interest of all the creditors.

---

[9] Cork Report (n 6) paras 1481–1484 (internal citation omitted).

At the same time, it is important not to make it more difficult for commercial enterprises to raise finance by unduly restricting the value of the security which they can offer in return; and it would be unjust to deprive the diligent creditor altogether of the priority for which he has had the prudence and foresight to bargain. There is a balance to be struck.

15.14   Some transaction avoidance rules, notably those dealing with transactions defrauding creditors, also have as part of their function the deterrence of malpractice. The same is obviously true of the possibility of parallel proceedings against directors for breach of fiduciary duty. A similar policy consideration is discernible in the differential treatment sometimes accorded to transactions with 'connected persons' involving the reversal of the burden of proof and extending the periods within which transactions must have occurred in order to be susceptible to being set aside.

15.15   Another policy objective is predictability. After the event retrieval should be a last resort because of the costs and inherent risks of litigation. An effective set of transaction avoidance rules should be sufficiently predictable to enable companies and their advisers to determine in advance, and refrain from undertaking, transactions which will offend those rules. That necessarily assumes that company directors are acting properly and it is no protection against those that are not despite the risks of personal liability and disqualification. In that connection, it is noticeable on a general review of the reported court decisions that there is a preponderance of cases dealing with individuals and small companies.

15.16   Finally, there is Dispositive transaction avoidance where the purpose is rather more pragmatic. The Cork Report said of a liquidator's power of disclaimer:[10]

> Among the assets of an insolvent, whether individual or corporate, there may be found items of property which are best regarded as a commercial liability. These include land subject to onerous obligations, unprofitable contracts, and other items not readily saleable ...
>
> A disclaimer by a liquidator releases the estate of the company being wound up, creates claims in the liquidation capable of proof and enables the liquidation to be completed.

3. Common law

15.17   Some insolvency transaction avoidance has common law origins but the subject has long since been largely the preserve of legislation (now the Act).[11] The answer to the question of how far, if at all, common law transaction avoidance now survives in English insolvency law, is that there is no room for discrete common law avoidance

---

[10]   Ibid at paras 1182 and 1186.

[11]   See, for example, Lord Campbell in *Rickards v AG* (1845) XII Cl & F 30 (HL) 42 holding that the Statute of Elizabeth dealing with fraudulent conveyances was merely declaratory of the common law.

in any area covered by the provisions of the Act[12] but that there is a continuing role for the common law in matters where the Act is silent, notably the anti-deprivation rule and the prohibition on contracting out of pari passu distribution.

Common law has been treated as a guide to the interpretation of statutory provi- **15.18** sions which have replaced it.[13] A modern example of this approach is the decision of the Privy Council in *Lewis v Hyde*, an appeal in which the issue was whether the New Zealand preference rules could be engaged in the absence of any actual preference. Lord Browne-Wilkinson, delivering the conclusions of the Board, said:[14]

> If the statute does not purport to state the whole law comprehensively, the basic common law assumption that an actual preference is necessary, which Lord Mansfield CJ plainly thought necessary, survives in the common law. The progression is as follows: Lord Mansfield CJ plainly treated an actual preference as a requirement; section 92 of the Act of 1869 was not a comprehensive code regulating fraudulent preference but to the extent that it was silent on the matter left the common law standing; the later statutory provisions (both in England and New Zealand) are simply re-enactments of section 92 of the Act of 1869 and must therefore receive the same construction. Therefore the common law rules of fraudulent preference which only applied where there had been an actual preference remains the law.

As to the residual importance of common law as a guide to interpretation in **15.19** England, it is thought that the English rules are now so detailed and comprehensively stated as to make recourse to pre-1869 case law unnecessary. The position is otherwise, however, in respect of those rules on transaction avoidance which are not codified. As stated, the most obvious examples are the rules on anti-deprivation and contracting out of pari passu distribution. Extra-statutory law also survives in the duties of directors (despite the general codification of those duties in the Companies Act 2006). Although transaction avoidance and directors' fiduciary duties are conceptually distinct, there is, in practice, a measure of overlap because breach of fiduciary duty can result in the recovery of property from directors and even, subject to defences, from third parties. In this connection, the courts are not constrained by the limits of statutory transaction avoidance. The interaction of those duties and transaction avoidance was examined by Newey J in *GHLM Trading Ltd v Maroo* where he said:[15]

> A director of a company has a duty to act 'in the way he considers, in good faith, would be most likely to promote the success of the company for the benefit of its members as a whole' (see s172 of the Companies Act 2006). Where creditors' interests are relevant, it will similarly, in my view, be a director's duty to have regard to the interests of the creditors as a class. If a director acts to advance the interests of a

---

[12] Applying the established test as summarized by Lord Sumption SCJ in *Singularis Holdings Ltd v PricewaterhouseCoopers* [2014] UKPC 36, [2015] AC 1675 [28].

[13] *Ex parte Blackburn; In re Cheesebrough* (1871) LR 12 Eq 358 (Court of Chancery); *Butcher v Stead* (1874–75) LR 7 HL 839 (HL); *Sharp v Jackson* [1899] AC 419 (HL).

[14] [1998] 1 WLR 94 (PC) 99 and 100.

[15] [2012] EWHC 61 (Ch), [2012] 2 BCLC 369 [168]–[172].

particular creditor, without believing the action to be in the interests of creditors as a class, it seems to me that he will commit a breach of duty. Whether or not s239 of the Insolvency Act 1986 (dealing with preferences) is in point cannot be determinative ... the fact that the conditions laid down by s239 are not all met should not, of itself, preclude a finding of breach of duty.

On the other hand, the applicability of s239 of the 1986 Act may have a bearing on what, if any, remedy is available in respect of a breach of duty ...

It seems to me that a company seeking redress in respect of a 'preference' to which s239 does not apply is likely to need to show: (a) that it has suffered loss, (b) that the director has profited (so that the 'no profit' rule operates), or (c) that the transaction in question is not binding on the company. In a typical case, the first of these may be impossible: if the 'preference' involved the discharge of a debt, the company's balance sheet position is likely to be unaffected. The second might well also be problematic if the company has not entered an insolvency regime: if, say, the 'preference' involved the discharge of a debt owed to a director, it could be hard to say whether or to what extent the director was better off than he would have been had he still been owed the money by the company.

As for whether the transaction is binding, ordinary agency principles indicate that a company can disavow a contract which a director has caused it to enter into if: (a) the director was acting in his own interests rather than those of the company, its members or (where appropriate) its creditors as a class, and (b) the other party to the contract had notice of the director's breach of duty ... The transaction may also be open to challenge on equitable principles ...

The better view appears to be that, where a director has caused his company to enter into a contract in pursuit of his own interests, and not in the interests of the company, its members or (where appropriate) its creditors as a class, and the other contracting party had notice of that fact, the contract is void rather than voidable ... On this basis, it is hard to see how it could matter whether the requirements of s239 of the 1986 Act are satisfied.

Were the relevant contract not void but voidable, the applicability of s239 would still be of no obvious significance.

15.20 Although this is transaction avoidance in the sense that it has a restorative function and, if successfully invoked, produces comparable results, it is distinguishable in that claims resulting from breach of fiduciary duty do not necessarily have any connection with solvency issues. Where, as in *GHLM Trading*, the claim arises out of a breach of the duty of the directors of an insolvent company to have regard to the interests of its creditors, the connection is merely circumstantial.

4. Retentive avoidance

a. Post-commencement dispositions

15.21 It would be inimical to the processes of either liquidation or administration for directors to retain any power to dispose of company property except in so far as they may be executing the wishes of the office-holder. Thus section 103 provides that, in a creditors' voluntary liquidation, all the directors' powers cease unless the liquidation committee (or the creditors if there is no committee) sanction their continuance. In administration, paragraph 64 of Schedule B1 provides that directors cannot exercise management powers without the consent of the administrator. In a company voluntary arrangement (CVA), everything depends upon the terms of the arrangement.

Paradoxically, the position in compulsory liquidation is more obscure because there **15.22** is no equivalent of section 103. In *Park Associated Developments Ltd v Kinnear*[16] the court treated transfers of land by directors after the making of a winding-up order as being ineffective on the ground that the directors had ceased to hold office when the order was made. It seems obvious that, regardless of questions as to the continuation of their offices, directors lack the capacity to make disposals of a company's property after the making of a winding-up order but this proposition is more safely grounded in section 127 as next discussed.[17] That section is not ordinarily thought to have any application after an order is made,[18] but that is because its application to a liquidator's own disposals would be inconsistent with the liquidator's express powers[19]—which should not prevent it being invoked to strike down any unauthorized transactions by directors.

Section 127 provides that any disposition of a company's property after the com- **15.23** mencement of its winding-up by the court is void unless the court otherwise orders. A precursor of section 127 was described by Lord Cairns in *Re Wiltshire Iron Co, ex parte Pearson* as being:[20]

> ... a wholesome and necessary provision, to prevent, during the period which must elapse before a Petition can be heard, the improper alienation and dissipation of the property of a company *in extremis*.

Section 127 can only properly be understood by reference to section 129 which provides that a compulsory liquidation commences with the presentation of the petition. In this respect, compulsory liquidation is distinguishable from both voluntary liquidation and administration which do not involve any retroactivity. The rationale for that distinction lies in the different nature of the proceedings. Voluntary liquidation is just that and it remains open to an aggrieved creditor to trigger the protection of section 127 by petitioning even though steps may be in hand for a voluntary liquidation. Administration is focused upon the preservation

---

[16] [2013] EWHC 3617 (Ch).

[17] See further Chapter 7.

[18] As originally enacted in section 153 Companies Act 1862, the provision only applied to the period between the presentation of a petition and the making of a winding-up order but the closure of the period with the making of the order was not re-enacted in section 173 Companies Act 1929 or later statutes.

[19] *Krextile Holdings Pty Ltd v Widdows* [1974] VR 689 (Supreme Court of Victoria) 696—a decision on the equivalent rule in Australian legislation.

[20] (1867–68) 3 LR Ch App 443 (CA) 446–447.

of going concerns and it would be inconsistent with that focus for an application for an administration order to have automatic effects equivalent to those flowing from a winding-up petition.

15.24 The court has a discretion to validate a transaction or even the more general continuation of trading. The discretion is at large and the circumstances in which a validation order may be sought are infinitely varied. That said, validation will only occur where the circumstances are exceptional and it is in the interests of the general body of creditors. The relevant authorities were reviewed by the Court of Appeal in *Express Electrical Distributors Ltd v Beavis* where Sales LJ said:[21]

> ... the policy of the law in favour of distribution of the assets of an insolvent company in the course of the liquidation process on a *pari passu* basis between its unsecured creditors is a strong one, and it needs to be shown that special circumstances exist which makes a particular transaction one in the interests of the creditors as a whole before a validation order will be made to override the usual application of the *pari passu* principle.
>
> Sometimes the court may be justified in making a validation order where the making of a payment or the supply of assets by the company is a way of, say, fulfilling its obligations under a particularly profitable contract where the eventual profits will exceed the consumption of the company's assets and will enure to the overall advantage of the general body of creditors ... Sometimes the court may be justified in making a validation order simply to allow the company to carry on its business in the usual way; but, as Buckley LJ pointed out [in *Re Gray's Inn Construction Ltd*], it will be more speculative whether this is really desirable in the interests of the general body of creditors and this 'will be likely to depend on whether a sale of the business as a going concern will probably be more beneficial than a break-up realisation of the company's assets'.

15.25 Property of the company which is recovered under section 127 is treated as if it had never left the company. Accordingly, it will be caught by a floating charge which applied to it at the time of the disposition.[22] This highlights an important distinction between transaction avoidance which treats transactions as void and other rules which merely enable an office-holder to mount a challenge.

b. Transactions offending the anti-deprivation rule

15.26 Agreements which purport to remove an asset from the debtor company's estate in the event of insolvency proceedings are void. This rule, which is considered in more detail in Chapter 21, is triggered by a deliberate intention to evade the operation of the insolvency scheme and it applies automatically from the commencement of

---

[21] [2016] EWCA Civ 765 [20], [21].

[22] *Mond v Hammond Suddards* [1996] 2 BCLC 470 (Ch), see also *Mond v Hammond Suddards* [2000] Ch 40 (CA) for further developments in this litigation where the issue was costs and the substantive decision as to the debenture-holder's entitlement was not challenged. See also Chapter 14 para 14.24.

insolvency proceedings. The rule prevents an outflow of value and therefore operates for the benefit of creditors holding security on the assets.

c. Transactions offending the pari passu rule

Agreements which would result in the debtor company's estate being distributed **15.27** amongst its creditors otherwise than in accordance with the statutory scheme are also void. This rule, which is related to the anti-deprivation rule in that they are both sub-sets of a more general prohibition on contracting out of the insolvency scheme, is concerned with effect not purpose and is not engaged unless and until the relevant procedure has become distributive in character (ie from the outset in liquidation but not until notice of a proposed distribution has been given in the case of administration). This rule is also considered in more detail in Chapter 21.

d. Late floating charges

Section 245 provides that charges granted by companies in liquidation or admin- **15.28** istration which, as created, were floating charges are invalid except as security for new value if granted within twelve months of the onset of insolvency (two years if in favour of a connected person) or while an administration is pending.[23] As against an unconnected chargee who took a charge other than when administration was already pending, the section only applies if the company was unable to pay its debts when the security was granted or became so as a result of the transaction under which the charge was granted.

Section 245 is the latest manifestation of a provision originally enacted as section **15.29** 13 of the Companies Act 1907 in response to the perceived injustice of floating charge security being enlarged at the expense of unpaid suppliers, which Buckley J had said in *Re London Pressed Hinge Company Ltd* required urgent attention.[24] As Mummery J said in *Re Fairway Magazines Ltd*:[25]

> … the general purpose of the provision is to prevent a company, which is on its last legs, from creating a floating charge to secure past debts or to secure moneys which do not go to swell its assets and become available for creditors.

Section 245 is, of course, only a partial answer to that problem because unpaid suppliers continue to swell the assets available to floating chargees in cases falling outwith the parameters of the section, but it seeks to strike a balance between the utility of floating charges as a form of security and the interests of other creditors.

---

[23] The phrase 'onset of insolvency' is very precisely defined in section 245(5) to cover various different circumstances applicable to the commencement of insolvency proceedings (as opposed to the financial condition of the company). Confusingly, a slightly different definition of 'onset of insolvency' is to be found in section 240. There is no apparent reason for this anomaly.
[24] [1905] 1 Ch 576 (Ch) 583.
[25] [1992] BCC 924 (Ch) 932.

15.30 New value, for the purposes of section 245, must comprise cash advances, the discharge of pre-existing debt, or the supply of goods or services at the same time as or after the creation of the charge.[26] The only apparent reason for excluding other forms of new value (eg a transfer of shares) is that section 245 is only intended to be a limited relaxation of the previous restriction (in section 617 of the Companies Act 1985) to 'cash paid to the company'. In the case of cash advances, the impact of section 245 is substantially reduced by the application of the rule in *Clayton's Case*[27] to a running account with the result that an active overdraft may rapidly comprise new money.[28] This can hardly be an inadvertent result since the model for the alternative approach already existed on the statute book in section 8(5) of the Agricultural Credits Act 1928 and a recommendation in the Cork Report[29] to reverse the previous law was ignored. However, section 245 cannot be circumvented simply by recycling an existing debt.[30]

15.31 Section 245 only makes the floating charge invalid in the liquidation or administration; it does not affect any previously completed repayment or enforcement.[31]

e. Unregistered charges

15.32 With limited exceptions, mortgages and charges created by debtor companies are void against liquidators, administrators, and other creditors if not registered within twenty-one days of their creation. Pending liquidation or administration, the charge remains valid as against the company itself but the liability secured by the charge is accelerated. The charged assets remain subject to any other (valid) securities granted by the company.[32]

15.33 This provision, which can be traced back to section 14 of the Companies Act 1900, is designed to give persons extending credit to a company the means of establishing their prospects of repayment (and redress if they are misled and insolvency proceedings ensue). Prior to the 1900 Act the only requirement had been that under section 43 of the Companies Act 1862, which required a company to maintain a private register which was accessible only by its own members and existing creditors and which had been held by the House of Lords not to affect the validity of the security.[33] In *Smith (Administrator of Cosslett (Contractors) Ltd) v Bridgend County Borough Council*, Lord Hoffmann said of the corresponding provision of the Companies Act 1985 that it:[34]

---

[26] *Re Shoe Lace Ltd* [1993] BCC 609 (CA).
[27] *Devaynes v Noble (Clayton's Case)* (1816) 1 Mer 572 (Court of Chancery).
[28] *Re Yeovil Glove Co Ltd* [1965] Ch 148 (CA).
[29] Cork Report (n 6) para 1562.
[30] *Re GT Whyte & Co Ltd* [1983] BCLC 311 (Ch).
[31] *Mace Builders (Glasgow) Ltd v Lunn* [1987] Ch 191 (CA).
[32] Section 859H Companies Act 2006; *Re Monolithic Building Co Ltd* [1915] 1 Ch 643 (CA); *Society of Lloyd's v Levy* [2004] EWHC 1860 (Comm), [2004] 3 CMLR 56.
[33] *Wright v Horton* (1887) 12 App Cas 371 (HL).
[34] [2001] UKHL 58, [2002] 1 AC 336 [19].

... was intended for the protection of the creditors of an insolvent company. It was intended to give persons dealing with a company the opportunity to discover, by consulting the register, whether its assets were burdened by floating and certain fixed charges which would reduce the amount available for unsecured creditors in a liquidation ... The plain intention of the legislature was that property subject to a registrable but unregistered charge should be available to the general body of creditors (or a secured creditor ranking after the unregistered charge) as if no such charge existed.

A detailed examination of these provisions (now in Part 25 of the Companies Act 2006) is outside the scope of this work which will consider only what is meant by a security being void as against a liquidator or administrator.

It is in the context of insolvency that the distinction between secured and unsecured debt matters most but in *Cosslett* the Court of Appeal had held that the avoidance against the office-holder meant that it could only be relied upon where the office-holder had a personal cause of action and not when proceeding to enforce the company's own rights in respect of its property. On the appeal to the House of Lords, Lord Hoffmann went on to deal with this 'startling and unorthodox' proposition in the following terms:[35]   **15.34**

> When a winding up order is made and a liquidator appointed, there is no divesting of the company's assets. The liquidator acquires no interest, whether beneficially or as trustee. The assets continue to belong to the company but the liquidator is able to exercise the company's right to collect them for the purposes of the liquidation.

> It must in my opinion follow that when [the relevant section in the Companies Act 1985] says that the charge shall be 'void against the liquidator', it means void against a company acting by its liquidator, that is to say, a company in liquidation ...

> On the other hand, once the company is in liquidation and can act only by its liquidator, there seems to me little value in a distinction between whether the charge is void against the liquidator or void against the company. It is void against the company in liquidation ...

> As in the case of liquidation, I consider that 'void against the administrator' means void against the company in administration or (another way of saying the same thing) against the company when acting by its administrator.

f. Liens on books and records

Liens on book, papers, and records (but not title documents) are unenforceable against administrators, liquidators, and provisional liquidators (but other proprietary rights are unaffected).[36] This rule is considered in conjunction with office-holders' investigation powers in Chapter 15.   **15.35**

---

[35] Ibid at [20], [21], and [31].
[36] Section 246. Such liens will most likely arise by operation of law. Where that is the case, it might be said that the lien is not a consensual dealing but section 246 warrants inclusion in the list of insolvency transaction avoidance rules because the parting with possession which gives rise to the lien will have been consensual even if the parties may not have had the creation of security in contemplation.

5. Restorative avoidance

a. Preferences

15.36 An administrator or liquidator can apply to the court for an order restoring the *status quo ante* if an insolvent company does something or suffers something to be done which has the effect of putting one or more of its creditors (or a surety for its debts) in a better position than that which he/she or they would have had in an insolvent liquidation and the company was influenced by a desire to produce that effect. There is a rebuttable presumption of the requisite desire where the creditor (or surety) is a connected person. The preference must have occurred within six months of the 'onset of insolvency'[37] or while an administration is pending, unless it was also a transaction at an undervalue or the preference of a connected person, in which case the period is two years.[38]

15.37 The court has a very wide discretion as to the nature of the orders which it can make and need not make any order at all.[39] Although, in principle, an order can be made affecting persons other than the person to whom the preference was given, there are protections for bona fide purchasers for value without notice. Thus, an interest in property acquired in good faith and for value from a person other than the company is protected and a person who receives a benefit from a preference in good faith and for value cannot be required to make a payment to the office-holder unless they were themselves a preferee. Any recoveries are made for the benefit of the general body of creditors and are not caught by any security granted by the company.[40]

15.38 *Re MC Bacon Ltd*,[41] the first reported decision on these provisions as amended and reformulated in the Act, remains crucial to a correct understanding of the current law on preferences. Some insolvency laws have preference rules based simply on the effect of the transaction in question, albeit usually subject to some form of ordinary course of business defence. English insolvency law approaches the subject from the perspective that it is only misconduct which needs to be negated. However, even in this respect, the Act introduced a profound change. Millett J said of the new law:[42]

> This is a completely different test. It involves at least two radical departures from the old law. It is no longer necessary to establish a *dominant* intention to prefer.

---

[37] The phrase 'onset of insolvency' is very precisely defined in section 240(3) to cover various different circumstances applicable to the commencement of insolvency proceedings (as opposed to the financial condition of the company). Confusingly, the definition of 'onset of insolvency' in section 240 is not exactly the same as that in section 245. There is no apparent reason for this anomaly.

[38] Sections 239 to 241.

[39] Section 241; *Re Paramount Airways Ltd* [1993] Ch 223 (CA) 239G.

[40] *Re Yagerphone Ltd* [1935] Ch 392 (Ch).

[41] [1990] BCC 78 (Ch).

[42] Ibid at 87D.

It is sufficient that the decision was *influenced* by the requisite desire. That is the first change. The second is that it is no longer sufficient to establish an *intention* to prefer. There must be a *desire* to produce the effect mentioned in the subsection.

This second change is made necessary by the first, for without it it would be virtually impossible to uphold the validity of a security taken in exchange for the injection of fresh funds into a company in financial difficulties. A man is taken to intend the necessary consequences of his actions, so that an intention to grant a security to a creditor necessarily involves an intention to prefer that creditor in the event of insolvency. The need to establish that such intention was dominant was essential under the old law to prevent perfectly proper transactions from being struck down. With the abolition of that requirement intention could not remain the relevant test. Desire has been substituted. That is a very different matter. Intention is objective, desire is subjective. A man can choose the lesser of two evils without desiring either.

It is not, however, sufficient to establish a desire to make the payment or grant the security which it is sought to avoid. There must have been a desire to produce the effect mentioned in the subsection, that is to say, to improve the creditor's position in the event of an insolvent liquidation. A man is not to be taken as *desiring* all the necessary consequences of his actions. Some consequences may be of advantage to him and be desired by him; others may not affect him and be matters of indifference to him; while still others may be positively disadvantageous to him and not be desired by him, but be regarded by him as the unavoidable price of obtaining the desired advantages. It will still be possible to provide assistance to a company in financial difficulties provided that the company is actuated only by proper commercial considerations. Under the new regime a transaction will not be set aside as a voidable preference unless the company positively wished to improve the creditor's position in the event of its own insolvent liquidation.

As is apparent from this passage, the purpose of the preference provision is to facilitate an attack on improper favouritism which interferes with pari passu distribution without preventing transactions which are being conducted in the interests of the company and its creditors generally. The comparatively high test imposed on the office-holder to establish that a putative preference was in fact influenced by a desire to prefer is substantially mitigated in the very cases where improper conduct is most likely to be found by the reversal of the burden of proof when the preferee is a connected party.

b. Transactions at an undervalue

15.39 An administrator or liquidator can also apply to the court for an order restoring the *status quo ante* if an insolvent company (a) makes a gift or (b) enters into some other form of transaction under which the consideration it receives is worth significantly less than that which it provides. The transaction must have occurred with two years of the onset of insolvency, or while an administration is pending. No order can be made if the transaction was entered into in good faith for the purposes of carrying on the company's business and there were reasonable grounds for believing that it would benefit the company.[43]

---

[43] Sections 238, 240, and 241.

15.40 The 'onset of insolvency' has the same meaning for these purposes as it does for preference. Here too the rules only apply if the company was already unable to pay its debts when it entered into the transaction or became so as a result of the transaction. However, in the case of transactions at an undervalue, in contrast to the preference rules, the burden of proof on the solvency question is reversed if the transaction is in favour of a connected party. The provisions as to the scope of the orders which may be made and the discretion of the court in that respect are the same as for preferences. It is generally accepted that, by analogy with the authority on preferences, any recoveries are for the benefit of the general body of creditors and are not caught by any security granted by the company.

15.41 The rules on preference and transactions at an undervalue are complementary. Transactions at an undervalue rules are focused on the preservation of the company's net worth for the benefit of its creditors. The preference rules deal with favouritism as between creditors and will usually be invoked where a genuine liability has been discharged (which should be neutral in terms of net worth). If something has been done other than in discharge of a genuine liability, then the transaction at an undervalue rules are in point. A given transaction can, of course, involve both as is recognized in the rules on the applicable hardening periods.

15.42 The focus on net worth raises a controversial question as to whether the grant of security to secure the debtor company's own liabilities (which can plainly amount to a preference) can be a transaction at undervalue. This possibility was initially dismissed by Millett J in *MC Bacon* where he said:[44]

> Section 238 of the Act is concerned with the depletion of a company's assets by transactions at an undervalue ...
>
> The granting of the debenture was not a gift, nor was it without consideration. The consideration consisted of the bank's forbearance from calling in the overdraft and its honouring of cheques and making of fresh advances to the company during the continuance of the facility. The applicant relies therefore on paragraph (b).
>
> To come within that paragraph the transaction must be:
>
> (1) entered into by the company;
> (2) for a consideration;
> (3) the value of which measured in money or money's worth;
> (4) is significantly less than the value;
> (5) also measured in money or money's worth;
> (6) of the consideration provided by the company.
>
> It requires a comparison to be made between the value obtained by the company for the transaction and the value of consideration provided by the company. Both values must be measurable in money or money's worth and both must be considered from the company's point of view.

---

[44] *MC Bacon* (n 41) 91–92. Applied in *National Bank of Kuwait v Menzies* [1994] 2 BCLC 306 (CA).

In my judgment, the applicant's claim to characterise the granting of the bank's debenture as a transaction at an undervalue is misconceived. The mere creation of a security over a company's assets does not deplete them and does not come within the paragraph. By charging its assets the company appropriates them to meet the liabilities due to the secured creditor and adversely affects the rights of other creditors in the event of insolvency. But it does not deplete its assets or diminish their value. It retains the right to redeem and the right to sell or remortgage the charged assets. All it loses is the ability to apply the proceeds otherwise than in satisfaction of the secured debt. That is not something capable of valuation in monetary terms and is not customarily disposed of for value.

In the present case the company did not suffer that loss by reason of the grant of the debenture. Once the bank had demanded a debenture the company could not have sold or charged its assets without applying the proceeds in reduction of the overdraft; had it attempted to do so, the bank would at once have called in the overdraft. By granting the debenture the company parted with nothing of value, and the value of the consideration which it received in return was incapable of being measured in money or money's worth.

The position is otherwise if the company is granting security (or entering into a guarantee) for third party debt in which case there could clearly be a transaction at an undervalue because the effect is to bring a new liability into the calculation of the company's own net worth.

The appealing logic of Millett J's analysis of the application of section 238 to the **15.43** grant of security in *MC Bacon* was doubted by the Court of Appeal in *Hill v Spread Trustee Co Ltd*.[45] *Hill* was a case where it was found that no consideration had been given and that paragraph (b) therefore did not apply. *MC Bacon* was distinguished on that account because Millett J had expressly referred to the provision of consideration in the form of forbearance in the passage from his judgment quoted above. In contrast to the facts of *Hill*, the simple grant of security by a corporate borrower to an arms' length lender will almost inevitably be accompanied by some forbearance. In such cases, it is suggested that the *MC Bacon* approach is to be preferred, that it is preference or nothing, and that section 238 should be confined to simple cases where there is no consideration even in the form of forbearance (and, possibly, more complicated cases where the provision of security is merely one aspect of the consideration provided by the company for the purposes a more complicated set of arrangements which together amount to a transaction[46]).

c. Extortionate credit transactions

Under section 244 an administrator or liquidator can apply to the court for an **15.44** order setting aside or varying a transaction involving the provision of credit to the company (and repayment of money paid or an account) if the terms required the

---

[45] [2006] EWCA Civ 542, [2007] 1 WLR 2404 [93], [138].
[46] Consider *Phillips v Brewin Dolphin Lawrie Ltd* [2001] UKHL 2, [2001] 1 WLR 143.

company to make grossly exorbitant payments or otherwise grossly contravened fair dealing principles. There is a rebuttable presumption that the transaction was extortionate. The transaction must have been entered into within three years of the company going into administration or liquidation. In principle, any recoveries should also form part of the general estate. The purpose is obvious but the practical impact is very limited.

15.45 Section 244 is modelled on sections 137 to 140 of the Consumer Credit Act 1974. In *Paragon Finance Plc v Nash*, Dyson LJ said of the test under the 1974 Act:[47]

> 'Extortionate' like 'harsh and unconscionable', signifies not merely that the terms of the bargain are stiff, or even unreasonable, but that they are so unfair as to be oppressive. This carries with it the notion of morally reprehensible conduct on the part of the creditor in taking grossly unfair advantage of the debtor's circumstances ... The jurisdiction seems to me to contemplate at least a substantial imbalance in bargaining power of which one party has taken advantage.

White v Davenham Trust Ltd was a case of a loan to finance the acquisition of property at an interest rate of 1.6 per cent per month which rose to 3 per cent per month in the event of a default. Floyd J referred to section 138 of the 1974 Act for guidance as to factors to be taken into account and to Dyson LJ's judgment before concluding that:

> The test for 'extortionate' in a commercial transaction of this kind, where the interest rates are spelled out at the outset must [be] a very stringent one.

and that a claim under section 244 would have had no realistic prospect of success.[48] It is unsurprising that such claims are rarely made despite the potential advantage to the office-holder of the reversal of the burden of proof.

d. Transactions defrauding creditors

15.46 An administrator, liquidator, CVA supervisor, and a victim of the transaction can all apply to the court for an order restoring the *status quo ante* and protecting the interests of the victims, if a company enters into a transaction at an undervalue for the purpose of putting assets beyond the reach of present or future creditors or otherwise prejudicing their interests.[49] Any application is made on behalf of all the victims.[50]

15.47 This is the classic form of transaction avoidance known in civil law systems as the 'Paulian action'.[51] Where the company is in liquidation or administration, a person wishing to apply as a victim requires the leave of the court.

---

[47] [2001] EWCA Civ 1466, [2002] 1 WLR 685 [67].
[48] [2010] EWHC 2748 (Ch), [2011] Bus LR 615 [43], [44], and [50] on appeal [2011] EWCA Civ 747, [2011] Bus LR 1442 but not on this point.
[49] Sections 423 to 425.
[50] The term is defined in section 423(5).
[51] Taking its name from the Roman law jurist Julius Paulus.

The test of what constitutes a transaction at an undervalue for the purposes of these   **15.48**
provisions is the same as that which applies for the purposes of section 238 applications. It is questionable whether the introduction of a requirement to establish
a transaction at an undervalue into the law on transactions defrauding creditors
was entirely helpful. Section 172 of the Law of Property Act 1925, which section
423 replaced, contained no such requirement. On the one hand, there is a logic
in restricting the remedy to situations in which there has been an outflow of value
but, on the other hand, it has necessitated a very wide interpretation of the meaning
of a transaction at an undervalue giving rise to the sort of conceptual difficulties
identified in *Hill v Spread Trustee Co Ltd*.[52]

The scope of the orders which can be made are also directly comparable, including   **15.49**
the protection for bona fide purchasers for value, although not couched in exactly
the same terms.

In contrast to the rules on preferences and 'ordinary' transactions at an undervalue,   **15.50**
there is no requirement to demonstrate contemporaneous inability to pay debts.
Instead, the requirement is to prove the improper motivation for the transaction—
namely to defeat or delay actual or potential creditors.[53] There is no hardening
period so, in theory, these provisions could be invoked to attack transactions which
had occurred significantly before insolvency. Indeed, one classic application of
these rules and their predecessors has been to challenge protective arrangements
made in anticipation of possible insolvency. As Arden LJ observed in *Hill v Spread
Trustee Co Ltd*:[54]

> It is one of the characteristics of transactions to which section 423 applies that they
> are entered into by a person when he is solvent just in case he becomes unable to
> pay his debts as they fall due later (as where a person is about to begin a new and
> risky business venture).

In reality, the greater the distance between the transaction and the advent of insolvency, the harder it will be to prove the requisite purpose. One obvious avenue
of enquiry concerns legal advice taken by the company, where there can be no
question of privilege against the office-holder. The office-holder may be able to
overcome privilege issues even where the privilege does not belong to the company
if he can show a sufficiently strong *prima facie* case.[55] The limits on privilege in this
context are consistent with the fact that entry into a transaction for the purpose of
defrauding creditors is serious misconduct which could, in a case involving dishonesty, lead to prosecution under section 207.

---

[52] [2006] EWCA Civ 542, [2007] 1 WLR 2404 discussed above in the context of section 238.
See also *Feakins v Department for Environment Food and Rural Affairs* [2005] EWCA Civ 1513,
[2007] BCC 54 (CA) and other cases referred to in the judgment of Jonathan Parker LJ.
[53] It is not necessary to prove dishonesty: *Pena v Coyne (No 1)* [2004] EWHC 2684 (Ch), [2004]
2 BCLC 703 [100].
[54] *Hill v Spread Trustee Co Ltd* (n 52) [111].
[55] *Barclays Bank Plc v Eustice* [1995] 1 WLR 1238 (CA).

15.51 The improper purpose need not be the sole or dominant purpose of the transaction; it is sufficient that it is a substantial purpose. As in the case of preferences, consequence must be distinguished from purpose. It is not enough that the transaction had the effect of disadvantaging creditors if it was entered into for some other (proper) reason.[56]

15.52 There are no hardening periods within which a transaction must have occurred in order to be susceptible to challenge as a transaction defrauding creditors but the claim must be brought within the applicable limitation periods under the Limitation Act 1980 (as must other transaction avoidance claims that necessitate proceedings). Since time will only begin to run against an office-holder when the company goes into administration or liquidation, this should not be a practical difficulty.[57]

6. Dispositive avoidance

a. Onerous property

15.53 A liquidator may, by notice, disclaim any onerous property. The disclaimer ends the obligations of the company but only affects others to the extent necessary to achieve the release of the company. Anyone suffering loss as a result of the disclaimer can prove in the liquidation. Persons with an interest in the disclaimed property or who have a liability in respect of it which is not discharged by the disclaimer, may apply to the court for an order vesting the disclaimed property in them.[58]

15.54 The power to disclaim is exercisable notwithstanding any intermediate use of the property (which may have given rise to an expense liability under the *Lundy Granite* principle[59]) unless a person interested in the property has applied to the liquidator to decide whether to disclaim and he has not done so within twenty-eight days (or such longer period as the court may allow).[60]

15.55 The function of the power to disclaim was explained by Lord Nicholls in *Hindcastle Ltd v Barbara Attenborough Associates Ltd* in the following terms:[61]

---

[56] *IRC v Hashmi* [2002] EWCA Civ 981, [2002] 2 BCLC 489; *4Eng Ltd v Harper* [2009] EWHC 2633 (Ch), [2010] 1 BCLC 176.

[57] *Hill v Spread Trustee Co Ltd* [2006] EWCA Civ 542, [2007] 1 WLR 2404.

[58] Sections 178 to 182; *Scmlla Properties Ltd v Gesso Properties (BVI) Ltd* [1995] BCC 793 (Ch). The history of this legislation is examined in the judgment of Chadwick LJ in *Re SSSL Realisations (2002) Ltd* [2006] EWCA Civ 7, [2006] Ch 610.

[59] See further Chapter 20.

[60] Section 178(2); *Re MK Airlines Ltd (No 2)* [2012] EWHC 2764 (Ch), [2013] Bus LR 243.

[61] [1997] AC 70 (HL) 86H–87B.

The fundamental purpose of these provisions is not in doubt. It is to facilitate the winding up of the insolvent's affairs …

Equally clear is the essential scheme by which the statute seeks to achieve these purposes. Unprofitable contracts can be ended, and property burdened with onerous obligations disowned. The company is to be freed from all liabilities in respect of the property. Conversely, and hardly surprisingly, the company is no longer to have any rights in respect of the property. The company could not fairly keep the property and yet be freed from its liabilities.

and in *Re Park Air Services Plc*, Lord Millett more succinctly stated the purpose thus:[62]

… the reason the liquidator is given the right to disclaim onerous property is in order to enable him to achieve an early closure of the liquidation.

'Onerous property' means, for these purposes, (a) any unprofitable contract and **15.56** (b) any unsaleable (or not readily saleable) property and any other property which gives rise to a liability to pay money or perform an onerous act.[63] The question of what is an unprofitable contract for a company in insolvent liquidation is potentially difficult: a contract giving rise to a liability is not *per se* 'unprofitable' for these purposes. In *Re SSSL Realisations (2002) Ltd*,[64] Chadwick LJ cited and applied the following five principles set out by Chesterman J in the Australian case *Transmetro Corporation Ltd v Real Investments Pty Ltd*:[65]

[1] A contract is unprofitable for the purpose of [the equivalent Australian legislation] if it imposes on the company continuing financial obligations which may be regarded as detrimental to the creditors, which presumably means that the contract confers no sufficient reciprocal benefit.

[2] Before a contract may be unprofitable for the purposes of the section it must give rise to prospective liabilities.

[3] Contracts which will delay the winding up of the company's affairs because they are to be performed over a substantial period of time and will involve expenditure that may not be recovered are unprofitable.

[4] No case has decided that a contract is unprofitable merely because it is financially disadvantageous. The cases focus upon the nature and causes of the disadvantage.

[5] A contract is not unprofitable merely because the company could have made or could make a better bargain.

Chadwick LJ (with who the other members of the court agreed) concluded that the critical feature of an unprofitable contract was that:[66]

---

[62] [2000] 2 AC 172 (HL) 184H.
[63] Section 178(3).
[64] *Re SSSL Realisations (2002) Ltd* (n 58) [36].
[65] (1999) 17 ACLC 1314 (Supreme Court of Queensland) at [21].
[66] Ibid at [42].

... performance of the future obligations will prejudice the liquidator's obligation to realise the company's property and pay a dividend to creditors within a
reasonable time ...

The second class of onerous property is more straightforward. The key is to determine whether the subject matter is 'property'. In *SSSL Realisations*, Chadwick
LJ upheld the first instance decision that there must be potentially at least, some
benefit or entitlement deriving from the thing in question so that a deed imposing
a negative obligation or disability did not qualify. As regards the composition of
'property', the courts will resist cherry-picking whereby liquidators seek to shed
only the disadvantageous aspects of a bundle of rights.[67]

15.57 Disclaimer of contracts is, in effect, unilateral repudiation. In the case of an ordinary executory contract, the appointment of a liquidator does not terminate the
contract as a matter of law and may not, depending on the terms of the contract,
even give the counterparty termination rights.[68] On the other hand, the liquidator
cannot usually be compelled to cause the company to perform its obligations. If the
liquidator unequivocally signals an intention that the company will not perform its
obligations, the company will thereby commit a repudiatory breach of the contract
giving the counterparty a right to elect to treat it as being at an end or as continuing (with, in each case, its rights against the company for the breach). If there is
a disclaimer, the loss for which the counterparty can claim in the liquidation is
assessed in the same way as damages.[69] Since the commercial realities are usually
apparent to both sides, the matter is often resolved by agreement and the liquidator
will only need to have recourse to his disclaimer powers to force termination upon
an unwilling counterparty (or to deal with other forms of property which are not
susceptible to a consensual termination).

15.58 The absence of any power of disclaimer in administration is usually explained on
the basis that it is not an appropriate power for inclusion in a proceeding from
which a company may emerge as a going concern under its own management.
However that pays little regard to the fact that a large number of administrations
have been 'liquidating' administrations since the changes in the procedure resulting from the Enterprise Act 2002 and the availability of a power to disclaim in such
cases would serve the same purpose as it does in a liquidation. In this connection
it is worth noting that a bank administrator has a liquidator's disclaimer powers.[70]
Bank administration is outside the scope of this work but the presence of the power

---

[67] *Re Fussell, ex parte Allen* (1882) 20 Ch D 341 (CA); *MEPC Ltd v Scottish Amicable Life Assurance Society* [1996] BPIR 447 (CA); *Environment Agency v Hillridge Ltd* [2003] EWHC 3023 (Ch), [2004] 2 BCLC 358.
[68] *British Waggon Co v Lea* (1880) 5 QBD 149 (QB).
[69] *Re Park Air Services Plc* [2000] 2 AC 172 (HL) 84C.
[70] Section 145 Banking Act 2009.

in that special procedure further undermines the rationale for its total exclusion from administration under the Act.

7. Conclusions

The rules do not form a homogenous group but they are all about defining the **15.59** insolvent estate and facilitating its distribution in a way that is fair as between creditors (and former creditors) even though, in their specific applications, they perform very different functions.

The analysis of transaction avoidance as relating to the concept of the insolvent **15.60** estate and its distribution is more difficult in the case of transactions defrauding creditors. Section 423 is, as already noted, capable of being applied outside insolvency proceedings. However, even though proceedings can be brought by any victim of the transaction without the need to obtain leave if there is no liquidation or administration on foot, such an application is always made on behalf of every victim of the transaction.[71] From this it would appear that any resultant order should not be for the benefit of the applicant alone (unless the applicant was the only victim). Indeed, it is difficult to see how it could be otherwise given an order on a section 423 application is for the purposes of restoring the *status quo ante* and protecting the interests of the victims generally. These unusual features of insolvency-related transaction avoidance initiated by an individual creditor can therefore be seen nonetheless to serve the purpose of reconstituting the debtor's estate if there is an estate and the next nearest thing to it if there is not.

---

[71] Section 424(2).

16

INVESTIGATION

1. Introduction

16.01   An office-holder cannot discharge his functions without a full understanding of the affairs, business, and property of the company. However, a significant prior professional relationship is regarded as posing a clear threat to the objectivity of an insolvency practitioner such as to make it inappropriate to accept appointment as an office-holder in insolvency proceedings relating to the company.[1] The requirement for an office-holder to be independent of the company therefore means that he may have little or even none of the requisite knowledge prior to his appointment.

16.02   It follows that familiarization with the facts is an important early task for the office-holder. Liquidators and administrators are supported in this respect by provisions of the Act which:

a) require officers and employees to co-operate with them;
b) enable persons capable of giving relevant information to be examined;
c) render liens on books and records unenforceable; and
d) provide summary remedies for the recovery of the company's books and records.

---

[1] See further *Insolvency Practitioner Code of Ethics* <https://www.gov.uk/government/publications/insolvency-practitioner-code-of-ethics> accessed 28 October 2016 and Chapter 13.

None of these provisions, which are discussed in more detail in the succeeding **16.03** sections of this chapter, apply to company voluntary arrangements (CVAs). There are two reasons why they are not needed for voluntary arrangements: first, the consensual (and therefore self-policing) nature of the procedure and, secondly, the finality of an approved arrangement. Rule 2.3 makes very detailed provisions for the information which a directors' proposal for a voluntary arrangement must deal with (and which must be accompanied by a statement of affairs) and rule 2.8 enables the nominee to call for additional disclosure. (A director who gives false information for the purposes of obtaining the approval of the arrangement commits an offence under section 6A.) A nominee who is not satisfied with the information which has been provided will note that fact in his report to the court on whether the proposal should be considered at a company meeting and by the creditors.[2] Once an arrangement has been approved the property which is affected by it and the supervisor's functions should be clear, such that no further special investigatory powers are required.

Some of the current provisions for investigation in liquidations and administra- **16.04** tions have no counterparts in the legislation which preceded the Act but the existence of some such special provisions dates back to the Companies Act 1862. In *Re Imperial Continental Water Corporation*, Lindley LJ said of the 1862 provisions:[3]

> The object of them all is to enable the company, through its liquidator, with a view to the benefit of the creditors or contributories, or both of them, to ascertain what has been going on, and what has been done with the assets of the company.

More recently, Megarry J said in *Re Rolls Razor Ltd (No 2)*:[4]

> The process under section 268 is needed because of the difficulty in which the liquidator in an insolvent company is necessarily placed. He usually comes as a stranger to the affairs of a company which has sunk to its financial doom. In that process, it may well be that some of those concerned in the management of the company, and others as well, have been guilty of some misconduct or impropriety which is of relevance to the liquidation. Even those who are wholly innocent of any wrongdoing may have motives for concealing what was done. In any case, there are almost certain to be many transactions which are difficult to discover or to understand merely from the books and papers of the company. Accordingly, the legislature has provided this extraordinary process so as to enable the requisite information to be obtained.

The reference to section 268 was a reference to the provision for private examination in the Companies Act 1948, but Megarry J's summary of the rationale for that

---

[2] See further *Re a debtor (No 140 IO of 1995)* [1996] 2 BCLC 429 (Ch) (an individual voluntary arrangement case where the details of the procedure differ but the nominee's role is analogous in this respect).

[3] (1886) 33 Ch D 314 (CA) 321.

[4] [1970] 1 Ch 576 (Ch) 591G.

particular power is equally applicable to the remainder of the provisions in the Act and to their application in administration as well as liquidation.

16.05   In some cases, these special powers even override privilege against self-incrimination.

2. The duty to co-operate

16.06   The starting point for an office-holder will usually be a statement of affairs. In a creditors' voluntary liquidation, the directors are required to send a statement of affairs to the creditors and deliver it to the liquidator.[5] In a compulsory liquidation, the official receiver can call for a statement of affairs and the administrator has a duty to call for such a statement in an administration.[6] A statement of affairs is essentially a statement of the company's assets and liabilities. A conscientiously prepared statement will be a useful starting point for the office-holder, but it will be no more than a starting point.

16.07   Under section 235, a liquidator or administrator can require a prescribed list of persons to give such information as he/she may reasonably require in respect of the promotion, formation, business, dealings, affairs, or property of the company.[7] This formulation of the scope of the potential requirement could scarcely be more widely drawn. The list of prescribed persons comprises principally past and present officers, those who have taken part in the formation of the company within the preceding twelve months, and persons who are either employed by the company or were employed within the preceding twelve months and who the office-holder thinks can give him information which he requires. A surprising (but justifiable) feature is that an 'employee' for these purposes includes a person retained under a contract for services: professional advisers are therefore covered. All these persons can also be required to attend on the office-holder at such times as he/she may reasonably require.

16.08   The prescribed persons are all 'insiders' and the office-holder has no need to go to the court to trigger their duties to co-operate. On the contrary, non-compliance without reasonable excuse is a criminal offence. It may nonetheless be necessary to compel compliance and the office-holder can do this by means of obtaining an order under rule 12.52.[8]

16.09   Privilege against self-incrimination is not available to persons subject to the section 235 duty to co-operate. A director of a company who had already been charged with criminal offences has been ordered to attend on the official receiver in compliance

---

[5] Section 99 and rule 6.3.
[6] Section 131 and Schedule B1 para 47.
[7] Section 235.
[8] *Re Wallace Smith Trust Co Ltd* [1992] BCC 707 (Ch).

with his section 235 duties in order to be asked questions.[9] In *Bishopsgate Investment Management Ltd v Maxwell*, Mann LJ said more generally:[10]

> The first duties of an office-holder who is a provisional liquidator are to trace and then to secure the assets of the company for the benefit of the creditors and (occasionally) the contributories. His ability to trace in a liquidation where assets are missing and the documentation does not disclose their whereabouts, must be heavily dependent upon his ability to use sections 235 and 236. Those sections could be useless for their purpose if the privilege against self-incrimination is not abrogated.

3. Examination powers

The importance attached to the investigatory aspects of insolvency law is demonstrated by the breadth of the examination powers available to liquidators and administrators. The examinations which are conducted pursuant to these powers are court procedures, not informal interviews. In the case of liquidation some examinations may be in public, but only private examination is available to an administrator. Subject to extra-territoriality considerations, these extraordinary powers can be used to compel assistance from literally anyone who is in a position to provide relevant information and, at least to some extent, they override privilege against self-incrimination. Although some such powers are to be found in other systems of insolvency law, the English powers are at the top end of the scale of severity. The counterbalance is that they are at all times subject to the control of the court which exercises its powers so as to prevent their being deployed in an oppressive manner. **16.10**

Public examination (pursuant to section 133) in a liquidation and private examination (pursuant to section 236) in both liquidation and administration serve slightly different purposes. Both are concerned with gathering information but public examination has a wider dimension. The Cork Report said:[11] **16.11**

> A public examination during the course of Compulsory Winding Up proceedings should ... be intended to serve three principal purposes:
>
> a) to form the basis of reports which the Official Receiver may have to submit to the Department concerning the affairs of the company; for example, concerning possible offences by officers of the company and others;
> b) to obtain material information for the administration of the estate which cannot as well be obtained privately; and

---

⁹ Ibid.
¹⁰ [1993] Ch 1 (CA) 60H, see also 63A. The position of a provisional liquidator is not materially different from that of a liquidator or administrator for these purposes. See further *R v Brady* [2004] EWCA Crim 1763, [2004] 1 WLR 3240 [23].
¹¹ Report of the Review Committee, *Insolvency Law and Practice* (Cm 8558, June 1982) para 655.

c) to give publicity, for the information of creditors and the community at large, to the salient facts and unusual features connected with the company's failure.

The focus on the consideration of conduct was emphasized, with an added hint of deterrence, by the contrasting summaries of the purposes of public and private examination which appeared in the ensuing White Paper:[12]

> The principal use of the public examination ... will in future be to aid the Official Receiver in establishing, where this has not been possible through other means, the true causes of failure and the existence of misconduct likely to warrant a criminal prosecution. It will also be an effective means of dealing with recalcitrant directors ... who do not co-operate with the Official Receiver ...

> The principal purpose of private examinations is to enable the liquidator ... to establish the circumstances relating to the company's ... property, dealings and affairs, with a particular view to recovering assets and ascertaining the validity of creditors' claims.

16.12 The mere existence of these residual powers will usually be sufficient to procure co-operation from prospective examinees. However, a prospective examinee who is subject to confidentiality obligations to third parties in respect of relevant information which it is holding (for example a bank) may ask the office-holder to obtain an order for private examination in order to protect the examinee from later claims that he has breached those obligations.

a. Public examination

16.13 The passages quoted above from the Cork Report and the White Paper refer to the official receiver and compulsory liquidations. Section 133 is an obvious adjunct to the official receiver's obligation to investigate and report to the court under section 132 but it only applies to persons falling within prescribed classes (as to which see below).

16.14 Under section 133[13] an application is made to the court by the official receiver and not by the responsible office-holder (if different) but a liquidator in a voluntary liquidation can apply under section 112.[14] Once satisfied that the company is in liquidation and the prospective examinee falls within one of the prescribed classes, the court must order a public examination unless satisfied that it would serve no useful purpose.[15] However, public examinations remain unusual.

16.15 Like section 235, section 133 is concerned with insiders but, in this case, the jurisdiction is concerned with officers of the company and those who have taken part

---

[12] Department of Trade and Industry, *A Revised Framework for Insolvency Law* (White Paper, Cm 9175, February 1984) paras 93 and 95.

[13] See also Part 7 Chapter 19 of the Rules.

[14] *Re Pantmaenog Timber Co Ltd* [2003] UKHL 49, [2004] 1 AC 158 [56].

[15] *Re Casterbridge Properties Ltd (No 2)* [2003] EWCA Civ 1246, [2004] 1 WLR 602.

in its management (excluding the employees who can be required to co-operate under section 235). The examination can be very wide-ranging, extending across the promotion, formation, and management of the company, and the conduct of its business and affairs, as well as the examinee's own conduct or dealings in relation to the company. As its name implies, public examination takes place in open court. In addition to the official receiver, the liquidator (if different), creditors, and contributories may all take part in the examination. (Specified majorities of the creditors and contributories can, unless the court otherwise orders, require the official receiver to apply for a public examination.) The ability of creditors to participate in the examination and have access to its results may lead them to favour public examination over a private examination.[16]

Subject to safeguards in respect of criminal proceedings, statements made by the examinee in the course of a public examination can be used in evidence against him.[17] The public interest in proper investigation was underlined by the Court of Appeal in *Re Seagull Manufacturing Co Ltd* where it was held that the jurisdiction of the court to order public examination of company officers in a compulsory liquidation is not subject to any territorial limitation. Peter Gibson J, giving the leading judgment in that case, prefaced his consideration of the territoriality issue with the following observations on the underlying policy of section 133:[18] **16.16**

> Where a company has come to a calamitous end and has been wound up by the court, the obvious intention of this section was that those responsible for the company's state of affairs should be liable to be subjected to a process of investigation and that investigation should be in public. Parliament could not have intended that a person who had that responsibility could escape liability to investigation simply by not being within the jurisdiction. Indeed, if the section were to be construed as leaving out of its grasp anyone not within the jurisdiction, deliberate evasion by removing oneself out of the jurisdiction would suffice. That seems to me to be a wholly improbable intention to attribute to Parliament.

b. Private examination

In practice, the private examination powers of official receivers, liquidators, and administrators under section 236 are much more important.[19] There is a similarly wide potential scope of an examination but private examination is not simply a private version of a public examination. In particular: **16.17**

a) the court has a discretion as to whether to order a private examination;
b) creditors cannot requisition a private examination and do not usually have any role to play in its conduct;

---

[16] As in *Re Richbell Strategic Holdings Ltd* [2001] BCC 409 (Ch).
[17] Section 433; *R v Sawtell* [2001] BPIR 381 (CA).
[18] [1993] Ch 345 (CA) 354G.
[19] See also Part 12 Chapter 4B of the Rules.

c) the record of the examination is not filed in the court and is not accessible by creditors without a court order;

d) (subject to extra-territoriality issues) anyone capable of giving relevant information can be examined, as can persons who are either suspected of being in possession of company property or who are supposed to be indebted to the company;[20]

e) an examinee can be ordered to produce relevant documents even though they do not belong to the company; and

f) the court can make a summary order under section 237 for the delivery up of company property or the payment of a debt due to the company.

16.18 As suggested by the statement of purpose in the White Paper which is quoted in paragraph 16.11, these powers are most frequently used in order to gain information about assets and liabilities. However, they exist for all the purposes of the proceeding. In *Re Rolls Razor Ltd*, Buckley J said:[21]

> The powers conferred by section 268 [the Companies Act 1948 analogue of section 236] are powers directed to enabling the court to help a liquidator to discover the truth of the circumstances in connection with the affairs of the company, information of trading, dealings, and so forth, in order that the liquidator may be able, as effectively as possible, and, I think, with as little expense as possible ... to complete his function as liquidator, to put the affairs of the company in order and to carry out the liquidation in all its various aspects, including, of course, the getting in of any assets of the company available in the liquidation. It is therefore appropriate for the liquidator, when he thinks that he may be under a duty to try to recover something from some officer or employee of a company, or some other person who is, in some way, concerned with the company's affairs, to be able to discover, with as little expense as possible, the facts surrounding any such possible claim.

The powers are equally applicable to the performance of the wider functions of the office-holder, for example in reporting on the conduct of directors for disqualification purposes.[22] As regards all these matters, information may be needed from persons who are not subject to the section 235 duty to co-operate with the office holder. As Chitty J said at first instance in *Re Imperial Continental Water Corporation*:[23]

> Those extensive powers are conferred upon the court for the beneficial winding up of the company, for sometimes it happens that the liquidator is unable to obtain from unwilling persons the information which he requires.

---

[20] But the risk of oppression is greater in the case of outsiders: *Shierson v Rastogi* [2003] EWCA Civ 1624, [2003] 1 WLR 586.

[21] [1968] 3 All ER 698 (CA) 700; cited with approval by Dillon LJ in *Re Esal (Commodities) Ltd* [1989] BCLC 59 (CA) and by Lord Slynn in *Re British & Commonwealth Holdings Plc (Nos 1 & 2)* [1993] AC 426 (HL).

[22] *Re Pantmaenog Timber Co Ltd* [2003] UKHL 49, [2004] 1 AC 158 (HL).

[23] (1886) 33 Ch D 314 (CA) 316.

In *Re British & Commonwealth Holdings Plc (Nos 1 & 2)*, the House of Lords held **16.19** that the legitimate scope of a section 236 order was not confined to reconstituting the company's own knowledge even though that might be one of the purposes most clearly justifying an order.[24] Whilst the courts are astute to prevent the office-holder from using examination powers simply to gain an unfair advantage in other proceedings against the prospective examinee, all cases require the court to conduct a balancing exercise to weigh up the conflicting interests of the office-holder and the prospective examinee.[25]

Although not conducted in public, private examination is nonetheless a formal **16.20** court procedure and the examinee's statements are admissible in evidence against him in the same way as statements made in the course of a public examination (and subject to the same safeguards as regards criminal proceedings). However, the office-holder is under a duty to use of the information which he obtains through a private examination only for the purposes of the proceeding unless leave is obtained from the court. This is an aspect of a general principle applicable to all private information obtained through the exercise or threat of compulsory powers.[26] In *Marcel v Commissioner of Police of the Metropolis* at first instance, Browne-Wilkinson V-C said:[27]

> Powers conferred for one purpose cannot lawfully be used for other purposes without giving rise to an abuse of power.

and later:

> ... there is a close analogy between documents obtained under statutory powers of compulsion and documents obtained on discovery ... the law imposes a duty on the party who obtains discovery not without the leave of the court to use the documents disclosed for any purpose other than the conduct of the action in which discovery is given. Since the whole process of discovery is conducted under the control of the court, this duty is imposed by means of an undertaking by the party to observe those conditions. But the underlying principle is that private information obtained under compulsory powers cannot be used for purposes other than those for which the powers were conferred.

Where application has been made for an examination order on information pro- **16.21** vided by a creditor, that creditor may, if the applicant does not object and the court permits, be allowed to put questions to the examinee through the applicant but creditors are not otherwise involved.[28]

---

[24] [1993] AC 426 (HL).
[25] *Shierson v Rastogi* [2003] EWCA Civ 1624, [2003] 1 WLR 586.
[26] See further Chapter 17.
[27] [1992] Ch 225 (CA) 234G and 237B. The Vice-Chancellor's judgment was substantially varied on appeal but for reasons relating to the functions of the police and the effect of subpoenas neither of which, it is submitted, invalidate the passages quoted in the context of insolvency examinations. As to leave, see *Re Esal Commodities Ltd (No 2)* [1990] BCC 708 (Ch); *Re a Company No 005374 of 1993* [1993] BCC 734 (Ch).
[28] Rule 12.20.

c. Privilege against self-incrimination

16.22 The leading case on privilege against self-incrimination in this context is *Bishopsgate Investment Management Ltd v Maxwell*. The case was concerned with private examination but the court's reasoning involved a review of the position on public examination. It was held that there is no privilege against self-incrimination available to examinees at a public examination and that those who are susceptible to public examination equally have no right to privilege against self-incrimination on a private examination. Dillon LJ said:[29]

> ... in practically every case in which an office-holder wants to examine a director of the company under section 236 of the Insolvency Act 1986 there will have been a failure to keep proper accounting records, whether due to fraud or incompetence. Otherwise, the office-holder would not be seeking further information from the director. But the object of the examination would be stultified if the director was entitled to rely on the privilege against self-incrimination. Therefore, by implication the plea is not available to any director or other officer of the company.

16.23 The question then arises as to whether the wider range of persons against whom private examination orders can be made but who are not susceptible to public examination would be entitled to privilege against self-incrimination. Within that class there are some who, whilst not officers of a company, nonetheless also share the statutory duty to assist a liquidator or administrator under section 235 and some others who are merely witnesses. Since privilege against self-incrimination does not apply in the context of section 235, it would be illogical if it were to be available to the same class of persons in the context of section 236. It is thought therefore that there is no distinction, for these purposes, between those who are amenable to public examination under section 133 and the wider class which has the section 235 duty to co-operate. Indeed, Mann LJ in *Bishopsgate* did not distinguish between the sections in the passage from his judgment quoted in paragraph 16.09.

16.24 Even as regards those with only knowledge and no responsibility, the case for treating privilege against self-incrimination as being abrogated is strengthened by the extension of the restrictions on the use of material obtained through these compulsory powers (to take human rights issues into account) which has taken effect since *Bishopsgate* was decided.[30] Broadly, the trend has been to reconcile the inherent tensions between the need for full investigation in insolvencies and the need to respect the rights of the examinee by facilitating the collection of information but imposing restrictions on its subsequent use.

---

[29] [1993] Ch 1 (CA) 32E.
[30] See section 433.

d. Legal professional privilege

There are also questions as to the extent to which legal professional privilege **16.25** can be invoked to resist examination powers. Just as with privilege against self-incrimination, so too legal professional privilege exposes tensions between competing principles—on the one hand that insolvency proceedings require effective investigatory powers and, on the other hand, that the administration of justice requires communications with legal advisers to be protected. Sir Thomas Etherton MR identified this tension in *Shlosberg v Avonwick Holdings Ltd* (when dealing with the question of whether privilege is property which vests in a trustee in bankruptcy) where he said:[31]

> The issue at the heart of this application and appeal concerns the inter-relationship between two public interest policies: the public interest that the trustees of a bankrupt are able to get in, realise and distribute the bankrupt's estate in accordance with statutory scheme in IA 1986, and the public interest that a person is able to consult their lawyer in confidence in the knowledge that what is told to the lawyer will never be revealed without their consent.

> It is not necessary to say much more about the first of those policies. It is an obviously vital factor in the economic prosperity and general welfare of the nation that creditors are duly paid and that, when an individual or company becomes insolvent, their assets are got in, realised and distributed among the creditors.

The first point to make in this respect is that legal professional privilege is gener- **16.26** ally no obstacle to the office-holder where the company was the client because the office-holder exercises the company's own rights in that respect. This means that, for example, where a company facing the possibility of insolvency proceedings takes legal advice on the propriety of proposed transactions or the duties of its directors (as often occurs), the advice given will be an open book to a subsequently appointed liquidator or administrator.

There are two aspects to the question of legal professional privilege. First, whether **16.27** a lawyer can refuse to answer questions on examination and, secondly, whether the client is entitled to claim privilege to withhold details of legal advice which he has received. Private examination orders can be made against legal advisers. The real question concerns the questions which a lawyer can be compelled to answer. Despite the long history of examination powers in insolvency law, these questions have rarely arisen in the courts. It is clear that lawyers can be required to disclose anything which their client can be required to disclose but this leaves open the question of what the client could refuse to disclose.[32] The weight of such authority as exists points to an examinee being entitled to legal professional privilege

---

[31] [2016] EWCA Civ 1138 [40], [41].
[32] *Re Murjani (A Bankrupt)* [1996] 1 WLR 1498 (Ch) (a bankruptcy case on section 366 but equally applicable to examinations in corporate insolvency proceedings).

according to the ordinary rules of law[33] but, significantly for some cases necessitating recourse to examination powers, fraud or 'iniquity' is an exception to those ordinary rules.[34]

e. Co-operation with prosecuting and regulatory authorities

16.28 An office-holder can pass on information which he has obtained through the exercise of his powers of compulsion to prosecuting and regulatory authorities.[35]

4. Liens on books and records

16.29 Section 246 provides that a lien on a company's books, papers, and other records is unenforceable against a liquidator or administrator. It does not apply to title documents.[36]

16.30 Where an office-holder can rely upon section 246, he will not need to use section 236 to gain access to the information that he requires. Hoffmann J dealt with the relationship between the two sections in *Re Aveling Barford Ltd* where he said:[37]

> An office-holder who is able to assert the company's proprietary right to a document under section 246 will have no need to obtain an order for its production under section 236. But that circumstance does not mean that when resort is had to section 236, it should be construed more narrowly than its ordinary meaning would require. For example, section 246 does not apply to 'documents which give a title to property and are held as such.' A solicitor who has a lien over such a document cannot be required to deliver it up to a liquidator. If the solicitor will not disclose the document and the liquidator wants to know what it says, he will have to seek an order under section 236.

Even where there remains an enforceable lien, the office-holder will usually be able to complete his investigations by means of examination. The efficacy of the lien will therefore impact more on his ability to make realizations than on his information gathering.

5. Summary remedies for getting in books and records

16.31 The remedies under sections 234 and 237, discussed under this heading, are concerned with the property of the company generally but it is their potential

---

[33] *Re Highgrade Traders Ltd* [1984] BCLC 151 (CA); *Re Brook Martin & Co (Nominees) Ltd* [1993] BCLC 328 (Ch).

[34] See, for example, *Barclays Bank Plc v Eustice* [1995] 1 WLR 1238 (CA) (a section 423 case where the scope of exception arose in the context of disclosure).

[35] See further Chapter 17.

[36] See further *Re SEIL Trade Finance Ltd* [1992] BCC 538 (Ch).

[37] [1989] 1 WLR 360 (Ch) 364H.

application to getting in the company's books, papers, and records which makes them relevant to the conduct of office-holders' investigations. Megarry J, in the passage from his judgment in *Re Rolls Razor Ltd (No 2)* which is quoted in paragraph 16.04, appears to have assumed that the office-holder will always have access to the company's books and records. Of course that should be the case, but it will not always be so and these remedies can be invoked when there is a difficulty.

Sections 234 and 237 overlap in this respect. Section 234 enables the office-holder **16.32** to apply for delivery-up of the company's books, papers, and records.[38] Section 237 enables the court to make an order for delivery-up when it appears on consideration of evidence obtained on a section 236 examination that a person is in possession of the company's property.[39]

In *Sutton v GE Capital Commercial Finance Ltd*, Chadwick LJ (giving the judg- **16.33** ment of the court) said 'the powers conferred by sections 234–236 can only be invoked for a legitimate purpose' namely the performance of the office-holder's own functions in relation to the insolvency proceeding.[40] *Sutton* was a case where the company's solicitors had voluntarily delivered up their files to the company's administrative receivers (to whom sections 234–236 also apply) and the administrative receivers had forwarded the files, unread, to their appointing debenture-holder for use in litigation against a guarantor. The court ordered the return of the files to the administrative receivers with all rights to confidence and privilege intact.

Whilst it is undoubtedly correct that examination under section 236 will only be **16.34** ordered for the purposes of the proceeding and the use of the evidence thereby obtained is similarly constrained, it is difficult to see why a liquidator or administrator's motives should have any bearing on the performance of his duty to get in the company's own property or his right to apply for relief for that purpose.[41] Elsewhere it had previously been held that, where a liquidator recovers possession of the company's own books, papers, and records then, absent any confidentiality obligations owed to third parties, he is free to disclose their contents to others if he considers that to do so would be in the interests of the estate,[42] but those decisions

---

[38] A liquidator in a compulsory liquidation can proceed in reliance upon rule 7.78 without the need for an application (but may need an application to enforce his/her requirement).

[39] Section 234 refers expressly to 'property, books, papers or records' whereas section 237 refers merely to 'property'. Given the breadth of that term, as defined in section 436, it is thought that books, papers, and records are property for these purposes and that the difference between the sections is merely another example of the infelicities of the drafting of the Act.

[40] [2004] EWCA Civ 315, [2004] 2 BCLC 662 [33].

[41] Administrative receivership may be distinguishable from liquidation and administration in this respect because an administrative receiver's interest in the company's property is governed by his equitable duty to act in good faith for the purpose of discharging the secured indebtedness (see further *Downsview Nominees Ltd v First City Corp Ltd* [1993] AC 295 (PC)).

[42] *Re ACLI Metals (London) Ltd* (1989) 5 BCC 749 (Ch); *Walker Morris v Khalastchi* [2001] 1 BCLC 1 (Ch).

were not referred to in the *Sutton* judgment. The Court of Appeal instead cited[43] passages from the judgment of Lord Millett in *Re Pantmaenog Timber Co Ltd*[44] and that of Lord Cameron in *First Tokyo Index Ltd v Gould*,[45] wrongly characterizing both as referring to section 234 when in fact both were referring only to section 236.

6. Conclusions

16.35 A well-advised liquidator or administrator will always prefer to secure voluntary co-operation if that is possible—if only to avoid the costs, formality, and potential delays of recourse to the courts. The deterrent effect of these various special powers should not be underestimated in that connection. Their mere presence in the armoury of an office-holder will usually be sufficient to procure co-operation from recalcitrant third parties as soon as they are advised as to the existence of the powers.

16.36 The courts have shown a robust approach to the use of the powers for all the purposes of the proceeding. The more obvious application of the powers is to getting in the company's own property. That includes investigating the possibility of transaction avoidance claims and misfeasance and other claims against directors. All that supports the interests of creditors in maximizing realizations and hence distributions. However, through linkage with the reporting functions discussed in Chapter 17, the powers are equally important in enabling wrongdoing by directors and others to be brought to book and the powers thereby also support the wider social interest in the efficacy of insolvency proceedings.

---

[43] *Sutton* (n 40) [33], [41].
[44] [2003] UKHL 49, [2004] 1 AC 158 [64].
[45] [1996] BPIR 406 (Court of Session, Outer House) 412D.

17

WRONGDOING BY DIRECTORS
AND OTHERS

1. Introduction

Both outright dishonesty and genuine misfortune are less common than is some- **17.01** times supposed; most insolvencies result from a degree of culpable mismanagement. Although the work of office-holders appointed in insolvency proceedings is primarily concerned with the administration of the insolvent estate, examination of the causes of insolvency and the punishment of malpractice are also important. Accordingly, insolvency law includes various provisions by means of which malpractice can be pursued. It is a statement of the obvious that failure to take proper action in respect of malpractice encourages degeneration in attitudes to debt. The treatment of malpractice is therefore central to the wider social and economic purposes of insolvency law. The Cork Report said of this:[1]

> It is a basic objective of the law to support the maintenance of commercial morality and encourage the fulfilment of financial obligations. Insolvency must not be an easy solution for those who can bear with equanimity the stigma of their own failure or their responsibility for the failure of a company under their management.
>
> … None of the directors or shareholders is normally liable for the debts of a company, but their freedom from liability is granted in return for:

---

[1] Report of the Review Committee, *Insolvency Law and Practice* (Cm 8558, June 1982) paras 191 and 193.

(a) an obligation on the part of those responsible for the management of the company's affairs to give an account of the reasons for the company's failure, and, if required, to submit their conduct of the company's affairs to impartial investigation; and

(b) subjection to such personal liability for the company's debts and such personal disabilities as may be appropriate in all the circumstances.

In its White Paper responding to the Report, the government endorsed this approach in blunt terms:[2]

> The fundamental objectives of the Department of Trade and Industry are to encourage, assist and ensure the proper regulation of British trade, industry and commerce, and to promote a climate conducive to growth and the national production of wealth. In pursuing these objectives, the principal role of the Insolvency Legislation is ... (iii) to deter and penalise irresponsible behaviour and malpractice on the part of those who manage a company's affairs ...

17.02   The difficulties of legislation in this area were well expressed in the report of the Greene Committee in 1926 and remain true today:[3]

> Many of the suggestions made to us show that the idea that fraud and lesser malpractices can be stopped by the simple expedient of a prohibition in an Act of Parliament, dies hard. Other witnesses with a view to making such malpractices impossible have advocated the imposition of statutory regulations and prohibitions calculated, not merely to put a stop to the activities of the wrongdoer, but to place quite intolerable fetters upon honest business. It is often forgotten that in dealing with a matter such as company law, which affects so closely the whole business life of the nation, a certain amount of elasticity is essential if the system is to work in practice ... We realise that the system of limited liability leaves opportunities for abuse. Some of these we consider to be part of the price which the community has to pay for the adoption of a system so beneficial to its trade and industry. It appears to us, as a matter of general principle, most undesirable, in order to defeat an occasional wrongdoer, to impose restrictions which would seriously hamper the activities of honest men and would inevitably react upon the commerce and prosperity of the country.

The ensuing Companies Act 1928, which was consolidated into the Companies Act 1929 before the relevant provisions took effect, nonetheless laid the foundations for the modern provisions dealing with malpractice. The problem is addressed in four ways:

a) prosecution leading to the imposition of fines or imprisonment;

b) reporting obligations;

c) civil liability to augment the insolvent estate; and

d) disqualification.

---

[2] Department of Trade and Industry, *A Revised Framework for Insolvency Law* (White Paper, Cm 9175, February 1984) para 2.

[3] Board of Trade, *Report of the Company Law Amendment Committee* (Cm 2657, 1926).

(Some of the law on transaction avoidance also addresses malpractice but those rules are treated as a separate subject in this book.[4])

Inevitably, the criminal provisions deal with dishonesty. The Act contains a discrete criminal code which applies only in the event of insolvency, but general criminal law remains equally applicable. The discrete insolvency provisions are mainly concerned with fraud. It is an unusual characteristic of these provisions that the commencement of formal insolvency proceedings is sometimes the final ingredient which must be established before an offence can be proved to have occurred ie, pre-proceedings conduct can, in such cases, only be attacked by virtue of subsequent proceedings and the offence is then deemed to have been committed earlier. **17.03**

On the other hand, the presence or absence of fraud has little to do with the operation of the civil aspects of English insolvency law. In other words, the prosecution of malpractice and the administration of the insolvent estate are separated and subjected to different approaches. Both nonetheless have, and are intended to have, important deterrent effects. **17.04**

2. Liquidation offences

As might be expected, the criminal provisions of the Act applicable to companies are detailed but broadly they make fraudulent conduct criminal, both in the period prior to the liquidation of a company and during the course of the liquidation.[5] Convicted persons are liable to imprisonment or a fine, or both. However, no concomitant civil redress is provided for where an offence is established: these provisions are only concerned with criminal sanctions.[6] **17.05**

The pre-liquidation offences are concerned with the concealment or removal of property, falsification of records and information, and transactions in fraud of creditors committed by officers of the company. The onus is on the accused person to prove absence of fraud in order to establish a defence. In one particular respect, creditors are also at risk. One of the offences concerns the fraudulent granting of security over or disposing of property obtained on credit which has not been paid for. Where that offence is established, any person taking the security or receiving the property with knowledge of the circumstances also commits an offence. **17.06**

The post-liquidation offences concern officers of the company dishonestly concealing property from the liquidator, giving misleading information, falsifying the **17.07**

---

[4] See Chapter 15.
[5] Sections 206 to 211.
[6] Unless a compensation order is made under the Powers of the Criminal Courts (Sentencing) Act 2000.

company's books, and making false representations to creditors for the purposes of obtaining consents. In the case of some but not all of these offences, the onus is again on the accused to show that no fraud was intended.

3. Reporting of offences

17.08 In every compulsory liquidation the official receiver has a duty to conduct a general investigation and to make such report as he thinks fit to the court.[7]

17.09 Much more specific provisions leading to the prosecution of offences committed by officers and members in corporate insolvency cases are to be found in section 218. First, the section confers a power on the court to direct the liquidator in a compulsory liquidation to refer perceived offences to the Secretary of State. This could be triggered by an official receiver's report made in performance of the duty already referred to. Secondly, in a compulsory liquidation where there is an insolvency practitioner acting as liquidator, the liquidator is required to report perceived offences to the official receiver. Thirdly, a voluntary liquidator is required to report perceived offences to the Secretary of State and to provide such further information and access to documents as may be required. All of this is designed to enable prosecutions to be brought in appropriate cases.

17.10 If it appears to the nominee or supervisor of a small company voluntary arrangement (CVA) where a moratorium has been obtained under Schedule A1 that an offence has been committed in connection with the moratorium or arrangement, then there is also a duty to report. Subject to that, in insolvency proceedings other than liquidations, the office-holder has no duty under the Act to report offences to the authorities.[8] However, that does not make it wrong to do so. Section 218 is not exhaustive.[9] The office-holder may wish to balance a sense of public responsibility for the pursuit of malpractice with the more commercial objectives of the appointment which he has undertaken if he needs some co-operation from those responsible. However, the office-holder's room for manoeuvre in this respect may be limited by obligations under the Company Directors Disqualification Act 1986 (CDDA) which require a liquidator or administrator to report any conduct indicating that a director is unfit to be concerned in the management of a company.

---

[7] Section 132.

[8] There may be duties under general law, for example in relation to money laundering and terrorist finance.

[9] *R v Brady* [2004] EWCA Crim 1763, [2004] 1 WLR 3240. See also Dear IP Chap 20 <https://www.insolvencydirect.bis.gov.uk/insolvencyprofessionandlegislation/dearip/dearipindex.htm> accessed 16 January 2017.

4. Investigation of malpractice: examination powers

The officers of a company in liquidation or administration have duties under sec- **17.11** tion 235 to co-operate with the office-holder and to provide an explanation of the assets and liabilities in the estate. For obvious reasons, these sources of information may not be wholly reliable where malpractice is concerned and then recourse may be had to examination powers under sections 133 and 236. Those duties and powers are considered in Chapter 16.

5. Co-operation with prosecuting and regulatory authorities

A question arises as to the extent to which office-holders can provide prosecut- **17.12** ing and regulatory authorities with relevant information obtained through these special rights and powers. This involves the so-called 'compulsion principle' under which material obtained pursuant to powers of compulsion which is not in the public domain is to be treated as confidential and used only for the purposes for which those powers were granted. Where the office-holder is himself under an enforceable duty to provide information obtained by examination, no question of public interest immunity arises so as to prevent compliance.[10] The potential tensions between the compulsion principle and such duties cannot be resolved on an office-holder's application for directions. The correct course is to challenge the decision to trigger the office-holder's duty, if necessary on a judicial review application.[11]

However, not all such disclosure involves any such tensions. The voluntary passing **17.13** of information obtained through an office-holder's powers to prosecuting authorities is consistent with the purpose for which those powers are granted. In *R v Brady*, Tuckey LJ (giving the judgment of the court) said:[12]

> Confidentiality is conceded, but it is necessary to examine why the information is confidential. It is not because the information provided is private, but because it has been obtained by compulsion in circumstances where the rule against self-incrimination cannot be invoked. The public interest requires that informa- tion obtained in this way should only be used for the purposes for which it was obtained. But wide use of such material can lawfully be made, as is apparent just

---

[10] *Hamilton v Naviede* [1995] 2 AC 75 (HL). Although the court retains formal control of access to the record of a section 236 examination under rule 12.21, it is not a proper exercise of the court's discretion to prevent prosecuting authorities from obtaining transcripts (their subsequent use in criminal proceedings being a matter for the trial judge).

[11] *Revenue and Customs Commissioners v Ariel* [2016] EWHC 1674 (Ch), [2016] BPIR 1144.

[12] [2004] EWCA Crim 1763, [2004] 1 WLR 3240 [23]. As to self-incrimination, see further Chapter 16.

from the terms of section 218 of the 1986 Act and the fact that it may be used for the purposes of a DTI prosecution or disqualification proceedings.

This was said of the use by the official receiver of material obtained pursuant to the duty of a company officer to co-operate with him under section 235. However, there is no reason to adopt a different approach as regards other office-holders or to distinguish between material obtained pursuant to the section 235 duty and material obtained through the use of office-holder examination powers. In *Re Pantmaenog Timber Co Ltd*, the House of Lords held that an office-holder's examination powers could be used for the sole purpose of gathering evidence for use in disqualification proceedings. Lord Millett said:[13]

> In my opinion, the only limitation which is implicit in section 236 is that it may be invoked only for the purpose of enabling the applicant to exercise his statutory functions in relation to the company which is being wound up. Whether the applicant is the official receiver or the liquidator or other office-holder these include the provision of information to the Secretary of State or the official receiver which is relevant to the bringing or continuing of disqualification proceedings.

If examination powers can be invoked for those purposes, it must follow that information obtained by means of such powers (whether exercised specifically for that purpose or not) can properly be provided to those charged with responsibility for disqualification proceedings and the propriety of also providing the same information to the prosecuting authorities in an appropriate case should also follow. This can be justified on the grounds that the investigation of criminal conduct must take priority and the rights of an accused are protected by the restrictions on the use that can be made of such material in criminal prosecutions.[14]

6. Fraudulent and wrongful trading

17.14 The most obvious area of possible malpractice in an insolvency concerns continued trading to the detriment of creditors. It is popularly supposed that 'trading while insolvent' in itself attracts sanctions but this is not correct. The immediate consequence of actual or anticipated insolvency is that the directors of a company must act with regard to the interests of the creditors of the company.[15] Many businesses nonetheless trade whilst they are either unable to pay their debts as they fall due or whilst the amount of their liabilities exceeds the realizable value of their assets. Start-ups, businesses experiencing temporary liquidity problems, and businesses undergoing restructuring all provide examples of where this might occur without

---

[13] [2003] UKHL 49, [2004] 1 AC 158 [67].

[14] Section 433 (which conforms with like protections in section 219 of the Act and section 20 of the CDDA).

[15] *West Mercia Safetywear Ltd v Dodd* [1988] BCLC 250 (CA); *GHLM Trading Ltd v Maroo* [2012] EWHC 61 (Ch), [2012] 2 BCLC 369; *BTI 2014 LLC v Sequana SA* [2016] EWHC 1686 (Ch).

necessarily involving any impropriety. Even though trading whilst insolvent does not, of itself, involve any exposure to liability, it is nonetheless a high-risk situation in which the rules on fraudulent and wrongful trading come into play.

Fraudulent trading involves a hybrid approach to the misconduct. Fraudulent trad- **17.15** ing is said to occur when the business of a company is carried on with intent to defraud creditors or for any other fraudulent purpose. There has to be actual dishonesty although that may be inferred where a company continues to carry on incurring credit when the directors know that there is no reasonable prospect of the creditors receiving payment.[16] Fraudulent trading does not happen in every case where an individual creditor is defrauded, but only in those cases where the business has been carried on with intent to defraud (even though, in the result, only one creditor may actually be defrauded by a single transaction).[17] Creditors, for these purposes, include future and potential creditors and the offence can be committed by deliberately taking unauthorized credit periods.[18] Under section 993 of the Companies Act 2006, such conduct constitutes a criminal offence carrying a maximum sentence of ten years. Formal insolvency is irrelevant in this context, so section 993 can also properly be regarded as part of the general criminal law. On the other hand, if in the course of liquidation or administration it appears that fraudulent trading has occurred, sections 213 and 246ZA empower the court, on the application of the liquidator or administrator, as the case may be, to order persons who were knowingly parties to the fraudulent trading to make such contribution to the company's assets as the court thinks fit.[19] There is therefore a criminal offence which is not insolvency related but which is coupled with civil or compensatory provisions which are only applicable in the event of insolvency proceedings. (Civil liability for fraudulent trading in administration, under section 246ZA, is a new development which resulted from amendments to the Act made by the Small Business, Enterprise and Employment Act 2015.)

The concept of fraudulent trading which involved both civil and criminal con- **17.16** sequences was introduced by the Companies Act 1928 but has not been without problems. The courts have consistently refused to impose civil liability without proof of dishonesty and have imposed a strict standard of proof on liquidators seeking to make recoveries from errant directors whose continued trading activities have inflicted losses on creditors. That led to a proposal in the Cork Report to replace the civil remedy for fraudulent trading with a new remedy under which personal liability could be imposed without proof of fraud or dishonesty and without a criminal standard of proof. The Cork proposal resulted in the enactment of

---

[16] *Re Patrick and Lyon Ltd* [1933] Ch 786 (Ch); *Re William C Leitch Bros Ltd* [1932] 2 Ch 71 (Ch).

[17] *Morphitis v Bernasconi* [2003] EWCA Civ 289, [2003] Ch 552.

[18] *R v Smith* [1996] 2 BCLC 109 (CA); *R v Kemp* [1988] QB 645 (CA); *R v Grantham* [1984] QB 675 (CA).

[19] The award is compensatory not penal: *Morphitis v Bernasconi* (n 17).

what is now section 214 and the introduction of liability for wrongful trading, but both the civil and criminal aspects of fraudulent trading were nonetheless retained. Section 246ZB, also resulting from the 2015 amendments, extends wrongful trading to administrations. Like fraudulent trading, wrongful trading is a statutory form of liability actionable by the office-holder but, instead of a test of dishonesty, it articulates a tortious standard of care.[20]

17.17   Sections 214 and 246ZB (which are in substantially the same terms) conspicuously fail to provide a definition of wrongful trading as such; instead, under that heading, they prescribe circumstances in which directors (and shadow directors) can be liable to contribute to a company's assets. This involves the concept of the directors knowing, or being in a position where they ought to have known, in advance of liquidation or administration (as the case may be), that insolvency proceedings were inevitable and that the company's assets would be insufficient for the discharge of its liabilities and the expenses of the proceeding. The position of each director is considered separately. The test of what a director actually knew is, of course, wholly subjective but, for the purposes of deciding what a director ought to have known, the test is partly subjective and partly objective. It has regard not only to the general knowledge, skill, and experience of the director in question but also that which can be expected of a person with the functions entrusted to that director.

17.18   Where wrongful trading is established on the part of directors, the court has a discretionary power to order them to contribute to the company's assets unless, by way of defence, they can establish that after the liquidation or administration could be seen to be inevitable, they took every step with a view to minimizing loss to individual creditors.[21] In the context of liquidation, it has been held that the correct approach is to establish whether the company suffered loss caused by the continuation of trading and that the starting point is to measure the increase in the net deficiency for unsecured creditors during the period between the first perception of inevitable liquidation and the eventual winding-up.[22] A more nuanced approach may be required in the case of administration. Where the administration is a liquidating administration, the liquidation approach is appropriate but it could be misleading where administration has been used as a step to effect a restructuring. Unless a more nuanced approach is adopted, the risk of liability might create a perverse incentive to avoid the use of administration even in cases where to do so would be in the interests of creditors.

17.19   The remedies for both fraudulent and wrongful trading provide for the contribution (if any) to be made to the company's assets. The award cannot be hypothecated to the claims of particular creditors.[23] This latter point arguably can lead to

---

[20] *Re D'Jan of London Ltd* [1994] BCLC 561 (Ch).
[21] *Re Ralls Builders Ltd* [2016] EWHC 243 (Ch), [2016] Bus LR 555 [245].
[22] Ibid at [241].
[23] *Brooks v Armstrong* [2016] EWHC 2893 (Ch) [120].

injustice in some cases since both fraudulent and wrongful trading will typically involve old creditors benefitting at the expense of new creditors.

It might be thought that, following the introduction of wrongful trading, civil **17.20** liability for fraudulent trading became redundant, but this is not so. In this connection it is important to appreciate first that the focus of the two remedies is fundamentally different. Fraudulent trading is not merely an aggravated form of wrongful trading. It is usually concerned with the propriety of incurring new liabilities. As interpreted by the courts, the test is whether there was a genuine belief in a reasonable prospect of those liabilities being discharged as they fell due. Wrongful trading is concerned with the reasonable prospect of a company avoiding insolvent liquidation or (now) administration. This is focused on the likely outcome for all creditors. Given the different nature of the tests it is possible, albeit unlikely, for fraudulent trading to be established without wrongful trading, for example in a case where directors were justified in thinking that a company could still avoid an insolvency proceeding through some form of consensual arrangement with its creditors but caused it to incur new liabilities in the meantime which they knew the company would be unable to discharge as they fell due. That said it is more likely that the remedies will overlap in any case where fraudulent trading has occurred and an office-holder who might make out both fraudulent and wrongful trading will inevitably prefer to address the lower standard of proof demanded in respect of the latter.

In some respects, however, the scope of fraudulent trading is wider and so it retains **17.21** a useful place in the office-holder's armoury. First, only directors (or shadow directors) can be liable for wrongful trading but fraudulent trading claims can be brought against any person who is 'knowingly a party to' the carrying on of the company's business with intent to defraud. In practice, the persons most likely to be party to fraudulent trading are directors but the remedy is not so restricted and, for example, a creditor could incur liability by accepting money known to have been procured by carrying on the business for the very purpose of making the payment because, as Templeman J graphically put it in *Re Gerald Cooper Chemicals Ltd*, 'a man who warms himself with the fire of fraud cannot complain if he is singed'.[24] (However, before an outsider can be held liable for fraudulent trading, it must be shown that someone who was actually responsible for carrying on the company's business was acting fraudulently. Thus a claim against a parent company, which had issued letters of comfort in respect of a subsidiary which were ultimately not honoured, was struck out where it appeared that the subsidiary's own management had believed that the support would be forthcoming.[25]) It is also possible for the knowledge of an employee to be attributed to his employer so as

---

[24] [1978] Ch 262 (Ch) 268F.
[25] *Re Augustus Barnett & Son Ltd* [1986] BCLC 170 (Ch).

to make the employer liable under sections 213 and 246ZA.[26] Secondly, the fraud does not have to be directed at the company itself or even the company's own creditors. If the business of the company is being conducted with intent to defraud the creditors of another person or for any other fraudulent purpose (for example, tax evasion) sections 213 and 246ZA apply.[27]

17.22   A declaration under either section 213 or section 214 that a person is liable to contribute to the company's assets as a result of either fraudulent or wrongful trading triggers a power to disqualify that person from acting as a company director under section 10 of the CDDA. Section 10 has not been amended to refer to sections 246ZA and 246ZB. There is, therefore, an anomalous distinction between liquidation and administration in this respect.

7. Disqualification of directors

17.23   Alongside exposure to civil liability for malpractice, company directors risk disqualification. In practice the most used ground for disqualifying directors is unfitness, which was introduced by the Insolvency Act 1985 and shortly afterwards consolidated with other disqualification provisions in the CDDA.[28] Disqualification on the ground of unfitness was one of the most controversial aspects of the 1985/86 reforms of insolvency law and the proposals in that respect were much changed during the process of enactment. However, the jurisdiction is now very well established and operates as a powerful deterrent.

17.24   The concept of disqualification in the absence of any material qualification is, at first sight, surprising but its origins also go back to the Companies Act 1928.[29] Until amendments made by the Small Business, Enterprise and Employment Act 2015 took effect, this was a purely prophylactic jurisdiction designed to protect the public from future misconduct. A director who had been disqualified could not act as the director of another company during the period of disqualification, or be concerned in its management, but there was no remedy for those who had suffered from the misconduct which gave rise to the disqualification. This is no longer the case because the court can now make a compensation order in addition to disqualification.[30]

---

[26]   *Bank of India v Morris* [2005] EWCA Civ 693, [2005] BCC 739.

[27]   *Re L Todd (Swanscombe) Ltd* [1990] BCC 125(Ch).

[28]   In addition to fraudulent and wrongful trading (as already mentioned) other grounds for disqualification are convictions, persistent breaches of companies legislation, other fraud, or breaches of competition law: see generally sections 1 to 10 CDDA.

[29]   The history of this branch of insolvency law was traced by Lord Millett in *Re Pantmaenog Timber Co Ltd* [2003] UKHL 49, [2004] 1 AC 158 [32]–[42].

[30]   Sections 15A and 15B CDDA; Compensation Orders (Disqualified Directors) Proceedings (England and Wales) Rules 2016 (SI 2016/890).

If a company becomes insolvent and unfitness is established, disqualification from **17.25** acting as a director is mandatory for a period of at least two years, subject to a maximum of fifteen years. Matters to be taken into account both in determining unfitness and in deciding upon the length of a disqualification order include the degree of responsibility for the company's insolvency and any misfeasance.[31] The courts have adopted three broad categories of disqualification orders. A top bracket of over ten years is reserved for particularly serious cases, for example where a respondent is being disqualified for a second time. A lowest bracket of two to five years is for cases which are not very serious and the bracket in between is for more serious cases which do not merit the top bracket. It might be thought that this categorization is not especially informative but it was first promulgated by the Court of Appeal in one of the early cases under the CDDA and has subsequently stood the test of time.[32]

For the purposes of disqualification on the ground of unfitness, 'director' includes **17.26** a shadow director.[33] Further amendments made by the Small Business, Enterprise and Employment Act 2015 closed a loophole by making it possible also to disqualify a person who directed or instructed conduct resulting in the disqualification of a single director (the 'main transgressor') even if their influence did not extend to the rest of the board.[34]

Flouting disqualification can result in imprisonment and personal liability for **17.27** debts of the company in respect of which the breach has occurred.[35]

A director who is accused of unfitness and who wishes to avoid the (consider- **17.28** able) costs of contesting disqualification proceedings can offer a disqualification undertaking, which has the same effect as an order.[36] Where an undertaking is offered before disqualification proceedings are brought, the Secretary of State will not usually demand payment of costs. An undertaking can still be given after the commencement of proceedings but in that eventuality the Secretary of State will normally seek his costs.[37] It remains questionable whether this system of plea bargaining between parties of such unequal strength is entirely just.

The average disqualification resulting from undertakings is lower than that result- **17.29** ing from orders. The Insolvency Service states that this is in recognition of saving the costs of proceedings and achieving earlier protection of the public but, presumably, it also reflects the fact that a bargain has been struck.

---

[31] Section 12C and Schedule 1 CDDA.
[32] *Re Sevenoaks Stationers (Retail) Ltd* [1991] Ch 164 (CA).
[33] Section 6(3C) CDDA.
[34] Section 8ZA CDDA.
[35] Sections 13 and 15 CDDA.
[36] Sections 1A and 7 CDDA.
[37] Dear IP Chap 10(4) (Issue No 2, March 2001) <https://www.insolvencydirect.bis.gov.uk/insolvencyprofessionandlegislation/dearip/dearipindex.htm> accessed 17 January 2017.

17.30   The jurisdiction to make disqualification orders is supported by online reporting obligations. The requirements apply whenever there is an insolvent liquidation or an administration. The gist of the reporting obligations is for the office-holder to provide, within three months, a report on the conduct of every person who has been a director within the preceding three years so as to enable the Secretary of State to decide whether disqualification proceedings should be brought.[38]

17.31   Compensation can be ordered, or an undertaking accepted, where a person is disqualified as a result of conduct which has caused loss to the creditors of an insolvent company. There is no prescribed limit to the amount of compensation that may be required but it must have regard to the relevant conduct and the amount of the loss caused. One striking distinction between compensation payable pursuant to the disqualification regime and amounts payable in respect of fraudulent and wrongful trading is that disqualification compensation can be made payable to particular creditors or classes of creditors. This raises the anomalous possibility that the destination of payments required as a result of fraudulent or wrongful trading could be different depending on whether the award is made under sections 213, 214, 246ZA, and 246ZB or by way of a compensation order (although the amount of a compensation order must have regard to any other financial compensation for the misconduct). However, the Insolvency Service has stated that there is no intention to usurp the asset recovery role of the office-holder.[39]

8. Conclusions

17.32   As the Greene Committee observed, there is a balance to be struck between the pursuit of malpractice and not discouraging what has more recently been called 'responsible risk taking'.[40] In modern English insolvency law, that balance is struck by facilitating corporate rescue whilst increasing the potential sanctions against errant directors (and others who may share their responsibility).

17.33   The sanctions also reflect a balance; in this case between redress for past misconduct and the prevention of future misconduct.

17.34   The milestones in the subsequent development of the original sanctions for malpractice have been the introduction of civil liability for wrongful trading and

---

[38] Section 7A CDDA; Insolvent Companies (Reports on Conduct of Directors) (England and Wales) Rules 2016 (SI 2016/180). Guidance on the use of the Director Conduct Reporting Service appears at: <https://www.gov.uk/government/publications/director-conduct-report-service> accessed 13 October 2016.

[39] See further sections 15A to 15C CDDA; Compensation Orders (Disqualified Directors) Proceedings (England and Wales) Rules 2016 (SI 2016/890); Dear IP Chap 10(46) (Issue No 73, October 2016).

[40] Department of Trade and Industry, *Insolvency – A Second Chance* (White Paper, Cm 5234, July 2001).

mandatory disqualification for conduct demonstrating unfitness resulting from the 1985/86 reforms, and the general tightening of the regime resulting from the amendments made by the Small Business, Enterprise and Employment Act 2015. One such amendment, not previously mentioned in this chapter but identified in the earlier consideration of office-holder recoveries and the insolvent estate,[41] is the power of the office-holder to assign fraudulent and wrongful trading claims which is contained in section 246ZD. This may well produce a new dynamic in the pursuit of such claims and, conversely, the risks for directors.

---

[41] See Chapter 14.

18

PHOENIXISM AND PRE-PACKING

1. Introduction

18.01 There is no necessary connection between phoenixism and pre-packing; each can occur without the other but it is the combination of both which attracts most controversy. 'Phoenixism' is the term used to describe the re-emergence, after insolvency proceedings, of the same business under the same management. Pre-packing is the process of executing a pre-arranged sale of a business immediately upon the appointment of an administrator. In practice, most pre-packs are sales to connected persons[1]—hence taking these subjects together for the purposes of this book.

2. Phoenixism

a. The issue

18.02 There is an inevitable tension between the office-holder's duty to maximize realizations and any measures which deter connected persons from bidding to buy assets because, in some cases, connected persons are the only viable purchaser. This happens, for example, in smaller companies which have few assets and where the

---

[1] 'Connected' is defined for the purposes of the Act by sections 249 and 435.

business model depends upon the participation of their founders who alone have the necessary skills and knowledge required to carry on the business.

The issue is not new. The Cork Report noted:[2]   **18.03**

> It has been made evident to us that there is a widespread dissatisfaction at the ease with which a person trading through the medium of one or more companies with limited liability can allow such a company to become insolvent, form a new company, and then carry on trading much as before, leaving behind him a trail of unpaid creditors, and often repeating the process several times. The dissatisfaction is greatest where the director of an insolvent company has set up business again, using a similar name for the new company, and trades with assets purchased at a discount from the liquidator of the old company.

The Cork Committee thought the dissatisfaction which it had noted was entirely   **18.04** justified but its proposals for reform, which centred on strengthening the disqualification regime and imposing personal liability, were thought by the government of the day to have gone too far. The difficulty lay in striking the right balance between dealing with malpractice and not stifling legitimate commercial activity:[3]

> The Government is concerned to remedy the abuse identified by the Review Committee and has considered the imposition on directors of a measure of personal liability for subsequent failures. It has, however, not been possible to adopt the Review Committee's proposals because the Government considers that they are too far reaching and whilst they would curb the activities of the delinquent director they would, at the same time, deter the genuine entrepreneur from risking his capital in a further venture. In addition the position of the non-executive or group director and the willingness of institutions to advance venture capital on a risk-taking basis (which may involve the appointment by the institution of a director) would be unwarrantably and adversely affected.

In the event, the disqualification regime was strengthened (entailing an exposure to personal liability when acting in breach of a disqualification order)[4] and new rules were introduced to regulate the use of similar company names.

b. The duty as to price

The starting point is the nature of the office-holder's duty when exercising a power   **18.05** of sale. Quite apart from an administrator's express statutory duty to perform his functions in the interests of the company's creditors as a whole[5] (which is also implicit in a liquidator's duties), both administrators and liquidators have a duty as to price when making their realizations. That duty is a duty in equity which flows

---

[2] Report of the Review Committee, *Insolvency Law and Practice* (Cm 8558, June 1982) para 1813. A deliberate pattern of the conduct described would raise fraudulent trading issues.
[3] Department of Trade and Industry, *A Revised Framework for Insolvency Law* (White Paper, Cm 9175, February 1984) para 55.
[4] See generally Chapter 17.
[5] Schedule B1 para 3(2).

from the office-holder's status as a fiduciary; it is a duty to take reasonable care to obtain the best price that is obtainable for the sale property. The duties of liquidators and administrators as to price are the same as the familiar duty of a mortgagee exercising power of sale but, unlike a mortgagee, the office-holder's duty extends to care in respect of the timing of a sale. Millett J compared and contrasted these duties in *Re Charnley Davies Ltd (No 2)* where he said:[6]

> It was common ground that an administrator owes a duty to a company over which he is appointed to take reasonable steps to obtain a proper price for its assets. That is an obligation which the law imposes on anyone with a power, whether contractual or statutory, to sell property which does not belong to him. A mortgagee is bound to have regard to the interests of the mortgagor, but he is entitled to give priority to his own interests, and may insist on an immediate sale whether or not that is calculated to realise the best price; he must 'take reasonable care to obtain whatever is the true market value of the mortgaged property at the moment he chooses to sell it': *Cuckmere Brick Co Ltd v Mutual Finance Ltd*. An administrator, by contrast, like a liquidator, has no interest of his own to which he may give priority, and must take reasonable care in choosing the time at which to sell the property. His duty is 'to take reasonable care to obtain the best price that the circumstances permit': *Standard Chartered Bank Ltd v Walker*.
>
> It is to be observed that it is not an absolute duty to obtain the best price that circumstances permit, but only to take reasonable care to do so; and in my judgment that means the best price that circumstances *as he reasonably perceives them to be* permit.

Lightman J, delivering the judgment of the Court of Appeal in *Silven Properties Ltd v Royal Bank of Scotland Plc*, added:[7]

> The administrator as agent for the company owes a duty of care to the company in the choice of the time to sell and (by parity of reasoning) in the decision whether to take the appropriate available advantageous pre-marketing steps which are calculated to achieve the best price.

For these purposes, the 'best' or 'proper' price is market value[8] but a failure to obtain market value does not, of itself, mean that the office-holder has breached his duty. First, as Millett J emphasized in *Charnley Davies (No 2)*, the duty is not absolute. The true question concerns the adequacy of the steps taken by the office-holder to achieve market value. Secondly, there will always be a bracket or margin of appreciation around what is market value and to be in breach the office-holder must plainly be on the wrong side of the line.[9]

---

[6] [1990] BCC 605 (Ch) 618 (internal citations omitted).

[7] [2003] EWCA Civ 1409, [2004] 1 WLR 997 [25]—a case about receiver's duties where the observation about administrators was obiter.

[8] Ibid at [19].

[9] See further *Michael v Miller* [2004] EWCA Civ 282, [2004] 2 EGLR 151 [131]–[141] and *Aodhcon LLP v Bridgeco Ltd* [2014] EWHC 535 (Ch), [2004] 2 BCLC 237 [154], [159] (both mortgagee cases).

It is to be observed that although the duty as to price so described can clearly **18.06** prevent the office-holder from carrying out a peremptory sale, the identity of the purchaser, whether a connected person or not, is wholly irrelevant. All other things being equal, if a connected person offers the office-holder the highest price, an administrator or liquidator's duty is to accept that offer in preference to lower bids. To qualify the office-holder's duty in some way so as prevent acceptance of the connected person's highest offer would be a very substantial departure from established principles.

In the circumstances it is not surprising that *Statement of Insolvency Practice* **18.07** *13: Disposal of Assets to Connected Parties in an Insolvency Process* makes no suggestion that there cannot or should not be a disposal to connected persons and concentrates instead on transparency:[10]

> It should be recognised that connected party transactions may be in the best interests of creditors but require adequate disclosure to creditors and other interested parties as soon as reasonably practicable.

The applicable principles are stated to be that the office-holder should provide sufficient information to enable interested third parties to conclude that the transaction was appropriate, be candid about his own role prior to his appointment, and avoid advising the purchaser side of the transaction.

The ordinary requirement for shareholder approval of substantial property trans- **18.08** actions with directors under section 190 of the Companies Act 2006 is disapplied by section 193 in the case of administrations and insolvent liquidations. This rule, which is for the protection of shareholders against self-dealing by directors and those connected with them, is redundant if it is creditors' interests which are at stake and the office-holder is protecting their interests. It would be wrong to allow shareholders to interfere with whatever disposals the office-holder wished to effect in the interests of the company's creditors. It is, however, essential for these purposes that the office-holder is acting with appropriate objectivity and independence.

It is equally important that the office-holder should consider the full extent of the **18.09** realizable value in the insolvent estate. Jacob J gave the following salutary warning in that respect in *Western Intelligence Ltd v KDO Label Printing Machines Ltd*:[11]

> Before I turn to the facts of this case, which is indeed a case of a phoenix company, it is worth remarking that sometimes this operation takes place through the innocent but perhaps gullible assistance of banks, receivers and accountants. In particular, as an intellectual property lawyer, I have noticed in many cases that the transfer of assets from the old company to the new company includes a passing of intellectual property from the old to the new for nothing. Very often the old and

---

[10] At para 2.
[11] [1998] BCC 472 (Ch) 473.

the new have virtually the same name, thereby transferring part of the goodwill of the old to the new for nothing. Very often the old company owns intellectual property rights of other sorts: design rights, rights in customer lists, reputation in telephone numbers and so on, all of which are allowed to pass from the old to the new for nothing.

Banks, insolvency practitioners, accountants, and anybody concerned with a transfer of business from one company to another should be alive to the fact that not all property consists of land and chattels. Making that mistake is one of the factors which enables the kind of people who operate through a series of phoenix companies to get away with it.

c. Prohibited names

18.10 The Cork Report, in the passage quoted in paragraph 18.03 above, referred to the public disquiet about the continuation of trading using similar company names. Sections 216 and 217 were introduced to address that particular aspect of phoenixism, although those measures were not themselves proposed in the Report. Moreover, as observed by Peter Gibson LJ in *Thorne v Silverleaf*:[12]

> … it is clear that the sections as enacted apply to a wider set of circumstances than the case of a person attempting to exploit the goodwill of a previous insolvent company.

In summary and subject to carve-outs, section 216 prohibits a person who was a director or shadow director of the company within the twelve months preceding its insolvent liquidation from being a director, or otherwise involved in the management of, another company or business using the same name, or another name which is sufficiently similar to suggest an association, within the following five years. Breach of section 216 is an offence and, under section 217, gives rise to joint and several liability for debts of the new company.

18.11 The court has jurisdiction to give a director leave to act where section 216 would otherwise apply[13] and rules 22.4 to 22.7 provide for three excepted cases where section 216 will not apply and no application to the court is needed. The three excepted cases cover cases where:

a) the business of the liquidating company is acquired from an office-holder (not merely the liquidator but covering also pre-liquidation acquisitions from administrators and supervisors) and creditors of that company have been given prior notice of the director's involvement in the successor business;

b) there is a pending (and promptly made) application to the court for leave; or

c) a successor company is using a name by which it was known for the full twelve months preceding the liquidation of the liquidating company.

---

[12] [1994] BCC 109 (CA) 113.
[13] Section 216(3) and rules 22.2 and 22.3.

In *Penrose v Secretary of State for Trade and Industry*, Chadwick J drew a distinction **18.12** between section 216 and the disqualification regime. The function of the latter was to protect the public from the activities of those whose misconduct has shown them to be unfit to be company directors whereas the function of section 216 was to prevent the public from being misled:[14]

> The purposes for which section 216 was enacted can be gleaned—in part at least— from the excepted cases under the rules. Rule 4.228 permits a director of an insolvent company to act as director of a new company with a prohibited name provided that the business of the insolvent company has been acquired under arrangements made by an insolvency practitioner and notice has been given to the creditors of the insolvent company.
>
> That rule identifies, and meets, two elements of mischief: first, the danger that the business of the old insolvent company has been acquired at an undervalue—or is otherwise to be expropriated—to the detriment of its creditors; and, secondly, the danger that creditors of the old company may be misled into the belief that there has been no change in the corporate vehicle. The phoenix must be disclosed as such.
>
> The third excepted case in rule 4.230 shows that the mischief is not thought to exist in a case where the company having a prohibited name has been established and trading under that name for a period of not less than 12 months before the liquidating company went into liquidation. The former director of the liquidating company can join, or can remain a member of, the board of such a company without restriction. That must be because the mischief is not perceived to exist when the company having a prohibited name is not a phoenix.

It followed that it was wrong in principle to approach an application for leave under section 216 in the same way as the court would approach an application for leave to act as a director notwithstanding disqualification and to impose restrictions as if there had been disqualification for misconduct. Leave was therefore given in *Penrose* where Chadwick J was satisfied that there was no risk to the creditors of the old company and none to the creditors of the new company (beyond that which was inherent in limited liability being available to those trading through the medium of under-capitalized companies).

Section 216 only applies where the company has gone into insolvent liquida- **18.13** tion. This was understandable when it was introduced as part of the 1985/86 reforms and administration was perceived as a rescue procedure. However, following the Enterprise Act reforms which facilitate 'liquidating' or 'distributing' administrations, the failure to extend section 216 to administrations is anomalous.

---

[14] [1996] 1 WLR 482 (Ch) 489G (the references to rules in the judgment are references to provisions of the Insolvency Rules 1986 which have been replaced by rules 22.4 to 22.7 of the 2016 Rules).

3. Pre-packs

a. The power to sell

18.14 In practice, pre-packs are a feature of administration and not liquidation because of the difficulties of securing the appointment of a liquidator with immediate power to act. Section 136 provides that the official receiver becomes the liquidator in a compulsory liquidation unless and until another liquidator is appointed. In a creditors' voluntary liquidation, the practitioner nominated by the members becomes the liquidator immediately upon the resolutions being passed for the winding up of the company and the appointment of the liquidator (which can be done on short notice with the requisite consents) but section 166 constrains his powers. It provides that during the period before the creditors nominate a liquidator or have had the opportunity to do so (any alternative nominee of the creditors then replacing the members' nominee), the liquidator cannot exercise his powers under section 165 and Schedule 4 (the general powers) without the leave of the court, save for taking the company's property into his custody, disposing of perishables and, more generally, protecting the company's assets. These restrictions put an end to the practice of 'centrebinding' which took its name from the decision in *Re Centrebind Ltd*[15] in which it had been held that, under the previous legislation, the members' nominee had full powers of disposal even though no creditors' meeting had been held. Although not necessarily undertaken for improper reasons, 'centrebinding' was too easily abused and fell into disrepute.

18.15 No such limitations apply to administrators. Indeed, the presence of any such limitations would be fundamentally inconsistent with the intended ability of an administrator to carry on the company's business. When administration was originally introduced, there were two potential questions in this respect: first, whether the administrator was in any way constrained by his duty to put proposals to the creditors and, secondly, as to whether any directions were required from the court in lieu of approved proposals. Both questions have been answered by the decided cases which show that (subject to any contrary directions from the court) the administrator is free to exercise his full powers from the outset. Some of these cases were cases on the pre-Enterprise Act version of Part II of the Act but they are equally applicable to Schedule B1.

18.16 It was recognized in one of the earliest administration cases that an administrator's disposals might pre-empt any decision on his proposals. In *Re Charnley Davies Business Services Ltd*,[16] where the administrator had realized the assets of a group

---

[15] [1967] 1 WLR 377 (Ch).
[16] (1987) 3 BCC 408 (Ch).

of companies without putting any proposals to their creditors, the court held that there could not be a meeting at which any proposals could be sensibly considered and discharged the administration orders. It was implicit in this decision that the administrator had had the power to make the realizations.

b. The role of the court

In *Re T&D Industries Plc*, Neuberger J carefully reviewed previous authorities **18.17** before concluding that, unless there was anything to the contrary in the administration order, an administrator was free to make disposals without the leave of the court. In doing so, he expressly recognized that on this interpretation of the legislation:[17]

> … an administrator could sell the whole undertaking of the company before the creditors even knew of his proposal to take that course.

He nonetheless went on to emphasize that, even in cases of urgency, administrators should do what they could to consult creditors and that there would be exceptional cases in which an application to the court for directions was appropriate. In other words, recognition of the scope of the administrator's powers did not carry with it any encouragement to exercise those powers in a cavalier manner. In *Re Transbus International Ltd*,[18] Lawrence Collins J confirmed that the same interpretation was correct in respect of a Schedule B1 case.

Those cases dealt with the generality of the administrator's powers. In substance, **18.18** albeit not in form, the result is to permit 'centrebinding' in administration. The gap which would otherwise exist between liquidation and administration in that respect is met by regulation. Specifically, for pre-packs, insolvency practitioners have been expected to observe *Statement of Insolvency Practice 16: Pre-packed Sales in Administrations* since January 2009 when the first version took effect. The current version, effective from November 2015, is discussed further below. The focus is again on transparency.

It follows from the court decisions already referred to that pre-packing may occur **18.19** without any court involvement but *Re Kayley Vending Ltd* examined the correct approach where an administration order is sought in circumstances where a pre-pack sale is intended to follow the making of the order. HH Judge Cooke noted the potential advantages of a pre-pack as follows:[19]

> The principal advantages of a pre-pack sale are well known; they are that the process enables a business to be sold quickly, with the minimum possible adverse impact from either the public knowledge of its insolvency or the restrictions imposed by the insolvency process itself. Employees can be retained who might leave, or have

---

[17] [2000] 1 WLR 646 (Ch) 653A.
[18] [2004] EWHC 932 (Ch), [2004] 1 WLR 2654.
[19] [2009] EWHC 904 (Ch), [2009] BCC 578 [6].

to be dismissed, once a formal insolvency starts. Continuity of customer and supplier contracts can be maintained. Even if a going concern sale might be achieved by an administrator, the period of trading in administration whilst it is negotiated requires to be funded and may in any event result in a damaging leaching away of business.

He went on to acknowledge the potential for abuse from those involved reaching a conclusion which served their own interests and not those of the creditors, in circumstances where credit may have been inappropriately incurred in the pre-appointment period and where the creditors are poorly placed to mount an after the event challenge. More specifically, in the context of an application for an administration order, he held that it was good practice for the information which would in due course be disseminated to creditors in accordance with SIP 16 to be before the court in so far as it was then known or ascertainable.[20]

18.20 It is clear on the authorities that there is no legal objection to pre-packing, as such, but that its acceptability or otherwise in any given case will depend upon the facts. Lewison J summarized the legal position in *Re Hellas Telecommunications (Luxembourg) II SCA* in the following terms:[21]

> It is not entirely easy to see precisely where in the statutory structure the court is concerned with the merits of a pre-pack sale. It seems to me that in general terms the merits of a pre-pack sale are for the administrator to deal with; and the creditors, if sufficiently aggrieved, have a remedy in the course of the administration to challenge an administrator's decision. It may on the evidence be obvious that a pre-pack sale is an abuse of the administrator's powers, in which event the court could refuse to make the administration order or could direct the administrators not to complete the pre-pack sale. At the other end of the spectrum it may be that it is obvious that a particular pre-pack is on the evidence the only real way forward, in which case the court could give the administrators liberty to enter into the pre-pack, leaving open the possibility that a sufficiently aggrieved creditor could nevertheless challenge the administrator's decision ex post facto. But in the majority of cases the position may not be clear; in which event the making of the administration order, even in the context of a pre-pack should not be taken as the court's blessing on the pre-pack sale.

c. The Graham Review

18.21 The approach described above failed to assuage public concern leading, in June 2014, to publication of the *Graham Review into Pre-pack Administration*.[22] The review, which was supported by empirical research, favoured regulatory reform over a legislative response and made a series of recommendations in that respect.

---

[20] Ibid at [11], [24]. See also *Re Halliwells LLP* [2010] EWHC 2036 (Ch), [2011] BCC 57 and *Re Hellas Telecommunications (Luxembourg) II SCA* [2009] EWHC 3199 (Ch), [2010] BCC 295.

[21] Ibid at [8]. See also *Re Hibernia (2005) Ltd* [2013] EWHC 2615 (Ch).

[22] See <https://www.gov.uk/government/publications/graham-review-into-pre-pack-administration> accessed 1 November 2016.

Unsurprisingly, the review found that a significant majority of pre-packs involved disposals to connected parties. A number of its key recommendations were focused upon protecting the interests of creditors where pre-packing is being undertaken. Thus it was recommended that a 'pre-pack pool' of experienced business people be established who could be consulted (on a voluntary basis) and whose function it would be to consider whether it was appropriate, in the circumstances of the case, to proceed with a pre-pack to a connected person—in other words to provide a level of independent scrutiny without forfeiting secrecy. Further recommendations, towards a like end, were to make the marketing process more robust and to improve the quality of any valuations which were being relied upon. There were also recommendations to revise and improve SIP 16 and to move the monitoring of SIP 16 reports from the Insolvency Service to the recognized professional bodies (whose job it is to take disciplinary action in the event of breaches of its requirements). The last of the review's key recommendations was directed to the viability of the purchasers. In this respect it was suggested that a connected person purchaser, again on a voluntary basis, should complete a viability review stating how the new company would survive for at least twelve months. This reflected a finding that a much higher proportion of connected person purchasers failed within three years of the pre-pack than was the case with unconnected purchasers. This last recommendation was fully justified by the terms of reference of the review, which had required it to consider the wider economic impact of pre-packing, but had little to do with the administrator's legal duty to accept the best available offer and to act in the interests of the creditors of the company in administration.

18.22 Although the review recognized that pre-packs tend to be undertaken in respect of smaller businesses, it thought it inappropriate to have a differential approach which might result in unintended consequences. It nonetheless adopted a modified version of the legal definition of connected persons with the aim of avoiding interference with pre-packs in the context of large company, or group, restructurings where typically only finance creditors are involved and a pre-pack may be used as a step in the process, for example to overcome the inability of a scheme of arrangement to cram down an entire class of creditors. Although such cases can be controversial as between rival groups of creditors struggling to preserve as much as possible of their respective positions in the ongoing business, they are not the cases which have provoked the generality of the public concern about pre-packing.

18.23 In the wake of the Graham Review, SIP 16 was revised and the Pre-pack Pool was established.[23] SIP 16 requires the insolvency practitioner to differentiate the roles that are associated with a pre-pack. An insolvency practitioner who is the architect of the pre-pack may not be the eventual administrator but, if he is proceeding with a view to accepting appointment, it is important that parties interested in

---

[23] The Pre-pack Pool's website is <www.prepackpool.co.uk> accessed 1 November 2016.

acquiring the business be encouraged to take independent advice. The administrator should provide creditors with sufficient information to enable them to judge whether a pre-pack was appropriate and that he has acted in their interests. SIP 16 notes that more detailed information may be required in a connected party transaction. The narrative and justification is known as the 'SIP 16 statement' and it is to be included in the administrator's statement of proposals filed at Companies House. In connected party transactions, the statement should say whether or not the Pre-pack Pool has been approached and with what result. It should also say whether a viability statement has been provided by the purchaser and, if so, the viability statement should be attached to the SIP 16 statement.[24]

d. Reserved power to legislate

18.24 In addition to the foregoing, Schedule B1 has been amended by the addition of a new paragraph 60A. Under this paragraph, the Secretary of State now has the power to make regulations to prohibit sales to connected persons in specified circumstances or to impose conditions. Conditions might include a requirement to obtain the approval of the court, creditors, or other specified persons. A modified version of the definition of connected persons would apply for these purposes. The power has not been exercised and is clearly intended as a last resort if the reforms resulting from the Graham Review fail to quell public concern.

4. Conclusions

18.25 The underlying problem is that the model of the Act, whereby an administrator is appointed who first formulates and then puts proposals to the creditors for achieving the purpose of the administration before proceeding in accordance with approved proposals, no longer meets the commercial needs of stakeholders. That problem has been exacerbated by the Enterprise Act reforms of the procedure and economic conditions. In practice, continued trading leads to a more expensive insolvency proceeding and requires funding. Lenders, who have lost their ability to control the process by appointing an administrative receiver, naturally favour the certainty and consequent cost control which pre-packs offer. The process also avoids the hiatus and potential damage to the business that can follow from the appointment of an administrator and the public marketing of the business.

18.26 What is required is a procedure which accommodates these needs in a way which fully protects the interests of the company's creditors. It is difficult to see how banning sales to connected parties could do other than further damage the financial

---

[24] See further <https://www.r3.org.uk/media/documents/technical_library/SIPS/SIP%2016%20 Version%203%20Nov%202015.pdf> accessed 1 November 2016.

interests of creditors. To make regulations to that effect would fundamentally affect the nature of an administrator's duties. This would be the more so if measures were taken to prevent sales to connected persons in order to quell concerns outside the stakeholder community about phoenixism because to do so would call into question the nature of administration as a collective insolvency proceeding. These are big questions.

In the meantime, pre-packing is a construct of insolvency practice which has been **18.27** developed to meet a need which is not adequately addressed by the legislation. Its propriety has been recognized by the courts (with suitable qualifications as to the manner in which it is conducted). It is also the subject of detailed and carefully considered regulatory measures—most of which are designed to give creditors more confidence in the process. If this is not sufficient to allay the concerns which have been expressed (and which were well rehearsed in the Graham Review) then it is suggested that some more radical solution would be required than the making of regulations pursuant to the paragraph 60A power.

19

DISTRIBUTION OF THE ESTATE

1. Introduction

19.01 Consistently with it being a terminal insolvency procedure, distribution of the insolvent estate amongst the company's creditors (and members in the event of a surplus) is the principal function of a liquidation.[1] Administration is not directly comparable in this respect. Where administration is used for the purposes of rescue or restructuring, there may be no need for the administrator to make distributions but, on the other hand, it may be a 'liquidating' or 'distributing' administration where the wider powers of an administrator are used to achieve a better result for creditors than that achievable in liquidation. As explained in Chapter 8, the latter form of administration was facilitated by the Enterprise Act remodelling of the administration provisions of the Act[2] and it is now common for an administrator with realizations available for distribution to creditors to use his own powers in that respect instead of putting the company into liquidation. The treatment of the claims of pre-proceeding creditors is the same whether distributions to them are made by an administrator exercising his own powers or by a liquidator appointed immediately following an administration.[3]

---

[1] Section 143 (for compulsory liquidation) and section 107 (for voluntary liquidation).
[2] Schedule B1 para 65.
[3] Rules14.1 and 14.2. (If the liquidation does not take place immediately following the administration, different cut-off dates will apply both for the purposes of identifying provable debts and for transaction avoidance purposes with the result that both the composition of the estate and the eligible claims may also differ.)

A company voluntary arrangement (CVA) is likely to involve distributions to **19.02** creditors by the supervisor but it depends entirely upon the terms of the arrangement. If the terms of the CVA provide for distributions, the basis on which the available funds will be distributed amongst creditors also depends on the terms of the arrangement. There is therefore no necessary correlation with the rules for pari passu distribution which apply in liquidation and administration—although an attempt to impose a different order of distribution on a dissenting creditor may provoke a challenge to the arrangement on the grounds of unfair prejudice (and the rights of secured and preferential creditors cannot be affected without their consent).[4] The commentary which follows is commentary upon the rules applicable to liquidation and administration. If and to the extent that a CVA applies those rules no further commentary is required but, where the terms of an approved arrangement apply different rules, the terms of the arrangement prevail.

Wherever there is a distributive function to be performed, as further explained **19.03** in Chapter 7, it is necessary to have rules for identifying both the creditors who are entitled to receive distributions ('dividends' in the language of the legislation) and the correct quantum of their claims. It is equally necessary for those rules to include a cut-off date for that purpose because, if the creditors remain an open-ended class, pari passu distribution between them is impossible. In summary, the cut-off date in either liquidation or administration is when the company went into the proceeding (unless liquidation was immediately preceded by administration, or vice versa, in which case the cut-off date for the first proceeding continues to apply for the purposes of the second).[5]

This chapter outlines the process of realization and the means by which creditor **19.04** claims are ascertained for the purposes of participating in distributions. The treatment of the expenses of the proceeding and the ranking and priority of creditor claims are then considered in Chapters 20 and 21.[6]

2. Realizations

In order to distribute the estate, the office-holder must convert non-cash assets **19.05** held in the estate into money. Receivables will naturally mature into money and, for the most part, the obvious method of realizing other assets will be sale. Both liquidators and administrators have powers of sale which give them a discretion as to the manner of sale (for example by choosing between auction

---

[4] Sections 4 and 6.
[5] Rule 14.1 and section 247.
[6] These questions are discussed in more detail in Hamish Anderson, Charlotte Cooke, and Louise Gullifer, 'National Report for England' in Dennis Faber, Niels Vermunt, Jason Kilborn, Tomás Richter, and Ignacio Tirado (eds), *Ranking and Priority of Creditors* (OUP 2016).

and private treaty sales) and as to the lotting of items for sale.[7] It may, however, be the case that a simple outright sale is not the method by which to maximize realizations.

19.06 In principle, an office-holder's powers are sufficient to enable him to pursue more sophisticated realization strategies when it is commercially expedient for him to do so. Under paragraph 13 of Schedule 4, a liquidator has 'power to do all such other things as may be necessary for winding up the company's affairs and distributing its assets'. In *Re Wreck Recovery and Salvage Company* the Court of Appeal considered the meaning of 'necessary' in the context of a liquidator's power under paragraph 5 'to carry on the company's business so far as may be necessary for its beneficial winding up' and concluded that:[8]

> ... we are not to take the word 'necessary' as importing an absolutely compelling force, but what may be called mercantile necessity, something which would be highly expedient under all the circumstances of the case for the beneficial winding-up of the company.

In *Connaught Income Fund, Series 1 v Capita Financial Managers Ltd*[9] the court applied this authority on the meaning of 'necessary' to the construction of the paragraph 13 power, which it interpreted as a free-standing power, and held that paragraph 13 had given liquidators the power to take assignments of claims with a view to generating realizations. The important point, in the context of liquidation, is the purpose for which the transaction is to be conducted (ie winding-up the company's affairs) and not the precise nature of the transaction. Purpose is unlikely to be an issue in administration because administrators' Schedule B1 paragraph 59 and Schedule 1 powers are so much wider, including both unrestricted powers to carry on the company's business and an express power 'to do all other things incidental to the exercise of the foregoing powers'.

19.07 In some situations it will be impossible to convert property into money even by engaging in more complicated transactions than outright sale. If this is because it is onerous property, a liquidator may resolve the problem by exercising his power to disclaim.[10] An administrator has no such power but may simply disregard the property. The same course is likely to be followed by both liquidators and administrators with property which, whilst not onerous, is of no commercial value. The existence of such property in an insolvent estate does not prevent the closure of either a liquidation or an administration. In *Re London and Caledonian Marine Insurance Company* James LJ said:[11]

---

[7] Schedule 4 para 6 (liquidation) and Schedule 1 para 2 (administration).
[8] (1880) 15 Ch D 353 (CA) 362 (Thesiger LJ).
[9] [2014] EWHC 3619 (Comm), [2015] 1 BCLC 241.
[10] As to which, see Chapter 15.
[11] (1879) 11 Ch D 140 (CA) 143–144. Se also, *Re Wilmott Trading Ltd (Nos 1 and 2)* [1999] 2 BCLC 541 (Ch). The position in administration is *a fortiori*.

… what was decided in the case to which I have referred was, that we could not put upon these words, 'as soon as the affairs of the company are fully wound up,' the construction contended for, namely, to make that a condition precedent and construe it to mean that everything had been done which was to be done. We are of the opinion that those words could not mean that if there were a single asset outstanding or a single debt unpaid, the affairs of the company were not to be considered as wound up … We must put some practical and sensible meaning on the words, and in my opinion they mean 'as far as the liquidators can wind them up;' that is, when the liquidator has done all that he can to wind up the company, when he has disposed of the assets as far as he can realise them, got in the calls as far as he can enforce them, and paid the debts as far as he is aware of them, and has done all that he can do in winding up the affairs, so that he has completed his business so far as he can, and is *functus officio.*

Upon the dissolution of the company, any remaining assets vested in the company belong to the Crown (subject to the Crown's own rights to disclaim).[12]

A potentially more difficult issue for the office-holder concerns assets of true value   **19.08**
which, for whatever reason, cannot be realized immediately. In a members' voluntary liquidation the members often wish to retain the assets and distribution in specie to them is permitted by section 107 if the articles of association so provide but this has no application to rateable distribution amongst creditors. Liquidators and administrators may instead have recourse to rarely exercised powers granted to them by the Rules.[13] The Rules permit the office-holder, with the consent of the liquidation/creditors' committee or, if none, the creditors, to divide assets which cannot readily or advantageously be sold amongst the creditors according to their estimated value. This would almost certainly be an unwelcome additional complication for unpaid creditors focused upon salvaging as much as possible in respect a bad debt, because it effectively outsources the office-holder's own function to the creditors in the interests of early closure of the case, and would be likely to be highly contentious if attempted on anything other than a wholly consensual basis.

In a voluntary liquidation, section 110 permits the liquidator, with the requisite   **19.09**
sanction, to transfer or sell the company's business and to receive in compensation shares or other interests in a transferee company for distribution among the members of a company in liquidation. Section 110 is quite frequently used for the purposes of solvent reconstructions and for partitioning family companies. Although technically available to a liquidator in a creditors' voluntary liquidation, the very fact that the power is focused on distributions to members means that it will be confined to creditor's voluntary liquidations which result in a surplus for members.

---

[12] Sections 1012 to 1015 Companies Act 2006.
[13] Rule 14.13.

3. Identifying claims

19.10 The onus is on creditors to submit their claims; an office-holder is not bound or even entitled to admit or make provision for claims which have not been advanced even if the company's own books suggest that they may be good claims.[14] On the other hand, the office-holder must take appropriate steps to solicit the submission of legitimate claims.[15]

19.11 In *Pulsford v Devenish* the issue was whether creditors of a company which had been dissolved following its liquidation, of which they had had no knowledge, had any remedy against its liquidator. In holding that they did, Farwell J said:[16]

> The [liquidator] took no steps whatever to ascertain the claims of any creditors against the [company in liquidation] except by inserting advertisements in six London newspapers. He knew of the existence of this claim by the plaintiffs for the payments under the licence; but he says that he did not know, and I accept his statement, of the existence of the claim for the lamps. If, however, he had performed that which I consider to be the duty of a liquidator, namely, not merely to advertise for creditors, but to write to the creditors of whose existence he knows, and who do not send in claims, and ask them if they have any claim, he would undoubtedly have received a claim, not merely for the instalments payable under the licence, but also for the purchase-money of the lamps.

> In *Re Armstrong Whitworth Securities Company Limited* a liquidator had advertised for creditors to submit claims under the provisions of the winding-up rules then in force but had taken no other steps to ascertain the claims of former employees. Jenkins J said:[17]

> ... his duty as liquidator was to take all steps reasonably open to him on the information in his possession to ascertain whether any of the former employees concerned did make any such claim. The obvious step open to [the liquidator] on the information in his possession was to send a notice to each such employee asking him whether he made any such claim.

19.12 The European Regulations make more specific provision for creditors in other member states. The office-holder has a duty to inform known creditors of the opening of the proceedings and rules as to the submission of their claims.[18]

---

[14] *Re Compania de Electricidad de la Provincia de Buenos Aires Ltd* [1980] Ch 146 (Ch). This general proposition must now be qualified by reference to the rules exempting small debts from the proof of debt procedures as described in the next section of this chapter.

[15] The extent of this duty depends on the nature of the claims, see further *Re London Scottish Finance Ltd* [2013] EWHC 4047 (Ch), [2014] Bus LR 424 [60], [61].

[16] [1903] 2 Ch 625 (Ch) 631. Applied in *James Smith & Sons (Norwood) Limited v Goodman* [1936] Ch 216 (CA). See also Chapter 11.

[17] [1947] Ch 673 (Ch) 691.

[18] Council Regulation (EC) No 1346/2000 of 29 May 2000 on Insolvency Proceedings [2000] OJ L 160/1 Chap IV to be replaced by Regulation (EU) 2015/848 of the European Parliament and of the Council of 20 May 2015 on Insolvency Proceedings [2015] OJ L 141/19 (RR) Chap IV.

The converse of an office-holder's duty to seek out and pay legitimate creditors is his **19.13** duty to proceed with their administration of the insolvent estate as expeditiously as possible and, in doing so, to reject all unmeritorious claims. In *Re House Property and Investment Co Ltd*, Roxburgh J said (in the context of a solvent liquidation):[19]

> Of course, a liquidator is not to distribute the property among the members before he has dealt with the liabilities. That is plain enough, but I am quite certain that, though it does not say so in express terms, the policy of the [Companies Act 1948] … carries the implication that he has to deal with the liabilities within [a] reasonable time, and deal with them finally within a reasonable time, and thereafter to distribute amongst the members within a reasonable time.

The principle that an office-holder must reject, and discharge his duties of distribution without reference to, claims that are not liabilities of the company is exemplified by the authorities on the inadmissibility of statute-barred debts.[20]

4. Proof of debt procedures

In the terminology of the Rules, 'proof of debt' is the process by which creditors **19.14** submit their claims. Not all creditors need to submit proofs of debt:

a) A secured creditor which is content to rely on its security need not submit a proof of debt. (Alternatively, a secured creditor can surrender its security and prove in full, value the security and prove for the balance, or realize the security and prove for any deficiency.[21])

b) Expense creditors will ordinarily be paid as their claims accrue and no proof of debt is required. The payment of expenses by a liquidator will, in any event, flow naturally from the priority accorded to liquidation expenses which must be respected by the liquidator when paying dividends. The position in administration is different because an administrator may not be making distributions. The legislation is silent on the duty of an administrator to pay expenses other than in the context of paying dividends but the statutory charge which arises at the end of an administration should inform the administrator's decision as to the application of funds during the currency of the proceeding and implies a duty to pay on vacation of office.[22]

c) Where administration immediately precedes liquidation, or vice versa, a creditor which proved in the first proceeding is deemed to have proved in the second.[23]

---

[19] [1954] Ch 576 (Ch) 612.

[20] *Re Art Reproduction Co Ltd* [1952] Ch 89 (Ch); *Re Fleetwood and District Electric Light and Power Syndicate* [1915] 1 Ch 486 (Ch).

[21] Rules 14.4 and 14.15 to 14.19. See also *Cleaver v Delta American Reinsurance Co* [2001] UKPC 6, [2001] 2 AC 328 [26].

[22] See further Chapter 20.

[23] Rule 14.3(2).

d) A creditor which is owed less than £1000 is deemed to have proved for the purposes of determination and the payment of dividend.[24]

19.15 The proof of debt procedure is the means by which unsecured creditors establish their claims in order to rank for dividend. The process of admitting proofs for the purpose of allowing creditors to receive dividends is not to be confused with the process of admitting proofs for voting purposes in creditors' decision procedures. Voting eligibility will often have to be determined before there has been a proper investigation of the validity of the putative creditor's claims and admission to vote for a given sum does not determine the amount of a provable debt or even status as a creditor.[25]

19.16 The Rules provide for what a proof of debt must state.[26] Foreign currency claims must be converted into sterling as at the cut-off date.[27]

19.17 Contingent claims must be valued by the office-holder as at the cut-off date and it is the estimated value which is the provable debt for the time being. However, the office-holder is free to vary his estimate by reference to new information or any change of circumstances.[28] Under the hindsight principle, if the amount of an estimated liability becomes certain before distribution or payment, then the actual amount becomes the value of the claim.[29] The hindsight principle also means that a creditor whose claim is discharged before the estate is distributed ceases to be entitled to receive dividends.[30]

19.18 A proof of debt may be submitted in respect of a debt which is not due for payment as at the cut-off date but the rate of dividend is adjusted to take account of acceleration.[31]

19.19 Most issues concerning the quantum of provable debts are resolved by agreement between the claimant and the office-holder but the Rules provide for a dissatisfied creditor (and indeed other creditors and the contributories) to challenge the office-holder's decision.[32] Although the relevant rules are headed 'Appeal against decision on proof', the resultant proceedings are not a true

---

[24] Rules 14.3(3) and 14.31.

[25] *Re Assico Engineering Ltd* [2002] BCC 481 (Ch); *Re Power Builders (Surrey) Ltd* [2008] EWHC 2607 (Ch), [2009] 1 BCLC 250.

[26] Rule 14.4.

[27] Rule 14.21. See further *Re Lehman Brothers International (Europe) (No 4)* [2015] EWCA Civ 485, [2016] Ch 50 (CA) (at the time of writing, the Supreme Court has heard an appeal from this decision but has not delivered its decision).

[28] Rules 14.14. See further Chapter 7.

[29] *Bwllfa and Merthyr Dare Steam Collieries (1891) Ltd v Pontypridd Waterworks Co* [1903] AC 426 (HL).

[30] *Wight v Eckhardt Marine GmbH* [2003] UKPC 37, [2004] 1 AC 147. See further Chapter 7.

[31] Rule 14.44.

[32] Rule 14.8.

appeal and the court makes a determination *de novo* on the evidence brought before it.[33]

5. Assignment of rights

Persons who are entitled to a dividend are free to assign their rights or to direct payment to a third party. The procedure is to give the office-holder notice of the name and address of the person to whom payment is to be made and the office-holder is then required to pay the dividend accordingly.[34] **19.20**

6. Unclaimed dividends

The office-holder is not obliged to hold money indefinitely for the persons who are entitled to it but have not collected it. The Insolvency Regulations 1994[35] provide that money held by the former administrator or liquidator of a dissolved company representing unclaimed dividends due to creditors or money held in trust for members or former members may, and in the case of a compulsory liquidation must, be paid into the Insolvency Services Account (an account kept by the Secretary of State at the Bank of England). The Secretary of State must be given particulars and a person claiming to be entitled to the money can apply to the Secretary of State for payment.[36] **19.21**

7. Conclusions

The broad purpose of the statutory scheme is to reduce an insolvent estate to cash for distribution purposes and then to distribute the fund in accordance with a waterfall of priorities. **19.22**

An office-holder has the necessary powers to realize assets but the completion of his role is not constrained by the continuing presence in the estate of unrealizable assets which can, according to circumstances, be the subject of disclaimer, distribution in specie or simply disregarded. **19.23**

The office-holder must be astute to ascertain the genuine claims against the estate but it is ultimately the responsibility of creditors to advance their claims. If they do not claim or do not collect their dividends, the office-holder is not responsible provided he has followed the correct procedures. **19.24**

---

[33] *Re Trepca Mines Ltd* [1960] 1 WLR 1273 (CA).
[34] Rule 14.43.
[35] SI 1994/2507.
[36] Regulations 3B, 18, and 32.

20

EXPENSES

1. Introduction

20.01 Insolvency proceedings inevitably entail cost. In addition to the office-holder's remuneration, there will be a wide range of other expenses—partly arising out of getting in the company's assets and making such distributions as the proceeds permit but also arising out of discharging compliance obligations. However, an office-holder does not generally have any personal liability for the expenses which he incurs unless he enters into a contract in his personal capacity or incurs costs in the unsuccessful pursuit of litigation brought in his own name.[1]

20.02 Even a small case involves significant costs and the smaller the case, the greater the risk that the costs will be disproportionate. It is not surprising that in many small cases there is nothing left for unsecured creditors after the costs and expenses of the proceeding have been paid, because the costs and expenses take priority to their claims. If this were not so, it would not be possible to conduct the proceedings at all. The priority of the costs and expenses of insolvency proceedings is consistent with trust and salvage law where, in both cases, the costs of administering an asset or estate for the benefit of others rank ahead of their own claims.

---

[1] *Stevensdrake Limited v Hunt* [2015] EWHC 1527 (Ch), [2015] 4 Costs LR 639 is an example of an exceptional case where a liquidator undertook a personal contractual liability for counsel's fees. (For subsequent developments in the same litigation, see *Stevensdrake Limited v Hunt* [2016] EWHC 342 (Ch), [2016] 2 Costs LO 187 where the same liquidator was held not to be liable for solicitors' fees.)

The possibility that costs and expenses will leave nothing for creditors does not **20.03** mean that the proceedings serve no useful purpose (or only serve the purpose of remunerating the office-holder) because of the wider social interests that are at stake and which require the law to provide the means by which the affairs of insolvent companies can be resolved.[2]

The rules for determining what constitutes an expense of the proceeding are sub- **20.04** stantially the same in liquidation and administration (the latter having been modelled on the former) even though the actual nature of the expenses can be very different because of the different underlying purposes of the proceedings. The general approach of the law in relation to both liquidation and administration expenses is to distinguish between liabilities which are incurred during the course of an insolvency proceeding and those which arise out of the state of the company's affairs at the commencement of the proceeding. The former will usually be expenses of the proceeding but the latter will be creditor claims in the proceeding (these two classes being generally, but not invariably, mutually exclusive). Due to the very wide definitions of 'debt' and 'liability' which apply for these purposes, most pre-commencement creditor claims will be provable debts ranking for dividend.[3] The commercial expectation is therefore that expenses will be paid in full whereas creditor claims will usually only attract a lower level of payment as determined by the funds available after the discharge of all the expenses. All this is consistent with recognition that expenses must inevitably take priority and with insolvency proceedings necessarily introducing a cut-off date for the purposes of determining the class of creditors who are entitled to participate in distributions by the office-holder.

In a company voluntary arrangement (CVA), the whole question of participating **20.05** claims and the priority of expenses is a matter to be determined by the terms of the arrangement. However, it is unlikely that a CVA will be proposed which does not accord expenses priority for precisely the reason identified above, namely that such priority is ordinarily necessary in order to enable the proceeding to take place. The remainder of this chapter therefore deals with only liquidation and administration expenses.

A liability will only rank as a liquidation or administration expense if: **20.06**

a) it is a liability which is identified as an expense in the Rules; or
b) it relates to costs ordered to be paid as such in the context of court proceedings; or
c) the *Lundy Granite* principle applies (whereby the attendant liabilities of the company are treated as if they were expenses of the proceeding if the

---

[2] As to which, see further Chapter 2.
[3] See further Chapter 21.

office-holder retains or makes use of property belonging to another for the purposes of the proceeding).

20.07   Expenses are subordinate to the claims of fixed charge creditors (consistently with fixed charge security being treated as standing outside the insolvent estate) but are generally payable out of floating charge assets, in addition to taking priority to the claims of unsecured creditors.[4] This is subject to one important refinement concerning litigation costs in respect of transaction avoidance proceedings and other office-holder applications which are incurred in the course of a liquidation, where approval or authorization from the affected creditor(s) (preferential creditors or the floating chargee as the case may be) or the court is required.[5] The consequence of this is that, where the floating chargee's recoveries are at risk from litigation costs in a liquidation, the chargee has an important measure of control over a potentially significant element of a liquidator's expenses which is not replicated in administration (where the administrator can utilize floating charge assets without any comparable requirement for authorization or approval). This creates a perverse incentive for a floating chargee to favour liquidation over administration in some cases—a result which is not consistent with the underlying policy of the Act to facilitate company rescue.[6]

2. The nature of expenses

20.08   The Rules state a general rule that the fees, costs, charges, and other expenses incurred in the course of a proceeding are expenses of that proceeding but this does little to elucidate the meaning of an expense.[7] Expenses fall into one of the three classes referred to above.

a. The Rules

20.09   The relevant rules are 7.108(4) (compulsory liquidation), 6.42(4) (creditors' voluntary liquidation), and 3.51(2) (for administration). Rules 6.42(4) and 3.51(2) are less detailed than rule 7.108(4), albeit modelled upon it, but only because of differences in the procedures which do not raise any points of principle.[8] There is common ground in that all the rules provide for the expenses of the office-holder

---

[4]   Section 175 and Schedule B1 para 65; *Re Nortel GmbH* [2013] UKSC 52, [2014] AC 209 [39].

[5]   Section 176ZA and Part 6 Chapter 7 and Part 7 Chapter 15 of the Rules.

[6]   This apparent anomaly results from section 176ZA having been enacted to reverse the effect of the interpretation of section 175 in *Buchler v Talbot* [2004] UKHL 9, [2004] 2 AC 298, but with safeguards for floating chargees, whereas floating chargees had always been at risk in respect of expenses in an administration.

[7]   Rules 7.108(1) (compulsory liquidation), 6.42(1) (creditors' voluntary liquidation), and 3.50(1) (administration).

[8]   The separation of rules 6.42(1) and 7.108(1) in the 2016 Rules is new.

in performing his functions,[9] any necessary disbursements incurred in the course of the proceeding,[10] and the office-holder's own remuneration.[11] The rules not only identify what constitutes an expense but also provide the order of priority in which such expenses are payable in the event of a deficiency, however this is subject to the power of the court to order different priorities.[12]

In *Re Toshoku Finance UK Plc* it was held that the listing of specific expenses in the 1986 analogue of rule 7.108(4) was both mandatory and definitive unless the liability related to the costs of proceedings or the *Lundy Granite* principle applied (as to both of which, see below).[13] David Richards J held in *Exeter City Council v Bairstow*[14] that the list in the analogue of rule 3.51(2) had to be similarly interpreted and that was common ground in *Re UK Housing Alliance (North West) Ltd*.[15] Having regard to the similarities between the rules and the background to the making of the latter (which was that the rule was introduced when making it possible for distributions to creditors to be made in the course of an administration), this seems uncontroversial. There is also no reason to distinguish the treatment of creditors' voluntary liquidation expenses under rule 6.42(4) (which was only separated out from compulsory liquidation expenses for the first time in the 2016 Rules). **20.10**

Most categories of expense listed in these rules are self-explanatory but there has been considerable difficulty over the meaning of 'necessary disbursements' which are incurred 'in the course of' the proceeding because of the very wide range of liabilities which can arise. Those difficulties were substantially resolved by the decision of the Supreme Court in *Re Nortel GmbH* where Lord Neuberger PSC said (*per curiam*):[16] **20.11**

> The word 'necessary' in rule 2.67(1)(f)[17] carries with it a legal obligation to pay (or, possibly, in exceptional cases, a moral obligation to pay ...) ... a liability may arise during an administration without falling within rule 2.67(1)(f), without being 'in the course of' the administration ...

---

[9] Rules 7.108(4)(a)(ii), 6.42(4)(a), and 3.51(2)(a).

[10] Rules 7.108(4)(m), 6.42(4)(f), and 3.51(2)(g) (the liquidator's functions are more specifically identified as preserving, getting in and realising assets, and conducting legal proceedings).

[11] Rules 7.108(4)(o), 6.42(4)(h), and 3.51(2)(i).

[12] Sections 112 and 156 (liquidation) and rule 3.51(3) (administration). The court will not ordinarily exercise its power to vary priorities as between expenses so as to give a liquidator's remuneration priority over other expenses to which it would not otherwise take priority: *Re Linda Marie Ltd* (1988) 4 BCC 463 (Ch). The same restraint can be expected in administration.

[13] [2002] UKHL 6, [2002] 1 WLR 671 [13]–[15].

[14] [2007] EWHC 400 (Ch), [2007] Bus LR 813 [79], [80].

[15] [2013] EWHC 2553 (Ch), [2013] BCC 752 [39]. (The same interpretation appears to have been assumed in *Re Nortel GmbH* [2013] UKSC 52, [2014] AC 209.)

[16] Ibid at [99] and [100]. Followed and applied in *Re PGL Realisations Ltd* [2014] EWHC 2721 (Ch), [2015] Bus LR 17.

[17] The analogue of rule 3.51(2)(g).

While it would be dangerous to treat any formulation as an absolute rule, it seems to me, at any rate subject to closer examination of the authorities and counter-arguments, a disbursement falls within rule 2.67(1)(f) if it arises out of something done in the administration (normally by the administrator or on the administrator's behalf), or if it is imposed by a statute whose terms render it clear that the liability to make the disbursement falls on an administrator as part of the administration – either because of the nature of the liability or because of the terms of the statute.

It follows that involuntary liabilities will not ordinarily be accorded the priority of expenses under this heading unless they are imposed by statute (but see the following paragraph as regards costs orders).

b. Costs associated with proceedings in court

20.12 Rules 7.110(2) and 6.43 provide an express qualification of rules 7.108 and 6.42 through a general saving of the powers of the court to make orders concerning the costs of court proceedings by or against the company. There is no directly comparable rule applicable to administration but paragraph 13(1)(f) of Schedule B1 enables the court to make any order it thinks appropriate on the hearing of an administration application and rule 3.12(2) gives the court jurisdiction to determine what costs shall be paid as an expense when it makes an administration order.[18] The case for some special treatment of court costs arises from the general public interest in the administration of justice and in the more specific need to ensure that companies and others involved in the commencement of insolvency proceedings by the court receive the advice and representation that they need. In *Re Portsmouth City Football Club Ltd,* the Court of Appeal summarized the legal position in relation to the costs associated with the commencement of insolvency proceedings in terms which are too detailed for this commentary, whilst robustly asserting the principle that the Rules are otherwise determinative (*Lundy Granite* not having been relevant).[19]

c. The *Lundy Granite* principle

20.13 Any concept of expenses which rests on a rigid demarcation between pre-proceeding obligations and new liabilities incurred during the course of the proceeding carries an obvious potential for injustice if it enables the office-holder to take the benefit or make use of property belonging to another without payment. The unwillingness of

---

[18] See also rule 3.11(2).

[19] [2013] EWCA Civ 916, [2013] Bus LR 1152 [41]. It remains to be seen how far costs payable pursuant to court orders truly constitute a discrete class of expenses or whether they are 'necessary disbursements'. The approach of Mann J in *Re Bickland Ltd* [2012] EWHC 706 (Ch), [2013] Bus LR 361, where costs payable pursuant to an order under Schedule B1 para 13(1)(f) were to be treated as an expense despite being outside what is now rule 3.51(2)(c), is unsustainable following *Portsmouth City* but the judgments do not explore the alternative approach of treating such an order as a necessary disbursement.

the courts to allow such a position to arise was summed up by Vaughan Williams J in *Re Oriental Bank Corporation (No 2)* where he said:[20]

> ... if a company which is in liquidation remains in beneficial occupation of a lease – that is to say, if it occupies the demised premises, or takes the rent, and thus obtains the benefit of the lease – the Court ought to do its very best to make the company pay the rent in full, and not merely a dividend.

The *Lundy Granite* principle, which takes its name from the decision of the Court of Appeal in *Re Lundy Granite Co, Ex parte Heaven*,[21] addresses what would otherwise be this lacuna. As explained by Lewison LJ in *Jervis v Pillar Denton Ltd*:[22]

> ... the rationale is a judge-made deeming provision under which the office holder is deemed to have incurred the liability in the course of the winding up or administration.

Like most of the reported cases on this subject, *Lundy Granite* and *Jervis v Pillar Denton Ltd* concerned unpaid rent under pre-liquidation leases but the principle applies to the retention (or consumption) of property of any description.

In *Lundy Granite* James LJ said:[23]   **20.14**

> ... if the company for its own purposes, and with a view to the realisation of the property to better advantage, remains in possession of the estate, which the lessor is therefore not able to obtain possession of, common sense and ordinary justice require the Court to see that the landlord receives the full value of the property.

In the slightly later case of *Re Oak Pits Colliery Company*, Lindley LJ more specifically identified what this meant in terms of liquidation expenses, saying:[24]

> When the liquidator retains the property for the purpose of advantageously disposing of it, or when he continues to use it, the rent of it ought to be regarded as a debt contracted for the purpose of winding up the company, and ought to be paid in full like any other debt or expense properly incurred by the liquidator for the same purpose ...

The modern position was summarized by Lord Hoffmann in *Re Toshoku Finance UK Plc* as being that:[25]

> The principle ... is thus one which permits, on equitable grounds, the concept of a liability incurred as an expense of the liquidation to be expanded to include liabilities incurred before the liquidation in respect of property afterwards retained by the liquidator for the benefit of the insolvent estate.

---

[20] [1895] 1 Ch 753 (Ch) 757. The case concerned provable debt under rules which are now different but the passage quoted nonetheless serves as a statement of principle which aptly describes when a liability should be treated as an expense.

[21] (1871) LR 6 Ch App 462 (CA).

[22] [2014] EWCA Civ 180, [2015] Ch 87 [77], [101].

[23] *Lundy Granite* (n 21) 466.

[24] (1882) 21 Ch D 332 (CA) 330.

[25] [2002] UKHL 6, [2002] 1 WLR 671 [29].

20.15 The *Lundy Granite* principle was an established feature of liquidation law long before administration was introduced and some uncertainty initially arose as to the application of the principle to administrations. The proposition that it did so was rejected by the Court of Appeal in *Re Atlantic Computer Systems Plc*[26] but that was a decision on the administration provisions of the Act as originally enacted, before there was any provision for administrators to make distributions and before what is now rule 3.51 existed. The problem addressed by the principle was, if anything, more acute in the context of administration because of the greater chance of premises (or other assets) being retained by an administrator for trading purposes as opposed to realization. Following the recasting of the administration provisions effected by the Enterprise Act and the introduction of provisions dealing with expenses in the Rules, it was accepted (obiter) by Briggs J in *Re Lehman Brothers International (Europe), Lomas v RAB Market Cycles (Master) Fund Ltd*[27] that the principle applies to administration and the same approach has been followed in later cases including the decision of the Court of Appeal in *Jervis v Pillar Denton Ltd*.[28]

20.16 The correct approach to the question of apportionment of ongoing liabilities was resolved by the Court of Appeal in *Jervis v Pillar Denton Ltd* where Lewison LJ said:[29]

> The true extent of the principle, in my judgment, is that the office holder must make payments at the rate of the rent for the duration of any period during which he retains possession of the demised property for the benefit of the winding up or administration (as the case may be). The rent will be treated as accruing from day to day. Those payments are payable as expenses of the winding up or administration. The duration of the period is a question of fact and is not determined merely by reference to which rent days occur before, during or after that period.

The decision overruled first instance decisions to the effect that there was no room for apportionment so that rent was only payable as an expense if the rent payment fell due during the period of the office-holder's retention of the property and without any relief if the property was relinquished before the end of the period to which a periodic payment of rent related. That had led to the unfortunate practice of delaying appointments until immediately after a quarter day so as to ensure a rent-free period (so far as expenses were concerned). There remain unresolved questions about the extent to which liabilities other than for periodic payments, for example dilapidations, must be treated as an expense.

---

[26] [1992] Ch 505 (CA).

[27] [2009] EWHC 2545 (Ch) [100].

[28] [2014] EWCA Civ 180, [2015] Ch 87; *Goldacre (Offices) Ltd v Nortel Networks UK Ltd* [2009] EWHC 3389 (Ch), [2010] Ch 455 [27]; *Leisure (Norwich) II Ltd v Luminar Lava Ignite Ltd* [2012] EWHC 951 (Ch), [2014] Ch 165 [16].

[29] Ibid at [77], [101].

The *Lundy Granite* principle means that a qualifying liability will, exceptionally, **20.17** rank both as an expense and as a provable debt. (It will not, of course, be paid twice. If or to the extent that it is discharged as an expense, the provable debt falls away.)

3. The duty to pay expenses

It should go without saying that an office-holder is intended to pay the expenses **20.18** which he incurs but it is a peculiarity of the Act that this important question is dealt with in terms of priorities. This approach pre-dates the introduction of administration and remains more appropriate for liquidation. Liquidation being a process for the realization of assets and the distribution of the resultant realizations, rules to the effect that expenses take priority to distributions to creditors substantially achieve the intended result because the underlying duty of the liquidator to make distributions will ensure that the priorities take effect. It is otherwise with administration which is much more likely to involve a period of continued trading and which may not involve any distributions. Here, although the law applies the same approach of simply providing priorities, it gives rise to a wider range of questions as to the nature of an administrator's duty to pay expenses outside the context of distributions.

Reverting to the question of liquidation expenses, the position is further confused **20.19** by the relevant provisions of the Act being different according to whether the liquidation is a compulsory or a creditors' voluntary liquidation (albeit to the same substantive effect). The priority of expenses in a compulsory liquidation is established through the combined effect of sections 143, 156, 175, and 176ZA of the Act. Section 143 requires a company's assets, in a compulsory liquidation, to be applied in satisfaction of its liabilities. Section 175 requires preferential creditors to be paid before other provable debts and expressly gives expenses priority to preferential debts (section 176ZA extends that priority to floating charge assets). Section 156 provides that, in the event of there being insufficient assets to pay all the expenses, the court has power to order the payment of expenses in such order of priority as it thinks fit (which assumes, without expressly so stating, that the expenses enjoy priority to all preferential and other provable debts).

The comparable provisions—sections 107, 115, 175, and 176ZA—dealing with **20.20** creditors' voluntary liquidation are clearer. Section 115 provides that the expenses of the liquidation are payable ahead of all other claims. Although this is merely a priority provision,[30] as are sections 175 and 176ZA, section 107 requires the liquidator to apply the estate in payment of the company's liabilities. The cumulative effect is that the liquidator has a duty to pay provable debts and a duty to pay

---

[30] *Re MC Bacon Ltd (No 2)* [1991] Ch 127 (Ch).

preferential creditors ahead of other provable debts which is subject to the priority of expenses. This is, in substance, if not in form, a duty to pay expenses.

20.21   In considering the liquidation rules, it should be borne in mind that the sections referred to above do not distinguish between the liquidator's remuneration and the other expenses of the proceeding (although rules 7.108(4) and 6.42(4) provide an order of priority of liquidation expenses which applies subject to section 156).

20.22   The framework in administrations is completely different. The starting point is paragraph 99(3) of Schedule B1 which provides that any expenses[31] of an administration which remain undischarged at its conclusion are secured by a charge on the estate which ranks pari passu with the administrator's remuneration but subordinate to like charges under paragraph 99(4) and (5) securing outstanding liabilities on contracts entered into by the administrator or liabilities on contracts of employment which were adopted. Paragraph 99 is supplemented by rule 14.38 which provides that, when an administrator proposes to make a distribution to creditors which will be a sole or final distribution, he must pay all liabilities which would otherwise be secured by the paragraph 99 charges.

20.23   Neither the Act nor the Rules offer any explanation of any duty on the part of an administrator to pay expenses outside the context of distributions. The status of a claim as an expense listed in rule 3.51(2) is not determinative of this question.[32] The statutory charge should nonetheless inform an administrator's decisions as to the application of funds during the course of the administration.[33] The same charge also implies a duty to pay on vacation of office which may be actionable as such.[34] In practice, an administrator will tend to discharge expenses as they fall due unless he has any reason to anticipate a deficiency. As Dillon LJ said in *Powdrill v Watson* in the Court of Appeal:[35]

> Although strictly sums payable are [under the statutory charge] only payable when the administrator vacates office, it is well understood that administrators will, in the ordinary way, pay expenses of the administration including the salaries and other payments to employees as they arise during the continuance of the administration. There is no need to wait until the end, and it would be impossible as a

---

[31]   Rule 3.50(4) provides that 'expenses' for these purposes are those identified in rule 3.51(2) but cannot have been intended to override the super-priority of contractual liabilities under Schedule B1 para 99(4).

[32]   *Goldacre (Offices) Ltd v Nortel Networks UK Ltd* [2009] EWHC 3389 (Ch), [2010] Ch 455 [28]; *Cheshire West and Chester BC, Petitioners* [2011] BCC 174 (Court of Session, Outer House) [32].

[33]   *Powdrill v Watson* [1994] 2 BCLC 118 (CA), on further appeal [1995] 2 AC 394 (HL); *Re Salmet International Ltd* [2001] BCC 796 (Ch). These cases were decided on differently worded legislation but remain relevant on this particular point.

[34]   *Re Maxwell Fleet and Facilities Management Ltd* [2001] 1 WLR 323 (Ch) (another case on earlier legislation which is equally relevant to that now in force); *Re Trident Fashions Plc* [2006] EWCA Civ 203, [2007] 1 BCLC 491. (As to the enforceability of any such duty, see Chapter 11.)

[35]   [1994] 2 BCLC 118 (CA) 142a.

practical matter to do that. What is picked up at the end are those matters which fall within the [charge], but have not been paid.

4. Conclusions

The question of what is and what is not an expense of the proceeding is one of con- **20.24** siderable importance in practice. From the point of view of a creditor, the distinction will in many cases be determinative of whether the liability is paid. From the point of view of the office-holder, any uncertainty as to whether a liability will rank as an expense raises the unwelcome possibility that an unbudgeted liability might rank in priority to his/her own remuneration giving rise to a shortfall. Insolvency practitioners have occasionally found themselves with just such a deficiency.

In the main, the rules on what will constitute an expense are now sufficiently clear **20.25** to enable insolvency practitioners to avoid deficiencies provided they have adequate information at the outset and, crucially, the available assets are correctly identified and realistically valued. Despite the lack of clarity over an administrator's duty to pay expenses, the more significant area of continuing difficulty concerns the *Lundy Granite* principle. It is comparatively easily stated but its outer limits are yet to be determined. The application of that principle to a much greater range of potential liabilities resulting from an administrator continuing a business in circumstances where it would be closed by a liquidator, means that its future development is likely to be in that context.

21

RANKING OF CLAIMS, PARI PASSU DISTRIBUTION, AND CONTRACTING OUT

1. Introduction

21.01 The order in which claims on the insolvent estate are discharged was summarized by Lord Neuberger PSC in *Re Nortel GmbH* where he said:[1]

> In a liquidation of a company and in an administration (where there is no question of trying to save the company or its business), the effect of insolvency legislation ... as interpreted and extended by the courts, is that the order of priority for payment out of the company's assets is, in summary terms, as follows:

> (1) Fixed charge creditors;
> (2) Expenses of the insolvency proceedings;
> (3) Preferential creditors;
> (4) Floating charge creditors;
> (5) Unsecured provable debts;
> (6) Statutory interest;
> (7) Non-provable liabilities; and
> (8) Shareholders.

---

[1] [2013] UKSC 52, [2014] AC 209 [39].

As the Law Commission observed when introducing a recommendation for some consumer claims to have preferential status:[2]

> These rules are set out in statute and reflect difficult political decisions about how to allocate losses between equally innocent parties.

The order of distribution reflects the following propositions: **21.02**

a) Property held by way of security (categories 1 and 4) does not form part of the insolvent estate which is available to unsecured creditors, except to the extent that floating charge security is statutorily subordinated to expenses, the claims of preferential creditors and the office-holder's duty to make 'the prescribed part' available to unsecured creditors.
b) Expense claims (category 2) are different in kind from the remainder of the classes of creditor claims in that they usually are not, and do not relate to, pre-proceeding obligations of the company.[3] They therefore take priority.
c) Equity ranks behind debt in an insolvency (category 8).
d) Most unsecured liabilities of the company relating to its pre-proceeding state of affairs will be provable debts (category 5).
e) Statutory interest, non-provable liabilities, and the claims of shareholders (as such) (categories 6, 7, and 8) are only relevant in the unusual case of the insolvent estate being sufficient to pay unsecured provable debts in full.

As stated by Lord Neuberger in introducing his eight categories, these are rules **21.03** for distribution in liquidation and administration. The scheme of distribution in a company voluntary arrangement (CVA) may be different except that the rights of secured and preferential creditors cannot be affected without their consent.[4] Such an arrangement can disapply the rights of unsecured creditors to the prescribed part.[5]

2. Lord Neuberger's eight categories

a. Fixed charge creditors

Fixed charge creditors enjoy overall priority because their security does not form **21.04** part of the insolvent estate. Lord Millett described the position of fixed charge creditors in *Buchler v Talbot* in the following terms:[6]

---

[2] The Law Commission, *Consumer Prepayments on Retail Insolvency* (Law Com No 368, 2016) para 8.4.
[3] With the exception of expenses recognized under the *Lundy Granite* principle discussed in Chapter 20.
[4] Section 4.
[5] Section 176A.
[6] [2004] UKHL 9, [2004] 2 AC 298 [51] (internal citations omitted). Fixed 'charges' in this context means any form of security which is not a floating charge.

Bankruptcy and companies liquidation are concerned with the realisation and dis-tribution of the insolvent's free assets among unsecured creditors. They are not concerned with assets which have been charged to creditors as security, whether by way of fixed or floating charge. Secured creditors can resort to their security for the discharge of their debts outside the bankruptcy or winding up. Assets subject to a charge belong to the charge holder to the extent of the amounts secured by them; only the equity of redemption remains the property of the chargor and falls within the scope of the chargor's bankruptcy or winding up. As James LJ observed in *In re Regent's Canal Ironworks Co* charge holders are creditors 'to whom the [charged] property [belongs] … with a specific right to the property for the purpose of paying their debts'. Such a creditor is a person who 'is considered as entirely outside the company, who is merely seeking to enforce a claim, not against the company, but to his own property' per James LJ in *In re David Lloyd & Co.*

(The decision in the case was subsequently reversed by the enactment of section 176ZA, with consequential effects so far as the passage quoted relates to floating charges (as to which see below), but without detracting from its authority in respect of fixed charges.)

21.05   A limited incursion on this overall priority may be made where an office-holder undertakes the process of realization on behalf of the secured creditor. In *Re Regent's Canal Ironworks Company*, James LJ said:[7]

> If the property is realised in the proceedings to which they are parties they must pay the costs of realisation, just as they would have had to pay them if they had their own suit for the purpose of realising it, or if they had employed a person out of doors. Those are charges to be deducted out of the proceeds of the property, and they are only entitled to the net proceeds of the property.

As the quoted passage makes clear, the court is merely concerned to see that the costs of realization are borne by the realized fund; that is not to elevate other claims which rank lower in Lord Neuberger's hierarchy.

b.   Expenses of the insolvency proceedings

21.06   The nature of liquidation and administration expenses is considered in Chapter 20 and the general priority enjoyed by those expenses is explained in the context of examining the nature of the office-holder's duty to pay expenses in Section 3 of that chapter. In short but subject to one important qualification, when making dis-tributions expenses take priority to all claims other than the rights of fixed charge creditors to their security.

21.07   The important qualification concerns floating charges and liquidation expenses. Priority for liquidation expenses under section 176ZA is subject to Part 6, Chapter 7 and Part 7, Chapter 15 of the Rules whereby certain litigation expenses in respect of office-holder proceedings must be approved or authorized by the creditors who

---

[7]   (1875) 3 Ch D 411 (CA) 427. (See also rule 18.38.)

will be affected (or the court) if the liquidator will need recourse to floating charge assets to meet those expenses. The Insolvency Service explained the rationale of the (then proposed) rules in the following terms:[8]

> The reason for putting in place Rules to restrict the application of the new section is to provide a better balance between the various stakeholders by providing that general liquidation expenses (including those discharged in fulfilling statutory obligations in the public interest) may be recovered out of floating charge assets where there are insufficient unencumbered assets to cover such expenses, whilst at the same time giving some control to the floating charge-holder and/or the preferential creditors to limit the nature and quantum of such expenses in certain circumstances.

> There was a clear consensus in the views expressed in response to the consultation in May 2006 that the only category of expense that should be restricted, are litigation expenses.

21.08 There is no equivalent provision for administrators' expenses and none is needed because of the more general power an administrator has always had to deal with floating charge assets as if they were free from charge—a necessary concomitant of his/her trading powers.[9]

c. Preferential creditors

21.09 Provision was first made by the Companies Act 1883 for preferential debts (comprising wages and salary claims) in a liquidation. The priority accorded to preferential creditors over other creditors was extended to priority over floating charges by the Preferential Payments in Bankruptcy Act 1897. Although the priority, as such, is therefore a very long-standing feature of corporate insolvency law, the categories of claim accorded that priority have changed from time to time reflecting changes in policy. Crown preference (preferential claims for taxes) was abolished as part of the Enterprise Act reforms.

21.10 Section 175 of the Act now provides priority for preferential creditors in liquidation and is applied to administration by paragraph 65 of Schedule B1. Section 175 was significantly amended in 2015[10] by the introduction of a sub-division of preferential debts into 'ordinary' and 'secondary' preferential debts, with the former taking priority to the latter. This was done in the context of adding new categories of preferential debt which relate to eligible deposits and the Financial Services Compensation Scheme (FSCS), and ordering priorities as between those debts. Insolvencies of credit institutions where those issues will arise are outside the scope of this book and the distinction between ordinary

---

[8] Consultation letter dated 16 August 2007 on the bringing into force of section 176ZA to reverse the decision in *Buchler v Talbot* (n 6).

[9] Schedule B1 para 70.

[10] Banks and Building Societies (Depositor Preference and Priorities) Order 2014 (SI 2014/3486). See also section 386.

and secondary preferential creditors will not be relevant elsewhere unless and until further amendments are made extending the distinction to other classes of preferential debt.[11]

21.11 The categories of preferential debt are listed in Schedule 6. Disregarding the deposit and FSCS categories of debt, the debts concern contributions to occupational pension schemes, remuneration of employees, and levies on coal and steel production.[12] These are all ordinary preferential debts. Section 387 identifies the date which determines the existence and amount of a preferential debt. This will usually be the same as the cut-off date that applies for the purposes of establishing a provable debt but the drafting of section 387 is more elaborate than that of rule 14.1 and different dates are possible (in which case rule 14.1 would apply as a free-standing test to any element of a creditor's claim which did not achieve priority under section 387).

d. Floating charge creditors (and the prescribed part)

21.12 Floating chargees are secured creditors but their position is not analogous to fixed charge creditors because their right to the proceeds of their floating charge security is subject to the payment of the expenses of the proceeding and preferential creditors (to the extent that the company does not have uncharged assets). Unless those claims are paid in full, the floating charge yields nothing for its holder. Even where there is a distributable fund, it must be shared with unsecured creditors (category 5) who are entitled to the prescribed part.

21.13 The prescribed part was introduced by the Enterprise Act reforms to the Act as part of the continuing legislative history of correcting the perceived imbalance between, on the one hand, the rights and interests of floating chargees and, on the other hand, the interests of other creditors. The result of this history has been to curtail the ability of floating chargees to leave nothing for unsecured creditors (which had had the effect of undermining confidence in the insolvency process and encouraging creditor apathy).

21.14 An earlier proposal to benefit unsecured creditors by providing for a 10 per cent fund was advanced in the Cork Report but not acted upon.[13] The critical change

---

[11] As appears to be contemplated by the recommendation of the Law Commission referred to in para 21.01.

[12] Preferential status for ECSC coal and steel levy debts, which appears anomalous, results from the Insolvency (ECSC Levy Debts) Regulations 1987 (SI 1987/2093) which were made to implement European Commission Recommendation 86/198/ECSC (OJ No L144, 29.5.86, 40).

[13] Report of the Review Committee, *Insolvency Law and Practice* (Cm 8558, June 1982) Chapter 36.

came with the abolition of Crown preference. It was announced in the following terms:[14]

> Finally, as an important and integral part of this package of measures, we will proceed with the abolition of Crown preference in all insolvencies. Preferential claims in insolvency originated in the late 19th century, but in recent years the trend in other jurisdictions has been towards restricting or abolishing Crown or State preference as, for instance, in Germany and Australia. We believe that this is more equitable. Where there is no floating charge-holder, the benefit of abolition will be available for unsecured creditors. Where there is a floating charge-holder (in relation to a floating charge created after the coming into force of the legislation), we would ensure that the benefit of abolition of preferential status goes to unsecured creditors. We will achieve this through a mechanism that ringfences a proportion of the funds generated by the floating charge.

21.15 The prescribed part is not a discrete claim; it is an allocation of part of the proceeds of floating charge realizations. Section 176A[15] requires a liquidator or administrator make 50 per cent of the first £10,000 and 20 per cent of the balance of the company's 'net property', up to a maximum of £600,000, available to unsecured creditors. Since net property is defined as being that which would otherwise be payable to the floating chargee, this naturally presupposes that expenses and preferential creditors have already been paid in full. If the office-holder thinks that the costs of distributing the prescribed part would be disproportionate, he can decide not to distribute if the net property amounts to less than £10,000 or, if over that figure, he obtains a court order relieving him from his obligation to distribute. Consistently with the background of abolition of Crown preference in order to benefit unsecured creditors, the courts are reluctant to sanction disapplication of section 176A.[16]

e. Unsecured provable debts

21.16 From a practical point of view, the concept of a provable debt is fundamental to the distribution of the estate amongst the general body of creditors—'proof of debt' being the terminology of the Rules describing the process for the submission of claims. The policy of the legislature has been to extend the class of unsecured claims which are entitled to participate in distributions such that there are now few claims which relate to the state of the company's affairs pertaining at

---

[14] Department of Trade and Industry, *Insolvency – A Second Chance* (White Paper, Cm 5234, July 2001) 2.19.

[15] Supplemented by the Insolvency Act 1986 (Prescribed Part) Order 2003 (SI 2003/2097).

[16] *Re International Sections Ltd* [2009] EWHC 137 (Ch), [2009] BCC 574. See also *Re Castlebridge Plant Ltd* [2015] CSOH 161 (Court of Session, Outer House).

the commencement of the proceedings which will not be provable debts. As Lord Neuberger PSC said in *Re Nortel GmbH*:[17]

> The notion that all possible liabilities within reason should be provable helps achieve equal justice to all creditors and potential creditors in any insolvency …

21.17 As explained in Chapters 7 and 19, the process of distribution necessitates the selection of a cut-off date for the purposes of ascertaining the company's liabilities. In *Stein v Blake*, Lord Hoffmann referred to:[18]

> … the general principle of bankruptcy law, which governs the payment of interest, conversion of foreign currencies etc, that the debts of the bankrupt are treated as having been ascertained and his assets simultaneously distributed among his creditors on the bankruptcy date: see *In re Dynamics Corporation of America*.

(The quantification of debts and the simultaneous distribution of the estate is, of course, notional. The function of the principle is merely to fix a point in time by reference to which assets and liabilities are ascertained.)

21.18 In principle (but subject to a few express exclusions[19]) claims of any description are provable provided that they existed at the relevant cut-off date or arise out of an 'obligation' incurred before that date:

a) For the purposes of liability in tort, a debt is provable if the cause of action accrued before the cut-off date or if all necessary elements of the tort existed except for actionable damage.[20]

b) The concept of a liability arising after the cut-off date by virtue of a pre-proceeding obligation is straightforward when considering contingent liabilities under contracts but much less so when considering statutory liabilities. Lord Neuberger PSC said of such liabilities:[21]

> … the mere fact that a company could become under a liability pursuant to a provision in a statute which was in force before the insolvency event, cannot mean that, where the liability arises after the insolvency event, it falls within rule 13.12(1)(b).[22] It would be dangerous to try and suggest a universally applicable formula, given the many different statutory and other liabilities and obligations which could exist. However, I would suggest that, at least normally, in order for a company to have incurred a relevant 'obligation' under rule 13.12(1)(b), it must have taken, or been subjected to, some step or combination of steps which (a) had some legal effect (such as putting it under some legal duty or into some legal relationship) and which (b) resulted in it being vulnerable to the specific liability in question, such that there would be a real prospect of that liability being incurred. If these two requirements

---

[17] [2013] UKSC 52, [2014] AC 209 [93].
[18] [1996] 1 AC 243 (HL) 252C (internal citation omitted).
[19] Rule 14.2(2).
[20] Rules 14.1(3) and (4).
[21] *Nortel* (n 17) [77].
[22] Now para (b) of the definition of 'debt' in rule 14.1(3).

are satisfied, it is also, I think, relevant to consider (c) whether it would be consistent with the regime under which the liability is imposed to conclude that the step or combination of steps gave rise to an obligation under rule 13.12(1)(b).

He went on to conclude that a liability to contribute to a group pension scheme deficit arising from actions taken by the Pensions Regulator after the commencement of administration was a provable debt.

f. Statutory interest

The Rules provide that interest on interest-bearing debts (and on a limited class of liabilities where interest has not previously been reserved or agreed) is provable in respect of the period up to the cut-off date but not in respect of any subsequent period.[23] However, where there is a surplus, statutory interest is payable on provable debts at a rate which is currently set at 8 per cent per annum.[24] **21.19**

g. Non-provable liabilities

Non-provable liabilities are legally enforceable claims which both fail to qualify as expenses and fail to conform to the definition of provable debts. Apart from the limited class of exceptional claims which are expressly debarred from proof by rule 14.2(2) (eg claims in respect of criminal confiscation orders), this category of liabilities exists because of the cut-off date which forms part of the definition of a provable debt and the Supreme Court's rejection in *Re Nortel GmbH* of the proposition that any liability arising after the cut-off date would then necessarily be an expense of the proceeding.[25] **21.20**

h. Shareholders

The deferral of shareholder claims is to ensure the maintenance of capital. A sum due to a member of a company by way of dividends, profits, or otherwise is not deemed to be a debt of the company, payable in competition with a debt due to a creditor, but any such sum may be taken into account for the purpose of the final adjustment of the rights of the contributories among themselves.[26] This rule relates to the claims of a shareholder which arise by virtue of the statutory contract and not to other claims which the shareholder may have against the company.[27] There is no doctrine of equitable subordination of shareholder claims. **21.21**

---

[23] Rule 14.23.

[24] Section 189 (liquidation) and rule 14.23 (administration). See section 17 Judgments Act 1838 and Judgment Debts (Rate of Interest) Order 1993 (SI 1993/564) as to the applicable rate. See also *Re Lehman Brothers International (Europe) (No 5)* [2015] EWHC 2269 (Ch), [2016] Bus LR 17.

[25] *Nortel* (n 17) [111]. See further *Re Lehman Brothers International (Europe) (No 4)* [2015] EWCA Civ 485, [2016] Ch 50 as to the range of non-provable liabilities (at the time of writing, the Supreme Court has heard an appeal from this decision but has not delivered its decision).

[26] Section 74(2)(f).

[27] *Soden v British & Commonwealth Holdings Plc* [1998] AC 298 (HL).

21.22 A shareholder who is also a creditor but whose shares are not fully paid up is further disadvantaged by the contributory rule. This rule precludes the shareholder from receiving anything in a liquidation in respect of the debt due to him unless he has first discharged everything which he owes as a contributory. The rule does not apply in administration because it presupposes a call already having been made (as opposed to the existence of a contingent liability to pay in respect of future calls) and an administrator has no power to make calls on shareholders.[28] In an appropriate case, an administrator would cause the company to go into liquidation so that a liquidator could make a call and thereby trigger the application of the contributory rule to prevent the shareholder creditor receiving dividends.

3. The principle of pari passu distribution

a. The principle and exceptions to it

21.23 In *Revenue and Customs Commissioners v Football League Ltd* David Richards J said:[29]

> The first principle in issue is the pari passu principle, which requires the assets of an insolvent person to be distributed among the creditors on a pari passu basis, subject only to such exceptions as the general law may permit. The pari passu basis of distribution means that all creditors will receive the same percentage of their debts out of the available assets. Parties are not free to contract out of the operation of this principle, except by the creation and, when required, registration of security over the debtor's assets.

21.24 The principle of pari passu distribution is less absolute than the foregoing statement might appear to suggest. It is subject to Lord Neuberger's eight categories of priority in the order of distribution. It is also subject to some priorities within those categories which are prescribed by the Act and Rules. It is best regarded as a residual principle, consonant with the general equitable principle that equality is equity, which applies to determine the ranking of unsecured claims within classes or subclasses in the absence of any contrary provision. Where it applies, observance is mandatory and attempts to gain an advantage by contracting out are void.[30]

21.25 The application of the pari passu principle is not straightforward in relation to any of Lord Neuberger's eight categories:

---

[28] *Re Kaupthing Singer & Friedlander Ltd (No 2)* [2011] UKSC 48, [2012] 1 AC 804 [52]; *Re Lehman Brothers International (Europe) (No 4)* above.

[29] [2012] EWHC 1372 (Ch), [2012] Bus LR 1539 [4].

[30] *British Eagle International Airlines Ltd v Compagnie Nationale Air France* [1975] 1 WLR 758 (HL). See further below.

a) Priorities as between fixed charge creditors (category 1) are determined by such inter-creditor and priority agreements as may exist between them and, in the absence of such agreements, by the general law governing such priorities.[31]

b) Liquidation and administration expenses (category 2) are payable in the order of priority prescribed by the Rules.[32] In each case the court has power to alter the order of priority in the Rules but that power will only be exercised in an exceptional case.[33] The principle should apply as between expenses falling within the same classes prescribed by the Rules.

c) Ordinary preferential creditors (category 3) take priority to secondary preferential creditors (also category 3) but debts in each sub-class of preferential debts rank equally amongst themselves.[34]

d) Like fixed charge creditors, priority as between floating charge creditors (category 4) is determined by agreement or, in default of agreement, by the general law. The claims of floating charge creditors are not only subordinated to expenses and preferential debts (categories 2 and 3) but also to the prescribed part.[35]

e) The Act and Rules provide for pari passu distribution as between creditors with unsecured provable debts (category 5).[36] However, not even this is unqualified because:

   i. Rule 14.2(4) makes provision for certain unsecured provable debts to be postponed to the remainder of category 5 debts and any statutory interest (category 6) paid on them. (The legislation is silent as to the ranking of postponed debts as between themselves and it is suggested that the pari passu principle applies.)

   ii. The court has a discretion to subordinate debts due to persons who are liable for wrongful or fraudulent trading.[37]

f) Claims to statutory interest (category 6) on debts proved in the proceeding rank equally regardless of the ranking of the underlying debts.[38] Although, at first sight, this would appear to be a particularly pure form of pari passu distribution, that is an illusion because rule 14.2(4), which postpones certain category 5 debts, achieves that postponement by providing that the debts

---

[31] *Cheah Theam Swee v Equiticorp Finance Group Ltd* [1992] 1 AC 472 (PC).

[32] Rules 7.108(4) (compulsory liquidation), 6.42(4) (creditors' voluntary liquidation), and 3.51(2) (administration).

[33] Sections 112 and 156 (liquidation), rules 7.110(1) (compulsory liquidation) and 3.51(3) (administration). See further *Re Beni-Felkai Mining Co Ltd* [1934] Ch 406 (Ch); *Re Linda Marie Ltd* (1988) 4 BCC 463 (Ch).

[34] Section 175.

[35] Section 176A. The distribution of the prescribed part is an ordinary distribution to unsecured creditors to which the pari passu principle applies.

[36] Section 107 and rule 14.12.

[37] Section 215.

[38] Section 189 (liquidation) and rule 14.23(7) (administration).

cannot be proved until the other category 5 debts have been paid in full with statutory interest.

g) The law relating to non-provable liabilities (category 7) is case law; the Act or Rules merely create the class of non-provable liabilities by prescribing what is and what is not provable. Unsurprisingly, therefore, the legislation makes no provision for the ranking of non-provable liabilities as between themselves but it is thought that the residual principle of pari passu distribution should apply.

h) Shareholders (category 8) claiming as such are subordinated to all creditors' claims. (This is a matter for a liquidator because the Act and Rules make no provision for distributions to members by administrators.) Their rights amongst themselves (in the event of all creditor claims having been paid in full) are determined by the articles of association.[39] In *Welton v Saffery*, Lord Watson said:[40]

> … it is, according to my apprehension, a lawful condition that, in the event of there being surplus assets when the company is wound up, such surplus shall be apportioned, according to any rule which may be agreed on, amongst the different classes of shareholders. The truth is, that all these are domestic matters, in which neither creditors nor the outside public have any interest, and with which, in my opinion, it is the policy of the Legislature not to interfere.

and Lord Simmonds said to the same effect in *Scottish Insurance Corporation Ltd v Wilsons & Clyde Coal Company Ltd*:[41]

> It is clear from the authorities, and would be clear without them, that, subject to any relevant provision of the general law, the rights inter se of preference and ordinary shareholders must depend on the terms of the instrument which contains the bargain that they have made with the company and each other.

> Where the articles make no relevant provision, any surplus will be applied first in the return of paid up capital (if there is unpaid share capital) and thereafter distributed in proportion to the shares held.[42]

b. Insolvency set-off

21.26 It is sometimes suggested that insolvency set-off is also an exception to the principle of pari passu distribution but insolvency set-off is mandatory and self-executing.[43] It therefore results in a net balance either to or from the insolvent estate and, where the balance is in favour of the company, is better regarded as

---

[39] Distribution 'according to their rights and interests in the company' per section 107.
[40] [1897] AC 299 (HL) 309.
[41] [1949] AC 462 (HL) 488.
[42] *Birch v Cropper* (1889) 14 App Cas 525 (HL).
[43] *National Westminster Bank Ltd v Halesowen Presswork & Assemblies Ltd* [1972] AC 785 (HL); *Stein v Blake* [1996] 1 AC 243 (HL).

part of the process of identifying the insolvent estate or, where the balance is in favour of a creditor, as part of the quantification of the company's liabilities, rather than as a distribution rule. It is nonetheless convenient to consider it in this context because, structurally, insolvency set-off is framed as part of the rules on proof of debt and only creditor claims which are susceptible of proof are brought into account.[44]

English jurisprudence regards insolvency set-off as being necessary in order **21.27** to do 'substantial justice' to creditors who are also indebted to the estate. Lord Hoffmann identified the function of insolvency set-off in *Stein v Blake* in the following terms (when contrasting it with other forms of set-off which are designed to avoid cross-claims):[45]

> [Insolvency] set-off, on the other hand, affects the substantive rights of the parties by enabling the bankrupt's creditor to use his indebtedness to the bankrupt as a form of security. Instead of having to prove with other creditors for the whole of his debt in the bankruptcy, he can set off pound for pound what he owes the bankrupt and prove for or pay only the balance. So in *Forster v Wilson*, Parke B said that the purpose of insolvency set-off was 'to do substantial justice between the parties.'

More recently, in *Re Kaupthing Singer & Friedlander Ltd*, Etherton LJ used the same phrase when saying:[46]

> The provisions for insolvency set-off are intended to promote speedy and efficient administration of the assets so as to enable a distribution to be made to creditors as soon as possible and in a manner which achieves substantial justice between the parties to the set-off and, so far as practicable, equality in the treatment of creditors.

Equal treatment of creditors is a more debatable point since it is arguable that the effect of insolvency set-off is to confer a preference at the expense of other creditors and, as Lord Hoffmann acknowledged in *Stein v Blake*,[47] other legal systems see justice as lying in the opposite direction.

Insolvency set-off raises some very difficult questions[48] but the underlying princi- **21.28** ple is straightforward. Insolvency set-off displaces all other forms of set-off which apply prior to insolvency proceedings (including contractual set-off). It applies to all debits and credits arising out of 'mutual' dealings between the company and its counterparty.[49] Mutuality means that the claims are between the same persons and

---

[44] Rules 14.25 (liquidation) and 14.24 (administration). *Secretary of State for Trade and Industry v Frid* [2004] UKHL 24, [2004] 2 AC 506 [13].
[45] [1996] 1 AC 243 (HL) 251E (internal citation omitted).
[46] [2010] EWCA Civ 518, [2010] Bus LR 1500, 1511B.
[47] *Stein v Blake* (n 45) 251F.
[48] See, by way of example, *Re Kaupthing Singer & Friedlander Ltd* [2009] EWHC 2308 (Ch), [2010] Bus LR 428; on appeal above.
[49] Mutual dealings do not include debts arising out of obligations incurred during insolvency proceedings or at a time when the creditor was on notice that insolvency proceedings were pending: rules 14.25(6) (liquidation) and 14.24(6) (administration).

in the same right (thus, for example, precluding trust claims from being set against personal debts). Subject to that requirement, insolvency set-off is at least as wide as any form of pre-insolvency set-off but the ouster of contractual set-off precludes claims of different group companies being consolidated for set-off purposes (as is quite commonly permitted in trading relationships with groups of companies) because such claims lack mutuality. As Lord Hoffmann stated in *Re Bank of Credit and Commerce International SA (No 8)*:[50]

> There can be no set-off of claims by third parties, even with their consent.

21.29 The Rules further protect the integrity of the process by precluding a debtor from relying for set-off purposes upon cross-claims against the company which are acquired by assignment after commencement of the insolvency proceedings or with notice that such proceedings are pending.[51]

21.30 Insolvency set-off has some additional complications in administration arising from the transposition of the liquidation rules into a procedure which may or may not be distributive in character and where the commencement of the proceeding may be followed by a period of trading during which new liabilities are being incurred. Whereas the liquidation rule applies to pre-liquidation mutual dealings, the administration rule addresses the fundamentally different circumstances of an administration simply by providing that it applies where the administrator has given notice under rule 14.29 of his intention to pay a distribution, upon which date the balance is to be struck. (The remainder of the rule follows the form of the liquidation rule.) The bifurcation of the 'cut-off date' (which, subject to the rules referred to in the preceding paragraph, remains the commencement of the proceeding[52]) from that 'set-off date' gives rise to some questions which are too detailed for consideration in this book.

4. Contracting out of the statutory scheme

a. The premise

21.31 It is a fundamental principle of English insolvency law that agreements which purport to disapply its rules are ineffective.[53] The issue arose in *British Eagle International Airlines Ltd v Compagnie Nationale Air France* where the liquidator

---

[50] [1998] AC 214 (HL) 223D.

[51] Rules 14.25(6)(d) (liquidation) and 14.24(6)(e) (administration). See further *Re Parkside International Ltd* [2008] EWHC 3554 (Ch), [2010] BCC 309 on the possible attack of earlier assignments on transaction avoidance grounds.

[52] *Re Lehman Brothers International (Europe)* [2016] EWHC 2131 (Ch).

[53] These questions are discussed in more detail in Charlotte Cooke, Hamish Anderson, and Louise Gullifer, 'National Report for England' in Dennis Faber, Niels Vermunt, Jason Kilborn, and Kathleen Van Der Linde (eds), *Treatment of Contracts in Insolvency* (OUP 2013).

of British Eagle successfully challenged clearing house arrangements between members of IATA under which monthly balances as between members were replaced by a single net sum due to or from IATA. Lord Cross said:[54]

> … what the respondents are saying here is that the parties to the 'clearing house' arrangements by agreeing that simple contract debts are to be satisfied in a particular way have succeeded in 'contracting out' of the provisions contained in [the relevant legislation then in force] for the payment of unsecured debts 'pari passu.' In such a context it is to my mind irrelevant that the parties to the 'clearing house' arrangements had good business reasons for entering into them and did not direct their minds to the question how the arrangements might be affected by the insolvency of one or more of the parties. Such a 'contracting out' must, to my mind, be contrary to public policy.

In *Belmont Park Investments Pty Ltd v BNY Corporate Trustee Services Ltd & Anor,* Lord Collins SCJ distinguished two sub-rules deriving from the principle:[55]

> The anti-deprivation rule and the rule that it is contrary to public policy to contract out of pari passu distribution are two sub-rules of the general principle that parties cannot contract out of the insolvency legislation. Although there is some overlap, they are aimed at different mischiefs … The anti-deprivation rule is aimed at attempts to withdraw an asset on bankruptcy or liquidation or administration, thereby reducing the value of the insolvent estate to the detriment of creditors. The pari passu rule reflects the principle that statutory provisions for pro rata distribution may not be excluded by a contract which gives one creditor more than its proper share.

b. The anti-deprivation rule

It is now established that the anti-deprivation rule applies from the outset in **21.32** both liquidation and administration but that the pari passu rule only takes effect when the proceedings are distributive. It therefore applies from the outset in liquidation but not in administration unless and until the administrator has given notice of intention to distribute in accordance with rule 14.29. This is because, in the words of David Richards J in *Revenue and Customs Commissioners v Football League Ltd*:[56]

> What matters as regards [the *pari passu* rule] is that there is to be a distribution pursuant to the insolvency legislation among creditors on a pari passu basis. What matters as regards the anti-deprivation rule is that the law has provided for an insolvency process which would be undermined by disposals to which the anti-deprivation rule would apply.

The classic form of transaction which offends the anti-deprivation rule is one **21.33** whereby a person agrees that, in the event of insolvency proceedings, property

---

[54] [1975] 1 WLR 758 (HL) 780G.
[55] [2011] UKSC 38, [2012] 1 AC 383 [1].
[56] [2012] EWHC 1372 (Ch), [2012] Bus LR 1539 [103] see also [89].

267

which that person owns shall belong to another. In *Whitmore v Mason*, Sir William Page Wood V-C said:[57]

> ... the law is too clearly settled to admit of a shadow of doubt that no person possessed of property can reserve that property to himself until he shall become bankrupt, and then provide that, in the event of his becoming bankrupt, it shall pass to another and not to his creditors.

Thus, in *Re Harrison, ex parte Jay*,[58] the Court of Appeal ruled that a term in an agreement for a lease between a landlord and a builder which provided materials on the land should become the property of the landlord in the event of the builder's default or bankruptcy before the lease had been granted was invalid.

21.34 Transactions providing for the gratuitous divestment of tangible property in the event of insolvency proceedings are unlikely to be encountered in arms' length commercial relationships but provisions for the termination of contracts or contractual rights are commonplace. Although contractual rights are not outwith the scope of the anti-deprivation rule, the courts have recognized a number of important practical limitations such that the rule has very limited relevance to ordinary commercial dealings. Thus:

a) Forfeiture provisions in leases escape the rule because a (much criticized) distinction is drawn between agreements which divest the debtor of property which is owned absolutely and grants of property which are limited from the outset so as to be defeasible in the event of insolvency. As Lord Collins observed in *Belmont*:[59]

> It would go far beyond the judicial function to hold that the distinction is indefensible. To hold that both types of determination are contrary to the anti-deprivation principle would be thoroughly destructive of commercial expectations in many areas.

b) Forfeiture rights will be upheld in the context of professional or business activities where insolvency is a disqualification and this treatment may extend to assets linked to the conduct of those activities.[60]

c) The anti-deprivation rule does not apply if deprivation takes effect for reasons other than insolvency (typically, the debtor's failure to perform its contractual obligations).[61]

---

[57] (1861) 2 J & H 204 (Court of King's Bench) 212.

[58] (1880) 14 Ch D 19 (CA).

[59] *Belmont* (n 55) [88]. This stops short of a general exclusion of all arrangements whereby assets revert to their original owner although the source of assets is a relevant consideration in deciding whether an arrangement was commercially justified and entered into in good faith such that it does not offend the rule [98].

[60] *Money Markets International Stockbrokers Ltd v London Stock Exchange Ltd* [2002] 1 WLR 1150 (Ch).

[61] *Belmont* (n 55) [80]–[83].

d) The rule is directed towards arrangements which are a deliberate attempt to evade the insolvency distribution rules.[62] Lord Collins said of this in *Belmont*:[63]

> That does not mean, of course, that a subjective intention is required, or that there will not be cases so obvious that an intention can be inferred, as in Ex p Jay. But it does suggest that in borderline cases a commercially sensible transaction entered into in good faith should not be held to infringe the anti-deprivation rule ...

e) A contract may also purport to suspend (possibly indefinitely) the counter-party's payment obligations in the event of insolvency. In *Lomas v JFB Firth Rixson Inc*, Briggs J distinguished between a payment obligation in respect of something done or supplied before insolvency and an obligation which related (in whole or part) to something yet to be done by the insolvent company, holding that the court would more readily conclude that the rule applies in the former situation.[64]

f) The rule does not apply where fair value is given for the deprivation.[65]

g) More generally, it appears that the courts will be reluctant to allow the rule to interfere with complex transactions which have been entered into in good faith.[66]

c. The pari passu rule

The essence of the pari passu rule is the prevention of arrangements whereby the **21.35** office-holder is to distribute otherwise than in accordance with the statutory scheme or which removes assets from the estate with the same results. In contrast to the anti-deprivation rule, where good faith and intention are crucial, the pari passu rule is concerned only with effects. In *Carreras Rothmans Ltd v Freeman Mathews Treasure Ltd*, Peter Gibson J said:[67]

> ... where the effect of a contract is that an asset which is actually owned by a company at the commencement of its liquidation would be dealt with in a way other than in accordance with [the statutory rules], then to that extent the contract as a matter of public policy is avoided, whether or not the contract was entered into for a considera-tion and for bona fide commercial reasons and whether or not the contractual provi-sion affecting that asset is expressed to take effect only on insolvency.

---

[62] As in *Mayhew v King* [2011] EWCA Civ 328, [2011] Bus LR 1327.

[63] Belmont (n 55) [79].

[64] [2010] EWHC 3372 (Ch), [2011] 2 BCLC 120 [108], see further on appeal [2012] EWCA Civ 419, [2013] 1 BCLC 27 [88]–[91].

[65] *Borland's Trustee v Steel Bros Co Ltd* [1901] 1 Ch 279 (Ch).

[66] *Belmont* (n 55) [108]–[113].

[67] [1985] Ch 207 (Ch) 226.

In *Revenue and Customs Commissioners v Football League Ltd* David Richards J said to like effect:[68]

> It is enough that the effect of the relevant contractual or other provision is to apply an asset belonging to the debtor at or following the commencement of the insolvency procedure in a non-pari passu way, as was the case in *British Eagle*. Contracts conflicting with the pari passu principle are void without any need to show that their purpose was to avoid a pari passu distribution. The purpose of the parties is irrelevant and, as in *British Eagle*, a contract may be void once an insolvency proceeding commences even though it is a bona fide commercial arrangement made for reasons unconnected with insolvency.

Although it is brought into play by insolvency proceedings, the relevant contractual trigger need not be those proceedings. Despite the ostensible rigour of this approach, there are two important qualifications:

a) the rule is confined to distributive proceedings; and
b) the rule is only engaged as regards assets forming part of the estate when it takes effect. Rights which would offend the pari passu rule can therefore be exercised prior to liquidation and before notice is given in administration without the risk of subsequent attack on that ground.[69]

d. Restating the principle

21.36 To state the principle underlying the anti-deprivation and pari passu sub-rules baldly in terms that contracting out of the statutory scheme offends public policy is an oversimplification:

a) Creditors can enter into 'non-petition agreements' whereby they bind themselves not to have recourse to insolvency proceedings or which by other means render a debtor 'bankruptcy remote'.[70]
b) It is open to creditors to contract out of pari passu distribution by taking security. Indeed, that is precisely the purpose of security. Subject to the effects of the transaction avoidance rules (and statutory priorities), the Act and Rules recognize the rights of secured creditors.
c) The principle is concerned with agreements which disturb the statutory scheme for the administration or distribution of the insolvent estate; there is

---

[68] [2012] EWHC 1372 (Ch), [2012] Bus LR 1539 [65]. (It is important to appreciate that the decision of the majority in *British Eagle* was premised upon the clearing house arrangements being a payment mechanism which did not change the underlying nature of the bilateral debts of members.)

[69] *Lomas v JFB Firth Rixson Inc* [2012] EWCA Civ 419, [2013] 1 BCLC 27 [97]; *Revenue and Customs Commissioners v Football League Ltd* (n 68) [89].

[70] *Re Colt Telecom Plc (No 2)* [2002] EWHC 2815 (Ch), [2003] BPIR 324 (see further Hamish Anderson, 'Non-petition Clauses' (2013) 1 NIBLeJ 3, (2014) 23 Nott LJ 85); *BNY Corporate Trustee Services Ltd v Eurosail-UK 2007-3BL Plc* [2013] UKSC 28, [2013] 1 WLR 1408.

no objection to agreements which prevent property from ever becoming part of the insolvent estate.[71]

d) The principle strikes down agreements which purport to confer an advantage on creditors; there is no objection to agreements by which creditors subordinate or forego what would otherwise be their rights to participate in the distribution of the estate.[72]

e) Inter-creditor agreements which disapply the pari passu principle as between the contracting creditors (for example by pooling and reallocating dividend rights), and which do not affect the rights of non-participating creditors, do not offend the principle.

f) Agreements and arrangements made in accordance with statutory procedures whereby a dissenting minority can be bound by the wishes of the majority creditors may depart from the statutory scheme for distribution (from which it would also appear that any agreement made by all interested parties could also disregard the statutory scheme).

The grounding of the principle in public policy is further undermined by arrangements which would otherwise offend the principle being expressly authorized in special cases.[73]

The principle is better stated in more limited terms as being one that it is not per- **21.37**
missible for a debtor and some (but not all) of its creditors to reach agreements to undermine the statutory scheme by either removing assets from the insolvent estate or displacing the distribution rules, unless the agreement results from an arrangement made pursuant to a procedure which binds all the creditors.

---

[71] *Barclays Bank Ltd v Quistclose Investments Ltd* [1970] AC 567 (HL); *Carreras Rothmans Ltd v Freeman Mathews Treasure Ltd* [1985] Ch 207 (Ch).

[72] *Re Maxwell Communications Corporation Plc* [1993] 1 WLR 1402 (Ch).

[73] Financial Markets and Insolvency (Settlement Finality) Regulations 1999 (SI 1999/2979); Financial Collateral Arrangements (No 2) Regulations 2003 (SI 2003/3226). See also *Belmont* (n 55) [13] (Lord Collins SCJ).

22

CROSS-BORDER INSOLVENCY

1. Introduction

22.01 In the practice of insolvency law, the usual challenge is to work out the answer to a problem as a matter of general law and then to factor in the consequences of one or more of the parties being insolvent. In cross-border insolvency cases, this exercise can be made considerably more complicated by choice of law issues. Ultimately, cross-border insolvency questions are all questions of private international law which are determined in accordance with specific rules where applicable or otherwise in accordance with general principles. The aims are to recognize properly grounded foreign insolvency proceedings, to act in aid of them where appropriate, to ensure that English proceedings will achieve extra-territorial recognition where necessary, and thereby to achieve fairness for all creditors everywhere by avoiding conflicts and confusions between jurisdictions.

22.02 'Cross-border insolvency' is not a legal term of art; it simply means insolvency with a foreign element. That could be because the debtor is a foreign corporation or because there are assets or creditors outside the jurisdiction. The key issues which arise from the presence of a foreign element are jurisdiction, recognition, and the need to identify the applicable law. Jurisdiction in this context means which court or courts will have jurisdiction to open insolvency proceedings in respect of the debtor (or where out of court proceedings can be commenced). Some laws take a narrow approach to this question but English law takes a broader view which means that it is possible to open liquidation proceedings in the English courts against foreign corporations. As a result, it is entirely possible to have insolvency proceedings taking place concurrently in England and another jurisdiction. Recognition is the issue which arises as soon as an office-holder has occasion to take some steps in a jurisdiction other than that in which he has been appointed. The issue is then whether, and if so to what extent, he will be recognized in that other jurisdiction as possessing any authority. In England, there is a tradition of recognizing and assisting foreign insolvency proceedings. Choice of law means that, wherever appointed, the office-holder must first address which law applies to whatever he is doing. To take a simple example, an English liquidator could be presented with a proof of debt from a creditor claiming under a contract which states that it is governed by foreign law. In such a case, the existence of any liability is a matter of contract to be determined by the application of the governing law clause but the eligibility and ranking of that claim in the English liquidation will be a matter of English insolvency law.

2. Modified universalism

Universalism is the principle of private international law that there should be one **22.03** set of insolvency proceedings applicable to all the debtor's assets and liabilities instead of potentially competing proceedings dealing with local pools of assets and liabilities. It is immediately apparent that universalism has both inward and outward facing aspects. Naturally states find it easier to espouse outbound universalism for their own proceedings than to accord full inbound effects to foreign proceedings, and England is no exception.

True universalism could only be achieved by international treaty but 'modified' **22.04** universalism is the unilateral pursuit of the same desirable goal, as far as is possible, having regard to local laws. Modified universalism incorporates two elements. The first is unity, which contrasts with plurality. Where the principle is applied it requires the debtor's affairs, business, and property to be subjected to a single procedure. Whilst the desirability of avoiding unnecessary plurality is a factor to be taken into account in exercising jurisdiction, the principle of unity lacks real force in English law which has continued to assert the power to open local liquidation proceedings notwithstanding the prior existence of foreign proceedings—except in those cases where its jurisdiction is curtailed by the European Regulations.[1] If anything, the complexity of modern cases has sometimes tended to promote plurality. The second element is universality, which contrasts with territoriality. A territorial proceeding will be concerned only with local assets whereas a universal

---

[1] Discussed below.

proceeding will, at least in theory, deal with the debtor's assets and undertaking worldwide. Modified universalism informs the English court's exercise of its common law jurisdiction and the exercise of its discretion in relation to its statutory powers.

22.05 Clearly, the domestic laws of a jurisdiction (be that England or any other) are incapable of applying the concepts of unity and universality in any absolute fashion because the outward facing consequences of their application will eventually become a matter for decision under the domestic laws of another jurisdiction. In *Re International Tin Council*, Millett J described the position in respect of an English order winding up a foreign company in the following terms: [2]

> Although a winding up in the country of incorporation will normally be given extra-territorial effect, a winding up elsewhere has only local operation. In the case of a foreign company, therefore, the fact that other countries, in accordance with their own rules of private international law, may not recognise our winding up order or the title of a liquidator appointed by our courts, necessarily imposes practical limitations on the consequences of the order. But in theory the effect of the order is world-wide.

22.06 Conversely, in the absence of an international framework, the undiluted application of universalism could lead to the English courts being called upon to give effect to the consequences of foreign laws which offended English public policy or were in some other way inimical to English concepts of justice. Modified universalism therefore recognizes the need for the protection of essential local interests which would be disadvantaged if exposed to the full effects of foreign proceedings. The best and most obvious example of the need for modification is the need to protect the priority of claims, for example the claims of preferential creditors, where the claims would not enjoy equivalent priority in foreign proceedings, but the circumstances in which universalism will be tempered by pragmatism remain open for consideration on a case by case basis.

22.07 Although universalism in English law, as a response to foreign insolvency proceedings, can be traced back to the eighteenth century, the role of modified universalism in modern English law has been reviewed and restated in a series of twenty-first century decisions of the House of Lords, Supreme Court, and Privy Council, starting with the decision of the Privy Council in *Cambridge Gas Transportation Corpn v Official Committee of Unsecured Creditors of Navigator Holdings Plc*. In that case, which can be seen as the high-water mark of inbound universalism, the Privy Council gave effect to a US Chapter 11 reorganization plan providing for the assets of an insolvent business to be transferred to its creditors, which involved divesting the shareholders of a Manx company of their shares and vesting them in a creditors'

---

[2] [1987] Ch 419 (Ch) 446G (on appeal [1989] Ch 309 (CA)).

committee. Lord Hoffmann explained the conceptual approach in the following terms:[3]

> The English common law has traditionally taken the view that fairness between creditors requires that, ideally, bankruptcy proceedings should have universal application. There should be a single bankruptcy in which all creditors are entitled and required to prove. No one should have an advantage because he happens to live in a jurisdiction where more of the assets or fewer of the creditors are situated ...

More specifically, and controversially, he went on to state that universalism meant that:[4]

> At common law ... the domestic court must at least be able to provide assistance by doing whatever it could have done in the case of a domestic insolvency. The purpose of recognition is to enable the foreign office holder or the creditors to avoid having to start parallel insolvency proceedings and to give them the remedies to which they would have been entitled if the equivalent proceedings had taken place in the domestic forum.

Lord Hoffmann returned to the subject in *Re HIH Casualty and General Insurance Ltd* where the House of Lords ordered provisional liquidators appointed in English winding-up proceedings in respect of an Australian insurance company to turn over reinsurance money in England for distribution in accordance with Australian rules (which differed from those which would have applied to an English distribution). Lord Hoffmann said:[5]

> The primary rule of private international law which seems to me applicable to this case is the principle of (modified) universalism, which has been the golden thread running through English cross-border insolvency law since the 18th century. That principle requires that English courts should, so far as is consistent with justice and UK public policy, co-operate with the courts in the country of the principal liquidation to ensure that all the company's assets are distributed to its creditors under a single system of distribution. That is the purpose of the power to direct remittal.

The authority of that, often quoted, statement of principle was significantly weakened by the fact that only one other member of the panel agreed with Lord Hoffmann's reasoning that there was a common law power to order remittal. Whilst all members of the panel agreed with the result, two based their conclusions on section 426 and the fifth declined to comment on whether remittal could have been ordered absent section 426.[6]

In the aftermath of *Cambridge Gas* and *HIH*, the lower courts began to take an **22.08** increasingly liberal approach to acting in aid of foreign proceedings. That movement was arrested by *Rubin v Eurofinance SA* where, by a majority, the Supreme

---

[3] [2006] UKPC 26, [2007] 1 AC 508 [16].
[4] Ibid at [22].
[5] [2008] UKHL 21, [2008] 1 WLR 852 [30].
[6] Section 426 is discussed further below.

Court refused to enforce a transaction avoidance judgment obtained in insolvency proceedings in the United States (which was not enforceable according to the ordinary rules of private international law applicable to foreign judgments) and declared *Cambridge Gas* to have been wrongly decided. Lord Collins SCJ, delivering the leading judgment, down-played universalism by describing it as 'only a trend'.[7]

22.09 *Rubin* was followed by *Singularis Holdings Ltd v PricewaterhouseCoopers* where the Privy Council further limited the (inbound) application of modified universalism to foreign proceedings. In *Singularis*, it was held that any common law power to assist foreign liquidators by making examination orders under local law was not exercisable where the liquidators did not have the powers which they needed under the law pursuant to which they had been appointed. The Board affirmed the principle of modified universalism but also prescribed limits. Lord Sumption SCJ said:[8]

> In the Board's opinion, the principle of modified universalism is part of the common law, but it is necessary to bear in mind, first, that it is subject to local law and local public policy and, secondly, that the court can only ever act within the limits of its own statutory and common law powers. What are those limits? In the absence of a relevant statutory power, they must depend on the common law, including any proper development of the common law. The question how far it is appropriate to develop the common law so as to recognise an equivalent power does not admit of a single, universal answer. It depends on the nature of the power that the court is being asked to exercise.

The proposition derived from *Cambridge Gas*, that there was a common law jurisdiction to do anything in aid of foreign proceedings that the court could have done in a domestic insolvency, was held to be insupportable.

22.10 Very shortly after its decision in *Singularis*, the Privy Council delivered its decision in *Stichting Shell Pensioenfonds v Krys*.[9] The issue was whether liquidators were entitled to an anti-suit injunction to require a foreign creditor, which had submitted a proof of debt, to relinquish a conservatory attachment which it had obtained in its own national courts. It was held that, in principle and subject to discretion, an anti-suit injunction is always available where it is required to serve the ends of justice and that preventing interference with the statutory scheme for distribution in an insolvency serves those ends. The person to be enjoined must be amenable to the jurisdiction but a creditor which submits a proof of debt renders itself amenable. The decision is not couched in terms of universalism but it is nonetheless a robust assertion of universalism, albeit in its easier outbound form.

---

[7] [2012] UKSC 46, [2013] 1 AC 236 [16].
[8] [2014] UKPC 36, [2015] AC 1675 [19].
[9] [2014] UKPC 41, [2015] AC 616.

English cases where the universalist nature of English proceedings would be in   **22.11**
issue are most likely to be cases over the nature and exercise of jurisdiction. This is
an area where, as discussed below, legislation now pays a significant role. However
the concept of an 'ancillary' liquidation, whereby the English liquidation of a foreign company is treated as being ancillary to a winding-up by the court of its domicile, predates that legislation. In such cases the powers and duties of the English
liquidator will, as a matter of judicial practice, be limited to collecting English
assets and settling a list of creditors.[10] Other cases can arise where, in the course
of applying a universalist approach to its own proceedings, the English court will
nonetheless recognize foreign priorities. In *Re Collins & Aikman Europe SA*,[11]
English administrators, who had discouraged foreign creditors from commencing
local proceedings by giving assurances that their position under local law would
be respected as far as possible, were given directions authorizing distributions in
European jurisdictions according to local law rather than English law. This was
another example of the principle of modified universalism even though the judgment was again not framed in those terms.

3. Cross-border insolvency laws

With that introduction to the nature of the issues raised by cross-border insolvency   **22.12**
cases—jurisdiction, recognition, and choice of law—and the overarching principle of modified universalism with which English law approaches those issues, it
is appropriate to turn to the applicable rules such as they are. This subject is now
one of even more complexity and uncertainty following the result of the United
Kingdom's 'Brexit' referendum on 23 June 2016, when the UK voted to leave the
European Union.

a. Sources

Aside from rules on jurisdiction over foreign debtors, the only legislation imme-   **22.13**
diately prior to the Act expressly dealing with cross-border insolvency was contained in the Bankruptcy Act 1914. This was a limited provision for the English
courts to act in aid of 'British' courts in personal insolvency cases which was a
relic of an earlier era when Bankruptcy Acts were Imperial statutes. That provision was remodelled and re-enacted as section 426 of the Act. The principal
changes were to create an open-ended class of other jurisdictions to be designated
for assistance and to extend it corporate insolvencies. However, section 426 was
clearly insufficient to deal with the issues which began to arise with increasing

---

[10] *HIH* (n 5) [8], [9].
[11] [2016] EWHC 1343 (Ch), [2007] 1 BCLC 182.

frequency and which led to judges identifying 'a crying need for an international insolvency convention'.[12]

22.14 In 2003, after a gestation period of approximately forty years, Council Regulation 1346/2000/EC finally took effect.[13] The Regulation is primarily directed to allocating the jurisdiction to open insolvency proceedings between member states of the European Union but it also deals with recognition and choice of law. After a review, Regulation 1346/2000 was revised and restated as Regulation (EU) 2015/848, usually referred to as the 'Recast Regulation'.[14] The Recast Regulation only applies to proceedings opened on or after 26 June 2017 (the EC Regulation continues to apply to proceedings opened before that date). In this book, references to the EC Regulation are references to the original Regulation 1346/2000, references to the Recast Regulation are references to the 2015 measure, and references to the European Regulations are references to both or either of them as appropriate. The continuing effect of the European Regulations depends on the terms and progress of Brexit.

22.15 In April 2006, the Cross-Border Insolvency Regulations 2006[15] took effect to adopt the Model Law on Cross-Border Insolvency, which had been promulgated by the United Nations Commission on International Trade in 1997 with a view to promoting internationally harmonized legislation governing instances of cross-border insolvency. The Model Law is principally concerned with recognition and does not attempt to regulate jurisdiction.

22.16 Alongside this legislation the common law rules, as restated by the Privy Council in *Singularis Holdings Ltd v PricewaterhouseCoopers*,[16] continue to apply.

22.17 This characteristically Anglo-Saxon cocktail of measures is largely complementary but, in case of conflict, there is a convoluted order of precedence which is described below. However, even cumulatively, the result falls far short of a coherent international convention. Instead the various powers and provisions work in a piecemeal, and sometimes haphazard, fashion.

b. Emerging international concepts

22.18 English law, with its concept of ancillary liquidation, has long recognized the primacy of insolvency proceedings in the place of domicile and that any local

---

[12] *Re Paramount Airways Limited* [1993] Ch 223 (CA) 239B (Nicholls V-C) and, earlier to the same effect, *Re Bank of Credit and Commerce International SA* [1992] BCLC 570 (Ch) 577c (Browne-Wilkinson V-C).

[13] Council Regulation (EC) No 1346/2000 of 29 May 2000 on Insolvency Proceedings [2000] OJ L 160/1.

[14] Regulation (EU) 2015/848 of the European Parliament and of the Council of 20 May 2015 on Insolvency Proceedings [2015] OJ L 141/19 (RR) as corrected by a Corrigendum [2016] OJ L 349/9.

[15] SI 2006/1030.

[16] [2014] UKPC 36, [2015] AC 1675.

proceedings should then be restricted to local assets. The same distinction between proceedings opened where the debtor is principally based and those opened elsewhere is adopted in the European Regulations and the Model Law, although the terminology varies. The general international trend is to accord primacy to proceedings which are taking place where the debtor is based and to treat those opened elsewhere as subordinated or meriting more limited assistance. This approach fits very comfortably with English jurisprudence and the principle of modified universalism.

To some extent, any determination of jurisdiction resolves the issues of recog- **22.19** nition and choice of law. Where the European Regulations apply so as to prescribe where insolvency proceedings can and cannot be opened, recognition of those proceedings elsewhere in the EU is the natural corollary. In other cases, for example the Model Law, the distinction between principal and subordinate proceedings is used to inform the approach to recognition. Choice of law is also, to some extent, consequential upon jurisdiction. The courts in every jurisdiction will ordinarily apply the insolvency laws of their own jurisdiction to all matters of procedure. However, the substantive rights of creditors and obligations of third parties may be governed by foreign law which will be applied as such within the insolvency proceedings.

Some forum shopping remains possible. This is particularly of interest to office- **22.20** holders seeking to attack antecedent transactions where the rules may differ markedly between jurisdictions. This is not usually 'choice of law' in the sense that the office-holder is able to exercise any wider choice than as to where to bring proceedings, but English law is unusual in this respect because there can be cases in which the English court has jurisdiction under section 426 to apply foreign law. Whether or not it will do so is, of course, a matter of discretion.

c. The European Regulations

The European Regulations[17] apply where the debtor's centre of main interests **22.21** (COMI) is located within the EU. In some respects these measures have constrained the traditional long-arm winding-up jurisdiction of the English courts but in other respects, where the Act itself did not previously confer jurisdiction, the Regulations have served to extend the jurisdiction over foreign debtors. This is because the Regulations provide that jurisdiction is exclusively determined by the location of the debtor's centre of main interests or the presence of any establishment in another jurisdiction. Where the Regulations confer jurisdiction, they do

---

[17] The European Regulations apply throughout the EU except for Denmark which exercised an opt-out. In this commentary references to the EU are references to all the member states with that exception. The EC Regulation has been amended from time to time to take account of the accession of new member states.

so even if, as in the case of administration, the procedure did not previously apply to a foreign company (and it matters not for these purposes whether or not the company was incorporated within the EU[18]).

22.22 The COMI is the central concept of the European Regulations. The expression has been defined for the purposes of the Recast Regulation in terms which codify previous case law from the Court of Justice. Thus COMI is the place where the debtor's interests are administered on a regular basis and which is ascertainable by third parties. There is a rebuttable presumption that the registered office of the company is its COMI (provided that the registered office has not been moved to another member state within the last three months[19]). In practice, the test is where the company's head office functions are performed.[20] In most cases, the location of the COMI is therefore straightforward but, ironically, a measure which was intended to inhibit forum shopping has afforded some scope for just that because the COMI is patently capable of being changed.[21] In particular, the focus on administrative control admits the possibility that groups of companies incorporated in different jurisdictions all have (or can be arranged to have) a single COMI. This is a beneficial result of the European Regulations which partly ameliorates the difficulty of achieving a co-ordinated insolvency administration of a European group whose constituent parts are incorporated in several different jurisdictions.[22] The potential issues in this regard are well illustrated by the decision of the European Court of Justice in *Re Eurofood IFSC Ltd (Case C-341/04)*[23] which discouraged an unduly liberal approach to identification of the COMI. Eurofood was the Irish subsidiary of Parmalat, an Italian parent company with subsidiaries in more than thirty countries. Insolvency proceedings were opened first in Ireland and then in Italy and the question was which proceedings should prevail. It was held that the presumption can only be rebutted if factors which are objective and identifiable by third parties enable it to be established that the true position is at variance from that which is deemed to be the case. That could be so where a company is not carrying on any business in the country where its registered office is located but the mere fact that economic choices are or can be controlled by its parent company elsewhere is not sufficient to rebut the presumption.[24]

---

[18] *Re BRAC International Rent-A-Car Inc* [2003] EWHC 128 (Ch), [2003] 1 WLR 1421.

[19] This proviso to the presumption did not feature in the EC Regulation.

[20] *Interedil Srl v Fallimento Interedil Srl (Case C-396/09)* [2011] ECR 1-9915 (European Court of Justice, First Chamber).

[21] See further: *Staubitz-Schreiber (Case C-1/04)* [2006] ECR I-701 (European Court of Justice); *Seagon v Deko Marty Belgium NV (Case C-339/07)* [2009] 1 WLR 2168 (European Court of Justice, First Chamber).

[22] As in *Re Daisytek-ISA Ltd* [2003] BCC 562 (Ch). See now also Chapter V of the Recast Regulation.

[23] [2006] Ch 508 (European Court of Justice).

[24] See also: *Rastelli Davide e C Snc v Hidoux (Case C-191/10)* [2011] ECR I-13209 (European Court of Justice, First Chamber).

Where the debtor's COMI is in a member state, then only that member state has **22.23** jurisdiction to open 'main' proceedings. Where main proceedings are opened in one jurisdiction on the basis that the COMI is located within that jurisdiction those proceedings must be recognized throughout the EU unless they offend public policy, and any challenge must be pursued in that same jurisdiction and not by opening new proceedings in another member state. Main proceedings are intended have universal scope unless other proceedings are permitted in another member state.

Where the company's COMI is in a member state, proceedings can only be opened **22.24** in another member state if the debtor possesses an establishment there (whether or not any main proceedings have been opened). 'Establishment' is a defined term meaning something in the nature of a branch.[25] The concept of local proceedings under the European Regulations therefore resembles the concept of an English ancillary liquidation. In both cases, the proceedings are restricted to the assets of the debtor which are situated in the jurisdiction where the establishment exists. The analogy extends to distributions because the European Regulations provide that assets collected in the local proceedings are distributed in those proceedings with only any residual surplus passing to the main proceedings (if any are taking place) and the present weight of authority is to the effect that, as a matter of English common law, distributions to creditors in an ancillary liquidation must be made in accordance with English law.[26]

Although the facility to open local proceedings admits plurality, the restriction of **22.25** such proceedings to local assets and other provisions of the European Regulations which contain mandatory rules for co-ordination are intended to achieve a form of unity within the EU. Universality is also imperfectly achieved through provision for EU-wide recognition of any insolvency proceedings opened in conformity with its rules on jurisdiction and the application of the law of the member state where proceedings are opened.[27] This covers all the ordinary incidents of the opening, conduct, and closure of insolvency proceedings but is subject to numerous exceptions which have the broad aim of protecting legitimate expectations and the certainty of transactions in other member states. Thus, for example, the proceedings do not affect rights *in rem* relating to the assets of a debtor which are located in another member state at the opening of proceedings or reservation of title rights where the relevant asset is in another member state. The effects of the insolvency proceedings on contracts relating to immoveable property are governed by the

---

[25] The definitions in the EC Regulation and the Recast Regulation are different. There are other important differences between the European Regulations in their treatment of 'secondary' and 'territorial' proceedings (both referred to, for convenience, as 'local' proceedings in this commentary).

[26] *Re Alitalia Linee Aeree Italiane SpA* [2011] EWHC 15 (Ch), [2011] 1 WLR 2049.

[27] See further *ENEFI Energiahatékonysági Nyrt v Direcția Generală Regională a Finanțelor Publice Brașov (DGRFP)* [2016] EUECJ C-212/15 (9 November 2016) (Court of Justice of the European Union).

law of the member state within which the property is located; the effects of the proceedings on contracts of employment remain governed by the proper law of the contract; and the effects of the proceedings on pending actions are governed by the law of the member state where the action is proceeding. The foregoing examples all disapply the law of the insolvency proceedings in favour of either the law of another member state or the general laws which would otherwise apply. The treatment of transaction avoidance under the European Regulations is different. Here the basic rule is that the law of the insolvency proceedings shall apply except where the transaction in question is governed by the law of another member state and it is unchallengeable under that law. Similarly, the law of the insolvency proceedings governs set-off but a creditor's rights of set-off are preserved where permitted under the law applicable to the insolvent debtor's claim.

d. Cross-Border Insolvency Regulations 2006

22.26 The Regulations are principally concerned with the recognition of foreign insolvency proceedings. This is a less ambitious objective than that of the European Regulations and results are correspondingly more straightforward.

22.27 The Regulations are the result of the UK's adoption of the UNCITRAL Model Law. The Model Law is a template or precedent. Legislation based on it has so far been adopted in a number of other countries including the United States, Japan, Australia, and Canada but not by any of the other major economic powers within the EU. It is important to remember that, in each case, the legislation is part of the domestic law of the enacting country, not the ratification of a treaty, and that the detail of the legislation varies. The adoption of the Model Law is not something done purely for the benefit of others; it is, on the contrary, one of the ways in which a state can position its laws as being favourable for inward investment.

22.28 The Model Law overtly draws on the EC Regulation as one of its sources[28] and the 2006 Regulations are to be interpreted with regard to their international origins and with a view to promoting uniformity of application. In this respect, one of the most important points is that the Regulations also use the COMI concept to identify 'main' proceedings and the presence of an 'establishment'[29] to identify other proceedings which will qualify for recognition. In general terms, the scheme of the Regulations is that recognition is available on application to the English court. Some consequences flow automatically from recognition of main proceedings whereas equivalent relief for foreign proceedings which are not main proceedings is only available on a discretionary basis. If the proceedings are main proceedings, recognition results in the debtor's power to deal with

---

[28] See the UNCITRAL *Guide to Enactment and Interpretation (2013)* <http://www.uncitral. org/pdf/english/texts/insolven/1997-Model-Law-Insol-2013-Guide-Enactment-e.pdf> accessed 3 November 2016.
[29] The definition of 'establishment' is slightly different to that in the EC Regulation.

assets being suspended and in a basic automatic stay of proceedings and execution which the court has a discretionary power to extend. [30] The court may also provide for the examination of witnesses, grant any additional relief available to an English office-holder, and entrust the realization and distribution of local assets to the foreign representative. If the foreign proceedings are not main proceedings but are taking place in a jurisdiction where the debtor has an establishment, the same consequences can flow from recognition but there is no automatic stay, everything is discretionary, and the court must be satisfied that the relief sought relates to assets which should be administered in the foreign proceeding or information needed in that proceeding.

An important aspect of these provisions is that, following recognition of a foreign proceeding, they enable the foreign representative to invoke some English transaction avoidance rules as if the debtor was the subject of English insolvency proceedings.[31] There is neither any requirement that English law be the governing law of the transactions in question nor that there be any equivalent rules which could be invoked under the law of the foreign proceedings but some test of sufficient connection must be implicit. In any event, in most cases, the court retains a discretion (under the terms of the Act[32]) as to any appropriate remedy and, if the foreign proceedings are not main proceedings, the court must again be satisfied that the assets in question are assets which should be administered in the foreign proceedings. **22.29**

A 'foreign representative', meaning an office-holder appointed in foreign insolvency proceedings, has the right to apply directly to the English court and to commence English insolvency proceedings (provided that the conditions for the commencement of such proceedings are otherwise met). So far as English office-holders acting abroad are concerned, the Regulations provide that the office-holder is authorized to act in a foreign state as permitted by the applicable foreign law. In fact, such an authority is, in any event, the natural concomitant of the universal nature of English insolvency proceedings and would not have been in doubt unless the office-holder had been given directions by the court to the contrary. The Regulations do not provide for the powers of the English court in this respect but the court has an inherent jurisdiction to issue a letter of request to a foreign court seeking its assistance in aid of English insolvency proceedings.[33] **22.30**

---

[30] There is no automatic stay if English proceedings are already taking place when the application for recognition is made; all relief is discretionary in such a case and must be consistent with the English proceedings.

[31] Sections 238 (transactions at an undervalue), 239 (preferences), 244 (extortionate credit transactions), 245 (avoidance of floating charges), and 423 (transactions defrauding creditors).

[32] Section 245 is an exception.

[33] *Re Nortel Networks SA* [2009] EWHC 206 (Ch), [2009] BCC 343.

e. Section 426 of the Act

22.31 This measure, which is the longest standing legislation under consideration, is in one respect the most radical. Under section 426, the English court has the power to apply either English law or the corresponding foreign law.

22.32 Section 426 also deals with co-operation between courts within the United Kingdom where, as might be expected, the section provides for reciprocal enforcement of orders. It is the provisions for acting in aid of other jurisdictions which are of more interest in the present context. In this respect, section 426 provides that the English court shall assist the courts exercising insolvency jurisdiction in a 'relevant country or territory'—which means the Channel Islands and the Isle of Man together with any other jurisdictions designated by statutory instrument. There have been three such instruments to date.[34] The most striking feature of the resulting list is the omission of the United States and all EU member states with the exception of Ireland. The explanation for these anomalies is that the original designations were made in some haste at the time of the Act coming into force and in order to preserve historical arrangements for co-operation in personal insolvencies with jurisdictions which either had or undertook to put in place reciprocal arrangements. The expectations of reciprocity have not always been realized. It remains to be seen whether there will be any perceived need to extend the list following Brexit.

22.33 One reason for doing so would be the unique facility afforded by section 426 whereby the English court can, in response to a letter of request from a foreign court, apply foreign insolvency law. This means, for example, that a foreign office-holder could use foreign examination powers to elicit information in England in circumstances where an English office-holder would not be able to use the equivalent English powers.[35] Conversely, section 426 also means that a foreign office-holder can use English transaction powers to set aside transactions which are not susceptible to challenge under the foreign insolvency law pursuant to which he has been appointed.[36] In *Re HIH Casualty and General Insurance Ltd*,[37] the House of Lords were unanimous that a turnover order should be made in response to a letter of request from the Supreme Court of New South Wales but evenly divided as to whether the order could have been made absent jurisdiction under section 426. The section can also be used to obtain administration orders in respect of foreign companies.[38] For all these reasons, it may therefore be a material advantage to be a relevant country or territory for section 426 purposes.

---

[34] Co-operation of Insolvency Courts (Designation of Relevant Countries and Territories) Orders 1986 (SI 1986/2123), 1996 (SI 1996/253), and 1998 (SI 1998/2766).

[35] *England v Smith* [2001] Ch 419 (CA).

[36] *Re Bank of Credit and Commerce International SA (No 9)* [1994] 2 BCLC 636 (Ch), on appeal [1994] 1 WLR 708 (CA) but not on this point.

[37] [2008] UKHL 21, [2008] 1 WLR 852.

[38] *Re Dallhold Estates (UK) Pty Ltd* [1992] BCLC 621 (Ch); *Re Tambrook Jersey Ltd* [2013] EWCA Civ 576, [2014] Ch 252.

However many future cases will now be resolved by the 2006 Regulations (which **22.34** did not apply in *HIH*).[39] Although the 2006 Regulations contain no power to apply foreign law,[40] other differences may be more apparent than real. Whereas a large part of the relief available under the 2006 Regulations is only available on a discretionary basis and section 426 says that the English court 'shall' assist, it is well established that the duty of the English court under section 426 is limited to what it can properly do.[41] It seems unlikely that the English court will feel compelled, as a matter of duty, to do that which it would not consider it appropriate to do as a matter of discretion. On the other hand, where there are concurrent proceedings in England and a foreign jurisdiction, then the 2006 Regulations provide that any relief consequent on the recognition of the foreign proceedings must be consistent with the English proceedings which could be interpreted as preventing the English court granting relief in a given situation where there is no equivalent restriction to relief under section 426. There are, therefore, important questions still to be addressed in respect of the overlap between section 426 and the 2006 Regulations.

f. Common law

Although the extent to which an English court will exercise a common law jurisdic- **22.35** tion to act in aid of foreign proceedings is limited by the ruling in *Singularis Holdings Ltd v PricewaterhouseCoopers*,[42] that decision does not affect the more fundamental point that the English court will recognize the authority of an office-holder appointed in proceedings which have been opened in the jurisdiction in which a foreign company has been incorporated. This is a simple application of the accepted rule of private international law that questions relating to the governance of foreign corporations are determined by the laws of the jurisdiction of incorporation.

The consequence of the approach adopted in *Singularis* is a double hurdle whereby **22.36** common law assistance is now confined to cases where relevant powers exist *both* in the jurisdiction where proceedings have been opened *and* in the jurisdiction which is being asked to act in aid. Even then it does not follow that the court will act in aid because the common law power of the court to act in aid is discretionary.

These are difficult questions. As Lord Neuberger PSC ruefully acknowledged in **22.37** *Singularis*:[43]

> The extent of the extra-statutory powers of a common law court to assist foreign liquidators is a very tricky topic on which the Board, the House of Lords and the

---

[39] In this connection, it should be noted that the 2006 Regulations contain a lengthy list of special types of company to which the regulations do not apply, eg, credit institutions, and that there is no equivalent list of exemptions from section 426.

[40] *Re Pan Ocean Ltd* [2014] EWHC 2124 (Ch), [2014] Bus LR 1041.

[41] *Hughes v Hannover Ruckversicherungs-Aktiengesellschaft* [1997] 1 BCLC 497 (CA).

[42] [2014] UKPC 36, [2015] AC 1675.

[43] Ibid at [154]

Supreme Court have not been conspicuously successful in giving clear or consistent guidance ...

before going on to say of the proposed assertion of a common law power to order the production of information (which he concluded did not exist but which was upheld by the majority):[44]

> The extreme version of the 'principle of universality', as propounded by Lord Hoffmann in *Cambridge Gas*, has, as Lord Sumption explains, effectively disappeared, principally as a result of the reasoning of Lord Collins speaking for the majority in *Rubin*, and speaking for the Board in this appeal. However, as with the Cheshire Cat, the principle's deceptively benevolent smile still appears to linger, and it is now invoked to justify the creation of this new common law power. It is almost as if the Board is suggesting that, while we went too far in *Cambridge Gas* and should pull back as indicated in *Rubin*, we do not want to withdraw as completely as we logically ought. In my view, the logic of the withdrawal from the more extreme version of the principle of universality is that we should not invent a new common law power based on the principle.

These reflections led Lord Neuberger to conclude:[45]

> The contention that judges should not be creating the Power is reinforced when one considers the extent of domestic statutory law and international convention law in the area of international insolvency ... In this highly legislated area, I consider that the power which is said to arise in this case is one which should be bestowed on the court by the legislature, and not arrogated to the court of its own motion.

22.38 The present difficulties appear to be more about the existence of jurisdiction than how to exercise jurisdiction once it has been found. One way in which the legislature could intervene to overcome these difficulties is by amending section 426 so as to expand its application to insolvency proceedings everywhere (ie to repeal its present restriction to relevant countries and territories). If doing so, it might be appropriate to make other changes including, as a safeguard, replacing the present qualified duty to assist where section 426 applies with a broad discretion. A measure along those lines would nonetheless give the courts the free-ranging powers to evaluate cases on merit and act in aid where appropriate with the added bonus of being able to choose between the application of English and foreign law.

g. Order of precedence

22.39 The European Regulations take automatic effect and override any contrary provision of English domestic law except to the extent that they would conflict with the operation of section 426 in respect of Commonwealth countries. It follows that the European Regulations prevail over the 2006 Regulations. This is unlikely to cause any difficulty because the provisions of the European Regulations are mandatory

---

[44] Ibid at [157].
[45] Ibid at [161].

whereas the 2006 Regulations are largely permissive. The 2006 Regulations prevail over English domestic law, including section 426. Section 426 formally prevails over common law but the unavailability of redress under section 426 will not preclude the exercise of the common law jurisdiction to assist (which is the default option if nothing else applies).[46]

This incoherent result can only be explained by reference to the different international and domestic origins of the various rules which co-exist. Unlike ordinary domestic legislation, which can be expected to exhibit a consistency of approach and to be capable of being codified if necessary, the superimposition of the European Regulations and the Model Law, which reflect different traditions and operate in each case as a form of overlay, precludes that ideal. The consequences of the European Regulations, which have direct effect, were unavoidable but the additional complexity might have been thought a reason for eschewing adoption of the Model Law (as may have been the case in some other EU member states). However, the resultant complexity is an acceptable price to pay for the flexibility which flows from retaining the old whilst also embracing the new. The practical application of the rules is nonetheless a form of legal archaeology in which the practitioner digs through successive layers of law in search of a solution. **22.40**

4. Co-operation and communication

One way of responding to the challenges of both group insolvencies and potentially competing proceedings in respect of single companies is the promotion of co-operation and communication between office-holders and courts. Apart from section 426 and its antecedents, an early English law example of cross-border co-operation arose in the administration of Maxwell Communication Corporation Plc which was concurrently the subject of US Chapter 11 proceedings. The unusual feature of the case was that neither proceeding was subordinate to the other. The potential conflicts were resolved by the office-holders in both jurisdictions entering into a protocol to harmonize their work. The English court authorized the administrators to enter into that agreement and the US court approved the agreement for the US examiner.[47] Protocols continue to be used where the need arises but bespoke arrangements of that sort are not an appropriate solution for the generality of more routine cases. **22.41**

---

[46] In practice, common law assistance is largely superseded by the 2006 Regulations: see *Singularis* ibid at [42]–[50] (Lord Collins).

[47] This solution is recorded in the first instance judgment of Hoffmann J in *Barclays Bank Plc v Homan* [1993] BCLC 680 (Ch) 684e. See also *Re Maxwell Communication Corporation Plc* [2016] EWHC 2200 (Ch).

22.42 The EC Regulation added little. Although it was a fundamental objective of the EC Regulation to control the exercise of competing jurisdictions by member states, this was achieved primarily by the allocation of jurisdiction to open main proceedings between member states. The residual issue of competing local proceedings where the debtor had an establishment was addressed by giving the office-holders qualified duties to provide each other with relevant information and to co-operate with each other.

22.43 More substantial provisions are contained in the Cross-Border Insolvency Regulations 2006 which make provision for co-operation and direct communication between courts and office-holders. This is expressed in terms that the court *may* co-operate and that both the court and an English office-holder *may* communicate but that an English office-holder *shall* co-operate to the maximum extent possible which is consistent with the performance with his English law duties. Co-operation and communication may be implemented by any appropriate means.[48] However, the concept of direct communication sits uneasily with the traditional role of an English judge in insolvency proceedings whose function is to resolve issues and to exercise judicial discretion in the giving of any directions. David Richards J expressed the following views on this subject in *Re T&N Ltd* (which pre-dated the 2006 Regulations):[49]

> At root I do not consider it appropriate for this court to enter into substantive discussions with the US court on matters of controversy between the parties which may come before the court for decision. As and when appropriate, the court should hear argument on the relevant issues and give its judgment on them. In the light of that judgment, inter-court communications may be appropriate.
>
> In adopting this approach, I am not seeking to nullify the process for inter-court communications before they have even started. That is not my intention. As I have said more than once already, I support the view that inter-court communications can have a vital role to play in major cross-border insolvencies such as these and I fully endorsed the efforts of the administrators and plan proponents to establish the formal procedures contained in the [a protocol entitled Procedures and Issues for Inter-Court Communications]. But in considering an application for inter-court communications the courts must necessarily proceed on a case-by-case basis, balancing the desirability of inter-court communications against other relevant factors. The circumstances of this particular application have led me to conclude that a direct inter-court discussion of the issues would not be appropriate at this stage.

These observations can be contrasted with the following (later) remarks of the same judge in *Re Lehman Brothers International (Europe)* with reference to a global

---

[48] See further: the UNICITRAL *Practice Guide on Cross-Border Insolvency Cooperation*, New York, 2010 <http://www.uncitral.org/pdf/english/texts/insolven/Practice_Guide_Ebook_eng.pdf> accessed 3 November 2016.
[49] [2004] EWHC 2878 (Ch), [2005] BCC 982 [26], [27].

settlement between two Lehman companies in respect of which he had been asked to give directions to English administrators:[50]

> I would like to endorse the view expressed by Judge Peck when approving the settlement agreement that it represents a truly remarkable achievement. It is right to acknowledge, as did Judge Peck, that this achievement is the result of the determination and good sense of the office-holders together with the skill and sheer hard work of their professional advisors. Above all, it very significantly accelerates and improves the prospect of distributions to clients and creditors which is, after all, the purpose of these insolvency proceedings.

> Judge Peck also remarked:

> 'One of the other notable aspects of this is that this is a cross-border problem, one in which no courts communicated with each other. We had no court-to-court communication. We had no need for coordination at that level. Rather, this is an example of pure negotiation with the avoidance of litigation risk, cost, and uncertainty driving a very creative outcome.'

> I would like to say that since he made those remarks and with the strong encouragement of the joint administrators and the trustee, Judge Peck and I have conducted a telephone discussion. We did so yesterday and were able to take stock of progress to date and to inform each other of what appear to be the principal outstanding matters in our respective jurisdictions. We agreed that, if appropriate and always with the knowledge of interested parties, we would be willing to have further communications. Whether they would be with or without the presence of other parties would depend upon the circumstances and on the views of those involved.

22.44 The 2006 Regulations make further provision for concurrent proceedings by ensuring that any relief given in consequence of recognition is compatible with the English proceedings. However, the most important aspect of these provisions is that, upon recognition of a foreign main proceeding, any English proceedings in respect of the same debtor be restricted to local assets. The practical effect of this is that the English tradition of ancillary liquidation has ceased to be a matter of judicial practice and has become a matter of formal requirement in cases to which the Regulations apply.

22.45 Even more extensive provisions are contained in the Recast Regulation. The provisions of the EC Regulation for co-operation and communication between office-holders are restated and expanded. They are also supplemented by new qualified duties requiring co-operation and communication between courts and between office-holders and courts. A more radical development is the introduction of new provisions for co-operation and communication where insolvency proceedings relate to two or more members of a group of companies. Those group provisions also impose new qualified duties on office-holders and courts. Finally, there are a series of new provisions for group co-ordination proceedings which do not provide for a group insolvency proceeding as such but rather, as the name implies,

---

[50] [2013] EWHC 1664 (Ch), [2014] BCC 132 [15]–[17].

a mechanism for independent co-ordination of discrete insolvency proceedings affecting companies within a group. All these new provisions are, as yet, untested because they do not apply to proceedings opened before 26 June 2017.

22.46 This is a rapidly developing field. In October 2016, judges from ten jurisdictions (which included England) held an inaugural meeting of the Judicial Insolvency Network in Singapore which resulted in the production of draft guidelines to facilitate communication and co-operation.[51]

5. Extra-territoriality and English insolvency proceedings

22.47 Extra-territoriality raises two broad questions, both of which are affected by the laws already considered: first, whether the English insolvency procedures are capable of applying to foreign companies and, secondly, whether such procedures (whether opened in respect of English or foreign companies) purport to have effect outside the jurisdiction.

a. English proceedings in respect of foreign companies

22.48 Subject now to the European Regulations, foreign companies can be wound up by the English courts as unregistered companies. A winding-up order will not be made unless there is a sufficient connection with England (usually, but not necessarily, meaning the presence of local assets), there is a reasonable possibility the order will benefit those applying for it, and one or more persons interested in the prospective distribution of assets are persons over whom the court can exercise jurisdiction.[52] Lawrence Collins J held in *Re Drax Holdings Ltd* that these are factors which go to the exercise of the court's discretion, not to its jurisdiction, whilst observing that:[53]

> In most cases the distinction will not matter. The English court will not wind up a foreign company where it has no legitimate interest to do so, for that would be to exercise an exorbitant jurisdiction contrary to international comity, and for that purpose it does not matter whether the preconditions are couched in terms of the existence of jurisdiction or the exercise of jurisdiction.

However, section 221(4) provides that no unregistered company can be wound up voluntarily except in accordance with the EC Regulation.[54] The European Regulations have had the curious effect of simultaneously curtailing the wind-up

---

[51] See further <http://www.supremecourt.gov.sg/news/media-releases/judicial-insolvency-network-discusses-guidelines-for-cross-border-insolvency-matters> accessed 20 October 2016.

[52] *Stocznia Gdanska SA v Latreefers Inc (No 2)* [2001] 2 BCLC 116 (CA).

[53] *Re Drax Holdings Limited* [2003] EWHC 2743 (Ch), [2004] 1 WLR 1049 [24].

[54] See further *Re TXU Europe German Finance BV* [2005] BCC 90. Section 221(4) has not yet been amended to refer to the Recast Regulation but the exception will nonetheless apply.

jurisdiction of the English courts and expanding the availability of voluntary liquidation.

Subject to the provisions of the European Regulations, a foreign company is only **22.49** a 'company' for the purposes of the administration and CVA provisions of the Act if incorporated in another EEA state or if, not being incorporated in an EEA state, it has its COMI in an EU member state other than Denmark.[55] A foreign company can also go into administration on the basis of a section 426 letter of request.[56]

b. Extra-territorial effects of English proceedings

This important subject is not directly addressed by the Act and the case law lacks a **22.50** coherent foundation, but the starting point is uncontroversial: universalism means that, in the eyes of English law and absent any contrary direction of the court (as in the case of an ancillary liquidation), English insolvency proceedings apply to the worldwide assets and liabilities of the company. As Millett J said of a winding-up order in *Re International Tin Council*:[57]

> The statutory trusts which it brings into operation are imposed on all the company's assets wherever situate, within and beyond the jurisdiction. Where the company is simultaneously being wound up in the country of its incorporation, the English court will naturally seek to avoid unnecessary conflict, and so far as possible to ensure that the English winding up is conducted as ancillary to the principal liquidation. In a proper case, it may authorise the liquidator to refrain from seeking to recover assets situate beyond the jurisdiction, thereby protecting him from any complaint that he has been derelict in his duty. But the statutory trusts extend to such assets, and so does the statutory obligation to collect and realise them and to deal with their proceeds in accordance with the statutory scheme.

This is reinforced by the definition of 'property' in section 436 which refers to 'every description of property wherever situated'.

In *Re HIH Casualty and General Insurance Ltd*, Lord Hoffmann said:[58]   **22.51**

> And in theory, such an order operates universally, applies to all the foreign company's assets and brings into play the full panoply of powers and duties under the Insolvency Act 1986 like any other winding up order ...

Lord Hoffmann's comment was directed to the distinction between ancillary and other liquidations but the reference to the 'full panoply of powers and duties' is potentially misleading if taken out of context because the more controversial question is how far such powers and duties do apply to questions involving a foreign element.

---

[55] Schedule B1 para 111(1A) and section 1(4).
[56] As in *Re Dallhold Estates (UK) Pty Ltd* (n 38) and *Re Tambrook Jersey Ltd* (n 38).
[57] [1987] Ch 419 (Ch) 446H (on appeal [1989] Ch 309 (CA)).
[58] [2008] UKHL 21, [2008] 1 WLR 852 [8].

On all these questions, the position in respect of liquidation and administration should, in principle, be the same.

22.52 The extra-territorial application of the respective stays in liquidation and administration is a convenient staring point. There is long-standing authority that the statutory stay on proceedings against a company in compulsory liquidation does not restrain proceedings in a foreign court.[59] This authority was relied on by the Court of Appeal in *Bloom v Harms Offshore AHT Taurus GmbH & Co KG* where the court thought, but did not conclusively determine, that the administration moratorium did not have extra-territorial effect.[60] The decision is questionable[61] but the law is now ostensibly that, subject to hotchpot, creditors are free to pursue claims through foreign proceedings unless they are amenable to an anti-suit injunction.

22.53 Under the hotchpot rule, a creditor seeking to participate in an English insolvency proceeding must account for recoveries made in foreign proceedings so as to preserve pari passu distribution in the English proceeding. In *Cleaver v Delta American Reinsurance Co*, Lord Scott described the effect of the rule in the case of concurrent insolvency proceedings in the following terms:[62]

> The authorities establish the principle that if a company is being wound up in an English liquidation and also in a liquidation in a foreign country, a creditor who has proved and received a dividend in the foreign liquidation may not receive a dividend in the English liquidation without bringing into hotchpot his foreign dividend.

However, the rule is not confined to the cases of concurrent insolvencies and the receipt of foreign dividends. It will apply to recoveries made through the pursuit of foreign proceedings notwithstanding an English stay. As Lord Selbourne said in *Banco de Portugal v Waddell*:[63]

> Every creditor coming in to prove under, and to take the benefit of, the English liquidation, must do so on the terms of the English law of bankruptcy; he cannot be permitted to approbate and reprobate, to claim the benefit of that law, and at the same time insist on retaining, as against it, any preferential right inconsistent with the equality of distribution intended by that law, which he may have obtained either by the use of legal process in a foreign country, or otherwise.

---

[59] *Re Oriental Inland Steam co, ex parte Scinde Railway Company* (1874) LR 9 Ch App 557 (CA); *Re Vocalion (Foreign) Ltd* [1932] Ch 196 (Ch).

[60] [2009] EWCA Civ 632, [2010] Ch 187 [22].

[61] See further Hamish Anderson, 'The Extra-Territoriality of the Statutory Stay in an English Administration' (2014) 23 Int Insol Rev 40 and, 'The Extra-Territoriality of the Statutory Stay in an English Administration – Revisited' (2015) 24 Int Insol Rev 165.

[62] [2001] UKPC 6, [2001] 2 AC 328 [18].

[63] (1880) 5 App Cas 161 (HL) 169.

The critical point is whether the assets held or received by the creditor from outside the English proceeding constitute assets which, in the eyes of English law, form part of the insolvent estate.[64]

The position in respect of examination powers, which is also not addressed by the **22.54** Act, is confusing and unsettled. In *Re Seagull Manufacturing Co Ltd*, it was held that the provisions of the Act for the public examination of officers and others under section 133 are not limited by territoriality. Peter Gibson J said:[65]

> I can see no reasons of comity which would prevent those who voluntarily were officers or otherwise participated in the formation or running of an English company to be capable of being summoned by the English court for the purposes of public examination. The fact that Parliament has provided for the compulsory winding up of foreign companies, knowing that those companies would only be wound up when there was a sufficient connection with the jurisdiction, and the fact that Parliament provided that section 133 should apply in such a case, seem to me to indicate that the officers of such companies who may well not be within the jurisdiction should be examinable publicly.

In reaching its decision, the Court of Appeal distinguished its own earlier decision in *Re Tucker*[66] in which it had held that there could not be a private examination under section 25 of the Bankruptcy Act 1914 (an analogue of section 236 of the Act) of a British subject resident in Belgium. The question of the extra-territoriality of section 236 itself has resulted in conflicting decisions. In Scotland (where the same power applies), the Court of Session made an order in respect of a non-resident, thereby adopting a literal reading of 'any person' in the relevant provision, but did so on the basis of a misunderstanding as to the enforceability of its order.[67] In England, David Richards J, in *Re MF Global UK Ltd*,[68] considered himself bound by *Tucker* and therefore declined to make a section 236 order against a French company, despite acknowledging that there would otherwise be much to be said for extra-territoriality. The case was distinguished shortly afterwards in *Re Omni Trustees Ltd (No 2)*[69] as regards making an order for the production of documents and the giving of an account (as opposed to oral examination) on the grounds that there were material differences in the structure of sections 25 and 236 and by reference to other authority not cited to David Richards J. The decisions are irreconcilable and the question must be resolved at an appellate level. In principle, and having regard to the purposes of examination as explained in Chapter 16,

---

[64] *Cleaver* (n 62) [26].

[65] [1993] Ch 345 (CA) 356E.

[66] [1990] Ch 148 (CA). See further: *Masri v Consolidated Contractors International Co SAL* [2009] UKHL 43, [2010] 1 AC 90 [19]–[24].

[67] *McIsaac, Petitioners; Joint Liquidators of First Tokyo Index Trust Ltd* [1994] BCC 410 (Court of Session, Outer House).

[68] [2015] EWHC 2319 (Ch), [2015] BCC 891.

[69] [2015] EWHC 2697, [2015] BCC 906 (an extempore judgment delivered on an unopposed application).

extra-territoriality is desirable—not least in order to avoid an anomalous distinction between public and private examination—leaving it to the court's discretion to avoid exercising an exorbitant jurisdiction.

22.55 The English courts have been readier to assert extra-territorial effect in relation to other provisions of the Act. Thus, in *Re Paramount Airways Ltd*,[70] it was held that the rules on transactions at an undervalue could be applied to a transaction with a Jersey bank. In *Jyske Bank (Gibraltar) Ltd v Spjeldnaes*,[71] the court applied the rules on transactions defrauding creditors to an Irish transaction between Irish companies and, in *Bilta (UK) Ltd v Nazir (No 2)*, the Supreme Court held that a Swiss company and a French resident could be liable for fraudulent trading in proceedings brought by the liquidators of an English company. In the last of those cases, Lord Sumption SCJ summarized (and endorsed) observations made by Sir Donald Nicholls V-C in *Paramount* as having been:[72]

> ... that current patterns of cross-border business weaken the presumption against extra-territorial effect as applied to the exercise of the court's powers in conducting the liquidation of a United Kingdom company; ...

22.56 According to the Act extra-territorial effect does not unleash an exorbitant jurisdiction which offends principles of comity because there is still a question as to whether the court will permit service of proceedings out of the jurisdiction and a discretion as to whether or not to grant relief. In both respects the presence or absence of connection with the jurisdiction will be a relevant factor. It is suggested that to uphold extra-territoriality subject to these mitigating factors is the approach which is most consonant with modified universalism and is therefore to be preferred.

---

[70] [1993] Ch 223 (CA).
[71] [2000] BCC 16 (Ch) on appeal, unreported 29 July 1999 but not on this point.
[72] [2015] UKSC 23, [2016] AC 1 (SC) [110].

INDEX